PHILIP SCHAFF

The portrait and signature are from *Berlin 1842–New York 1892.*
The Semi-Centennial of Philip Schaff (privately printed, 1893).

PHILIP SCHAFF

Historian and Ambassador
of the Universal Church
Selected Writings

edited and with introductions by
KLAUS PENZEL

MERCER
MP

ISBN 0-86554-376-3

Philip Schaff: Historian and Ambassador of the Universal Church
Copyright ©1991
Mercer University Press, Macon, Georgia 31207
All rights reserved
Printed in the United States of America

We gratefully acknowledge permission to reprint previously published material:

Excerpts from "Church History in Context: The Case of Philip Schaff," by Klaus Penzel, in *Our Common History as Christians: Essays in Honor of Albert C. Outler,* ed. John Deschner, Leroy T. Howe, and Klaus Penzel, 217-60. Copyright ©1975 by Oxford University Press, Inc. Reprinted by permission.

Excerpts from "The Reformation Goes West: The Notion of Historical Development in the Thought of Philip Schaff," by Klaus Penzel, in the *Journal of Religion* 62 (July 1982): 219-41. Copyright ©1982 by the University of Chicago. Reprinted by permission.

"Philip Schaff—A Centennial Appraisal," by Klaus Penzel, in *Church History* 59 (June 1990): 207-21. Copyright ©1990 by the American Society of Church History. Reprinted by permission.

The paper used in this publication meets the minimum requirements
of American National Standard for Information Sciences—
Permanence of Paper for Printed Library Materials, ANSI Z39.48-1984.

Library of Congress Cataloging-in-Publication Data

Schaff, Philip, 1819–1893.
    Philip Schaff, historian and ambassador of the universal church : selected writings / edited and with introductions by Klaus Penzel.
    lxviii + 391pp. 6 × 9″ (15 × 23cm.)
    Includes bibliographical references and index.
    ISBN 0-86554-376-3 (alk. paper)
    1. Church history—Historiography. 2. Theology—19th century. 3. Christian union. 4. Schaff, Philip. 1819–1893. I. Penzel, Klaus. II. Title.
BR138.S29   1990
285.7′092—dc20   90-43814
                                                                                    CIP

CONTENTS

PART I
Formative Influences

PART II
Major Themes—The Mercersburg Years (1844–1863)

PART III
Major Projects—The New York Years (1863–1893)

To my teachers
Wilhelm Pauck
and
Robert T. Handy
who also introduced me to Philip Schaff

✳ ✳ ✳

If unconstrained universality of the sense is the first and original condition of religion, and also, as is natural, its ripest fruit, you can surely see that, as religion advances and piety is purified, the whole religious world must appear as an undivisible whole.

The impulse to abstract, in so far as it proceeds to rigid separation, is a proof of imperfection. The highest and most cultured always see a universal union, and, in seeing it, establish it.

—Friedrich Schleiermacher,
On Religion. Speeches to its Cultured Despisers,
trans. John Oman, Harper Torchbooks
(New York, 1958) 154.

Probably never until now has the world been ready to conceive the true idea of a comprehensive Christianity. Nor is it ready now, save in part. The idea itself is yet in its twilight, dimly seen, only by a few—by none save those who are up to watch for the morning.

—Horace Bushnell,
"Christian Comprehensiveness,"
New Englander 6 (January 1848): 82.

PREFACE

Philip Schaff's life (1819–1893) spans two continents and nearly a whole century. Born in Switzerland and educated in Germany at a time of brilliant creativity there especially in theology, philosophy and historical studies, he rose to prominence in the United States, first at the Seminary of the German Reformed church at Mercersburg, Pennsylvania, then at Union Theological Seminary in New York. Incredibly productive throughout his long and distinguished career, his scholarly and practical contributions touched almost every aspect of religious scholarship and interest in the United States in the second half of the nineteenth century. As a matter of fact, his life is a window into nearly a whole century of religious developments not only in the United States but in western Europe as well. The so-called Mercersburg Theology, which he and his colleague John W. Nevin developed, added a remarkable new chapter in the history of American theology, for it introduced American Protestants to the new German modes of thought that had been created and shaped in the era dominated by Schleiermacher, Hegel and Ranke. Later Schaff played a leading role in the Evangelical Alliance and the World Alliance of Reformed Churches, in the revision of the English Bible initiated by the Church of England and in the creed revision of the Presbyterian churches. He pioneered the internationalization of theology, especially as the editor of a translation and adaptation of Lange's German Bible Commentary, which was the first comprehensive and complete English-language Bible commentary, and of the *Schaff-Herzog Encyclopedia*. He was also a brilliant interpreter of religion in America. As a church historian he distinguished himself as the author of the three-volume *Creeds of Christendom* and a multi-volume *History of the Christian Church*. He founded the American Society of Church History in 1888, and shortly before his death initiated that Society's first major project, the American Church History Series. His most popular book was a Life of Jesus, *The Person of Christ*. George L. Prentiss, who had been his oldest American friend and a colleague at Union Theological Seminary, later wrote of him as follows: "He surpassed all the men I ever knew in the extent, variety and fruitful results of his practical, literary, and theological activities. One is fairly staggered in reading over a list of the books he wrote, the journeys he made, the societies he founded, the plans he formed, the addresses he delivered, the funds he raised, and the solid, lasting effects he produced in furtherance of good learning, Christian union and fellowship, and other vital interests of the cause and kingdom of Jesus Christ."[1] As the historian and ambassador of the universal church, Schaff was without peers in his own time.

When I arrived in this country as an immigrant from Germany at the age of twenty-five, just like Philip Schaff, and settled into my graduate studies at Union Theological Seminary in New York, I was soon looking for a dissertation topic in the history of American Christianity that would reward my daring entry into the strange world of American religion but still leave me with a secure foothold in the Old World. I also wanted to combine my historical interest in the nineteenth century with my theological concern that the past be evoked to illuminate our contemporary efforts at developing an understanding of the Christian faith appropriate to the present historical moment and at addressing the ever urgent task of the renewal and unity of the church. The life and work of Philip Schaff qualified on each count. From time to time I later returned to Schaff, deepening my understanding of selected aspects of his life's work. Where appropriate, I have drawn upon my earlier Schaff essays in this present work. During those same years I also witnessed excitedly an increased attention to Schaff's work. This renewed interest manifested

---

[1]George L. Prentiss, *The Union Theological Seminary in the City of New York, Its Design and Another Decade of Its History* (New York, 1899) 421.

itself in new editions or reprints of some of his more important publications, and in more books and articles about him as well. In 1988 the observance of the Centennial of the American Society of Church History was focused on the work and continuing significance of the Society's founder and first president. This occasion prompted the publication of George Shriver's new biography *Philip Schaff: Christian Scholar and Ecumenical Prophet* (1987) and of Henry W. Bowden's edition of a remarkable collection of essays entitled *A Century of Church History: The Legacy of Philip Schaff* (1988).

Most recent studies of Schaff, my own included, as well as all the recent editions of Schaff's writings, have limited their attention to the Mercersburg period of his career. Thus they have left out of view what James H. Nichols has called Schaff's "second career," those thirty years he spent in New York City.[2] The earlier interest in the Mercersburg Theology or Mercersburg Movement, which Nevin and Schaff had evolved in the German Reformed church, then the backwaters of antebellum American Christianity, was no doubt largely prompted by the ecumenical movement and the neo-orthodox theological revival in the decades following the Second World War. Both movements had a close affinity to many of the concerns and efforts that engaged Nevin and Schaff at Mercersburg. The "evangelical renaissance" of our time, however, is likely to make more pertinent the evangelical character of Schaff's scholarship and churchmanship especially during the later New York period of his life.

Hence I believe that the time has now come to see Schaff whole. In this volume I have therefore attempted to create a clear profile and useful summary of Schaff's whole career and work and their continuing significance by bringing together representative selections from his published writings and some additional unpublished materials. In doing so, I have tried to strike a balance between emphasizing the full orbit of Schaff's scholarship and churchmanship and highlighting what will appear to be of particular relevance to today's readers, Protestants and Catholics, "liberal" and "evangelical" Christians,

---

[2]James H. Nichols, *Romanticism in American Theology: Nevin and Schaff at Mercersburg* (Chicago, 1961) 309.

scholars, ministers and laity alike. Of course, what is to be considered to be of continuing significance is to some extent a matter of personal preference, which the editorial introductions will attempt to explain and justify more fully. No one will dispute, however, that Schaff occupies an important place in the history of the Reformed tradition in this country, and that, beyond this denominational appeal, his life and work can help to illuminate many of the themes and concerns that loom large in the ecumenical endeavors, historical scholarship, and evangelical theology and churchmanship of our own time. Indeed, he should be of particular interest to all those of us who want to test or to appropriate a liberal and ecumenical evangelicalism. And even in the late twentieth century he continues to hold out an impressive and suggestive program for the reform and renewal of the church. Finally, when he pioneered efforts at the internationalization of theology, he can once again be our guide, as we ourselves venture forth, as today we must, into the still larger world of Christianity in its global setting. Much of his work is most certainly, therefore, of more than passing historical interest.

Schaff's career itself suggests the three sections into which this book has been divided: the formative influences of his German years of study (part I); the characteristic themes of his scholarship which he established at Mercersburg (part II); the remarkable variety of projects into which he channelled his considerable energies during the final New York years of his life (part III). Though these selections represent all four major motifs that gave form and direction to his life's work: the biblical, historical, ecumenical and apologetic, it was unavoidable that not every aspect and facet of his long career could be equally honored, for no selection of his writings, however carefully chosen, can adequately mirror a life so rich in its many and varied accomplishments. The editor of this volume therefore cheerfully concedes the possibility that others might have chosen some other texts from among Schaff's many publications. As to the text itself, I want to add that I have retained only selectively, as appropriate, Schaff's own footnotes. It should also be noted that all translations, especially from the German, are my own unless otherwise indicated.

Finally, a word also about my own approach to the study of the past. By preference and training it is that of an intellectual historian.

This approach is reflected in this volume. Without neglecting the important events of Schaff's life and career, I therefore aim to sketch an intellectual portrayal of Schaff, highlighting and appraising what is theologically significant in his career and publications as well as placing his life in the larger context of the history of nineteenth-century theology and the churches on both sides of the Atlantic. In this sense, this volume may be viewed as an attempt to complement the two available biographies of Schaff: David S. Schaff, *The Life of Philip Schaff, in Part Autobiographical* (1897), and George Shriver's recent Life of Schaff.

I owe much to the staff of the Bridwell Library at Perkins School of Theology, of the Burke Library at Union Theological Seminary, and of the Philip Schaff Library and the Evangelical and Reformed Historical Society at Lancaster Theological Seminary. Whenever I needed help, which was often, it was always offered graciously and readily. Terry Smith typed the manuscript and stored it, as it evolved and went through various revisions, in her Wang word processor. I am grateful to all of these helpers. I am also in debt to the copyright holders of my earlier Schaff essays for permission to make use of these essays in this present work. Finally, I would like to express my gratitude to the American Society of Church History for having commended this work in observation of its Centennial Year, 1988.

I dedicate this volume to those two teachers, Wilhelm Pauck and Robert T. Handy, who first introduced me to Philip Schaff and who together, like Philip Schaff himself, taught me not only to appreciate what continues to be best in the scholarly traditions of both Germany and the United States but also to build bridges between European and American Christianity.

EDITORIAL INTRODUCTION

Whoever sets out to survey the exceptional career of Philip Schaff is bound to notice three issues of particular interest, two of which represent a noteworthy repetition of the same kind of development. One can trace in Schaff's early life a remarkable educational progression that led a poverty-striken boy, fatherless and left behind in an orphan home by his mother, from his birthplace in the mountains of Switzerland to the beginnings of a professorial career at the University of Berlin. Though founded in 1810, this university was at that time already acknowledged to be Germany's foremost institution of higher learning. Two decades later a similar progression occurred in the United States. There Schaff advanced from the narrow confines of the struggling Mercersburg Seminary in western Pennsylvania and a small denomination, the German Reformed church, to a position on the faculty of the prestigious Union Theological Seminary in New York, to membership in the theologically and socially powerful Presbyterian church, and to a leading role in American and even world Protestantism. At the very end, in 1893, at the World's Parliament of Religions, which he heartily endorsed, he even entered eagerly the still wider orbit of the great religions of the world. Of course, there also occurred those events that marked the turning point in Schaff's life: the transition in 1844 from the Old World to the New, so that his life is of primary importance also, as Perry Miller correctly observed, for anyone interested in "the history of that mysterious process called 'Americanization'."[1] Schaff himself once drew the sum of

---

[1]Schaff, *America: A Sketch of Its Political, Social, and Religious Character*, ed. Perry Miller (Cambridge MA, 1961) xxxv.

his life as follows: "Germany could easily spare me, while the German churches in America were in great need of educated ministers. I had no idea, at that time [when he arrived], that my labors would gradually extend to the English speaking churches as well, and that Mercersburg would prepare me for New York."[2] These, then, are the most important issues that any brief survey and evaluation of Schaff's life would need to address: his German education, the Mercersburg period of his career, his "Americanization," and his further evolution as a chief spokesman and representative of the dominant evangelical Protestantism in the decades following the Civil War.

I

In 1819, the year of Schaff's birth,[3] Johann Wolfgang von Goethe enthusiastically exclaimed to a friend: "If we were twenty years younger, we would set sail for America."[4] There was nothing in the circumstances of Schaff's birth to indicate that twenty-five years later he himself would set sail for the New World as one of Germany's most promising younger theologians. He was born in the town of Chur in the Swiss canton Graubünden (or Grison). His mother, a simple peasant woman, who had deserted her first husband, had to go to court to force the elder Philip Schaff (he spelled his name "Philipp Schaaf") to accept the paternity of the child to whom she was about to give birth. After the authorities had ordered the mother, on

---

[2]Schaff, "Autobiographical Reminiscences" (unpaginated ms., The Evangelical and Reformed Historical Society, Lancaster Theological Seminary, Lancaster PA) chap. "Call to America." Schaff wrote this ms. intermittently from 1871 to 1890. A paginated copy was prepared for Schaff by Carl M. Adler in 1882 (also at Lancaster Theological Seminary). All further citations are from the Adler copy, unless indicated otherwise.

[3]The name was originally spelled "Philipp Schaf." Schaff soon dropped the second p from his first name, but he changed his surname by adding a second f only in the United States in 1847. See Wilhelm Julius Mann's letter of 30 November 1847, in which he humorously commented on the change of his friend's name, quoted by Adolf Spaeth, *D. Wilhelm Julius Mann* (Reading PA, 1895) 45.

[4]Quoted by Thomas Mann, "Goethe und die Demokratie," in *Reden und Aufsätze,* vol. 9 of *Gesammelte Werke* (Frankfurt, 1974) 778.

account of her scandalous behavior, to leave the town, which she did, but without the child, and after the father's untimely death a year after the child's birth, young Philip became a ward of the town of Chur, growing up in an orphan home. At the local schools he stood out as a gifted student, yet he suffered the indignity of being dismissed from school after he and some classmates were caught committing what their elders then darkly called "the secret sin," that is, masturbation.[5] There are no references to this incident, nor to the tragic circumstances of his illegitimate birth, in any of Schaff's writings (neither is there any indication as to when Schaff learned of his illegitimate birth), unless one suddenly detects more meaning in Schaff's passing remark in his "Autobiographical Reminiscences" that in Chur "I was surrounded by uncongenial and dangerous influences."[6] The deviation from the established and sternly guarded sexual norm led in 1834 to Schaff's removal, through the good services of the senior pastor at St. Martin, the Reverend Paul Kind, from Chur to a boarding school at Kornthal near Stuttgart in the kingdom

---

[5]We owe all the new information about the unusual circumstances of Schaff's birth and childhood in Chur to the researches of Professor Ulrich Gäbler of the University of Basel. See his article "Philip Schaff in Chur, 1819-1834," *Zwingliana* 18, nos. 1 and 2 (1989): 143-65. A shorter English version, "Philip Schaff at Chur, 1819-1834," appeared in *Probing the Reformed Tradition: Historical Studies in Honor of Edward A. Dowey,* ed. E. A. McKee and B. Armstrong (Louisville KY, 1989) 408-23.

The prevailing narrowly restrictive and misguided sexual attitudes of the times, and presumably not just of the pietists, were presented in a popular book written by Sixtus Carl Kapff, Schaff's pastor at Kornthal and his life-long friend. First published in 1841, it had passed through 20 editions by 1902! An English translation, from the 6th German edition, appeared under the telling title: *Admonitions of a Friend of Youth, against the most dangerous enemy of youth; or instructions in regard to secret sins; their consequences, cure, and prevention. Commended to the affectionate consideration of the young and their teachers* (Philadelphia, 1858). No translator or editor is mentioned. But since the publisher was Schäfer and Koradi, publisher also of Schaff's magazine *Der deutsche Kirchenfreund,* one is tempted to speculate that Schaff might have had a hand in the American edition.

[6]For this and the immediately following quotations from Schaff's "Autobiographical Reminiscences," see below, pp. 18, 21.

of Württemberg. Kornthal had been founded in 1819 by Württemberg pietists as a community modelled after the Moravian settlement at Herrnhut and the apostolic church.[7] Schaff's later claim that his removal to Kornthal was "an experimental argument for the mystery of predestination" carries obviously more meaning than he was ever willing publicly to admit.

Even though Schaff spent no more than six months at Kornthal, this community became his "spiritual birthplace," for here, at the age of fifteen, he experienced an intense conversion in a forest "at three o'clock in the morning." This experience obviously also gave him a cleansing and vivifying release from the shame and guilt engendered by his immediate past. On Easter Sunday he was confirmed in a Lutheran service (he had been baptized in the Reformed church), and on that occasion he dedicated himself—no doubt under the influence of the able young pastor Sixtus Carl Kapff, who became his life-long friend—to the service of God in the ministry of the church. For the next two years he attended the Stuttgart *Gymnasium*, lodging in the hospitable home of the Mann family, one of those merchant families in Stuttgart who had kept alive the older traditions of Württemberg pietism. At that time he also came to know the leading younger ministers who were bringing the spirit of the Awakening (*Erweckungsbewegung*), that early nineteenth-century revival movement which swept across much of continental western Europe, to Württemberg's capital.[8]

In his study of Ferdinand Christian Baur (who would soon be one of Schaff's teachers at the University of Tübingen) Wilhelm Dilthey correctly observed that the religious milieu of Baur's youth, a thoughtful, solid supernaturalism, adhered to Baur wherever his rev-

---

[7]For the Kornthal community, see Sixtus Carl Kapff, *Die Württembergischen Brüdergemeinden Kornthal und Wilhelmsdorf, ihre Geschichte, Einrichtung und Erziehungsanstalten* (Kornthal, 1839), and art. "Kornthal," *Realencyklopädie für protestantische Theologie und Kirche*, 3rd ed., 11:38-47.

[8]See Karl Müller, *Die religiöse Erweckung in Württemberg am Anfang des 19. Jahrhunderts* (Tübingen, 1925), and Heinrich Hermelink, *Geschichte der evangelischen Kirche in Württemberg von der Reformation bis zur Gegenwart* (Stuttgart and Tübingen, 1949) 330-415.

olutionary researches into the origin and history of Christianity would later take him, "forming, as it were, the background of his world of thought."[9] One is equally justified to say of Schaff that the religious outlook and ethos of the Württemberg Awakening—what Schaff liked to call the "childlike faith" of his youth—was to form the permanent background of the imposing scholarship and churchmanship of his American career. In Württemberg he embraced a warmly emotional piety that firmly clung to the supernatural beliefs of traditional Christianity, expressed itself in moral rectitude, and was intent on the active pursuit of whatever tasks appeared to hasten the coming of God's kingdom. Four other elements were also added to the formation of his theology. Foremost were the emphasis on the "converted heart" as the true mark of the Christian and of Christian fellowship and—the other side of the coin—a broad-minded ecumenical outlook and outreach that downplayed denominational particularities in favor of the spiritual unity of all of God's true children. When around 1850 American Methodists started evangelizing in Württemberg, pietistic ministers in the established church called the Methodists' work "blessed and not exaggerated" and countered all opposition with the characteristc response: "First the salvation of the soul, then the church."[10] Schaff also embraced an eschatological realism. After all, at Kornthal the so-called "Jerusalem carriage" stood ever ready to get the pietists to Jerusalem in time for the expected triumphant return of Christ.[11] Still, the faithful were warned against dating Christ's return too precisely when they discovered that the eighteenth-century pietistic leader Johann Albrecht Bengel had mistakenly predicted this event to occur in 1836. Finally, Schaff also acquired the ambiguous, moralizing attitude of Württemberg pietism toward human culture—even the classicism of Goethe and Schiller—which was at all times to be subservient to and informed by the

---

[9]Wilhelm Dilthey, "Ferdinand Christian Baur," *Gesammelte Schriften*, vol. 4, 3rd ed. (Stuttgart and Göttingen, 1963) 419.

[10]See Müller, *Die religiöse Erweckung in Württemberg*, 29.

[11]*Pietismus und Neuzeit*, vol. 7 of *Ein Jahrbuch zur Geschichte des Neueren Protestantismus* (Göttingen, 1982) 187.

Christian faith, preferably as pietists understood it. Schaff had every right to call Württemberg his "second fatherland," especially since he also was to spend the next two years, 1837-39, at the divinity school of Württemberg's famous university at Tübingen.

Before we follow Schaff to Tübingen, however, a brief survey of the larger German scene is called for. During the years of Schaff's university studies one of the most extraordinary periods in the history of German culture was drawing to its close. One needs only to remember that Beethoven had died in 1827, Hegel in 1831, Goethe in 1832 and Schleiermacher in 1834. It is the Age of Goethe, the Age of German Idealism. It is the towering culmination of what Friedrich Meinecke has simply called "the German movement," from Leibnitz to Goethe, and has hailed as the second great achievement of the German mind after the sixteenth-century Reformation. It was the genius of this age to create what Ernst Troeltsch has suggestively described as "the second great type of modern thought," besides the Enlightenment.[12] Many, indeed, were the new ideas which this age turned into potent cultural forces. In the setting and under the impact of this exceptional age German Protestantism also was transformed. It now made the transition from the Enlightenment of the previous century, when it had lost much of its dogmatic substance and of the intensity of its faith, to a new religious climate which was to be permeated by the optimism and exultant mood that began to govern "the philosophy of religion through Hegel, theology through Schleiermacher, and faith itself through the theologians of the Awakening."[13] When in 1841 the philosopher Schelling categori-

----

[12]Friedrich Meinecke, *Die Entstehung des Historismus*, vol. 3 of *Werke*, ed. C. Hinrichs (Munich, 1965) 2; Ernst Troeltsch, "Der deutsche Idealismus," in *Gesammelte Schriften*, vol. 4 (Tübingen, 1925) 535. -Three monumental works offer brilliant and comprehensive surveys of the history of German culture in the first half of the nineteenth century: Franz Schnabel, *Deutsche Geschichte im neunzehnten Jahrhundert*, 4 vols. (latest editions, Freiburg, 1949-55); H. A. Korff, *Geist der Goethezeit*, 5 vols. (Leipzig, 1964 edition); Wilhelm Lütgert, *Die Religion des deutschen Idealismus und ihr Ende*, 4 vols. (2nd ed., Gütersloh, 1923).

[13]Werner Elert, *Der Kampf um das Christentum. Geschichte der Beziehungen zwischen dem evangelischen Christentum in Deutschland und dem allgemeinen Denken seit Schleiermacher und Hegel* (Munich, 1921) 34.

cally declared: "In Germany the fate of Christianity will be decided," he eloquently testified to the new-found intellectual self-consciousness and self-confidence of German Protestantism.[14]

Schaff was to share fully this spirit of expectancy, this exultant and optimistic mood. Moreover, the creative forces of this age—the Awakening, Schleiermacher, Hegel and Schelling, and the new historical consciousness and historiography associated with such names as Herder, Wilhelm von Humboldt, Savigny, Ranke and Hegel—were to determine permanently his own intellectual and religious outlook and orientation. Indeed, he was first and foremost an *heir* of this great age. Like all the members of his generation he now faced the crucial question as to what principle of selection, correction, combination and application he was to use in channeling the wealth of new ideas and aims into the life of his mind. An eclectic and more practical attitude began to prevail. Also, as Jacob Burkhardt is reported to have remarked, after 1830 everything had begun to be "more common."[15] Even so, the years prior to the revolution of 1848 were still full of the hope and promise of greater things yet to come.

Nevertheless, when in 1842 Schaff applied at the University of Berlin for the *venia legendi* (the right to give academic lectures), he wrote in smooth, almost Ciceronian Latin that the position of a professor of theology, to which he now aspired, was not only very beautiful but also most difficult. For, as he continued, "Some theologians, who are endowed with brilliant powers of mind, are eager to overthrow not only parts of lighter weight but the whole historical and dogmatic foundation of our saving faith, and even those theologians who are loyal to the Sacred Scriptures and to the church disagree greatly among themselves."[16]

Why suddenly this jarring and discordant note? These remarks indicate that Schaff was also to be a *participant* in what Karl Marx

---

[14]F. W. J. Schelling *Sämmtliche Werke*, ed. F. K. A. Schelling (Stuttgart and Augsburg, 1856-61) sec. 2, 4:320.

[15]Quoted by Karl Löwith, *From Hegel to Nietzsche*, trans. D. E. Green (New York, 1964) 67.

[16]University of Berlin, "Akten" (unpublished records).

would later call—in a grand but singularly fitting phrase—the "decay of the Absolute Spirit," that is, the disintegration of Hegel's school of philosophy.[17] This process began in 1835 with the publication of David Friedrich Strauss's sensational *The Life of Jesus Critically Examined.* A brilliantly gifted Hegelian, this young instructor at the University of Tübingen's divinity school presented the Gospel story as the fanciful, mythical invention of Christ's first disciples and, in doing so, suddenly revealed Hegel's philosophy as potentially being one of traditional Christianity's worst enemies. The Tübingen church historian Ferdinand Christian Baur later wrote: "One must have lived at the time when Strauss's book appeared to have any idea of the commotion it provoked."[18] Together with the germs of dissension that were nourished by the unavoidable frictions between the Awakening, Schleiermacher's theology and Hegel's philosophy, this book therefore also contributed to the speedy formation and subsequent confrontation of three schools of theology that were to dominate German Protestantism until the advent of Ritschlianism: the "free" or "radical theology for which Baur and Strauss stood, the mediating theology and the orthodox theology of a resurgent Lutheran confessionalism.

Schaff was to hear some of the dark rumblings caused by the disintegration of Hegel's school, by such other revolutionary Hegelians as Ludwig Feuerbach and Karl Marx, besides David Friedrich Strauss. But he was not to understand the fateful development in German culture that led "From Hegel to Nietzsche" (Karl Löwith). Those developments that were at war with the prevailing spirit of the age were in the end to him nothing but swiftly moving clouds casting no more than a passing shadow on this new and glorious age, the Gilded Age, in which a progressive, smugly self-satisfied western bourgeoisie was comfortably at home. Indeed, to the end of his life Schaff remained a faithful, innocent child as well as an articulate

---

[17]From Karl Marx and Friedrich Engels, *Die deutsche Ideologie* (1845-46), quoted by Löwith, *From Hegel to Nietsche,* 100.

[18]Ferdinand Christian Baur, *Kirchengeschichte des 19. Jahrhunderts,* ed. E. Zeller (Tübingen, 1862) 363.

spokesman of the nineteenth century's unbounded optimism. The exhilarating New World experience, of course, invigorated still further his optimistic outlook. The contemporary divisions of German Protestantism, however, were to affect immediately and lastingly the life of his mind and his career. For he was to learn to fear those "free" and "radical" theologians, in particular the Tübingen school of Baur and Strauss, whom he held to be chief among those who are "eager to overthrow . . . the whole historical and dogmatic foundation of our saving faith." He was to enter fully into the discussions and quarrels of those whom he considered to be the friends of true Christianity: the representatives of the mediating theology and of the Lutheran confessional theology.

When Schaff began his university studies at Tübingen in 1837, one could well have wondered how he would weather the transition from the narrow, intense pietism of his youth into the bracing air of the German university and the bombshell caused by Strauss's *Life of Jesus Critically Examined*. After all, this book was written in the very heart of pious Württemberg and published when Schaff was still a student at the Stuttgart *Gymnasium*. At Tübingen, it was especially the influence of Isaac August Dorner, another young instructor and rising star who was then beginning work on his monumental *History of the Development of the Doctrine of the Person of Christ*, which would assure that Schaff was one of those young men for whom, as Schleiermacher had hoped, the intense pietism of their youth was "but a transition to a worthier freedom of the spiritual life."[19] According to Schaff, Dorner labored "to prove the harmony of Christian theology and sound philosophy" and to make "the dialectics of Schleiermacher and Hegel subservient to the defense of the truths of revelation."[20] Thus Dorner, and later others of like mind, succeeded, certainly in Schaff's case, in satisfying "the wants of those advanced

---

[19]Friedrich Schleiermacher, *On Religion. Speeches to Its Cultured Despisers*, trans. J. Oman (New York, 1958) 145 (from an explanatory note to the 3rd ed. of 1821).

[20]Schaff, *Germany: Its Universities, Theology, and Religion* (Philadelphia, 1857) 376.

students who wished to master the speculative and critical problems of the age without losing their Christian faith."[21]

As to Strauss, Schaff took his cue from the Württemberg pietists' first shocked reaction, as in the following years and even to the end of his life he too would wage an unremitting war against "Straussian infidelity." For the faithful, even in the German theological faculties, Strauss stood first among those "critical terrorists" (an apt phrase later coined by one of Schaff's friends) who boldly practiced a nonmiraculous interpretation of Christian origins.[22] And like his pietistic friends Schaff immediately protected himself from the assaults of these "critical terrorists" by retreating into the bulkwark of the experience of his own spiritual rebirth. He would always believe that the truth of orthodox Christian dogmas is sufficiently demonstrated by Christianity's power to convert sinners and to give them the Spirit-induced experience of Christ's saving presence. Shortly before leaving Tübingen he confided into his diary that during the past year Christ "has been wonderfully present ... proving to me indeed that he lives and that his holy Gospel is not a garland of myth which abortive effort has sought to bind around his brow, and keeping me from erring in the labyrinth of the wisdom of the age."[23] It is this "evangelical" notion of the significance of Christ's saving presence that continued to distinguish Schaff's whole career. The experience of spiritual rebirth remained for him an epistemological principle that itself was no longer subject to any higher authority. Furthermore, it was the prerequisite for understanding the nature of Christianity itself, as it was also the final arbiter for deciding the extent of the mediation that was to be both permissible and mandatory between the inherited Christian faith and the critical, intellectual currents of contemporary culture. In short, the "childlike faith" of Württemberg pietism was to become, so to say, the work-

---

[21]See below, p. 27.

[22]Johann Peter Lange, *Das Evangelium nach Johannes* (Bielefeld and Leipzig, 1880) vii.

[23]David S. Schaff, *The Life of Philip Schaff: in Part Autobiographical* (New York, 1897) 25.

horse of Schaff's mature theology, pulling all sorts of heavy doctrinal loads throughout his whole career and pulling them, after the Civil War, increasingly against the main currents of modern intellectual thought.

At Tübingen Schaff was immediately drawn into the confrontation between the two hostile camps, which he felicitously dubbed the "critical" and the "evangelical."[24] The commanding figure of the church historian Ferdinand Christian Baur dominated the "critical" camp. Its members were committed to remaining free of all restrictive dogmatic presuppositions while they employed brilliantly the categories of Hegel's philosophy in their study of the origins and history of Christianity. The "evangelical" camp was gathered around such teachers as Dorner and the New Testament professor Christian Friedrich Schmid. From Schmid, and later from August Neander as well, Schaff learned to distinguish the three apostolic types of Peter, Paul and John and to accept this distinction as the key to understanding the history of the apostolic church.[25] It is obvious that Schaff lost no time in joining the "evangelical" camp—and of this camp he remained a life-long member, even though, if one is to do justice to Schaff's whole career, the term "evangelical" will always warrant most careful definition, both in the German and the American context and for the various stages of Schaff's development as well. During the years of Schaff's studies most members of the "evangelical" camp showed an eager, though always cautious openness toward the creative new thought that was bursting forth in theology, philosophy and historical studies. Soon there emerged the so-called *Vermittlungstheologie* or mediating theology, which, standing as it did in the long shadow of Schleiermacher and Hegel, had set itself the goal of mediating between the creative intellectual currents of early nineteenth-century German culture and the inherited supernaturalism of

---

[24]See below, p. 24.

[25]Schmid and Neander actually distinguished the four doctrinal types of James and Peter (which Schaff combined) and Paul and John. See Christian Friedrich Schmid, *Biblische Theologie des Neuen Testaments* (Stuttgart, 1853), and August Neander, *Geschichte der Pflanzung und Leitung der christlichen Kirche durch die Apostel*, 5th ed. (Gotha, 1862).

the Christian dogmatic tradition, all assaults of the modern consciousness against this traditional Christian position notwithstanding. The mediating theology therefore came to represent what we
might well call a progressive orthodoxy or liberal evangelicalism,
which then was also to become a powerful shaping influence in Schaff's
life, helping to refine as well as to define his character as an "evangelical" scholar. The periodical *Theologische Studien und Kritiken,* the
major organ of this school, had in its first issue programmatically declared that at no time, and least of all at this time, can there be "too
much of true mediations."[26] This understanding of the theological
task was to become the dominant motif also of Schaff's own theology
and churchmanship. The story of his American career is, therefore,
in one sense best told as the story of a transplanted German mediating theologian. This viewpoint alone, I believe, can adequately explain Schaff's later activity and thought and the unity underlying his
whole life's work in its various stages of development. One might
note that the first instance of such a "mediation" in Schaff's life was
his acceptance of Hegel's developmental theory of history in Baur's
class-room at Tübingen; the first literary evidence of this position was
his doctoral dissertation *The Sin Against the Holy Spirit* (1841).

Like the mediating theologians generally, Schaff too, at the end
of his German years of study, had become firmly grounded in the
biblical faith and historical Christianity and had simultaneously absorbed many of the potent cultural ideas of the romantic-idealistic
era. He had embraced, in particular, the romantic-idealistic philosophy of history, which combined critical attention to the historical
detail and a philosophical approach to history centered in "ideas" as
the necessary components of historical research. It was firmly anchored in the principle of historical development and even viewed all
history, in one sense or another, ultimately as the revelation of God.
He too tried eagerly—at times almost obsessively—to mediate between conflicting or polar forces and positions; but he too could be
evasive and vague at the points of real intellectual conflict. As he

---

[26]Quoted by Horst Stephan, *Geschichte der deutschen evangelischen Theologie seit
dem deutschen Idealismus,* 2nd rev. ed. by Martin Schmidt (Berlin, 1960) 188.

would soon state as much in self-defense as in self-explanation: he would rather be "too churchly at the expense of science than too scientific at the expense of the church."[27] Furthermore, Schaff showed the mediating theology's characteristic combination of apologetics and polemics, skillfully defending evangelical Christianity while attacking its enemies, such as Baur's Tübingen School with its alleged "rationalism" and "pantheism" on the left and later the stiffening orthodoxy of Lutheran confessionalism on the right. He also did battle with various contemporary manifestations in politics and society of what today we would broadly call a "secular humanism." Equally characteristic were the historical interest, the ability and eagerness to harvest the rich results of the scholarship of the age, and a practical, highly successful churchmanship. Finally, Schaff himself, more than anyone else, was to bear out the truth of Emanuel Hirsch's observation that the mediating theology in the nineteenth century "awakened an appreciation and understanding for the fact that there is a world-wide Protestant community."[28]

But what has been said in criticism of the mediating theology— for example by Baur, Troeltsch, Barth and Hirsch—must be equally applied to Schaff.[29] On the whole, the mediating theology, whether

---

[27]Schaff, "Die Studien und Kritiken," *Der deutsche Kirchenfreund* 1 (1848): 82.

[28]Emanuel Hirsch, *Geschichte der neueren evangelischen Theologie im Zusammenhang mit den allgemeinen Bewegungen des europäischen Denkens,* vol. 5 (Gütersloh, 1954) 414.

[29]Ferdinand Christian Baur spoke contemptuously of the mediating theologians' "insipid and flat theology which availed itself of Schleiermacher's name merely to cover its scientific shortcomings" (*Kirchengeschichte des 19. Jahrhunderts,* ed. E. Zeller, 426). Ernst Troeltsch referred still more acidly to the "petty harmony and unctious inaccuracies of the so-called mediating theology which fraudulently used Schleiermacher's name for its own purposes" (*Gesammelte Schriften,* vol. 7 [Tübingen, 1913] 202). Karl Barth judged the theology of Alexander Schweizer, whom he called "the prototype of the mediating theologian," to be "boring," and he concluded that while the mediating theology reigned supreme in German Protestantism systematic theology tended "to hibernate" and, consequently, the best minds gave up systematic theology for church history (*Die protestantische Theologie im 19. Jahrhundert,* 2nd. ed. [Zollikon/Zurich, 1952] 516, 522). Hirsch, *Geschichte der neueren evangelischen Theologie,* 5:410-14, offers in a brief compass the most

we think of its German representatives or even of an American like Schaff's later colleague Henry B. Smith, lacked the power of truly creative thought (Karl Barth even called its theology "boring") and therefore managed to arrange no more than a temporary truce between Christian faith and modern criticism. To be sure, this theology "kept open all questions and decisions and in the breathing space thus gained (did) helpful intellectual work according to its best abilities" (and, adds Hirsch, what more can be asked?).[30] Nevertheless, most of these theologians came to represent in their work an unstable eclecticism, for "the personal union (*Personalunion*) of theological motifs did not lead to an actual, substantial union (*Realunion*)."[31] One might add that later developments would prove such a critical appraisal to be true. For the coming fissure between liberalism and fundamentalism, and still later the divergent paths followed by the Federal (then National) Council of the Churches of Christ and the National Association of Evangelicals, certainly marked the end of what then turned out to have been only a temporary truce in late nineteenth-century American Protestantism, with which Schaff had come to identify himself so confidently.

Schaff encountered teachers similar in spirit and theological orientation to Dorner and Schmid at the University of Halle, where he spent the winter semester of 1839/40. He had the good fortune of being at once employed as the *amanuensis* (a kind of social and academic assistant) by Friedrich Tholuck, the leading theologian of the Awakening alongside of August Neander in Berlin. Julius Müller, author of a monumental study of the doctrine of sin (hence students had dubbed him *Sünden-Müller*), equally impressed Schaff. Nevertheless, Schaff was unable to resist for long the attraction and brilliance of the University of Berlin, where, as Friedrich Engels enthusiastically proclaimed in 1841, "there are daily spoken words

---

balanced evaluation. For the best systematic discussion of the theology of this school one should turn to Ragnar Holte, *Die Vermittlungstheologie: Ihre theologischen Grundbegriffe kritisch untersucht* (Uppsala, 1965).

[30]Hirsch, *Geschichte der neueren evangelischen Theologie*, 5:430.

[31]Stephan, *Geschichte der deutschen evangelischen Theologie*, 189.

to which the boundaries of Prussia, yea of all the German-speaking countries cannot set a limit."[32] The various university departments had brilliantly capable teachers: the historian Ranke, the jurist Savigny, the geographer Ritter and, since 1841, the philosopher Schelling.

Schaff arrived in the Prussian capital in the spring of 1841. Ernst Hengstenberg, the Old Testament professor and editor of the influential *Evangelische Kirchenzeitung,* who also was the leader of the "evangelical" camp in Berlin, obtained at once for Schaff the position of tutor to the only son of the widowed Baroness von Kröcher. This position provided him with the necessary financial security and the leisure for completing sucessfully, in the spring of the following year, his doctoral dissertation, "The Sin Against the Holy Spirit." He passed the doctoral examinations with the grade *non sine laude* ("not without praise").[33] Schaff had apparently little contact with Philip Marheineke, a conservative Hegelian. August Twesten, Schleiermacher's successor in systematic theology, however, initially influenced Schaff deeply. The church historian August Neander would soon enter his life and then leave his permanent mark on Schaff.

In the early summer of 1841 the von Kröchers and their young tutor embarked on an Italian journey that was a fitting conclusion to the years of Schaff's academic apprenticeship. In Rome, where Schaff officiated for several weeks as the chaplain at the Prussian embassy, he participated in the solemnities and excitement of Passion week and even had an audience with the reactionary Pope Gregory XVI. On this journey, which lasted fourteen months and extended as far south as Sicily, Schaff already displayed to the fullest those two traits that would enrich and characterize his whole career. He demonstrated his native ability of associating easily with all kinds of people—peasants and church dignitaries, artists and theologians, Catholics and Protestants—always eagerly drawing out from each what was instructive and would increase the pleasures of sociable companionship. He also

---

[32]Quoted in art. "Berlin," *Die Religion in Geschichte und Gegenwart,* 3rd ed., 1:1057.

[33]University of Berlin, "Akten."

put to good use his great linguistic skills: at Chur he had grown up speaking both German and Italian, and at the Stuttgart *Gymnasium* he had acquired his knowledge of Latin, Greek, Hebrew and French, to which, beginning in 1843, he would add English. After his return to Berlin, in the summer of 1842, he hurriedly prepared his inaugural dissertation (required as a qualification for an academic career) on a topic of minor interest, "The Relationship of James, the Lord's Brother, to James, the Son of Alphaeus, Anew Exegetically and Historically Investigated." During the first week of December he delivered two trial lectures, one in German, the other one in Latin. Some thirty years later he still sighed: "I passed safely through the ordeal of the professorial examinations."[34] In the winter semester of 1842/43, Schaff, at the age of twenty-three, proudly began his academic career as a *privatdozent* (a non-tenured assistant professor whose sole university source of income are student fees) in the theological faculty of Germany's foremost university.

However, during the next two years—the last years Schaff was to spend in Germany, as it turned out—two new developments occurred in his life. He came under the powerful influence of what is best designated as the Prussian High-Orthodoxy, and he now attached himself firmly and permanently to the church historian August Neander.[35] The Prussian High-Orthodoxy represented the confessional theology of a resurgent Lutheran orthodoxy. It had grown out of the Berlin Awakening and, in the reign of king Friedrich Wilhelm IV, had forged an alliance between the Awakening and the forces of political reaction. Despite its deep roots in the Awakening, in the early 1840's it had sharply turned against the old pietism, when it began to accuse both pietism and rationalism of a "subjectivism" that it held to be destructive of the historical, confessional church as the "Body of Christ," as the pillar of all Christian truth and the mother of all true believers. Its Lutheran confessional orthodoxy, however, had been uniquely tempered, at least for the time being, by an ecu-

---

[34]Schaff, "Autobiographical Reminiscences," 13.

[35]Hans Joachim Schoeps, *Das andere Preussen,* 2nd ed. (Honef, 1957) 220 and passim.

menical outlook that was nourished and shaped by the romantic-idealistic currents of that time.

It is important to realize that when Schaff embraced the aims and ideas of the Prussian High-Orthodoxy he was caught up in yet another phase in the evolution of German Protestantism. Beginning in the early 1840's, this phase was dominated by what was broadly called "the church question." Emanuel Hirsch has called attention to the "peculiarity" in the history of nineteenth-century German Protestantism that "to an extent which was not known to an earlier age, not even to the Reformation, the church itself—its nature, its task, its structure and order, its relationship to the state and the common life in general—becomes the object, if not the center, of theological and ecclesiastical consideration and activity."[36] Soon there evolved two contrasting ecclesiological positions which Hirsch labelled "neo-protestant"— variously combining the Enlightenment, Schleiermacher and Hegel as the major forces—and "neo-pietist"—primarily represented by the revived orthodoxy of Lutheran confessionalism. Wilhelm Löhe, a leader of the Lutheran party in Bavaria, spoke the truth, though hardly the whole truth, when he exclaimed in 1845: "Everybody is talking about the church in our time."[37] And "talking about the church" was now also Schaff.[38] Having embraced both the high-church and ecumenical views of the Prussian High-Ortho-

---

[36]See Hirsch, *Geschichte der neueren evangelischen Theologie,* 5:145, and the whole chapter 49, "The Controversy about the Concept of the Church." Also helpful is Gyula Bárczay, *Ecclesia semper reformanda. Eine Untersuchung zum Kirchenbegriff des 19. Jahrhunderts* (Zurich, 1961), which distinguishes the three ecclesiological positions of the liberal, mediating and confessional theologies.

[37]Wilhelm Löhe, *Drei Bücher von der Kirche* (Stuttgart, 1845) preface.

[38]It is possible to date rather accurately the beginning of Schaff's interest in the "church question." In his diary for August 15, 1844, he excitedly remarked that his Mercersburg colleague John William Nevin had shown complete understanding of his views of the church, with which he, Schaff, had been preoccupied "for one year" ("Tagebuch 1844." All of Schaff's extant diaries are in the Schaff Collection, Union Theological Seminary, New York). Schaff's first literary contribution to the "church question" was his article "Katholizismus und Romanismus," *Literarische Zeitung* (Berlin) 1843, nos. 87 (October 31) and 100 (December 16).

doxy (Hirsch's "neo-pietist" position), he too now firmly believed
that contemporary Protestantism stood in dire need of a "churchly,"
sacramental and liturgical renewal which would gather in the rich
harvest of the universal church of all ages and would in due time issue
both in the "catholic" perfection of Protestantism and the "evangelical" perfection of Roman Catholicism. Then the unity of the
Christian church would be visibly restored and made manifest by what
Schaff and his friends liked to call an "evangelical catholicism," the
grand synthesis of Roman Catholicism and Protestantism, both having left behind their respective imperfections.

Later the jurist Friedrich Julius Stahl became the most influential leader of this group of theologians, politicians and Prussian
junkers whose political conservatism continued to be matched by their
high-church views. In the early 1840's, however, Hengstenberg and
the jurist Ludwig von Gerlach, a Prussian nobelman of great charm
and persuasive power, were the leading representatives of this party,
and it was their influence that won Schaff over.[39] But it was Schelling, Hegel's successor in Berlin, who provided Schaff with the most
suggestive ecumenical vision. In the last two lectures of his course
"The Philosophy of Revelation," which he taught for the first time
in Berlin in the spring of 1842, he distinguished in the history of
Christianity the "petrine church" of Roman Catholicism and the
"pauline church" of Protestantism and predicted their coming reconciliation in the "johannean church" of Love, which will then be
the final embodiment of that hoped-for "evangelical catholicism."[40]
It was only after Schaff had already departed for the United States
that the members of the Prussian High-Orthodoxy discovered the
incompatibility of the orthodoxy and high-church views of their Lu-

---

[39]For Ludwig von Gerlach's views, see Schoeps, *Das andere Preussen*; Eugen Je-
dele, *Die kirchenpolitischen Anschauungen des Ernst Ludwig von Gerlach* (Ansbach,
1910); and esp. *Ernst Ludwig von Gerlach: Aufzeichnungen aus seinem Leben und Wirken, 1795-1877*, ed. Jakob von Gerlach, 2 vols. (Schwerin, 1903).

[40]Schelling's two lectures can be found in *Sämmtliche Werke*, ed. K. F. A. von
Schelling (Stuttgart and Augsburg, 1856-61) sec. 2, 4:294-334. For a translation
of these lectures see Klaus Penzel, "A Nineteenth-Century Ecumenical Vision: F.
W. J. Schelling," *Lutheran Quarterly* 18 (November 1966): 362-78.

theran confessionalism and the broad ecumenical ideals and aims of their "evangelical catholicism." In reaction especially to the revolution of 1848 they then firmly embraced an exclusive Lutheran confessionalism.

During those same two years Schaff also attached himself to Neander personally, and under his growing influence and in his spirit he finally committed himself to the study of church history as his professional goal. In applying for his doctoral examinations in 1841, when he was still influenced by such teachers as Dorner, Tholuck and Twesten, he had named New Testament exegesis and dogmatic theology as his primary interests.[41] Two years later, in his letter accepting the Mercersburg position, he singled out biblical exegesis and church history as those two fields to which he was professionally committed, and indeed would remain committed throughout his long career. Nevertheless, in two important respects—the high-church views of the Prussian High-Orthodoxy and Hegel's "speculation"— Schaff found himself at first forced to go beyond Neander's position. Reference is to these developments when I broadly characterize Schaff's theological position at the end of his German years of study as the provocative and exciting fusion of a high-church pietism and the romantic-idealistic philosophy of history.

By dint of hard work, a sociable personality and a brilliant mind, and with the steady financial support of his many friends and patrons, Schaff had risen from obscure beginnings in the Swiss mountains to what promised to be the beginning of an outstanding academic career either at a German or Swiss university.

But in the summer of 1843 the New World suddenly and unexpectedly beckoned to this young scholar, when he received a call from across the Atlantic Ocean to assume the professorship of Biblical Exegesis and Church History at the Seminary of the German Reformed church at Mercersburg in Pennsylvania. This was to be the turning point of his life. For this invitation was to him "a divine call that came to me with irresistible force."[42] Shortly before leaving for

---

[41]University of Berlin, "Akten."

[42]From Schaff's ordination sermon, ms. in the collection of The Evangelical and Reformed Historical Society, Lancaster Theological Seminary.

the New World in April of 1844, he was ordained to the ministry in
the Reformed Church at Elberfeld, but under the auspices of the
Prussian Union church, and commissioned to his American work by
the "Langenberg Society," an outgrowth of the Lower Rhineland
Awakening, which supported all Protestant German-language
churches in the United States. Leaving Germany, he spent six weeks
in England, where he laid the foundations for his thorough knowledge of English affairs, both past and present, and for his working
friendship with leading representatives of that nation's churches and
theological faculties. With ease and impartiality he called upon two
leading prominent combatants in the Established Church: Frederick
Denison Maurice, a chief proponent of "Broad-Church" views, and
Edward Bouverie Pusey, the leader of the Anglo-Catholic revival,
better known as Puseyism or Tractarianism. End of May Schaff set
sail for the New World. On July 28 he finally caught sight of the
New Jersey coast and exclaimed: "The evidences of civilisation are
here, as in the land we left,"[43] Soon he would boast, "I am a Swiss
by birth, a German by education, and an American by adoption."[44]

   If we cast another backward glance at Schaff's formative years,
we should first note how important at almost every significant turn
of his life the network of the "awakened" or evangelical Christians
in Switzerland and Germany had been. By supporting and directing
him, they had kept him firmly within the orbit of their own piety
and world view. The *Deutsche Christentumsgesellschaft*, which had been
founded in Basel in 1780 as a countermeasure against the rationalistic spirit then rampant in the churches of continental Europe, provided the link between the pietists of eastern Switzerland and southern
Germany, facilitating Schaff's removal from his native Chur to
Kornthal, Stuttgart and Tübingen. Tholuck at Halle and Hengstenberg at Berlin found employment for him and kept close to him. And
soon the leading representatives of the "evangelical" camp at Halle
and Berlin unanimously recommended the young scholar for the
Mercersburg position in the United States. In pietistic fashion Schaff

---

[43]David S. Schaff, *Life of Schaff*, 90.

[44]See below, p. 15.

saw the guiding hand of divine providence in all of these events. The historian, however, will simply point to the network of these "awakened" Christians, who firmly believed that they were doing God's will and furthering the coming of His kingdom when they supported young men of their own persuasion for the ministry and an academic career—and withheld with equal determination their support from others of a different outlook! Richard Rothe later bitterly remarked of his erstwhile pietistic friends: "Their kingdom of heaven is a religious fraternity."[45] Indeed, the "fraternity spirit" of the Awakening, more than any other influence, guided Schaff's early life and in the end helped to shape the character of his scholarship and his whole career. But we must also emphasize once more the importance generally of Schaff's German years of study for his American career. His whole life, to an extent that is quite remarkable, bears out the truth of Arthur Schopenhauer's observation: "The impression which the world makes on the individual mind, and the ideas with which such a mind, after it has gone through the process of education, reacts to that impression, all this is over and done with by the thirtieth year: what comes later are only the developments and variations of the same theme."[46] This observation, however, becomes fully applicable to Schaff only when the first few years of his American career—when the impressions of the New World on his receptive and creative mind—are also included. After all, he was to turn thirty five years after his arrival in the New World.

II

When Schaff left Berlin for the United States in 1844, he had every reason to think of himself as "a missionary of science."[47] In-

---

[45] Adolf Hausrath, *Richard Rothe und seine Freunde*, vol. 1 (Berlin, 1902) 168.

[46] *Arthur Schopenhauers Briefwechsel und andere Dokumente*, ed. Max Brahn (Leipzig, 1911) 61.

[47] Schaff, *Das Princip des Protestantismus* (Chambersburg PA, 1845) 10 (cf. *The Principle of Protestantism*, trans. John W. Nevin [1845], Lancaster Series on the Mercersburg Theology, vol. 1, ed. Bard Thompson and George H. Bricker [Philadelphia, 1964], 54).

deed, his ordination sermon had shown eloquently that the missionary and ecumenical impulses of the Awakening were deeply embedded
in his consciousness.[48] The life of this young scholar was energized
by the same spirit that had found its beautiful expression in Wilhelm
Löhe's remark: "Mission is nothing but the one church of God in its
movement—the realization of the one universal, catholic church."[49]
Schaff was especially conscious of the task, though he hardly already
perceived its true dimensions, of building bridges between the
churches of the two continents.

The "mission field" he was about to enter was a new nation,
barely fifty years old, committed to the great experiment of a democracy governed by majority rule, with a wide-open and continuously expanding western frontier, and with immigrants arriving in
ever larger numbers at its eastern seaports. Recent immigration had
made the Roman Catholic church the largest Christian body, and it
now even appeared to threaten the religious and social hegemony that
the Protestant churches had been able to maintain and to increase since
colonial times. Moreover, after the revolutionary principle of religious liberty and the separation of church and state had firmly been
anchored in the Constitution of the new republic, American Christianity was in ferment: the life of the churches centered around "the
great alternative" of the voluntary principle;[50] sects multiplied; and
revivalism, that new missionary technique, ran wild—or so it ap-

---

[48]Schaff concluded his sermon with the stirring words (abridged): "What is
wanted is that members of the same faith take hands as brothers, both in spirit and
in body, on this and the farther shore of the great ocean. What is wanted is the
firm union of all true members of the evangelical, apostolic, and therefore only
true catholic Church. What is wanted is to have Europe and more especially Protestant Germany, the heart of Europe, live, thrive, and bloom in America, so as to
bring the new world, pregnant with the future, closer to the old and aging world.
Then the time will come when both hemispheres will understand each other in
their love for the crucified One and take hands across the sea in a spirit of love and
everlasting peace" (see n. 42 above).

[49]Löhe, *Drei Bücher von der Kirche*, 15.

[50]Robert Baird, *Religion in America*, ed. Henry W. Bowden (New York, 1970)
chap. 33: "The Voluntary Principle the Great Alternative."

peared at least to Schaff when he contrasted these revivals with the mission efforts of the stately, churchly German Awakening. Later many, surprised, would conclude that "religious liberty opened the highway to a greater uniformity than the Church of Rome ever contemplated."[51] European visitors and immigrants, however, often found the sad consequence of religious liberty to be sectarian anarchy, or, in the words of a recent study, "a disorderly and theologically uninspiring pluralism."[52]

The German Reformed church was one of the smaller Christian tribes in this new nation.[53] Limited to the middle section of the eastern seaboard region, in the early 1840's it had 75,000 members, 600 congregations, 184 ministers, and two institutions of higher learning, Marshall College and the Seminary. Recently formed, both institutions, since the mid-thirties, were located at Mercersburg in western Pennsylvania in the western foothills of the Appalachian mountains. The village of Mercersburg with its 1000 inhabitants had recommended itself as the ideal site for both college and seminay because of its scenic beauty, its safe distance from urban distractions and a road much travelled by stage coaches. In its early years the seminary was continuously burdened with financial difficulties, and its student enrollment was small, between ten and twenty students. Four years prior to Schaff's arrival, the Presbyterian John Williamson Nevin had been called into the service of the German Reformed church, where he joined Frederick A. Rauch, a native German, both teaching at the seminary and the college. Rauch, who had been educated at the University of Heidelberg, had first introduced the new German philosophy and theology into the German Reformed church,

---

[51]Perry Miller, *The Life of the Mind in America: From the Revolution to the Civil War* (New York, 1965) 68.

[52]R. Laurence Moore, *Religious Outsiders and the Making of Americans* (New York and Oxford, 1986) ix.

[53]For background see esp. J. M. J. Klein, *The History of the Eastern Synod of the Reformed Church in the United States* (Lancaster PA, 1943), and George Warren Richards, *History of the Theological Seminary of the Reformed Church in the United States, 1825-1934, Evangelical and Reformed Church, 1934-1952* (Lancaster PA, 1952).

and it was his untimely death at the age of thirty-five in 1841 that two years later led to Schaff's Mercersburg appointment.

This, then, was the strange, new world to which Schaff brought the distinctive and substantial theological program he had acquired during his German years of study. Small wonder that Schaff's theology clashed with America's pre-Civil War evangelical Protestantism, what Perry Miller called its "indigenous passions," that is, its virulent anti-Catholicism, its biblicism and individualism, its emotional and contrived revival techniques, and its disregard for and hence ignorance of the history and traditions of the universal church.[54] The wonder, however, is that Schaff's lone Mercersburg colleague, John Williamson Nevin, had independently, through his own study of Neander's works, arrived at a position quite similar to Schaff's.[55] It was, indeed, a strange coincidence that Nevin should have opened himself in the United States to the same German theological influences as his German-trained colleague.

A few months before his death, when Schaff visited the First Reformed Church in Reading, Pennsylvania, for the last time, he remarked nostalgically: "Here I stood fifty years ago and flung out a firebrand. However, I did it unintentionally."[56] The "firebrand" was his inaugural lecture, which a year later had grown into a book, *The Principle of Protestantism.* Later Schaff also liked to claim that *The Principle of Protestantism* was "a harmless book," and he averred that "I had not the remotest thought, when I delivered my address, that I was out of accord with the views of the Reformed Church in this country."[57] In 1847 he reassured his German friends that he had not "passed off his whole point of view as something original," but had "declared it to be essentially identical with the standpoint of the

---

[54]Schaff, *America,* ed. P. Miller, xx.

[55]James H. Nichols has shown well the liberating impact of Neander's church history on Nevin, whose church history teacher at Princeton had used "Mosheim for facts and Milner for piety" and had judged everything "polemically from Princeton's orthodox point of view" (*Romanticism in American Theology,* 43).

[56]David S. Schaff, *Life of Schaff,* 114.

[57]Ibid.

evangelical-churchly theology of present-day Germany."[58] Nevertheless, the new German theology and historiography were bound to excite and disturb the members of the German Reformed church, as well as the American Christian public at large. Nevin and Schaff were to initiate what came to be known as the "Mercersburg movement" and the "Mercersburg theology," fanning not only a long-lasting controversy in the German Reformed church but also adding a remarkable new chapter in the history of American theology.[59]

In the German Reformed church the battle lines were already drawn when in the opening sermon at the synod in October of 1844, a week before Schaff's inaugural lecture, the synod president, Dr. Joseph Berg, set forth those notions then commonly held by American Protestants: the Reformation was a direct return to New Testament Christianity; Roman Catholicism had been an apostate church from the beginning; the line of historical succession from apostolic times to the Reformation and beyond had therefore run only through the medieval sects, the Waldensians in particular. This "Waldensian theory" Schaff explicitly rejected in thesis thirty-one of the "Theses for the Time," which he appended to *The Principle of Protestantism.* The following year Berg too published an enlarged version of his address under the telling title *The Old Paths, or, A Sketch of the Order and Discipline of the Reformed Church Before the Reformation, as Maintained by the Waldenses Prior to That Epoch, and by the Church of the Palatinate in the Sixteenth Century.* Here he categorically asserted: "If we admit that the Church of Rome has ever been the Church of Christ, you concede the entire ground."[60] Soon Berg and the Philadelphia Classis charged Schaff and Nevin with serious deviations from the Reformed faith, hurling against both men the grave accusation of "Romanizing tendencies," an epithet considered most damaging at

---

[58]*Palmblätter,* ed. Friedrich Krummacher, 4 (1847): 84.

[59]For a masterful interpretation of the Mercersburg theology, though mostly of Nevin, we are indebted to James H. Nichols, *Romanticism in American Theology: Nevin and Schaff at Mercersburg* (Chicago, 1961), and, as editor, *The Mercersburg Theology* (New York, 1966).

[60]Joseph Berg, *The Old Paths . . .* (Philadelphia, 1845) viii.

that time by the defenders of Protestant orthodoxy, both in Europe
and America. In the heresy trial that followed in October of 1845,
the Synod of the German Reformed church stood by its two professors, acquitting them honorably of all the charges brought against
them. Two months later Schaff married Mary Elizabeth Schley (1822–
1901), his lifelong companion, who gave birth to eight children of
whom five died in their youth.

A second heresy trial threatened Schaff a year later, when an unauthorized translation of his speculative views on a "middle state,"
which he had set forth in his dissertation *Die Sünde wider den Heiligen
Geist* (1841), again offended the orthodox stalwarts. Schaff had
claimed that all those pagans, who had not already here on earth encountered the gospel, would be given the opportunity to hear the
gospel after their death, in a middle state of sorts between heaven and
hell, though even then they would be saved only by faith in Christ.
This time, however, the Synod of the German Reformed church refused to take any formal action at all.[61] In the midst of continuing
controversy, Berg in 1852 departed for the Dutch Reformed church,
which itself was in the process of severing all official ties with her
German sister church, accusing it of being led astray by the "Mercersburg theology" of Nevin and Schaff.

Schaff later declared that the Mercersburg theology was mainly
developed by Nevin.[62] The evolving relationship between these two

---

[61]For Schaff's two heresy trials, see Shriver's chapter "Philip Schaff: Heresy at
Mercersburg," in *American Religious Heretics,* ed. George H. Shriver (Nashville and
New York, 1966) 18-55. William R. Hutchinson's claim needs to be corrected
that it was later Newman Smyth, drawing upon August Dorner, who introduced
"the startling and controversial possibility of a second chance, after death, for those
who had not attained salvation in this life," into the American theological discussion (*The Modernist Impulse in American Protestantism* [Cambridge MA and London, 1976] 84). Obviously the notion of a middle state, which was of a kind with
the notion of the salvation of unbaptized children, proved increasingly attractive
to evangelical sensibilities offended by the stern character of the exclusivist and
elitist Calvinist system. For Schaff's last word on the middle state, now more cir-
cumspect and cautious, see *Lange's Commentary on the Holy Scriptures,* ed. Philip Schaff
(New York and Edinburgh, 1868-1880), vol. 1 of the New Testament (Matthew,
228-29).

[62]See below, p. 7.

men—their collaboration, their influence upon each other, their differences—and the impact each had upon the German Reformed church and the Christian public at large present some intriguing questions that still await a fuller answer. Nevin, who was Schaff's senior by sixteen years, was the theologian and polemicist; Schaff was the historian, by temperament and outlook conciliatory, though he too could at times be quite pugnacious. Observers noted a curious reversal of roles, for Nevin, with his powerful mind and angular, grave personality, appeared to be the "German," while Schaff, with his agile mind and lively, active personality, impressed many as the "American." When Nevin resigned from the Seminary in 1852, Schaff offered a moving testimony to their common life. He had, he wrote, "after almost eight years of collaboration, whose harmony has never even for a moment been disturbed, the melancholy feeling that, humanly speaking, he will hardly find again a colleague in every respect so able, experienced and worthy."[63]

Schaff's Mercersburg theology is in any case best presented by itself.[64] Its most important ingredients were the high-church notion of the church as the Body of Christ, the *Christus prolongatus*; the romantic-idealistic philosophy of history with its novel principle of historical development; the Neander-Schmid distinction of the three apostolic types of Peter, Paul and John as the key to understanding the nature and history of the New Testament church; and the romantic vision of an "evangelical catholicism." He articulated this program in three books—*The Principle of Protestantism* (1845), *What is Church History?* (1846), and *History of the Apostolic Church* (German, 1851; English translation, 1853)—as well as in his numerous contributions to the journal *Der deutsche Kirchenfreund*, which he founded in 1848 and edited for the next six years. This journal proclaimed itself on every title page to be the "Organ for the Common Interests of the American German Churches."

---

[63]Schaff, "Kirchenchronik," *Der deutsche Kirchenfreund* 5 (March 1852): 127.

[64]For a fuller discussion of Schaff's theological program, see my article "The Reformation Goes West: The Notion of Historical Development in the Thought of Philip Schaff," *Journal of Religion* 62 (July 1982): 219-41.

It is significant that Schaff's first two major works—*The Principle of Protestantism* and *History of the Apostolic Church*—dealt with those two issues that were then most hotly contested between the "evangelical" and "critical" camps of German Protestantism: the origin and nature of Christianity and of Protestantism.[65] This fact already explains the polemical and apologetic features so conspicuous in both works. In addressing first the question of the origin, development and nature of Protestantism in *The Principle of Protestantism,* Schaff skillfully and eclectically tried to synthesize orthodox, romantic and idealistic views, as chapter 2 will show in greater detail. When he next turned his attention to the question of the origin and nature of Christianity, he naturally chose to follow in Neander's footsteps, to whose memory he had dedicated the original German version of his book. Like Neander he pitted the traditional, supernaturalistic understanding of the apostolic church against its modern counterpart, the nonmiraculous interpretation and radical reconstruction of the apostolic literature of Baur's Tübingen School. One should add, though, that Neander no less than Baur, and Schaff as well, employed, each in his own fashion, the best critical tools of contemporary historical scholarship.

The controversies and discussions prompted by the questions of the origin and nature of Christianity and of Protestantism had, of course, a profound bearing on the third contested issue, the "church question." Schaff agreed with the Lutheran Theodor Kliefoth that the most important task theology faced in the nineteenth century was

---

[65]One should note, for instance, how closely the literary labors of Schaff's Tübingen classmate, Heinrich Thiersch, paralleled Schaff's own: Thiersch's *Vorlesungen über Katholizismus und Protestantismus* (1846) was followed by the first volume of a projected history of the Christian church, *Die Kirche im apostolischen Zeitalter and die neutestamentliche Literatur* (1852). One with Schaff in attacking Baur, his program for the renewal of the church, however, differed greatly from Schaff's, since already in 1847 he had joined the Irvingite movement, hoping for the miraculous restoration of apostolic Christianity. Another rising German scholar, Albrecht Ritschl, whom Schaff was to notice only several decades later, wrote at this time under Baur's influence *Die Entstehung der altkatholischen Kirche* (1850), although in the second edition of 1857, precisely over the question of the origins of Christianity, he broke with Baur and began to chart his own independent course.

the doctrine and the renewal of the church.[66] Modern Protestantism, because of what Schaff alleged to be its one-sided "subjectivism," was as diseased and in need of reformation as Roman Catholicism had been in the sixteenth century. Schaff identified this diseased or "pseudo-Protestantism," broadly speaking, with the ethos of the European Enlightenment and the denominational fragmentation of Anglo-American Christianity. But he was also firmly convinced that Christianity at that very time stood on the eve of a new reformation which would occur in North America, where it would be brought about through an organic combination of the new German theology and the practical and organizational skills of American Christians. This coming reformation will then issue in an "evangelical catholicism," though Schaff soon came to suspect that its perfect manifestation may have to await the triumphant return of Christ. Other contemporary movements aiming at the renewal of the church, such as Irvingism, Puseyism and Lutheran confessionalism, he welcomed to the extent that they represented the needed tendency toward "objectivity" in Protestantism. Nonetheless, he rejected all of them, since each in its own way ran afoul of his cherished principle of the historical development of Christianity, by looking backward only, to some allegedly perfect state of the church in the distant past. Still other efforts at church renewal and unity, such as Samuel S. Schmucker's *Fraternal Appeal* (1838) and the Evangelical Alliance founded in London in 1846, he opposed as representing what he considered to be the anti-Catholic, unchurchly and unhistorical tendencies of British and American Protestantism.

It is obvious that center place in Schaff's theological program belonged to the romantic-idealistic theory of historical development, which in his understanding faithfully mirrored Schleiermacher's "Protestant view" of the Christian church "as a whole that is capable of motion, progress and development, with the single restriction without which Christianity would collapse . . . namely, that such progress is nothing but a better understanding and a more perfect

---

[66]Theodor Kliefoth, *Einleitung in die Dogmengeschichte* (Parchim and Ludwigslust, 1839) 94.

appropriation of what is founded in Christ."[67] The theory of historical development, essential as it is for understanding the nature and history of Christianity, is therefore misapplied if such development is assumed to lead beyond "what is founded in Christ." Like Neander he identified this permanent foundation with the apostolic age, the "century of miracles."[68] Utilizing the distinction between "idea" and "manifestation," between object and subject, he insisted that Christianity is complete objectively, as an "idea" embodied in the apostolic church. Development, therefore, takes place only in the changing historical manifestations of that "idea," only as the apostolic faith is subjectively ever more fully appropriated and unfolded in the consciousness of the successive generations of Christian believers. It should further be noted that he eclectically combined idealistic and romantic notions, and hence interpreted church history both as following the laws of idealistic dialectics and as representing a self-unfolding organic process.[69] And over against the Tübingen School of Baur and Strauss he insisted that a "right application" of the principle of historical development depended entirely on a "right view of positive Christianity," that is, on the traditional supernaturalistic understanding of Christianity.[70] The other English publication that just then also espoused a theory of de-

---

[67]Friedrich Schleiermacher, *Die christliche Sitte nach den Grundsätzen der evangelischen Kirche im Zusammenhang dargestellt,* ed. L. Jonas, in *Sämmtliche Werke,* sec. 1, vol. 12, 2nd ed. (Berlin, 1884) 72.

[68]This phrase, which was especially dear to Schaff, had apparently been coined by the Swiss historian Johannes von Müller. See Schaff, *History of the Apostolic Church,* trans. E. D. Yeomans (New York, 1853) 675.

[69]Hegel himself discussed the contrast between the romantic and dialectical concepts of development in *Die Vernunft in der Geschichte,* in *Sämmtliche Werke,* ed. J. Hoffmeister, vol. 18 A (Hamburg, 1955) 151-52. See also Ernst Troeltsch, "Über den historischen Entwicklungsbegriff und die Universalgeschichte," *Gesammelte Schriften,* vol. 3 (Tübingen, 1922) 283. There Troeltsch emphasized that one must carefully "distinguish between the concept of development of the organological school and that of the dialectical school," although in reality they frequently fused—as, for instance, in Schaff's mind.

[70]Schaff, *History of the Apostolic Church,* 91.

velopment—John Henry Newman's *An Essay on the Development of Christian Doctrine* (1845), written as its author was about to convert to Roman Catholicism—Schaff guardedly welcomed as making "a concession in favor of Protestant science" but faulted for allowing the development "to hold only in the Roman Catholic direction."[71]

One might well claim that the so-called Mercersburg theology was on Schaff's part, in one sense, nothing but an attempt to adjust the German Reformed church, and the other American churches as well, to the present transitional stage of church history. One may even assert that during those first Mercersburg years Schaff confidently believed himself to be at the very center of the progress of church history, precisely where God's spirit—or Hegel's "world spirit"— was now at work, for at this tiny Pennsylvania seminary, and especially in his own person and that of his colleague Nevin, the new German theology and the practical bent of American Christianity were being fused for the larger purpose of ushering in the johannean age of church history. Of course, Schaff knew that "much pauline struggle will yet be necessary before the johannean festival of reconciliation among the various Christian confessions can be celebrated."[72] Perceiving his own time as a period of such "pauline struggle" that will lead to the ultimate goal of the "johannean festival of reconciliation," is, indeed, the broad thematic frame within which all of Schaff's efforts, theological and practical alike, at Mercersburg and later at New York may be placed.

In practical terms this meant that at Mercersburg Schaff pursued above all three goals: (1) to introduce the new German theology into American Christianity, beginning with the German-language churches (his program of 'anglogermanism'); (2) to bring together the Lutheran and Reformed churches in the United States on the

---

[71]Schaff, *What is Church History? A Vindication of the Idea of Historical Development,* trans. John W. Nevin (Philadelphia, 1846) 46n.

[72]Schaff, *Amerika,* 2nd ed. (Berlin, 1858) 219. Quotations from the German edition are from sections omitted in the English editions.

model of the Prussian union of 1817;[73] and (3) to achieve that larger goal of the "catholic" perfection of Protestantism and the "evangelical" perfection of Catholicism, which in God's own good time will result in the ultimte union of both. As a biblical scholar and church historian, he had come to believe in a deeply felt ecumenism that the restoration of the unity of the church is "the supreme task of church history."[74]

By 1851, however, disappointment set in. On the one hand, Schaff took note of the growing strength of an exclusive Lutheran confessionalism, both in Germany and the United States. American Lutherans, it appeared to him, had in fact heeded the admonition to return to their historical roots. They had recovered the orthodox, churchly and historical identity of their church. But, ignoring the Hegelian dialectic, they had sadly failed to go forward as well toward that final goal of an "evangelical catholicism." In 1852, in articles in *Der deutsched Kirchenfreund*, Schaff sharply criticised the direction in which Lutherans at St. Louis, Gettysburg and Philadelphia—and German Lutherans at Erlangen, Leipzig and Berlin—now seemed to be moving.[75] On the other hand, he was equally dismayed by the continuing virulent anti-Catholicism of American Protestantism, a chief manifestation of which was to him the Presbyterian rejection of the validity of baptism in the Roman Catholic church at Cincinnati in 1845. More passionately than ever he pressed the case for an informed and generous appreciation of the historical significance and Christian character of Roman Catholicism.

---

[73]Even the title of Schaff's inaugural lecture, "The Principle of Protestantism," was expressive of this hope. According to Ragner Holte, this phrase itself "becomes one of the key words in the mediating theology for motivating the unitive efforts that were of such burning interest among Lutherans and Calvinists in nineteenth-century Germany" (*Die Vermittlungstheologie*, 152).

[74]Schaff, *Amerika*, 2nd ed., 262.

[75]To what extent Schaff (and Nevin) contributed to the recovery of American Lutherans of their own unique tradition, and why in the end he failed to turn Lutherans in the direction of an inclusive, ecumenical confessionalism, is a question that has yet to receive the scholarly attention it deserves.

The generally unfavorable reaction to those sharply polemical articles of 1852 was typified by Schaff's friend Julius Mann. In letters to his friend he exclaimed in exasperation (August): "When one sometimes hears you, one might well think that the Roman curia has offered you a cardinal's hat." He confessed his "inner disquiet" (September) and wrote again unhappily (October): "You astonish me. You think you must undeceive Puritanism. Desist, my friend. It will yet in the course of a great historical praxis find its way." Then he added words that must have carried much weight with Schaff: "If in American Protestantism you shut more doors than you open for German theology, then the day will come when you will realize that you have been truly useful neither to the Roman nor the Protestant church."[76] Soon Scribner warned Schaff that his controversial views might hurt the sale of his *History of the Apostolic Church*.[77] The publisher of *Der deutsche Kirchenfreud,* Schäfer and Koradi in Philadelphia, feared losing subscribers, for, as Mann also wrote Schaff, his views were out of line with the thinking of by far the largest part of the journal's readers.

Impressed, no doubt, by these voices of concern, Schaff resigned from the editorship of *Der deutsche Kirchenfreund* at the end of 1853, gladly accepting Julius Mann as his successor. In a "Farewell" to the readers he declared that in all essentials the leading principles of his theological program were still the same: He continued to hope for the coming organic union of the English and German nationalities in America, of the Reformed and Lutheran churches, of Protestantism and Catholicism. Nevertheless, he conceded obliquely that his mediating position "might have its own peculiar dangers and be open to much reproach, especially in the manner in which we until now represented it according to the talents we were given."[78] But when

---

[76]Letters of Mann to Schaff, quoted by Spaeth, *D. Wilhelm Julius Mann,* 61-65.

[77]Letter of Schaff to Theodore Appel (23 June 1853). See Nichols, *Romanticism in American Theology,* 224.

[78]Schaff, "Abschied von den Lesern des Kirchenfreundes," *Der deutsche Kirchenfreund* 6 (December 1853): 471.

this "Farewell" was published, Schaff was already on his way to Europe, celebrating Christmas 1853 aboard the steamship "The City of Glasgow" on a storm-tossed ocean en route from Philadelphia to Liverpool. The Synod had granted him a year's leave of absence, which was a much deserved respite for a scholar who had shouldered an enormous workload during the previous ten years and had just recently begun to establish an international reputation as a church historian of great promise with the publication of his *History of the Apostolic Church*. In 1853 the parents had also watched helplessly the suffering and death of their two-year-old son Philip William.

Though Schaff was to revisit Europe fourteen times—in the nineteenth century obviously an amazing number of transatlantic journeys for a scholar— none of these journeys was more significant for Schaff's development—and almost another turning point—than the first one, in 1853/54.[79] In England he was surprised to discover that Roman Catholicism was by far not as strong as he had apparently been led to believe at Mercersburg. Moreover, he found Puseyism limited to small circles of the clergy and aristocracy, and their piety characterized by a pedantry "which the genuine Protestant consciousness cannot get used to."[80] England, he now realized, was, after all, a thoroughly Protestant country. Even more important were the changes he encountered in Germany. The inherently unstable "paradox" of the Prussian High-Orthodoxy, which had uneasily combined Lutheran confessional and ecumenical tendencies, was, as already noted, to be finally resolved after the revolution of 1848.[81] His former Berlin mentors now embraced an exclusive Lutheran

---

[79]None of Schaff's fourteen European journeys is more fully documented than the first one, thanks to a series of lengthy letters in German Schaff wrote for the readers of *Der Deutsche Kirchenfreund*. The first one, "From Philadelphia to Liverpool" ["Reisebriefe No. 1: Von Philadelphia nach Liverpool"], appeared in the February 1854 issue, and the last one, "Letter from Trent" ["Reisebilder für den Kirchenfreund: Trient"], in the October 1855 issue.

[80]Schaff, "Reisebriefe No. 5: Oxford," *Der deutsche Kirchenfreund* 7 (June 1854): 212.

[81]See Schoeps, *Das andere Preussen*, 72.

confessionalism, while Schaff, on the contrary, turned in the other direction of an inclusive "evangelical catholicism."

One might say that the final break with his former Berlin mentors occurred as late as 1857, when the orthodox party in Prussia's capital opposed the Berlin conference of the Evangelical Alliance— Ernst Hengstenberg and Friedrich Julius Stahl, the leaders, ostentatiously leaving the city for the duration of the conference and Stahl even resigning in protest his official position in the government of the Prussian church. As recently as 1853, Schaff too had still rejected the Evangelical Alliance as a misguided ecumenical effort.[82] But a year later, in Germany, he suddenly joined his evangelical friends, such as Tholuck and Kapff, in hearty support of the Evangelical Alliance. And though he was unable to be personally present at the Berlin conference in 1857, it was on that occasion that he sent his first report on the state of Christianity in the United States to an Evangelical Alliance conference. To Stahl's rhetorical question, "Shall we give up our fellowship with Augustine, Gregory the Great, Bernard of Clairvaux, [the Catholics] Fenelon and Sailer, in exchange for the fellowship with a Baptist preacher?",[83] Schaff could have honestly replied that his outlook had grown to be broad enough to allow him to be at home with the fathers of the early and medieval church, later Roman Catholic theologians, and the Baptist preachers in America. At a conference of the Basel Mission in 1854 he noted a speaker's remark, offered in response to visitors from Berlin, who had come to support the pietistic Basel Mission out of opposition to the exclusive orthodoxy of the Berlin Mission: "Mount Zion is higher than every church steeple."[84] In the section on the German-Ameri-

---

[82]Even though Schaff acknowledged that the London conference of the Evangelical Alliance in 1846 had been a manifestation of the widespread desire for Christian unity, he once again (and for the last time!) denounced the Evangelical Alliance as a "total failure" because of its anti-Catholicism; limiting Christ's kingdom to Protestantism was "an enormous stupidity" ("Ein Blick in die kirchlich-religiöse Weltlage," *Der deutsche Kirchenfreund* 6 [March 1853]:107).

[83]Friedrich Julius Stahl, *Der Protestantismus als politisches Prinzip* (Berlin, 1853) 119.

[84]Schaff, "Correspondenz," *Der deutsche Kirchenfreund* 7 (September 1854): 330.

can churches in *Amerika* Schaff immediately agreed: "In the interest of the kingdom of God which is elevated above all individual confessions—Mount Zion extends beyond the highest church steeples—we can only rejoice that so many Germans in America wear the robe of Christ's righteousness, even if they wear over it the Presbyterian or Puritan or Methodist or Baptist coat, instead of the Lutheran, Reformed or United."[85] The religious individualism and activism of Europe's and America's evangelical Protestantism were beginning to outrun the high-church views of Schaff's Berlin and early Mercersburg years. Schaff now made his choice. He was going to plant himself firmly and lastingly in the broad camp of "evangelical" Protestantism, whose growing strength and unity he also witnessed at the Frankfurt *Kirchentag* in 1854. He returned from his first European trip, as he wrote, hinting at that further evolution in his theology and outlook, "probably a better Protestant and American."[86]

Schaff continued at his Mercersburg post for almost another decade, until 1863, when the turmoil of the Civil War interrupted seminary activities and he permanently settled with his family in New York. In the winter of 1862/63 he taught at Andover Seminary. During those last Mercersburg years he was a major force in the formulation of a new liturgy for the German Reformed church, which, as James H. Nichols correctly put it, was "the most specific practical expression" of the peculiar Mercersburg views of Nevin and Schaff.[87] This new liturgy was to cause a serious and long-lasting controversy in the German Reformed church, in which Schaff, however, no longer actively participated. The horizons of his scholarship, after all, were growing ever wider and his interests were turning elsewhere. He continued to work on the volumes of his *History of the Christian Church.* Two of his other publications were of special significance. *Amerika* (1854; English translation, 1855) was his first book in which he la-

---

[85]Schaff, *Amerika,* 2nd ed., 214.

[86]See below, p. 121.

[87]Nichols, *Romanticism in American Theology,* 281. Jack Martin Maxwell, *Worship and Reformed Theology: The Liturgical Lessons of Mercersburg* (Pittsburgh, 1976), is the best study of the Mercersburg liturgy.

bored free of the long shadow of his German teachers; he was now even eager to be their teacher in turn. For determined as he was to bring the fruits of German scholarship to the United States, he was equally eager to spread knowledge of the history, present conditions and future prospects of the United States and her churches in Germany. Characteristically, he next published *Germany* (1857), which was the greatly expanded version of the 1852 series of articles on German theology in *Der deutsche Kirchenfreund,* but without the polemics. It also was the first book he wrote in English without the benefit of a translator. He also prepared a German Hymnbook, a German Catechism, and a volume on the Heidelberg Catechism in connection with the tercentenary celebrations of that catechism in the German Reformed church in 1863. Ten years earlier he had already rejoiced that the German Reformed church had now gained "a clear consciousness of its origin, and of its character as a Melanchthonian, conciliatory medium between Lutheranism and Calvinism," for which he gave the credit to Nevin.[88] However, he felt increasingly isolated at Mercersburg, especially after Marshall College was moved in 1853 to Lancaster, a larger town and more centrally located, while the Seminary, as Schaff bitterly complained, was foolishly left behind (the Seminary was removed to Lancaster in 1871). After a two-years leave of absence and a second European journey, Schaff officially resigned from his Mercersburg position in 1865.

It is obvious that the Mercersburg period of Schaff's career can be properly understood only back to back with the last Berlin years in his education and as that stage of his life when in his experience as an immigrant the American context and the new German modes of thought first met—and clashed, and then gradually began to merge. I would like to suggest, however, that some additional perspectives can be brought to bear on this important period of his life. Historians of the immigrant experience in American culture remind us that the first phase of immigrant alienation is usually soon followed by the no less typical reaction of immigrant fervor. One might therefore view, for instance, Schaff's two books—*The Principle of Protestantism* and a

---

[88]Schaff, *History of the Apostolic Church,* 133n.1.

decade later *America*—as the literary manifestations of those two typical immigrant reactions, first of alienation and then of fervor, so that
Schaff's *America,* as Perry Miller claimed, not only "by its objectivity" but also by its "affectionate power is as fine a tribute to America
as any immigrant ever paid."[89] And if I may indulge for a moment
in psychohistory, then one may also view the Mercersburg period in
Schaff's life, in particular his high-church views, as a belated stage
of rebellion in his otherwise so smoothly continuous development. It
was a healthy reaction of doubt and resistance that was directed against
the "fathers," men like Tholuck and Neander, who represented the
German Awakening, so that, with his sense of adult independence
and self-identity strengthened and confirmed, he later typically re-
joined their company even more firmly and faithfully. By the time
of his first European journey he had also come out from under the
influence of the older Nevin's dominant personality.

But one more remark is called for. Lord Acton is reported to have
said of John Henry Newman's *Essay on the Development of Christian
Doctrine* (1845) that more than any other book at the time it made
the English "think historically, to watch the process as well as the
result."[90] These same words can be applied with equal justification
to Schaff's Mercersburg publications and their impact upon American Protestants. One should therefore single out as perhaps Schaff's
greatest achievement at Mercersburg that here his historical learning, rooted as it was in the romantic-idealistic philosophy of history,
helped to prove Newman's famous dictum to be no longer applicable
even to American Protestants. "To be deep in history is to cease being
a Protestant."[91]

III

The final stage in Schaff's development is obviously also a part of
the complex story of his "Americanization." His adaptive person-

---

[89]. Schaff, *America,* ed. P. Miller, xxxv.

[90]See Owen Chadwick, *From Bossuet to Newman: The Idea of Doctrinal Development* (Cambridge, 1957) x.

[91]John Henry Newman, *An Essay on the Development of Christian Doctrine,* 6th
ed. (London, 1890) 8.

ality and scholarly eclecticism, his Hegelian idealism and American pragmatism, no doubt, helped to ease his way into the mainstream of American life. After all, Schaff was only too ready to march in the rear of what he was wont to call, in good Hegelian fashion, "the objective force of history."[92] Believing firmly that God's Spirit manifests itself in the actual flow of historical events, he always listened more eagerly to the powerful language of historical facts than to the philosophical theories emanating from the scholar's ivory tower. "The powerful proof of historical facts must finally cause the most stubborn opposition to fall silent," so he asserted, for instance, in 1848.[93] Schaff's own evolution became therefore a part of the remarkable story of the evolution of American Protestantism itself: from the evangelicalism of the nineteenth century's first half, which Schaff and Nevin used to deride as "Puritan" and "Methodist," to the evangelicalism of the postbellum years. The latter became increasingly "liberal" and "ecumenical" because (among other things) it was increasingly informed by those new German modes of thought, especially the historical consciousness of nineteenth-century German culture. James H. Nichols correctly observed that Nevin and Schaff led the German Reformed church through a transition that the Presbyterians and Congregationalists experienced only in the 1880's and 1890's, and that the Mercersburg movement should therefore be viewed as "a kind of paradigm before the Civil War of what would happen to the American Reformed churches generally by the end of the century," when the New England theology and that of the Presbyterian Old School finally collapsed.[94] And as Schaff was a driving force in the earlier transformation of the German Reformed church, so he was an equally active participant in the later transformation of the evangelical denominations of American Protestantism, while his own theological program evolved still further as well.

---

[92]Schaff, *What is Church History?*, 118.

[93]Schaff, "Prolegomena zur Kirchengeschichte der Vereinigten Staaten," *Der deutsche Kirchenfreund* 1 (December 1848): 358.

[94]Nichols, *Romanticism in American Theology*, 310.

The complex story of Schaff's "Americanization" is therefore much more than an instructive example of how in the end American "facts" will overcome European "theories" in the immigrant's mind. This conclusion holds true in still another respect. When Schaff, for instance, embraced the prevailing millenialism, messianism and even racism of nineteenth-century American religion and society, when he soon welcomed—and no longer condemned—the denominational diversity of American Christianity and then celebrated its lively, active mass of individual Christianity, then these changes in outlook obviously manifested Schaff's growing accommodation to the reality of America's dominant evangelical Protestantism and his new-found appreciation of its pietistic core. But I now want to emphasize what is less obvious: these changes also revealed the renewed impact of certain German categories of thought and influences that had, as it were, for a time merely lain dormant in his mind. A few examples must suffice as evidence.

Perhaps most significant was a shift in Schaff's ecumenical views. At the beginning of his Americn career Schaff had shouted: "Away with human denominations, down with sects!", which was the pointed expression of his rejection of the Free-Church tradition of Anglo-American Protestantism as a diseased stage in the historical development of Christianity.[95] Later, however, he drew a careful distinction between "denomination" and "sect" and he then affirmed the denominational diversity of American Christianity as a "blessing."[96] This important reorientation in his ecumenical outlook was, on its intellectual side, nothing but a shift from the dialectics of German idealism to the individualizing approach of German romanticism, both being a part of the German background of his thought.

In keeping with the logic of idealistic dialectics, Schaff had at first posited the "reunion of Christendom" as the *end result* of the historical process, and, moreover, had conceived this process as the unfolding of the "great European dialectic"—to use Johann Adam

---

[95]Schaff, *Das Princip des Protestantismus*, 101 (cf. *The Principle of Protestantism* [repr. 1964] 155.

[96]See below, p. 309.

Möhler's apt expression—of Roman Catholicism and Reformation Protestantism.[97] Hence he had denigrated the American denominations as wild shoots on the stem of Reformation Protestantism. Furthermore, orienting his ecumenical thought at first to the high-church notion of the visible church as the "Body of Christ," he had also insisted that the coming unity of the universal church is to be made manifest in a visible structure. Later, however, he returned to Neander's (and Schleiermacher's) conception of Christianity as "life," to the romantic understanding of the whole Christian world with its multiplicity of distinct historical phenomena as being but the necessary individualization of the Christian spirit. This understanding then led him to affirm that diversity itself belongs to the very nature of Christianity and that diversity is therefore also essential to Christian unity. "Unity in diversity, and diversity in unity," this slogan would be the ecumenical battlecry of Schaff's later years. Only those romantic notions and not the idealistic understanding of history corresponded to his own experience of the strength of evangelical Protestantism in the second half of the nineteenth century, as that strength manifested itself both in the diversity of the evangelical denominations and in their underlying unity as expressed in a common spirit and in voluntary missionary cooperation. Correspondingly, Neander's concept of the invisible church or the "kingdom of God" rather than the high-church notion of the Church as the "Body of Christ" now became the focal point of orientation not only for his ecumenical thought but also for his conception of the nature and task of church history. Those historians who look for "the true architects of the denominational theory of the Church" should therefore not only look to the Dissenting Brethren in the Westminster Assembly or to nineteenth-century American Evangelicals but also to Schleiermacher and

---

[97]See, for instance, Hegel's characteristic declaration that "the true is the whole," which, properly understood, means that everything is *"only in the end* what it is in truth" (*Phänomenologie des Geistes,* vol. 2 of *Sämmtliche Werke,* ed. H. Glockner [Stuttgart, 1951] 24; italics are mine). — Johann Adam Möhler, *Theologische Quartalschrift* 13 (1831): 655.

Neander—and to Philip Schaff, who finally came to embrace fully
and represent their views.[98]

Again, when Schaff joined the chorus of American voices that ex-
tolled the racial superiority and singular virtues of the Anglo-Saxon
and the German, he was inspired also by German romantic notions,
namely, that nationality is a determining factor in history, that history is always borne along on the shoulders of one or two dominant
ethnic groups or nations, and that all life is but the continuous interplay of the principles of polarity and totality. And even Schaff's
eager endorsement of American millenialism and messianism had
deep roots in German soil, above all in the adventism of Württemberg pietism and the millennial schemes and expectations of such
idealistic philosophers as Schelling. As a matter of fact, it is this peculiar confluence of German and American currents of thought that
makes Schaff's voice so unique in the swelling chorus of Americans
praising and affirming the messianic role of the United States among
the nations of the world. Finally, even the apparent ease with which
Schaff embraced the American principle of the separation of church
and state points to the separatist tendencies Schaff had encountered
among Württemberg pietists, in particular at the separatist com-

---

[98]See Winthrop S. Hudson, *American Protestantism* (Chicago, 1961) 37, and
Sidney E. Mead, "Prospects for the Church in America," in *The Future of the American Church,* ed. Philip Hefner (Philadelphia, 1968) 17.

It is characteristic of Schaff's eclecticism that he never reflected systematically
on these ecumenical options, nor was he apparently aware of a shift in his ecumenical thought. A comparison with his German contemporary Richard Rothe,
who offered the most carefully reasoned combination of these ecumenical positions
(cf. *Theologische Ethik,* 3 vols. [Wittenberg, 1845-48] pars. 998, 1186) is therefore
instructive. Rothe held the idealistic dialectics to be applicable only to the Roman
Catholic-Protestant relationship, while he employed Schleiermacher's romantic
principle of individuality as a means only for comprehending the denominational
diversity of Protestantism. Rothe believed, however, that for the modern period
Christians of all churches should more and more embrace a third ecumenical alternative, that of an ethical union only of all those individuals who are working
for the final, world-encompassing triumph of the kingdom of God. This was an
ecumenical orientation that soon such liberal theologians as Albrecht Ritschl and
Adolf Harnack—and even Schaff himself—would find congenial.

munity of Kornthal, but also to the preference for the principle of religious freedom and separation of church and state of such German theologians as Schleiermacher, Neander and Rothe.[99] Thus it should be obvious that Schaff's so-called "Americanization" is indeed a "mysterious," a very complex process that should invite still further exploration.

IV

It is for these and still other reasons that Schaff, especially after he moved to New York in 1863, increasingly identified himself with the goals and aspirations of the broad tradition of post-Civil War evangelical Protestantism in the United States, of the Broad-Church party in England, and of the center party in German Protestantism, warily observing all the while the growing strength of the ultramontane party in the Roman Catholic church. He now liked to think of himself as a "broad-churchman," whom he described as follows:

---

[99]Schleiermacher, for instance, was favorably impressed by the lack of political interference in religious affairs and the constant process of religious diversification and re-unification which he had found to be characteristic of American Christianity (*On Religion. Speeches to Its Cultured Despisers*, trans. J. Oman, 196-97). And Schaff spoke later of Neander's love of American Christianity, precisely because there Christianity was free of state control and hence could exhibit the full compass of Christian truth in the most diverse forms of piety and church life (see Schaff, *Saint Augustin, Melanchthon, Neander* [New York, 1885] 147). Schaff had a long conversation with Richard Rothe in 1854, when he argued forcefully that Rothe's well-known but singular theory of the gradual disappearance of the church into the state was contradicted by the historical fact of the American separation of church and state. Rothe, however, according to Schaff, "denied the force of the objection, inasmuch as in the United States Christianity had ceased to be a power and organization over against the people, or outside of it, . . . and had become, or promised to become, a truly national concern, the voluntary expression of the people's will, an inherent element of the general life, and that was the very thing he wanted." Rothe here obviously anticipated the twentieth-century notion of America's "civil religion," and it is too bad that the significance of these remarks escaped Schaff, who, instead, posited the final triumph of the church over the state, a theocracy, as the ultimate goal of history (*Germany: Its Universities, Theology, and Religion* [Philadelphia, 1857] 374).

"truly evangelical, Catholic, moderate, comprehensive, humble and in hearty sympathy with all that is pure and good and Christian."[100]

It was in keeping with the character of such a "broad-church-man" that during the last decades of his life Schaff was content to reduce the task of theology, as he now saw it, to the maintenance of a minimal set of doctrinal principles and to their conciliatory application, still battling polemically, however, some of those movements and forces that were outside the broad orbit of a liberal and cooperative evangelical Protestantism. More than ever, his guiding principle was the firm belief of the pietism of his youth that the spiritual reality behind theological concepts is primary and alone essential. As he put it in 1884: "The piety of the heart often protests against the theology of the head, and love is better than logic."[101] Compared with the sparkling presentation of innovative ideas in the literary output of his Mercersburg years, his later theological contributions— however substantial and prominent the continuities— are indeed (to quote Karl Barth once more) "boring." A cursory comparison, for instance, of *The Principle of Protestantism* with a collection of his essays and addresses published forty years later under the title *Christ and Christianity* will confirm such an assessment. Even the volumes of the final edition of his church history are richly but also drily "factual"; they are no longer animated by the fresh power of keen insights and suggestive ideas. The direction of his theological interests had also changed. The contrast between his inaugural lectures at Mercersburg and at Union Theological Seminary is at this point revealing. In 1871 he no longer singled out the "church question" as the great issue that confronted theology and the churches in the nineteenth century, as he had done at the beginning of his American career. Instead, he informed his New York audience that "Christology in its historical aspects and Bibliology in its relation to modern criticism and science" are "the burning questions."[102] In this

---

[100]David S. Schaff, *Life of Schaff*, 323.

[101]Schaff, *Christ and Christianity* (New York, 1885) 308.

[102]Schaff, "The Theology of Our Age and Country" (1871), in *Christ and Christianity*, 11.

sceptical age it had become his highest ambition "to strengthen the faith in the immovable historical foundations of Christianity and its victory over the world."[103]

All these changes may tempt the historian to offer separate evaluations of Schaff's Mercersburg theology, that scintillating fusion of a high-church pietism and the romantic-idealistic philosophy of history, and the theology of his New York years, which one might loosely characterize as follows: a sometimes superficial but always well-intentioned combination of various and at times quite disparate and even already antiquated elements, which Schaff himself once characteristically described as the "liberal and progressive evangelical orthodoxy."[104] The fact is that during the last three decades of his life he would be a "doer" rather than a "thinker." He would primarily pursue, actively and energetically and in the end almost always sucessfully, an amazing range of scholarly and practical projects, in which all four major motifs that gave form and direction to his life's work came fully into play: the biblical, historical, ecumenical and apologetic. In 1882 Julius Mann hailed his great friend as "the presiding genius of international theology" and then added that Schaff's mind was distinguished not so much by "imagination and creative-active power" as by "memory and the critical and organizing ability of assimiliation." Perhaps we can even conclude with Julius Mann that if Schaff had had both he would have been "without a rival" at the height of his career.[105] It would be difficult to think of a more suitable designation for calling attention to what was at the heart of Schaff's professional self-understanding and gave a unique cast especially to the New York period of his career than that phrase his friend had coined—"the presiding genius of international theology."

Schaff believed that Mercersburg had prepared him for New York. But the contrast must have almost overwhelmed him. He had moved

---

[103]Schaff, *History of the Christian Church*, vol. 1 (New York, 1882) vi.

[104]Schaff, *Theological Propaedeutic* (New York, 1894) 228.

[105]Letter of Mann to Schaff (3 October 1882) quoted by Spaeth, *D. Wilhelm Julius Mann*, 73.

to the country's largest metropolis, its teeming population at that time already exceeding one million. Moreover, in the second half of the nineteenth century the city's dominant intellectual culture was, as a recent study observed, a lively and stimulating combination of the literary culture of Paris and the academic culture of Berlin. But fifty percent of the city's population lived in 1876 in the unhealthy squalor of tenements, suffering from a disproportinately high death rate, so that it also could be asserted: "Perhaps in no other great city, whether European or American, was social inequality so extreme."[106] This darker side of the great city during the Gilded Age Schaff failed to notice. What mattered most to him, too, was that New York "stood foremost as a centre of American evangelicialism," where the headquarters for many of the major Bible, missionary and educational societies of evangelical Protestantism were located, and that it was also the "religious publishing centre for the whole country."[107]

In 1870, after he had already lived in New York for seven years, Schaff was appointed to the faculty of Union Theological Seminary. In the same year he was received into the New York Presbytery when he joined the Presbyterian church, of which he had written admiringly in 1854 that it "is without question one of the most numerous, respectable, worthy, intelligent, and influential denominations, and has a particular strong hold on the solid middle class."[108] He joined the Presbyterian church at a most important juncture in its history. Just a year earlier the division of 1837 had been healed when the Old School and New School, the conservative and progressive wings, were reunited (except for the southern constituency, which established itself as the Presbyterian church in the United States).[109] The old ri-

---

[106]See Thomas Bender, *New York Intellect: A History of Intellectual Life in New York City, from 1750 to the Beginnings of Our Time* (New York, 1987) esp. 169-71.

[107]George L. Prentiss, *The Union Theological Seminary in the City of New York: Historical and Biographical Sketches of its First Fifty Years* (New York, 1889) 38.

[108]Schaff, *America*, ed. P. Miller, 118.

[109]For a helpful discussion of these and later developments, see Leffert A. Loetscher, *The Broadening Church. A Study of Theological Issues in the Presbyterian Church since 1869* (Philadelphia, 1954).

valry between Union and Princeton, however, continued. Union Theological Seminary had been founded by New School men in 1836, and though it had been formally independent, it had continued to play a leading role in New School Presbyterianism. Furthermore, it was Henry Boynton Smith, Schaff's Union colleague, who not only had imbued New School thought with the tenets and spirit of the mediating theology which he had embraced during his German years of study, but who also was the acknowledged leader of the movement for reunion. Princeton, by contrast, under the continuing, forceful leadership of Charles Hodge, had remained the theological center of the Old School and had led the opposition to the proposed reunion. A temporary peace was finally established at the first General Assembly of the reunited church in 1870. In that year Union also gave up its independence, when it officially affiliated itself with the reunited Presbyterian church and granted its General Assembly the right to veto faculty appointments.

In 1870 Union was still located at its original site at 9 University Place, though during Schaff's tenure, in 1884, it was to move uptown to much larger and impressive new quarters at 700 Park Avenue. According to the Founders' design, Union was to be a Seminary "around which all men, of moderate views and feelings, who desire to live free from party strife, and to stand aloof from all extremes of doctrinal speculation, practical radicalism, and ecclesiastical domination, may cordially and affectionally rally."[110] Schaff could not have hoped to find a more congenial place to work. He had distinguished colleagues of outlook and sympathies similar to his own, except that from time to time there were friendly clashes with William G. T. Shedd, an Old School man who, since 1874, taught systematic theology. At Union Seminary the versatile and erudite Schaff occupied the chairs of Encyclopedia and Christian Symbolics (1870), Hebrew (1873), Biblical Literature (1874) and Church History (1887). In the end he was to stand out as "the most conspicuous scholar at Union during the period of Union's life as an official denominational sem-

---

[110]Quoted by Robert T. Handy, *A History of Union Theological Seminary in New York* (New York, 1987) 9.

inary."[111] During the final years of his life he loyally defended his former student and colleague Charles A. Briggs at his trial for heresy, and he welcomed the steps that finally led to Union's separation from the Presbyterian church and its independence in 1892.

The chapters of Part II of this volume selectively present texts related to the most important "projects" that occupied Schaff's attention during the New York period of his life. Since a fuller discussion of those endeavors will be found in the editorial introduction to each chapter, I will here offer no more than a brief enumeration of the various "projects" of Schaff's New York years. For the first several years he was the corresponding secretary (or executive director) of the New York Sabbath Committee, which, as he believed, "just in the time of the greatest danger, in 1857, God raised up" to save the Anglo-American Sabbath against "the increasing tide of foreign Sabbath desecration."[112] With the arrival of ever larger numbers of foreign immigrants, the American sabbath, he claimed, "was in danger of being crucified between two thieves— Irish wiskey and German beer."[113] Schaff's decision to give so much of his time and energy to the preservation of the sabbath—a battle soon to be lost— was prompted by his deep conviction that the sabbath, the Bible and the churches were the chief institutions for securing the Christian character of the American republic. During his second European journey in 1865 he labored mightily for the revival of a stricter sabbath observance even on the European continent. In 1865 he published a Life of Jesus, *The Person of Christ: The Perfection of His Humanity Viewed as a Proof of His Divinity,* a kind of Christology "from below," without originality but written with great apologetic fervor for the benefit of "doubters," which turned out to be his most popular book, re-edited repeatedly and translated into many languages.

The major editorial project of his career was, no doubt, the American edition of Lange's German Bible Commentary, the first comprehensive and complete English-language Bible commentary,

---

[111]Ibid., 51.

[112]Schaff, *Christ and Christianity,* 269.

[113]David S. Schaff, *Life of Schaff,* 226.

which occupied his attention for sixteen years (1864-1880) and involved the collaboration of more than fifty scholars, representing a novel and pioneering effort at scholarship by team-work, both international and interdenominational. Remarkably, he is said to have retained the good-will of all of his collaborators. This trail-blazing effort, however, soon proved to be no more than a minor footnote in the history of biblical scholarship, for the twenty-five volumes of this Bible commentary excelled in textual criticism but consistently skirted the burning issue of the "higher" or historical-literary criticism of the Bible. In 1880 Schaff also helped to found the Society of Biblical Literature and Exegesis. As a later Memorial Resolution of this Society stated: "His name stands on the first page of our book of records,—the first name found there."[114] Once more Schaff tried to transfer the harvest of German scholarship across the Atlantic when he prepared the American edition of the Herzog-Plitt-Hauck *Encyklopädie,* now known, after a further revision, as the *New Schaff-Herzog Encyclopedia of Religious Knowledge.*

Schaff showed himself equally adept at cooperating with British scholars in the revision of the King James Version of the English Bible. Although his native tongue was not English, he was for twelve years (1872-1884) the President of the American Committee for Bible Revision, which worked alongside of the British Committee, and in the end he was hailed for his signal contributions to this transatlantic effort as organizer, fund-raiser, exegete and skillful ecumenical ambassador. He was a founder of the American branch of the Evangelical Alliance in 1867, and until his death it was this organization to which he contributed in numerous ways, for he viewed it as the chief instrument at hand in the quest for Christian unity. He was also a major force in the World Alliance of Reformed Churches since its formation in 1875. More than anyone else he contributed to the success of the International Conference of the Evangelical Alliance held in New York in 1873, the largest international gathering of Christians on American soil prior to the Evanston Assembly of the World

[114]Quoted by Ernest W. Sanders, *Searching the Scriptures: A History of the Society of Biblical Literature, 1880-1980* (Chico CA, 1982) 10.

Council of Churches several generations later, in 1954. He pursued another project of adapting old creeds to nineteenth-century evangelical sensibilities in two ways, working, though in the end he was unsuccessful, toward a consensus creed in the larger setting of the World Alliance of Reformed Churches and toward creed revision in the Presbyterian church in the United States.

Finally, there were his contributions as a church historian. Having published the three-volume *Creeds of Christendom* in 1877 (which remains a contribution of lasting value), he spent the last ten years of his life bringing out the final edition of his *History of the Christian Church*. He had twice unsuccessfully made a beginning, in 1853 and 1859/67. Now he covered the history of the church down to Gregory VII in four volumes. He also completed two volumes on the history of the Protestant Reformation, one volume each for Luther's Germany and his native Switzerland. However, he was unable to find the time for completing his presentation of the history of medieval Christianity. This task he left to his son David, who, after the father's death, added two more volumes. Schaff's hope that Arthur C. McGiffert, his student and successor as Union Theological Seminary, would be "the finisher of my life work" by adding the remaining volume on the history of modern Christianity was not to be fullfilled.[115] It was an unrealistic expectation in any case, since during his German years of study McGiffert had become the disciple of Adolf Harnack, acquiring a theological and scholarly outlook in several respects quite different from Schaff's. It must have given Schaff some satisfaction that at the end of his life he had returned with those two volumes on the Reformation to the subject matter with which he had made his debut as a church historian in 1845, *The Principle of Protestantism*. In 1886 he also began work, as coeditor, on the edition of a *Select Library of the Nicene and Post-Nicene Fathers of the Christian Church*. In 1888 he organized the American Society of Church History, of which he remained the president until his death. At the very last he initiated in that Society the *American Church History Series*.

---

[115]Letter of Schaff to McGiffert (11 May 1891) quoted by Arthur C. McGiffert, Jr., "The Making of an American Scholar: Biography in Letters," *Union Seminary Quarterly Review* 24 (November 1968): 43.

During those same years he journeyed to Europe thirteen times, mostly in pursuit of his various projects, for example Bible Revision, the conferences of the Evangelical Alliance and of the World Alliance of Reformed Churches, archival work in preparation for the volumes of his church history. At times he would range as far afield as Spain, Moscow and the Holy Land, and almost always he would make time to vacation with the Heusser family, close friends since his student days, amid the splendor of the Swiss Alps. Not only a brilliant mind but also robust health and an obsessive work habit made it possible for him to sustain the hectic tempo of his life. He once exclaimed that "the only rest I can really enjoy (is) change of work."[116] He also carried the heavy burden of many family afflictions: the death of five children, his wife's severe illness in 1872, a son's marital distress and nervous break-down. His last major publication was an encyclopedic survey of the full orbit of theological disciplines, *Theological Propaedeutic*, which mirrored, in manner and spirit, the widely influential and durable theological encyclopedia of Karl Rudolf Hagenbach, a fellow mediating theologian.[117] In the end he did not have enough time left for one more book he had planned to write, on Symbolics. His last public utterance, which he delivered at the World's Parliament of Religions at Chicago in September of 1893, was the ecumenical address "The Reunion of Christendom." It also was a telling and grand summary of his life's work. He died in his home in New York on 20 October 1893.

V

In concluding this introduction to the life and thought of Philip Schaff, a few more brief comments are called for. I have tried to show that his theological program issued from the unique confluence of

---

[116]Schaff, "Autobiographical Reminiscences," 65.

[117]Karl Rudolf Hagenbach, *Encyklopädie und Methodologie der theologischen Wissenschaften* (Leipzig, 1833; 12th ed. by Max Reischle, 1889). George R. Crooks and John F. Hurst published an English translation and adaptation (which failed to distinguish between the original and the additions): *Theological Encyclopaedia and Methodology. On the Basis of Hagenbach* (New York, 1884).

German and American traditions and is best characterized as a progressive orthodoxy or liberal evangelicalism that was given further
distinction by the ecumenical vision of an evangelical catholicism,
all of which makes his career uniquely instructive. In the strength of
this program and to the best of his considerable abilities, he attempted throughout his long career to mediate between conflicting
and diverse forces, positions and national traditions in order to achieve
or maintain an evangelical consensus and to restore the unity of the
church, viewing both as means toward the ultimate goal of establishing God's kingdom on earth. A postmillenialist and ardent
American, he tended to conceive of the kingdom of God as a global,
English-speaking Christian civilization. The key to his career is that
he used scholarly and practical means for evangelical ends and his liberal evangelicalism for the accomplishment of ecumenical goals. In
the nineteenth century there were few—perhaps there was no one—
on either side of the Atlantic who surpassed him in contributing (to
use Schaff's own words) "toward the mutual understanding and appreciation of European and American divines, and toward the great
cause of Christian union."[118]

But in the end, it turned out that Schaff had been less successful
in mediating between the past and the future. By this I mean that it
is true enough that he built bridges in various fields and in several
different directions, but many of them he did not cross himself (as
did his students Arthur C. McGiffert, Charles A. Briggs and William Adams Brown). William G. McLoughlin has described, perhaps somewhat too neatly and schematically, three phases in the
nineteenth-century evolution of American evangelicalism: Common
Sense Evangelicalism, Romantic Evangelicalism and Evangelical
Liberalism.[119] Correspondingly, one might say that Schaff clashed

---

[118]Schaff, "Autobiographical Reminiscences," 15.

[119]See *The American Evangelicals, 1800-1900: An Anthology*, ed. William G.
McLoughlin (New York and Evanston, 1968) "Introduction," 1-27. The "evangelical" world in which Schaff was at home is, in its intellectual and social aspects,
especially well portrayed in Louis L. Stevenson's recent study *Scholarly Means to
Evangelical Ends: The New Haven Scholars and the Transformation of Higher Learning
in America, 1830–1890* (Baltimore and London, 1986).

with the first phase, represented and helped to shape the second phase, and in the end stood uneasily, with his back partially, if not mostly, turned to the future, at the point of transition where the second phase merged into the third. Certainly this conclusion holds true especially of those two fields—the biblical and historical—that were of such great interest to him and in which he did some of his major work. In his work both as a Biblical scholar and a church historian there is much that we must now judge as transient, even though Lange's Bible Commentary and his church history, both recently reissued by evangelical publishing houses, admittedly do contain a wealth of still useful materials. Most of us, however, will find their basic point of view to be dated and hence of strictly historical interest only. Indeed, Schaff turned his back on most of the many new forces in church and society: Ritschl's theology; the "higher criticism"; the new orientation in historical studies for which Adolf Harnack's name as well as the temporary cessation of the life of the American Society of Church History in 1896 may stand; the rise of the modern university with its specialization, professionalism, and liberal culture and the concomitant "Collapse of American Evangelical Academia"; and finally the growing industrialization with its attendant social problems and tensions.[120] Shortly before his death, though, Schaff publicly embraced Darwin's theory of evolution, affirming it as the counterpart in the natural sciences to his cherished notion of historical development. So profound were the impressions of his German years of study, and so little had his basic theological position been changed in the course of a long career, that at his life's end he could still claim both admiringly and nostalgically that Schleiermacher and the mediating theologians formed "a generation of thinkers and scholars such as had not been seen in the Church since the sixteenth century."[121]

More permanent, at least as an impetus, we may want to judge his work in creed and Bible revision, and, perhaps above all, his ecu-

---

[120]See George Marsden's informative essay "The Collapse of American Evangelical Academia," in *Faith and Rationality: Reason and Belief in God,* ed. Alvin Plantinga and Nicholas Wolterstorff (Notre Dame and London, 1983) 219-64.

[121]Schaff, *Theological Propaedeutic,* 227.

menical endeavors—from his contributions to liturgics and symbolics to his leading role in the Evangelical Alliance and the World Alliance of Reformed Churches—inspired, as all of these endeavors were, by his grand dual vision of an "evangelical catholicism" and the "internationalization of theology." In his quest for Christian unity and cooperation—despite the time-bound nature of the romantic-idealistic notions that shaped his ecumenical views—he was unusually insightful and truly prophetic. Indeed, his whole career may be called a nineteenth-century prelude to the ecumenical movement of our time. One should finally mention that remarkable collection of essays entitled *A Century of Church History: The Legacy of Philip Schaff* (1988), for this book offers abundant proof that the versatile Schaff's pioneering work has helped to stimulate the scholarship and research of later generations in a great variety of ways and in many different fields.

Finally, I want to cite Friedrich Schleiermacher's definition of what he called "the idea of a prince of the Church": "If one should imagine both a religious interest and a scientific spirit conjoined in the highest degree and with the finest balance for the purpose of theoretical and practical activity alike, that would be the idea of a 'prince of the Church.' "[122] This volume is meant to salute Philip Schaff as "the presiding genius of international theology," as a biblical scholar, church historian, apologist of Christianity and fervent advocate of the reunion of Christendom, who in his long and distinguished career truly was such a "prince of the Church."

---

[122]Friedrich Schleiermacher, *Brief Outline on the Study of Theology,* trans. Terrence N. Tice (Richmond VA, 1966) 21 (par. 9).

INTRODUCTION

RETROSPECT AND FAREWELL

EDITORIAL INTRODUCTION.

In October 1844, shortly after his arrival in the United States, Schaff was received into the Synod of the German Reformed church then meeting at Allentown, Pennsylvania. Nearly half a century later, on 24 October 1892, he addressed the Eastern Synod of the Reformed church (the 'German' was dropped from the denomination's name in 1869) on the last day of its annual meeting, which was held in St. Paul's Reformed Church at Lancaster, Pennsylvania. He had recovered with remarkable speed from his first stroke, which he had suffered a few months earlier in July of 1892, while he vacationed, as was his custom during these later years of his life, at Lake Mohonk in upstate New York. Less than a year later, a second crippling stroke broke his health. He died in his home in New York City on 20 October 1893.

It is fitting that Schaff's retrospective farewell should be his first rather than his last word. For it focuses on the events that marked the turning point of his life: the transition from the Old World to the New World, from the University of Berlin in the capital of the kingdom of Prussia to the struggling, isolated seminary in the foothills of the Appalachian mountains at Mercersburg in Pennsylvania. In addition, looking back, Schaff in his own words here offers the reader a preview of the first twenty years of his American career, until his removal to New York City in 1863. The text of the address is from stenographic notes as published in Lancaster

newspapers and the *Reformed Church Messenger* (24 November 1892),
which Schaff then revised. For the Synod's "Welcome and Greet-
ing," to which Schaff's address was the response, see *Berlin 1842—
New York 1892. The Semi-Centennial of Philip Schaff* (Privately
Printed, 1893) 20-22.

FAREWELL ADDRESS TO THE EASTERN SYNOD
OF THE REFORMED CHURCH IN THE UNITED STATES*

Your address touches the springs of my heart, and revives the
memories of my youth connected with my call to America. Feeble as
I am, I must venture on a few reminiscences which will interest my
friends and pupils assembled before me.

I see the two delegates of your special Synodical meeting held at
Lebanon, in January, 1843, the Rev. Dr. Hoffeditz, of German birth,
and as polite as a courtier, and the Rev. Dr. Schneck, a fine specimen
of a native American-German, of unusual height (hence called 'the
high priest of the German Reformed Church').[1] They called at my
study in Berlin, in the summer of 1843, and informed me that the
Theological Professors of Halle and Berlin, especially Tholuck, Julius Müller, and Neander, had unanimously directed them to me as
a suitable person to fill the German Professorship in your Theological Seminary, then located at Mercersburg.[2] Their mission excited
considerable attention by its novelty and boldness, and the prospect
which it seemed to open for the transplantation of German theology

---

*"Dr. Schaff's Reply and Farewell to the Synod," *Berlin 1842–New York 1892.
The Semi-Centennial of Philip Schaff* (Privately Printed, 1893) 23-28.

[1](Ed.) Theodore L. Hoffeditz held various pastorates in the German Reformed
church. Benjamin S. Schneck (1806–74) was for many years the editor of both *The
Weekly Messenger* and the German language *Reformirte Kirchenzeitung* of the German
Reformed church; from 1855 until his death he was the pastor of a congregation
in Chambersburg, Pennsylvania.

[2](Ed.) Friedrich August Gottreu Tholuck (1799–1877) and Julius Müller
(1801–1878) at Halle and August Neander (1789–1850) at Berlin were three of
Schaff's favorite teachers.

to America. King Frederick William IV invited your delegates to the palace, and showed his interest in your Seminary by a liberal gift of fifteen hundred dollars. The House of Hohenzollern, you know, is originally German Reformed, and still uses the Heidelberg Catechism, though strictly devoted to the Evangelical Union of the Lutheran and Reformed Confessions since the third centennial of the German Reformation.

In December I received a call from your Synod held in Winchester, Va. It was signed by the President, the Rev. Dr. Berg, of Philadelphia, who soon afterward raised the charge of heresy against me;[3] while the only member of the Synod who opposed the call, from fear of foreign influence and German neology, became a good friend.

In the spring of 1844 I left Berlin, was ordained at Elberfeld, in the church of Dr. Krummacher, before a large congregation, and preached an ordination sermon, which he published in his *Palmblätter,* and which gave rise to bitter attacks from infidel German papers in America.[4] I had thus on my arrival a warm reception from friends and foes.

Before sailing for my adopted country I spent seven weeks in London and Oxford. What I heard and saw in the May-meetings at Exeter Hall, and in the mediaeval Colleges of the venerable University of Oxford, was to me a revelation, and prepared me for my work in America. I made the personal acquaintance of the leaders of the

---

[3](Ed.) Joseph Frederick Berg (1812–71), who was born to a Moravian missionary couple in the Caribbean, was ordained to the ministry in the German Reformed church in 1835 and was the pastor of the Race Street German Church in Philadelphia until 1852 when he joined the Dutch Reformed church. Author of several anti-Roman Catholic books and tracts. He was appointed professor of theology in the Dutch Reformed Seminary at New Brunswick in 1861.

[4](Ed.) Friedrich Wilhelm Krummacher (1796–1868), a leading representative of the Lower Rhenish Awakening, had been pastor of the Reformed Church at Elberfeld since 1834; he was called to the prestigious Trinity Church in Berlin in 1847 and appointed court preacher at Potsdam in 1853. Schaff's ordination sermon appeared in *Palmblätter* ("Palm Leaves"), ed. F. Krummacher, 1 (May–June 1844); English translation in *The Weekly Messenger* (4 September 1844): 1869–70.

Tractarian movement, (Pusey, Newman, Marriott),[5] but especially of some of the future leaders of the Broad Church School (as Dean Stanley, Professor Jowett), and other rising scholars of liberal tendency, who treated me with cordial hospitality.[6] A year afterward, Dr. Newman, the singer of "Lead, kindly Light," headed the Anglo-Catholic secession to Rome. He was remarkably reserved when I saw him, for half an hour, at Littlemore, as if he was then seriously contemplating that decisive step which marks an epoch in modern church history, as the secession of Dr. Döllinger from Rome, a quarter of a century later, marks another epoch in the opposite direction.[7]

After a voyage of forty days, in a sailing vessel, I safely reached New York, in July, 1844. There Dr. Wolf, the model of a courteous, kindhearted, Christian gentleman, who afterward became my colleague, met me, and accompanied me to Easton, where he was then

---

[5](Ed.) Edward Bouverie Pusey (1800–82), Regius professor of Hebrew and canon at Christ Church, Oxford, joined the Tractarian movement in 1835 and henceforth was considered its leader. The movement was therefore commonly known as Puseyism. John Henry Newman (1801–90), the early leader of the Tractarian movement, withdrew from Oxford to Littlemore (just outside Oxford) in 1842, resigning the next year the living of St. Mary's, the university church at Oxford, where he had been appointed vicar in 1828. A year after Schaff met him, he published his *Essay on the Development of Christian Doctrine* and converted to Roman Catholicism. Ordained to the priesthood in 1846, he was made cardinal by Pope Leo XIII in 1879. Charles Marriott (1811–58), appointed sub-deacon at Oriel College at Oxford in 1841, a close disciple of Newman, took Newman's place as spiritual advisor to students after his mentor's conversion to Roman Catholicism.

[6](Ed.) Arthur Penrhyn Stanley (1815–81), prolific author and the leading Broad-Church theologian of his time, since 1863 dean of Westminster. Benjamin Jowett (1817–93) was appointed tutor at Balliol College at Oxford in 1842 and ordained to the Anglican priesthood in 1845. Regius professor of Greek since 1855, he was one of the contributors to the controversial *Essays and Reviews* (1860). In 1870 he became master of Balliol College.

[7](Ed.) Johann Josef Ignaz von Döllinger (1799–1890), distinguished German Roman Catholic historian, professor of church history and ecclesiastical law at the University of Munich. He broke with his church over the dogma of papal infallibility, was excommunicated and joined the Old Catholic church. Newman's defection to, and Döllinger's secession from, the Roman Catholic church were to Schaff two memorable events which he never failed mentioning together.

pastor.[8] The next day, Dr. Hoffeditz took charge of me, on my leisurely journey through East Pennsylvania, stopping at Kutztown, Reading, and Tulpehocken with Rev. Dr. Leinbach, the father of three ministers, now among my dear pupils. The manners and customs of the people and the Pennsylvanian German dialect (which my friend, the sainted Harbaugh, partly at my suggestion, immortalized in song), were exceedingly interesting to me.[9] Passing through Lebanon to Harrisburg, I met there the delegates of a convention between the German and Dutch Reformed Churches, and for the first time saw Dr. Nevin, with whom I was to be so intimately connected as colleague. I was struck with his commanding and dignified presence, his familiarity with modern German thought, and his churchly tendency. He preached on that occasion the sermon on "Catholic Unity," which foreshadowed his peculiar theology.[10] I was most cordially received and hospitably entertained in Harrisburg by Judge Bucher.[11] On arriving at Mercersburg, on the evening of August 12th, the students of the College and Seminary, by way of encouragement and in vague expectation of great things to come, surprised me, who had done nothing as yet, with a torchlight procession and speeches of welcome in German and English.

---

[8](Ed.) Bernard Crouse Wolff (1794–1870) was pastor of German Reformed churches in Easton, Pa., and Baltimore, Md., and then professor of theology at the Seminary at Mercersburg (1854–64).

[9](Ed.) Henry Harbaugh (1817–67), professor of theology at Mercersburg since 1863, author of *Harbaugh's Harfe* (Philadelphia, 1870), a collection of poems written in "Pennsylvania German."

[10](Ed.) John Williamson Nevin (1803–86), a Presbyterian, joined the German Reformed church in 1840 when he was appointed professor of theology at the Seminary at Mercersburg, retaining this position until 1853. He founded and edited *The Mercersburg Review* (1849–53), was president of Marshall College (1841–53), professor at Franklin and Marshall College (1861–66 and 1868–76), and also president of that College (1866–76). The sermon "Catholic Unity" was first published in the weekly papers of both the German and Dutch Reformed churches and then included, upon Schaff's request, in his *Principle of Protestantism*.

[11](Ed.) John C. Bucher (1792–1851), a leading layman of the German Reformed church, member of Congress (1831–33) and Associate Judge, Dauphin County, Pa. (1839–51).

In October I was received into your Synod, at Allentown, and delivered, in Dr. Bucher's church, at Reading, my inaugural address on the "Principle of Protestantism," in the German language, which some hearers misunderstood for Latin or Greek. It was a vindication of the Reformation on the theory of progressive historical development, which was then regarded as dangerous, but is now very generally accepted.

This address, which Dr. Nevin translated into English, with a polemical introduction, became the innocent occasion of a long theological controversy. A year after its delivery I was accused of heresy by the Classis of Philadelphia, under the lead of Dr. Berg, who denied the validity of Roman Catholic ordinances, and had shortly before rebaptized an Irish monk. About the same time the Old School Assembly of the Presbyterian Church, at its meeting in Cincinnati, had by a resolution unchurched the Roman Catholic Church and declared her baptism invalid;[12] against this decision, however, her most eminent divines, under the lead of Dr. Charles Hodge, of Princeton, vigorously protested.[13] The Synod of York in 1845 was occupied several days with hearing the charge and defence. Dr. Berg delivered an eloquent popular argument to convict me of a Romanizing tendency. Dr. Nevin disproved the charge in a weighty reply. I made a German address in self-defence, but as it was not generally understood, I had to attempt another speech, in broken English, which was much shorter but more effective. So much for being brief and for speaking

---

[12](Ed.) The General Assembly of the Old School Presbyterian church, meeting at Cincinnati in 1845, declared that the Roman Catholic church is utterly corrupt and hopelessly apostate and that its baptisms are invalid.

[13](Ed.) Charles Hodge (1797–1878) was the influential defender of historic Calvinism throughout his long career at Princeton Theological Seminary. In 1825 he founded the *Biblical Repository and Princeton Review,* of which he remained the editor for forty years. He had studied at Halle and Berlin (1826–28), where the same two men who later influenced Schaff, Friedrich Tholuck and Ludwig von Gerlach, had impressed him by the warmth and depth of their piety more than any of the other Germans—he even kept their pictures in his Princeton study to the end of his life. However, having closed his mind to the new currents of German theology and philosophy, he became a friendly but persistent critic of the Mercersburg theology of Nevin and Schaff.

English. The Synod, after every delegate had given his opinion, acquitted me with an overwhelming majority.

With such a record I thought I might venture upon the honorable estate of matrimony, and married a Mary from Maryland, which I have never regretted; but this is a private matter.

Then followed the development of the "Mercersburg Theology," so called, mainly by Dr. Nevin, in books and through *The Mercersburg Review*. His pessimistic view on the divided state of Protestantism, with which I could never quite agree, misled a few ministers into Romanism; but this was merely incidental and temporary. The Mercersburg movement, in its spirit and aim, was hopeful and progressive, and resulted in the consolidation of the Church and a deeper and broader theology.

In 1846, I was threatened with a second heresy trial on the subject of the middle state between death and the resurrection, and the hope of the salvation of all children dying in infancy and of such heathen as would have accepted the gospel if it had been offered to them in this world. The charge of heresy was founded on a garbled translation of extracts from my book on "The Sin Against the Holy Ghost," written in Germany, in 1841; but the matter was satisfactorily settled by the Board of Visitors. In 1848, I ventured on publishing the first American theological periodical in the German language, the *Kirchenfreund*, for which I had to import from Philadelphia a printer and printing apparatus. The first German edition of my "History of the Apostolic Church" was also printed in Mercersburg, and soon afterward translated into idiomatic English by my dear departed friend, Dr. Yeomans.[14] I soon learned that I could

---

[14](Ed.) Edward Dorr Yeomans (1829–68), a Presbyterian, served as pastor at several churches, the last one at Orange, N.J. He translated Schaff's *History of the Apostolic Church, America* (except for Part III which was translated by Thomas C. Porter), *History of the Christian Church*, vol. 1, and at the time of his death was working on a translation of the Commentary on John in Lange's *Bibelwerk*, of which Schaff was preparing an English edition. Schaff was most fortunate to have found so tireless and brilliant a collaborator at the beginning of his American career, for Yeoman's translations were widely praised as having "the idiomatic character of original compositions" (*Appleton's Cyclopedia of American Biography*, vol. 6 [1889]

double my influence, if I taught and wrote in the ruling language of the country. In 1849, the Committee for the Preparation of a New Liturgy was appointed, of which I was chairman for seven years. The result was the "Provisional Liturgy" of 1857. You also intrusted me with the compilation of a German Hymn-book, which was completed in 1859, without any help, and is still used in your churches. For your service I prepared a history, and tercentennary edition of the Heidelberg Catechism in German (1863), and a small German Hymn-book, and a German and English Catechism for Sunday-schools (1864).

In 1850, the removal of the Institutions from the retired village of Mercersburg to a more eligible location began to be agitated, and resulted in the union of Franklin and Marshall Colleges in Lancaster (1853). The Seminary unfortunately was left behind in lonely isolation. You refused to let me accept the call to the presidency of the united Colleges, and I declined other attractive invitations. I appreciated your reluctance to spare me from the Seminary, and obeyed.

After a visit to Europe (1854), I returned to the Seminary and served it ten years longer, hoping in vain for its removal to Lancaster, which was not effected till 1870. In those years, though overburdened with lectures, I made preparations for a general Church history, and an English reproduction of Lange's "Bible-work."

During the Civil War, Mercersburg was constantly exposed to ravaging raids of the Confederate cavalry. After the battle of Gettysburg, in July, 1863, the Seminary building was turned into a military hospital for a thousand wounded Confederate soldiers, who were captured on their retreat to Virginia.

At this juncture I felt at liberty to remove to New York, where I could hope with the help of large libraries to execute my literary projects. After a second visit to Europe (1865), I was, in the providence of God, assigned a large field of usefulness in the Union Theo-

---

641). After his friend's death, a grateful Schaff quoted an English reviewer of his *History of the Christian Church*: "In point of style and general structure there is nothing to indicate that the book is a translation from the German. Indeed in this respect it will stand a favorable comparison with the best English classics" (vol. 3 of the New Testament section of Lange's *Commentary on the Holy Scriptures*, xii, n.).

logical Seminary at New York in congenial companionship with honored and beloved colleagues.

But my affections remained with you undiminished. I followed with interest your growth and prosperity. And now, when I appear before you, I heartily rejoice in your bright prospects. The Seminary and College are once more united, never to be separated again, and are steadily advancing in efficiency. When I arrived in Mercersburg I found but half-a-dozen theological students; now you have sixty-four. Then there were but two professors, who had to divide their time between the Seminary and the College; now there are four professors wholly devoted to the Seminary, with a fifth professor just elected, and a new building in prospect for recitation-rooms and a library, to be erected on a commanding site in this city. Then there was but one Reformed congregation in Lancaster, one in Reading, and two in Philadelphia; now their number in these cities is sixfold. Your Synod, which is the Mother Synod, has given birth to half-a-dozen daughters in the West. Your membership has increased in proportion, and is steadily growing in intelligence and influence. Your theology and order of worship, and the education of your ministry are far in advance of the crude and unsettled state of things fifty years ago. You have been brought into living contact with the other Reformed Churches of Europe and America through the Pan-Presbyterian or Reformed Alliance, and were duly represented at all the Councils—at Edinburgh, Philadephia, Belfast, London, and Toronto.

Under such favorable auspices it is my rare privilege to meet your Synodical assembly once more, and probably for the last time. I thank you for your kind sympathy with me in the severe illness which interrupted me last summer in the midst of work. The stroke of paralysis was a warning, and a blessing in disguise. It taught me two cheering lessons: how many friends I have at home and abroad; and how easy it is to die—"the readiness is all." In the kind providence of God I am so far restored to health that I am able just now to read the last proofs of the seventh volume of my "Church History," which is devoted to the story of the Reformation in my native Switzerland, and the great labors of Zwingli and Calvin, the chief founders of the Reformed Churches.

Providence may still have a few years of usefulness in store for me. The autumnal storms are followed by the Indian summer with its bright sunshine and balmy air, before nature goes to sleep till the resurrection of the spring. But whether one year or ten years may yet be granted to me, I shall never forget the sweet memories of this day, and it is with profound gratitude that I bid you, my old and dear pupils and friends, an affectionate farewell till we meet again, in the general assembly of the first-born in heaven. There (in the words of my sainted friend, Dr. William A. Muhlenberg, written about sixty years ago in this very city, where he was then rector of the Episcopal church)

> The saints of all ages in harmony meet,
> Their Saviour and brethren transported to greet;
> While the anthems of rapture unceasingly roll,
> And the smile of the Lord is the feast of the soul![15]

---

[15](Ed.) William A. Muhlenberg (1796–1877), episcopal clergyman and founder of St. Luke's Hospital in New York City, wrote during his ministry at Lancaster, Pa., in 1824, the poem "I would not live alway—live alway below!" of which the cited verse is part of the fifth stanza. The poem was adopted by the Episcopal church as a hymn, "I would not live always, I ask not to stay," which was popular in the nineteenth century.

PART I
Formative Influences

CHAPTER 1

"A Swiss by Birth,
a German by Education"

EDITORIAL INTRODUCTION

Schaff reviewed twice for American readers the larger German scene that was the context of the formative years of his life: initially in a series of articles, "Gallerie der bedeutendsten jetzt lebenden Universitätstheologen Deutschlands," in *Der deutsche Kirchenfreund* (April–September 1852), and then again in *Germany: Its Universities, Theology, and Religion* (1857). The "Autobiographical Reminiscences," a manuscript he commenced writing on the last day of 1871, was also conceived as a review "of my youth till my Arrival in America" but for the benefit of his children only. With his memory even in his old age as crisply retentive as ever, he worked intermittently for almost twenty years on this manuscript (which his son David in the biography of his father frequently, though not always fully, quoted, but as "Personal Reminiscences"). He incorporated several lengthy chapters that dealt with events of the years just past, so that he wrote the chapters on Stuttgart and Tübingen as late as 1884. He added the final three chapters on Halle, Berlin and his arrival in America in 1890. The original manuscript, as well as an incomplete but clean and paginated copy which Carl M. Adler prepared for Schaff in 1882 (to which Schaff made some additions in 1884), are in the archives of the Evangelical and Reformed Historical Society at Lancaster Theological Seminary,

Lancaster, Pennsylvania. The selections here included are from the Adler copy.

Neander's death in 1850 prompted Schaff's first assessment of his teacher's work and its significance but also revived memories of a more personal nature. The concluding paragraphs of the article "Recollections of Neander," which have been corrected in a few places from the original German, show Schaff's growing but by no means uncritical attachment to Neander as well as some of the theological crosscurrents that were agitating both faculty and students at Berlin at that time. Toward the end of his life, on the occasion of the approaching fiftieth anniversary of Neander's death, Schaff offered still another portrayal and assessment of Neander, in *Saint Augustin, Melanchthon, Neander* (1886). By then, he had come to be counted among Neander's most prominent disciples. Neander, of course, also looms large, as does Ferdinand Christian Baur, in those sections from the "General Introduction to Church History" of Schaff's *History of the Apostolic Church* (1853) in which the focus was sharply narrowed to the exciting scene of German Protestant historiography. Here Schaff introduced and discussed those church historians who as his teachers, fellow students or more distant contemporaries helped to shape his own evolving position as a church historian. It should be added that Schaff's spirited and learned account paralleled and repeatedly drew upon Theodor Kliefoth's article series, "Die neuere Kirchengeschichtsschreibung in der deutsch-evangelischen Kirche."[1] Both accounts may even today be considered unequalled as introductions to German Protestant church historiography in the first half of the nineteenth century. But Schaff's account is also indispensable for understanding the formative influences of contemporary German scholarship upon his own mind. As our selection clearly shows, he had learned to do church history in the shadow of Schleiermacher and Hegel by grafting Baur and the Prussian High-Orthodoxy on Neander—just as Baur, in Lord Acton's apt characterization, "grafted Hegel on Ranke"[2]—and by studiously ignoring Strauss's *Life of Jesus*.

---

[1] *Allgemeines Repertorium für die theologische Literatur und kirchliche Statistik* (1845), 48:105-18; 49:18-29, 106-13, 207-15; 50:18-24.

[2] Lord Acton [John Emerich], "German Schools of History," *Historical Essays and Studies* (London, 1908) 368.

The following three selections trace, therefore, not only the outlines of a period of brilliant intellectual creativity and ferment in German Protestantism but also Schaff's own remarkable progress from his birthplace in the Swiss mountains to the beginnings of an academic career at the University of Berlin.

AUTOBIOGRAPHICAL REMINISCENCES*

I am a Swiss by birth, a German by education, an American by adoption. I always loved Switzerland as my fatherland, and love it all the better for having left it. We learn to appreciate a thing from a distance which "lends enchantment to the view." I would rather visit my native land occasionally than live there permanently. It is, like Scotland and New England, a good land to emigrate from and to cleave to in fond recollection.

In many respects America is an extended Switzerland. I found it much easier to fall in with American institutions and to feel at home in this country than the immigrants from monarchial Germany, who are apt either to retain a preference for a more centralized form of government, or more frequently to run into an excess of democracy, especially on the Sunday question. Restraint of individual freedom, regard for law and custom, self-government and discipline are indispensable to the permanency and prosperity of a Republic. I doubt, whether we could maintain our liberty for six months, without our Christianity, our Churches, our Bible and our Sabbath. They are the moral pillars of our nationality. Take them away, and we will become a mere sham republic, like Mexico, and soon degenerate into anarchy and military despotism.

I was born January 1, 1819 at Coire (Chur, from the Roman Curia), the capital of the Canton de Grisons (Graubündten), and was

---

*"Autobiographical Reminiscences" (ms. written intermittently 1871–1890, The Evangelical and Reformed Historical Society, Lancaster Theological Seminary) 20, 24-25, 32-35, 49-58, 111-17, 120-22 (paginated copy by Carl M. Adler [1882] of the unpaginated original manuscript).

baptized January 7, 1819, according to the rite of the Reformed church to which my ancestors belonged. The Grisons were for a long time an independent republic before their annexation to Switzerland. The Canton borders on the Tyrol in the East and on Italy in the South, and contains some of the grandest and most romantic scenery, but was comparatively unknown to travellers till toward the middle of the nineteenth century.

I was born and bred in poverty and obscurity. I can boast of no illustrious ancestors and kindred. I can truly say: "Of the grace of God I am what I am" [1 Cor. 15:10]. Inestimable is the blessing of a refined Christian home, warmed by the sunshine of parental care, and brotherly and sisterly affection; it is the best discipline of mind and heart, and the nursery of every virtue and grace. But poverty has its redeeming features: it stimulates energy, breeds industry and develops the spirit of self-reliance and manly independence. It is often a better capital to start with than wealth and prestige. I have nothing to complain. What my parents lacked, was not their fault, and God has overruled the disadvantage of my early childhood for my own good.

My father was a carpenter in humble condition, and much esteemed, as I was told by those who knew him, but he died very young, February 9, 1820. He lies buried in the graveyard of Coire. My mother who was born in the year of the French Revolution (1789), . . . belonged to a large family of farmers at Zizers, a small village near Coire, and had several sisters, one of whom I remember as being very kind to me. She married again, soon after my father's death, a widower with several children near Coire, and afterwards moved to the neighboring Canton Glarus. This, I suppose, was the reason for my early separation from her, for I was left in an orphan home at Coire.[1] She was nevertheless much attached to me, her only child, and would have followed me to America, had she not been bound by

---

[1](Ed.) This sentence is crossed out in the manuscript, though it is still legible. In the biography of his father, David S. Schaff does not mention that the young child was left behind in an orphan home.

family ties. She is a woman of fine appearance, strong constitution, good mind, independent will and native wit, but she never enjoyed the advantages of education and had a hard and checkered life, struggling with poverty and various misfortunes. It is a great comfort to me that I can contribute something to her comfort in her declining years.

I received my early education in the public schools at Coire. I spent three years in the classical high school or Gymnasium (Cantonschule) of the Grisons, made rapid progress (standing first in my class) and gained the esteem and affection of my teachers. When fourteen or fifteen years of age, I began to give elementary instruction to the children of a wealthy family, distantly connected with me. Afterwards I borrowed money from kind friends who appreciated my desire for a University education, and before I emigrated to America, I was able to return it with interest. I must except, however, certain donations which were transmitted to me by an unknown friend in Basle, whom I afterwards learned to esteem and love as the Rev. Mr. Passavant, a liberal friend of students for the ministry.[2]

My best patron in Coire whom I shall always gratefully remember, was the Rev. Paul Kind, Antistes or chief pastor of the city.[3] He was an able and faithful preacher of the gospel, and for this reason unpopular among his rationalistic or indifferent colleagues, though generally esteemed for his irreproachable character. It was a peculiar satisfaction to me to greet this venerable servant of Christ once more in 1869 and again in 1871, when, bowed down with the weight of more than four score years and totally blind, he still clearly remembered me and the scenes of my youth with the affection of a father and rejoiced in my prosperity. . . .

The greatest service for which I am indebted to Antistes Kind was that he sent me to a Christian institution in Kornthal, near

---

[2](Ed.) Theophil Passavant (1787–1864), pastor at Basel, who provided a link between the pietists of Switzerland and southern Germany.

[3](Ed.) Paul Kind (1783–1875) was professor at the *Gymnasium* (1808) and since 1832 senior minister at St. Martin Church in Chur.

Stuttgart, where my moral and religious interests were much better provided for than in the College of my native place. . . .

Had I remained in Switzerland, my life would probably have taken a very different turn. Some of my fellow students became respectable and useful men, but others, no worse than I, went sadly astray. I was surrounded by uncongenial and dangerous influences. The religious instruction I received, made no impression on my heart, and I was sorely vexed by doubts. . . .

I regard it therefore as a merciful Providence that I was transferred to a different atmosphere. This was to me always an experimental argument for the mystery of predestination. After all it is the sovereign mercy of God which shapes our destinies and controls the course of our life.

———————————

I spent five years in the interesting country [Württemberg] which has become to me a second fatherland. I can look back upon that period of my youth with unalloyed pleasure. I have a great many friends there whom I can never forget and whom I hope to meet in heaven. To Würtemberg I owe, under God, my spiritual life and the best part of my education.

It was in September 1834, that I left my native town and friends on my way to Würtemberg, with mingled feelings of sadness and hopefulness. I carried all my possessions in a knapsack ("omnia mea mecum portans") and travelled alone and on foot to Ragatz, Sargans, Werdenberg and down the valley of the Rhine to Rorschach, where I took the boat across Lake Constance to Friedrichshafen on the German shore. The sight of a lake and the entrance into the first German town made me forget all the fatigues of the journey and was the first sensation in my life. I took a refreshing bath in the beautiful lake near the castle, the summer residence of the king of Würtemberg.

Twenty seven years later, in July 1871, I visited Friedrichshafen again, but no more as a poor, homeless orphan boy, but as the president and spokesman of thirty seven delegates from all branches of the Evangelical Alliance including such men as Bishop McIlvaine, Rev. Dr. Adams. the Hon. William E. Dodge, the Hon. Nathan Bishop, Mr. Cyrus W. Field, Rev. Dr. Washburn, Rev. Dr. Schenck, of America, Rev. Dr. Stean of England, Baron van Essen of Sweden, Dr. van Oosterzee of Holland, Dr. Coulin of Geneva, Prof. von Tischendorf of Germany, carrying a memorial to the Emperor Alexander II of Russia—then on a visit to King William and Queen Olga (his sister) at the celebration of their silver wedding—and pleading before his Prime minister Prince Gortschakoff the cause of the persecuted Lutherans in the Baltic provinces and of religious liberty in that vast Empire.[4] "Truth is sometimes stranger than fiction," or as the French say, "Le vrai n'est pas toujours vraisemblable."[5] That deputation, like similar deputations of the Evangelical Alliance in behalf of religious liberty, has not been in vain.

A kind friend in Friedrichshafen to whom Antistes Kind had given me a letter of introduction, facilitated my journey. In two or three days I reached Kornthal by way of Urach, Reutlingen, Tübingen and Stuttgart.

Kornthal is a neat and quiet village a few miles from Stuttgart. It resembles in origin and character a Moravian settlement such as Herrnhut, Gnadau, Königsfeld, Barby in Germany, or Bethlehem, Nazareth, Lititz in Pennsylvania. It is a strictly religious colony founded in 1819 by Mr. Hoffmann, a very remarkable man, who under different circumstances might have become the founder of a monastic order or a new sect.[6] It was refuge for Pietists who were dissatisfied with the prevailing indifferentism and rationalism of the state church in Würtemberg and wished to realize their idea of a self-supporting and self-governing Christian community after the apostolic model. They did not separate, however, from the pious minority in the established church and retained the Augsburg Confession as their creed. The colony flourished and acquired a wide reputation

---

[4](Ed.) Cf. Schaff, "Report of the Deputation of the American Branch of the Evangelical Alliance, Appointed to Memorialize the Emperor of Russia in Behalf of Religious Liberty," *Evangelical Alliance Document* 6 (1871).

[5](Ed.) "The truth is not always believable."

[6](Ed.) Gottlieb Wilhelm Hoffmann (1771–1846), a layman and one of the leaders of Württemberg pietism, remained the director of Kornthal until his death.

by its literary and benevolent institutions. The school for boys and
young men, then under the superintendence of Mr. Kullen, a man
of considerable ability and most devoted piety, attracted pupils from
different countries of Europe.[7]

In this school I spent six months to great advantage. My favorite
teacher was the Rev. Mr. Schönthaler who took special interest in
me, but died soon afterwards in the prime of his life. . . . The most
important part of my education there was religious, especially the
catechetical instruction I received from Dr. Kapff, then Pastor in
Kornthal, now Prelate and Stiftsprediger in Stuttgart.[8] He is one of
the noblest, purest, and loveliest men I ever knew, a true disciple of
St. John, the apostle of love. He is universally esteemed and loved
by the Würtemberg "Pietists," as the more determined Christians
are called there, and has great influence in Southern Germany. He
confirmed me in the church at Kornthal after a thorough course of
catechetical instruction; and I shall never forget the deep impressions
which were made on me at this solemn act in the Passion week of
1835. Since that time I looked up to him as a spiritual father.

Regeneration is as much a mystery in the order of grace as birth
is in the order of nature. No one knows the time and manner of his
birth except from the testimony of others. But the fact itself is in-
disputable in one case as well as in the other. Spiritual life which is
brought into existence by the second birth is as real and manifest as
natural life. The blind man knew this one thing that he was born
blind, but that Jesus had opened his eyes, and he believed in him.

As far as I can trace my spiritual life, it originated under the religious instructions and influences I received at Kornthal. At all events
it assumed there a definite shape and form. I was never irreligious,

---

[7](Ed.) Johannes Kullen (1787–1842), whose family had deep roots in Württemberg and a long tradition of service as teachers, was the founder and headmaster
of the boys' school at Kornthal. There were also two schools for girls.

[8](Ed.) Sixt Karl Kapff (1805–79) was the pastor of the separatist Kornthal congregation for ten years (1833–43), but later assumed leadership in the state church
of Württemberg. In his own career he thus represented and helped to make possible the triumph of neopietism in Württemberg by the middle of the nineteenth
century.

but somewhat skeptical and lacked that childlike faith without which no one can enter into the kingdom of heaven. During the first weeks of my residence in Kornthal, I felt very miserable. Swiss homesickness seized me in all its intensity and filled me with disgust of life. But God in his mercy overruled this trial for my benefit and directed my desires towards a higher and better home.

In 1869 I had the pleasure, in company with General Superintendent Dr. Hoffmann of Berlin (the son of the founder of Kornthal), Praelat Kapff of Stuttgart, Pastor Blumhard of Boll and other friends, to take part in the semicentennial celebration of the founding of Kornthal.[9] My son David was also with me. In the address I made, I thus alluded to the change which thirty-five years previously had taken place in me while studying there (I translate from a report in the "Christenbote"):[10]

"Thirty five years ago, A.D. 1834, a youth from Switzerland, who was born in the same year as Kornthal (1819) and therefore has a twofold share in this semicentennial festival, arrived at this place and entered the institute of Mr. Kullen to be prepared for the Gymnasium in Stuttgart. At first he felt lonely and discontented, and was seized by that homesickness which is peculiarly strong in the Swiss and which no one can properly appreciate without personal experience. One day at three o'clock in the morning this stranger in a strange land went away to the neighboring forest and prayed and cried in intense agony and trembled on the brink of despair. His heart was

---

[9](Ed.) Wilhelm Hoffman (1806–73) was appointed court preacher by King Friedrich Wilhelm IV in 1853 and soon was the most influential churchman in Prussia. He provided on occasion for his friend Schaff a ready entree to the royal, later imperial, court of Prussia. Johann Christoph Blumhard (1805–80), charismatic revival preacher and faith healer, friend of the poor and distressed, founded in 1853 Bad Boll in Württemberg, an asylum for the afflicted.

[10](Ed.) The translation is from the text in "Christlicher Volksbote aus Basel" (15 September 1869), a publication of the Basel *Missionsverein*. Schaff mistakenly referred to "Der Christenbote," the house organ of Württemberg pietism (since 1831), where the account of the celebrations at Kornthal on 9 July 1869 contains only a one-paragraph summary of Schaff's address (cf. *Der Christenbote* 39 [18 July 1869]: 183).

without rest because it had not yet found its rest in God. He was wretched and miserable because he had not yet experienced the forgiveness of sins. He longed to die because he was a stranger to the only true life which is eternal. But God had mercy upon him and heard his cries. His homesickness was the pain of a new birth from above. He began for the first time to realize what it is to have peace with God through the atoning blood of Jesus which cleanses from all sin. By the faithful instruction and pious example of Kullen, Schönthaler and Kapff he was introduced into the mysteries of evangelical truth, and dedicated himself at this very altar to the service of God. Never, never will he forget the day of his Confirmation on Easter Sunday 1835, and the solemn vow he then made. May he ever be faithful to it to the end! I shall not give you the name of this pupil of Kornthal, who lives in a far distant land, but he begged me on this occasion to thank you for the unspeakable benefit which he owes to this his spiritual birthplace."

From Kornthal where I spent a short, but important period of my youth, I went in the spring of 1835 to the Gymnasium (College) at Stuttgart, the capital of the kingdom of Würtemberg, and I remained there till the autumn 1837. This city is very dear to me for many associations. The Gymnasium is one of the best, if not the very best in Southern Germany. I received thorough instruction in the classical and other liberal studies by competent and kind teachers. . . . I heard the best evangelical preachers of their day, Wilhelm Hofacker (the brother of the revival preacher Ludwig) and Albert Knapp (the poet), and derived much benefit from personal intercourse with them. . . .[11]

Among my fellow students I was most intimate with William Julius Mann and the two sons of Gustav Schwab who remained my

[11](Ed.) Ludwig (1789–1828) and Wilhelm (1805–48) Hofacker were both popular and influential revival preachers in Württemberg. Wilhelm was appointed dean of St. Leonhard Church in Stuttgart in 1835. Albert Knapp (1798–1864), poet, hymn writer and evangelical preacher, held various pastorates in Stuttgart.

friends to this day.[12] By a singular providence we all met again in America. Gustav Schwab (the younger son of the poet) came to New York as member of an importing house in 1844, the same year in which I followed a call to Mercersburg in Pennsylvania, and he rose to be one of the most honored merchants in this great commercial metropolis, agent of the Bremen Lloyd, and prominently connected with several philanthropic institutions. I know no German layman in America who surpasses him in intelligence, information, integrity, liberality, and quiet usefulness. He is a member of the Episcopal Church in Fordham. Dr. Mann came to America first on a visit at my invitation in 1845 and spent three months with me in Mercersburg, as I had spent three months in the house of his worthy parents in Stuttgart. He was called to the chief German Lutheran congregation in Philadelphia and afterwards to a professorship in the Lutheran Theological Seminary of the same city. He fills both these responsible positions with marked ability and with acceptance. Both he and Schwab are fine specimens of Americanized German gentlemen. We see each other from time to time, though not as often as we could wish. We are full of work. I had the pleasure of dedicating the third revised volume of my Church History (1883) to these my oldest and lifelong friends in America. They acknowledged the compliment in touching letters. . . .

After passing through the upper classes of the Stuttgart Gymnasium I entered the University of Tübingen and studied there philosophy and theology for two years. It was a very exciting period in the history of that venerable University.

The philosophy of Hegel ruled without a successful rival among the students and filled them with enthusiasm for absolute knowl-

---

[12](Ed.) Wilhelm Julius Mann (1819–92), though his education in Württemberg was similar to Schaff's, in the United States championed confessional Lutheranism and became a friendly critic of his friend's "unionistic" tendencies (cf. A. Spaeth, D. Wilhelm Julius Mann [Reading PA, 1895] esp. ch. 5, "Freundschaft mit Dr. Philip Schaff"). Gustaf Schwab (1792–1850), Swabian poet and pastor, was one of Schaff's teachers at the Stuttgart Gymnasium; on Easter Monday in 1837 Schaff preached his first sermon in Schwab's church in the village of Gomaringen near Stuttgart.

edge. They thought they could reconstruct the whole universe by re-thinking the thoughts of God who comes to his self-consciousness in man.

Theology was divided into two hostile camps, the evangelical school of Dr. Schmid, and the critical school headed by Dr. Baur. The whole theological world had just been stirred to its depth by the publication of the famous "Life of Jesus" (1835 and 36) of Strauss, a pupil of Baur and Repetent at Tübingen.[13] He was removed from his place. Schwegler, another of his pupils, who subsequently distinguished himself by his "Post-Apostolic Age," and his "History of Philosophy," was my classmate and an intense student who worked himself to an untimely death.[14] Baur himself, the founder of the so-called "Tübingen School," was then in the prime of life and working out his critical reconstruction of the history of the apostolic and post-apostolic ages, which has created such a revolution in this department. I cannot enter here into a discussion of these problems, as I have done elsewhere.[15] I confine myself simply to a few personal reminiscences.

---

[13](Ed.) David Friedrich Strauss, *Das Leben Jesu, kritisch bearbeitet*, 2 vols. (Tübingen, 1835–36; and later editions); English trans. (from the 4th German ed.) Marian [Mary Ann] Evans (George Eliot), *The Life of Jesus Critically Examined*, 3 vols. (London, 1846). At the time he wrote this book which was to ruin his academic career, Strauss (1808–74) was a member of an unusually diverse and distinguished group of theological tutors (*Repetenten*) at Tübingen, which included Wilhelm Hofacker, Sixt Karl Kapff and Wilhelm Hoffman (who, as already mentioned, in later years became influential evangelical churchmen and preachers) and Isaak Dorner (see below), later one of the great mediating theologians. Strauss spent the rest of his life as an independent writer and publicist, rejecting the Christian faith entirely in his last book, *Der alte und der neue Glaube* (1872).

[14](Ed.) Friedrich Carl Albert Schwegler (1819–57), unable to gain a position on the theological faculty, became professor of Roman literature and ancient history at Tübingen. *Das nachapostolische Zeitalter in den Hauptmomenten seiner Entwicklung*, 2 vols. (Tübingen, 1846), was not translated into English, unlike his *A History of Philosophy in Epitome*, trans. Julius H. Seelye (New York, 1856; many later editions).

[15](Ed.) See, for instance, below, pp. 205-12.

Professor Schmid was a profoundly learned, pious, conscientious, and estimable scholar, but modest to a fault.[16] He published nothing of importance in his lifetime, and posthumous publications on Christian Ethics and the Theology of the New Testament (as I could prove from my own notes of his lectures) do not do justice to him. His forte lay in exegesis. He combined, like Bengel, deep reverence for the Word of God with accurate philology and critical discernment.[17] He sympathized with Neander, and independently wrought out a similar reproduction of apostolic teaching under the four leading types of James, Peter, Paul, and John.[18] The essential results of these joint labors of Neander and Schmid have since become general property of exegetical and historical theology. His likeminded pupil and friend, Dr. Oehler (whom I likewise knew very well) applied the same method to the Theology of the Old Testament which has become a text book in several American Seminaries (in the revised English Version of my friend Dr. Day of New Haven, 1883).[19] I revered and loved Dr. Schmid as a fatherly friend, and his views gave me most satisfaction.

---

[16](Ed.) Christian Friedrich Schmid (1794–1852) taught at Tübingen since 1826. Both of his posthumously published books are available in English: *Biblical Theology of the New Testament,* trans. (from the 4th German ed.) G. H. Venables (Edinburgh, 1870), and *General Principles of Christian Ethics,* trans. and abridged by William Julius Mann (Philadelphia, 1872).

[17](Ed.) Johann Albrecht Bengel (1687–1752), a Württemberg pietist and clergyman, pioneered the modern textual criticism and exegesis of the Bible.

[18](Ed.) The distinction of "apostolic types" in the New Testament which Schmid and Neander had worked out was to be very important for Schaff, as his claim of its universal acceptance as late as 1884 (when he wrote the Tübingen chapter of his "Autobiographical Reminiscences") makes clear. For Neander's *History of the Planting and Training of the Christian Church,* see below, p. 37n29.

[19](Ed.) Gustav Friedrich Oehler (1812–72), a remarkable linguist, was a *Repetent* at Tübingen when Schaff began his studies there. He returned to Tübingen in 1852 as professor of the Old Testament; his *Theologie des Alten Testaments,* 2 vols. (Tübingen, 1873–74), was edited by his son and translated and edited by George E. Day, *Theology of the Old Testament* (New York, 1883).

Dr. Baur filled me with intellectual admiration for his rare genius and scholarship.[20] He had great magnetism as a teacher. He handled the most difficult problems of Gnosticism with the grip of a giant. He elaborated his lectures with conscientious care and read them very closely, but with intense earnestness and inspiring enthusiasm. He was at that time, next to Neander, the most influential academic teacher in Germany. I heard his lectures on the history of Christian Doctrine, and his Symbolics. He gave me the first idea of historical development, or a constant and progressive flow of thought in the successive ages of the church. He made sad havoc with the literature of the apostolic age, and transferred all the writings of the canon, except the four great Epistles of Paul and the Apocalypse of John, down to the postapostolic age, as elements in the growth of the Catholic system out of the conflicting tendencies of Petrinism and Paulinism. But his bold critical researches stimulated an immense activity in every direction and led to many valuable results. His personal character was above reproach and among all the modern opponents of traditional orthodoxy he is the ablest and most honest and earnest. On his deathbed he is said to have prayed: *Herr mach's sanft mit meinem Ende!*[21] . . .

One more teacher nearer and dearer to me personally than all the Tübingen professors, I must mention. It is Dr. Dorner, now in Berlin, the well known author of an exhaustive history of Christology, and of a System of Theology, both of which rank among the profoundest works that German scholarship has ever produced.[22] He was called to a professor's chair in 1837. I heard his first course of lectures

---

[20](Ed.) Ferdinand Christian Baur (1792–1860) taught at Tübingen since 1826.

[21](Ed.) "Lord, grant me a peaceful end."

[22](Ed.) Isaak August Dorner (1809–84) left Tübingen already in 1839. After various other teaching positions, he was appointed professor of systematic theology at the University of Berlin in 1862. His *Entwicklungsgeschichte der Lehre von der Person Christi,* 3 vols., 2nd ed. (Stuttgart, 1845–56) was translated by W. I. Alexander and D. W. Simon, *History of the Development of the Doctrine of the Person of Christ,* 5 vols. (Edinburgh, 1861–63); his *System der christlichen Glaubenslehre,* 2 vols. (Berlin, 1879–81) was translated by A. Cave and J. S. Banks, *A System of Christian Doctrine,* 4 vols. (Edinburgh, 1880–82).

on Apologetics and Dogmatics. He combined in some measure the excellencies of Baur and Schmid, the speculative and critical faculty of the former and the Christian piety and Scriptural soundness of the latter. He knew as much of history as Baur, was much more just and sober in his judgment, but fell short of him in boldness, originality and force, and in mastery of style. He passed through the training of Hegel and Schleiermacher, and was just the man to satisfy the wants of those advanced students who wished to master the speculative and critical problems of the age without losing their Christian faith. I met him repeatedly since in Kiel, Berlin and other places, and remained in regular correspondence with him. I had the pleasure of inviting and inducing him and his son to visit America as delegates to the General Conference of the Evangelical Alliance of New York in 1873. His visit greatly strengthened his previous love for our institutions and religious activities. He was everywhere received with the greatest respect. He is one of the purest and noblest men I know, and combines the highest scientific culture with Christian faith, simplicity and humility. . . .

My sojourn in that University on the charming banks of the Neckar fell in a period of extraordinary intellectual activity and commotion, which left a permanent impress upon the theological development of Germany and the whole Protestant world. I never lived in a place where there was more earnest and intense study as in Tübingen between 1837 and 1839.

I shall always gratefully and affectionately remember Tübingen and Würtemberg where I received so much hearty kindness and so much useful instruction.

RECOLLECTIONS OF NEANDER*

It will be perceived that this very imperfect sketch rests upon something more than a mere literary interest in Neander. The writer

---

*"Recollections of Neander," *The Mercersburg Review* 3 (January 1851): 88-89. This is a translation from the original German, "Erinnerungen an Neander," *Der deutsche Kirchenfreund* 4 (January 1851): 33-34.

did not belong indeed to the more intimate circle of his disciples and followers. When my acquaintance with him commenced, I had already nearly completed my theological studies, under wholly different influences in part, at Tübingen and Halle, and my attendance on his lectures was limited to the third part simply of his course in church history, reaching from the Reformation down to the present time. I admit that the constant vilifying of several of his most unoriginal admirers of Hegel, on the one hand, and of Hengstenberg (whom I learned personally to esteeem highly and to love), on the other hand, was repugnant to me, so that I never attended his evening circle where his students gathered around him, as much as I would have liked to go for his sake.[23] The relation besides in which I stood to speculative theology and church orthodoxy, was not exactly what he could approve. The first I then held, and still hold, to be highly necessary, for the full solution of certain great problems of the present time, particularly the christological question, or at least for bringing them nearer to their final solution; the second I regard not merely as a barrier to the destructive tendencies of unbelief, but as a wholesome counterpoise also to that onesided subjectivity, which is the fault of our modern Protestantism generally. If the later evangelical theology then, among whose founders the highly gifted Schleiermacher must be allowed at least to hold a prominent place, is ever to accomplish its mission, it may never renounce connection with the faith of the fathers, and it must show itself also in the widest sense practical and churchly; that is, it must lead to a new construction of the general life of the Church, in which shall be happily united and preserved the results of all earlier history, the bloom and fruit of the past both Protestant and Catholic. Notwithstanding these differences however, which touch not indeed the substance of the Christian faith, Neander always treated me, as a student, and then in the exercises connected with the taking of my degree, and as *privatdocent,* with the greatest friendship and with a love I may say which was truly pater-

---

[23](Ed.) Ernst Wilhelm Hengstenberg (1802–69) was professor of Old Testament at Berlin and since 1827 the editor of the influential *Evangelische Kirchenzeitung,* which soon aggressively represented an orthodox Lutheran position and the political views of the conservative party at the Prussian court.

nal. He was ever ready to direct and assist me in my studies. It was my privilege to spend many precious hours, partly alone with him in his study and partly at his dinner table, to which his particular friends were so often invited; and I count it a special favor of the Lord, that he permitted me to come so closely to such a theologian, in whom learning and piety were so harmoniously blended, and from whose frail body the life of Jesus Christ was reflected with such unearthly beauty, and to impress upon my memory his beloved image, as a powerful monition to simplicity, to gentleness, to humility, to love, and to a heavenly mind. When accordingly in the year 1843, partly by Neander's recommendation, I was called altogether unexpectedly to Mercersburg, he gave me at parting his warm shake of the hand, his hearty benediction, which I cannot call to mind without grateful emotion. And although my situation since has of necessity brought me into relation negatively and positively with the Anglo-American theology and religion, and I have accustomed myself to look at the history both of the world and the church, so to speak, from the American or more correctly from the Anglo-German standpoint; I have still continued in almost daily connection with Neander's works, and have learned from them, particularly as regards the patristic period, more than from any other historian. When I made up my mind accordingly a year and a half since to publish my own Church History, I held it a simple duty of gratitude to dedicate the first volume to my venerated teacher and fatherly friend. . . .

The Evangelical Catholic Period
of Organic Development
in German Protestant Historiography*

Evangelical Catholic Period of Organic Development

German Protestantism, like the prodigal son, gradually became ashamed of the husks, on which it had long fed, (and on which, in

---

*History of the Apostolic Church, with a General Introduction to Church History, trans. Edward D. Yeomans (New York, 1853) 86-87, 90-124.

some places, it still tries to live), smote upon its breast in penitent sorrow, and resolved to return to its father's house, to the old, and yet eternally young faith of the church. As the deistical or vulgar Rationalism gained prevalence and power towards the end of the last century by the cooperation of different causes and influences; so men of various callings and tendencies, as Herder, Hamann, Jacobi, the romantic school of Schlegel, Tieck, and Novalis, the philosophers Schelling and Hegel, and still more the theologian Schleiermacher, each did his part towards overthrowing its dominion in the scientific world, and preparing the way for a new theology, pervaded by the life of faith. To their exertions must be added the reawakening of moral earnestness and religious life, occasioned partly by the after-working of Pietism, and of the Moravian movement; partly by the deep concussions of the Napoleon wars, and the patriotic enthusiasm of the popular struggles for freedom, accompanied by an effort, though somewhat vague, for a universal regeneration of Germany; in part, finally, by the third centennial Jubilee of the Reformation, A.D. 1817, and the important and pregnant fact, connected with it, of the *Evangelical Union* between the hitherto separated sister churches of the Lutheran and Reformed confessions, first in Prussia, and afterwards, in pursuance of this example, in Württemberg, Baden, and other parts of Germany. From these causes, and in bold, unintermitted, and victorious warfare, first against the older popular Rationalism, and afterwards against the speculative forms of it proceeding from the Hegelian school, arose the modern *evangelical* theology of Germany; displaying in all departments of religious knowledge, especially in exegesis, church history, and doctrine history, a noble and still lively and productive activity; and, of all Protestant theological schools of the present day, unquestionably the first in learning, acumen, spirit, vigor and promise.

This period has done proportionally more than any other for the advancement of our science, as to both matter and form. Within the last thirty years in Germany historical theology has engaged an extraordinary amount of diligence and zeal, the effects of which will long be felt, and will be found increasingly beneficial, also, in other lands, particularly in the various branches of English and American Protestantism. . . .

With these explanations and qualifications, we proceed to point out those *general* features of modern German historiography which give it a decided superiority over that of the preceding periods.

1. Its most prominent excellence, as to *form* and method, we take to be its *scientific* structure and that *spirited, lifelike* mode of representation, which springs from the idea of an *organic development*. History is no longer viewed as a mere inorganic mass of names, dates, and facts, but as *spirit and life,* and therefore as process, motion, development, passing through various stages, ever rising to some higher state, yet always identical with itself, so that its end is but the full unfolding of its beginning. This makes church history, then, appear as an organism, starting from the person of Jesus Christ, the creator and progenitor of a new race; perpetually spreading both outwardly and inwardly; maintaining a steady conflict with sin and error without and within; continually beset with difficulties and obstructions; yet, under the unfailing guidance of providence, infallibly working towards an appointed end. The idea of organic development combines what was true in the notion of something permanent and unchangeable in church history, as held by both the Catholic and Old Protestant Orthodoxy, with the element of truth in the Rationalistic conception of motion and flow; and on such ground alone it is possible to understand fully and clearly the temporal life of Christianity. A permanent principle, without motion, stiffens into stagnation; motion, without a principle of permanence, is a process of dissolution. In neither case can there properly be any living history. The conception of such history is, that, while it incessantly changes its form, never for a moment standing still, yet, through all its changes, it remains true to its own essence; never outgrows itself; incorporates into each succeeding stage of growth the results of the preceding; and thus never loses anything, which was ever of real value.

The idea of an organic, steadily improving development of humanity, according to a wise, unalterable plan of providence, is properly speaking as old as Christianity, meets us in many passages of the New Testament (Matt. 13:31, 32; Eph. 4:12-16; Col. 2:19; 2 Pet. 3:18), and in occasional remarks of the early fathers, such as Tertullian and Augustine, and was brought out in the eighteenth century with peculiar emphasis and freshness by the genial *Herder,* in his

"Ideas for the Philosophy of the History of Humanity" (1784),[24] so highly valued by the gifted historian of Switzerland, John von Müller.[25] The more mature and philosophical conception of it, however, and the impulse which it gave to a deeper and livelier study of history, are due especially to the philosophy of *Schelling,* and, still more, of *Hegel.* With Hegel, all life and thought is properly development, or a process of organic growth, which he calls *Aufhebung*; that is, in the threefold sense of this philosophical term so much used by him; (1) an abolition of the previous imperfect form (an *aufheben* in the sense of *tollere*), (2) a preservation of the essence (*conservare*), and (3) an elevation of it to a higher stage of existence (*elevare*). Thus as the child grows to be a man, his childhood is done away, his personal identity is preserved, and his nature raised to the stage of manhood. So, as Judaism passes into Christianity, its exclusive character, as a preparatory establishment, is lost; but its substance is transferred into the gospel, and by it completed. Christ is, on the one hand, the end of the law and the prophets, while, on the other, he says: "I am not come to destroy, but to fulfill" [Matt. 5:17]. This is no contradiction, but only the exhibition of the same relation in different aspects.

The general idea of development, however, takes very different forms from different standpoints; as faith, authority, freedom, nay, even Christianity itself are liable to the most contradictory definitions. How far apart, for example, are Neander and Baur, though both apprehend and represent church history as a process of life! How different again from both the Roman Catholic convert Newman, who has likewise a theory of development of his own! Hegel's development in the hands of his infidel followers, is, at bottom, merely an intellectual process of logical thinking, in which, in the end, the substance of the Christian life itself is lost. As once Platonism was, for Origen, Victorinus, Augustine, Synesius, and others, a bridge to Christianity, while, at the same time, the Neoplatonists and Julian

---

[24](Ed.) *Ideen zur Geschichte der Menschheit,* 4 vols. (Riga and Leipzig, 1784–1791).

[25](Ed.) Johannes von Müller (1752–1809), author of a history of Switzerland and a universal history, impressed Schaff in particular by his appreciation of the Middle Ages.

the Apostate used it as a weapon against the Christian religion; so, also, the categories of modern philosophy, (not only German, but English too), have subserved purposes and tendencies diametrically opposite. *The right application of the theory of development depends altogether on having beforehand a right view of positive Christianity, and being rooted and grounded in it, not only in thought, but also in heart and experience.* With this preparation a man may learn from any philosophical system without danger, on the principle of Paul, that "all things are his" [1 Cor. 3:22]. Here, too, we may say: *Amicus Plato, amicus Aristoteles, sed magis amica veritas.*[26]

But when this mode of viewing history is adopted, it cannot fail to have its influence on the *representation*. If history is spirit and life, and, in fact, rational spirit, the manifestation and organic unfolding of eternal divine ideas; its representation must likewise *be full of spirit and life,* an *organic reproduction.* A mechanical and lifeless method, which merely accumulates a mass of learned material, however accurately, is no longer enough. The historian's object now is, to comprehend truly the events, leading ideas, and prominent actors of the past, and to unfold them before the eyes of his readers, just as they originally stood; to know not only *what* has taken place, but also *how* it has taken place. The old pragmatic method, too, of referring things merely to accidental subjective and psychological causes and motives, has become equally unsatisfying. A higher pragmatism is now demanded, which has paramount regard to the objective forces of history; traces the divine connection of cause and effect; and, with reverential wonder, searches out the plan of eternal wisdom and love.

2. With this view of history, as an inwardly connected whole, pervaded by the same life-blood and always striving towards the same end, is united the second characteristic; which we look upon as the greatest *material* excellence of the most important historians of modern Germany; viz., the spirit of *impartiality* and *Protestant catholicity.* Here, also, *Herder,* with his enthusiastic natural sensibility to the beautiful and the noble in all times and nations, was the mighty pioneer. By the recent development of theology and religious life in

---

[26](Ed.) "Plato is dear to me, Aristotle is dear to me, but dearer still is the truth."

Germany the barriers of prejudice, which separated the Lutheran and
Reformed churches, have been, in a great measure, surmounted, and
by the Prussian Union, (which, without such inward development,
would be an unmeaning governmental measure), these barriers have
been, in a certain degree, also outwardly removed, and almost all the
great theologians of the day in Germany now stand essentially upon
the basis of the Evangelical Union. Nay more. Protestantism has also
been forced to abandon forever her former one-sided posture towards
Catholicism. The old view of the Middle Ages especially, whose
darkness Rationalism in its arrogant pretensions to superior light and
knowledge (*Aufklärung*) could not paint black enough, has been entirely repudiated, since the most thorough research has revealed their
real significance in poetry, art, politics, science, theology and religion. It is now generally agreed, that the Middle Ages were the necessary connecting link between ancient and modern times; that this
period was the cradle of Germanic Christianity and modern civilization; that its grand, peculiar institutions and enterprises, the papacy, the scholastic and mystic divinity, the monastic orders, the
crusades, the creations of sacred art, were indispensable means of ed-
ucating the European races; and that, without them, even the Reformation of the sixteenth century could not have arisen. Here, of
course, the ultra-Protestant fanatical opposition to the Catholic
church must cease. The general disposition now is to break away from
the narrow apologetic and polemic interest of a particular confession
or party, the colored spectacles of which allow but a dim and partial
view of the Saviour's majestic person. We wish to be guided solely
by the spirit of impartial truth; and truth, at the same time, always
best vindicates itself by the simple exhibition of its substance and
historical course. Christianity can never be absolutely fitted to the
last of a fixed human formula, without losing her dignity and majesty; and her history may claim, for its own sake, to be thoroughly
investigated and represented, *sine ira et studio,* without any impure
or loveless designs.[27] The greatest masters in this field become more
and more convinced, that the boundless life of the church can never

---

[27](Ed.) "without anger or zeal."

be exhausted by any single sect or period, but can be fully expressed only by the collective Christianity of all periods, nations, confessions, and individual believers; that the Lord has never left himself without a witness; that, consequently, every period has its excellencies, and reflects, in its own way, the image of the Redeemer. A Neander, for example, reverentially kisses the footprints of his Master, even in the darkest times, and bows before the most varied refractions of his glory. Hence, within the last thirty years, almost every nook of church history has been searched with amazing industry and zeal; the darkest portions have been enlightened; and a mass of treasures brought forth from primitive, medieval, and modern times, to be admired and turned to the most valuable account by present and future generations.

In short, the investigations of *believing* Germany in the sphere of church history are inwardly and irresistably pressing towards an evangelical catholic, central, and universal position, which will afford a fair view of all parts of the vast expanse. They are making men see, how the flood of divine light and life, emanating from Jesus Christ, the central sun of the moral universe, has been pouring, with unbroken effulgence, on all past centuries, and will continue to pour upon the world in ever new variegations. For this reason, the study of our science is continually acquiring a greater practical importance. Church history is the field, on which are to be decided the weightiest denominational controversies, the most momentous theological and religious questions. It aims to sketch forth from the old foundations of the church the plan for its new superstructure. In truth, the spirit of the modern evangelical theology of Germany seems to have already risen, in principle, above the present sad divisions of Christendom; and to foretoken a new age of the church. It can reach its aim, and find complete satisfaction only in the glorious fulfillment of the precious promise of one fold and one shepherd.

Having noticed these general features, which, however, as already intimated, by no means belong to all the German church historians of our day, we must now characterize more minutely the most prominent authors; and, in so doing, we shall have occasion at the same time to explain our own relation to them, especially to Dr. Neander.

Among the latest German ecclesiastical historians, who stand at
the head of their profession, we must distinguish two widely different schools, which, as to their philosophico-theological basis, attach
themselves to the names of the two greatest scientific geniuses of the
nineteenth century, *Schleiermacher* and *Hegel.* They bear to each other,
in some respects, the relation of direct antagonism, but partly, also,
that of mutual completion; and are well matched in spirit and learning. They are: (1) The school of *Schleiermacher* and *Neander,* with Dr.
Neander himself at its head, as the "father of modern church history." For Schleiermacher was, properly, no historian: and his posthumous lectures on church history amount to no more than a loose
unsatisfactory sketch. But his philosophical views of religion, Christianity, and the church, have indirectly exerted a very important influence upon this department of theology, as well as upon almost all
others. (2) The *Hegelian* school. This, however, falls again into two
essentially different branches, viz.; (a) an *unchurchly* and *destructive*
branch, the *Tübingen* school, as it is called, the chief representative
of which is Dr. Baur, of Tübingen; and (b) a *conservative* branch, devoted to the *Christian faith,* among the leaders of which must be
named with special prominence Drs. Rothe and Dorner. Since this
later school, however, combines with the objective view of history
and the dialectic method of the Hegelian philosophy, the elements,
also, of the Schleiermacherian theological culture, it may as well have
an independent place, as a third school, intermediate between the
two others. [28]

Dr. Neander and his School

Dr. Augustus Neander forms an epoch in the development of
Protestant church historiography, as well as Flacius in the sixteenth

---

[28]In the following review of these schools we will not forget the debt of personal gratitude we owe to their leaders, *Neander, Baur,* and *Dorner,* who were our
respected instructors; the first, in Berlin, the last two, previously, in Tübingen.
But this cannot induce us to withhold a decided and uncompromising protest
against the dangerous and antichristian extravagances of the skeptical school of Baur.
All personal considerations must be subordinated to the sacred interests of faith
and the church.

century, Arnold at the close of the seventeenth, Mosheim and, somewhat later, Semler in the eighteenth; and was, accordingly, by general consent, distinguished, even before his death (1850), with the honorary title, "Father of (Modern) Church History." From him we have a large work, unfortunately not finished, on the general history of the Christian church; extending from the death of the Apostles almost to the Reformation. Next a special work on the apostolic period, which, together with one on the life of Christ (1837, 5th ed. 1849), serves as a foundation for the main work. Then, several valuable historical monographs on Julian the Apostate (1812), St. Bernard of Clairvaux (1813, 2nd ed. 1849), the Gnostic Systems (1818), St. John Chrysostom (1821, 3rd ed. 1848), the Anti-Gnostic Tertullian (1825, 3rd ed. 1849). Finally some collections of smaller treatises, mostly historical, in which he presents single persons or manifestations of the Christian life, on the authority of original sources, indeed, but in a form better adapted to meet the practical religious wants of the public generally. The most important of these is his *Denkwürdigkeiten aus der Geschichte des christlichen Lebens* (3 vols., 1822; 3rd ed. 1845), a series of edifying pictures of religious life in the first eight centuries.[29]

Neander was fitted, as few have been, for the great task of writing the history of the church of Jesus Christ. By birth and early training an Israelite, and a genuine Nathanael too, full of childlike simplicity, and longing for the Messianic salvation; in youth, an enthusiastic student of the Grecian philosophy, particularly of Plato, who became, for him, as for Origen and other church fathers, a sci-

---

[29](Ed.) Most of Neander's major works were soon made available in English: *General History of the Christian Religion and Church*, trans. J. Torrey, 8 vols. (Edinburgh, 1847–1852); 5 vols. (Boston, 1847–1854); *History of the Planting and Training of the Christian Church*, trans. (from the 3rd German ed.) J. E. Ryland (Philadelphia, 1844); *Life of Jesus Christ*, trans. (from the 4th German ed.) J. M'Clintock and C. E. Blumenthal (New York, 1848); *The Emperor Julian and His Generation*, trans. G. V. Cox (New York, 1850); *The Life and Times of St. Bernard*, trans. M. Wrench (London, 1843); *Genetische Entwicklung der vornehmsten gnostischen Systeme* (Berlin, 1818); *Antignostikus; or Spirit of Tertullian*, trans. (from the 3rd German ed.) J. E. Ryland (London, 1851); *Memorials of Christian Life in the Early and Middle Ages*, trans. J. E. Ryland (London, 1852).

entific schoolmaster, to bring him to Christ—he had, when in his seventeenth year he received holy baptism, passed through, in his own inward experience, so to speak, the whole historical course, by which the world had been prepared for Christianity; he had gained an experimental knowledge of the workings of Judaism and Heathenism in their direct tendency towards Christianity; and thus he had already broken his own way to the only proper position for contemplating the history of the church; a position, whence Jesus Christ is viewed as the object of the deepest yearnings of humanity, the centre of all history, and the only key to its mysterious sense. Richly endowed in mind and heart; free from all domestic cares; an eunuch from his mother's womb, and that for the kingdom of heaven's sake (Matt. 19:12); without taste for the distracting externals and vanities of life; a stranger in the material world, which, in his last years, was withdrawn even from his bodily eye,—he was, in every respect, fitted to bury himself, during a long and uninterrupted academical course, from 1812 to 1850, in the silent contemplation of the spiritual world, to explore the past, and to make his home among the mighty dead, whose activity belonged to eternity. In theology, he was at first a pupil of the gifted Schleiermacher, under whose electrifying influence he came during his university studies at Halle, and at whose side he afterwards stood as colleague for many years in Berlin. He always thankfully acknowledged the great merits of this German Plato, who, in a time of general apostacy from the truth, rescued so many young men from the iron embrace of Rationalism, and led them at least to the threshold of the holiest of all. But he himself took a more positive course, rejecting the pantheistic and fatalistic elements which had adhered to the system of his master from the study of Spinoza, and which, it must be confessed, bring it, in a measure, into direct opposition to the simple gospel and the old faith of the church. This was, for him, of the greatest moment. For only in the recognition of a personal God, and of the free agency of individual men, can history be duly apprehended and appreciated. But apart from this he was, in his own particular department, entirely independent. For Schleiermacher's strength lay in criticism, dogmatics, and ethics, far more than in church history; though, by his spiritual intuitions, he undoubtedly exerted on the latter science also a quickening influence.

Thus, from the beginning of his public labors, Neander appeared as one of the leading founders of the new evangelical theology of Germany, and its most conspicuous representative on the field of church and doctrine history.

His first and greatest merit consists in restoring the *religious* and *practical* interest to its due prominence, in opposition to the coldly intellectual and negative critical method of Rationalism; yet without thereby wronging in the least the claims of science. This comes out very clearly even in the preface to the first volume of his great work, where he declares it to be the grand object of his life, to set forth the history of Christ, "as a living witness for the divine power of Christianity; a school of Christian experience; a voice of edification, instruction, and warning, sounding through all ages, for all, who will hear."[30] True, he is second to none in learning. With the church fathers, in particular, many years of intercourse had made him intimately familiar. And though, from his hearty dislike for all vanity and affectation, he never makes any parade with citations, yet, by his pertinent and conscientious manner of quoting, he everywhere evinces a perfect mastery of the sources: for the genuine scholar is recognized, not in the number of citations, which, at any rate, may be very cheaply had from second or third hand; but in their independence and reliability, and in the critical discernment, with which they are selected. With the most thorough knowledge of facts he united, also, almost every other qualification of a scientific historian; a spirit of profound critical inquiry, a happy power of combination, and no small talent for genetically developing religious characters and their theological systems. But he diffuses through all his theoretical matter a pious, gentle, and deeply humble, yet equally earnest spirit. Like Spener and Francke, Neander views theology, and with it church history, not merely as a thing of the understanding, but also as a practical matter for the heart; and he has chosen for his motto: *Pectus*

---

[30](Ed.) Neander, *General History of the Christian Religion and Church*, vol. 1, preface.

est quod theologum facit.[31] This gives his works a great advantage over
the productions of the modern Tübingen school, as well as over the
text book of *Gieseler,* which, in learning and keen research, is at least
of equal merit; though in the case of the latter object, and by his invaluable extracts from sources compensates in part for the lack of life
in the dry skeleton of his text.[32] Neander moves through the history
of the church in the spirit of faith and devotion; Gieseler, with critical acumen and cold intellect. The one lives in his heroes, thinks,
feels, acts, and suffers with them; the other surveys their movements
from a distance, without love or hatred, without sympathy or antipathy. The former reverently kisses the footsteps of his Lord and Saviour, wherever he meets them; the latter remains unmoved and
indifferent even before the most glorious manifestations of the Christian life.

The spirit of Christian piety, which animates Neander's historical writings, and rules his whole habit of thought, is further characterized by a comprehensive *liberality* and evangelical *catholicity.*
Arnold and Milner, in their subjective and unchurchly pietism, had
like regard, indeed, to a practical utility; but they could find matter
of edification, for the most part, only in heretics and dissenters. From
these historians Neander differs, not only in his incomparably greater
learning and scientific ability, but also in that right feeling, by which,
notwithstanding his own disposition to show even too much favor to
certain heretics, he still traces the main current of the Christian life
in the unbroken line of the Christian church. From the orthodox
Protestant, rough, polemical historians of the seventeenth century,
on the other hand, Neander differs in the liberal spirit with which,
though constitutionally inclined rather to the German Lutheran type
of religious character in its moderate, Melanchthonian form, he rises
above denominational limits, and plants himself on the basis of the
Union, where Lutheran and Reformed Protestantism become only

---

[31](Ed.) "It is the heart that makes the theologian."

[32](Ed.) Johann Karl Gieseler, *Lehrbuch der Kirchengeschichte,* 6 vols. in 11 (Bonn,
1844–1857); trans. (from the 4th German ed.) S. Davidson and revised by Henry
B. Smith, *A Textbook of Church History,* 5 vols. (New York, 1857–1880).

parts of a higher whole. But his sympathies go far beyond the Reformation, and take in also the peculiar forms of *Catholic* piety. With him, in truth, the universal history of the church is no mere fortuitous concourse of outward facts, but a connected process of evolution, an unbroken continuation of the life of Christ through all centuries. He has won, in particular, the priceless merit of having introduced a more correct judgment respecting the whole church *before* the Reformation; above all, of having presented to the Protestant mind, not in the service of this or that party, but in the sole interest of truth, and in an unprejudiced, living reproduction, the theology of the *church fathers* in their conflict with the oldest forms of heresy. This he did first in his monographs. In his *Tertullian,* he drew a picture of the African church of the second and third centuries, and taught the true value, hitherto so much mistaken, of this rough, but vigorous Christian, the patriarch of the Latin theology. In his *John Chrysostom,* he portrayed the greatest orator, interpreter, and saint of the ancient Greek church. In his *Bernard of Clairvaux,* he described with warm, though by no means blind admiration, the worthiest representative of monkery, of the crusades, and of the practical and orthodox mysticism, in the bloom of the Catholic Middle Ages, previously so little known and so much decried. He felt thus at home in all periods, because he met the same Christ in them all, only in different forms. By such sketches, drawn from life, and then by the connected representation in his large work, he contributed mightily to burst the shackles of Protestant prejudice and bigotry, and to prepare the way, in some measure, for a mutual understanding between Catholicism and Protestantism on historical ground. He adopted the significant words of the Jansenist Pascal, one of his favorite authors: *En Jésus-Christ toutes les contradictions sont accordées.*[33] And in these great antagonisms in church history, he saw no irreconcilable contradiction, but two equally necessary manifestations of the same Christianity; and he looked forward, with joyful hope to a future

---

[33](Ed.) "In Jesus Christ all contradictions are resolved." Pascal, *Pensées,* fragment 683.

reconciliation of the two, already typified, as he thought, in St. John, the apostle of love and of the consummation.[34]

These large views of history, however, and this candid acknowledgement of the great facts of the ancient and medieval church—views, which may lead, in the end, to practical consequences even more weighty, than he himself could foresee or approve—spring, in Neander's case, by no means from a Romanizing tendency. Such a disposition was utterly foreign to him. His liberality proceeds partly from his mild, John-like nature, and partly from his genuine Protestant toleration and high regard for individual personality; or from such a *subjectivity,* as formed a barrier against ultra-Protestant and sectarian bigotry, no less than against Romanism, where individual freedom is lost in the authority of the general. In this he is a faithful follower of Schleiermacher, who, though he based his philosophy on the pantheistic system of Spinoza, had neverthless an uncommonly keen eye and a tender regard for the personal and individual. What Schleiermacher thus asserted mainly in the sphere of speculation and doctrine, Neander carried out in history. He was fully convinced that the free spirit of the gospel could never be concentrated in any one given form, but could be completely manifested only in a great variety of forms and views. Hence his frequent remark, that Christianity, the leaven, which is to pervade humanity, does not destroy natural capacities, or national and individual differences, but refines and sanctifies them. Hence his partiality for diversity and freedom of development, and his enmity to constraint and uniformity. Hence his taste for monographic literature, which sets a whole age concretely before the eye in the person of a single representative; of which invaluable form of church history Neander is to be accounted the proper father. Hence the love and patience and scrupulous fidelity with which he goes into all the circumstances of the men and systems he unfolds, to whatever nation, time, or school of thought they may belong; setting forth their defects and aberrations, as well as their vir-

---

[34]Compare the closing words of his *History of the Apostolic Church,* and the Dedication of the second edition of the first volume of his larger work to Schelling, where he alludes with approbation to that philosopher's idea of three stages of development answering to the three apostles Peter, Paul and John.

tues and merits; though without neglecting the duty of the philosophical historian, to collect the scattered particulars again into one complete picture, and refer them to the one unchanging idea. Finally this sacred reverence for the image of God in the persons of men, and for the rights of individuals, accounts for the esteem and popularity, which this equally pious and learned church father of the nineteenth century commands, more than any other modern theologian, in almost all sections of Protestantism, not only in Germany, but also in France, Holland, England, Scotland and America, nay, so far as difference of ecclesiastical ground at all allows, among liberal-minded scholars of the Roman Catholic church itself. In this view he stands before us, amidst the present distractions of Christendom, as an apostle of *mediation,* in the noblest sense of the word; and as such, he still has, by his writings, a long and exalted mission to fulfill.

To sum up what has now been said; the most essential peculiarity, the fairest ornament, the most enduring merit of Neander's church history consists in the *vital union of the two elements of science and Christian piety,* and in the exhibition of both in the form, not of dead narrative, or mechanical accumulation of material, but of *life and genetic development.* The practical element is not a mere appendage to the subject in the way of pious reflection and declamation, but grows out of it as by nature. It is the very spirit, which fills and animates the history of Christianity as such. Neander is Christian, not *although,* but *because* he is scientific; and scientific, *because* he is Christian. This is the only form of edification which *can* be expected in a learned work; but such *must* be expected, where the work has to do with Christianity and its history. And this gain, therefore, ought never to be lost. A church historian without faith and piety can only set before us, at best, instead of the living body of Christ, a cold marble statue, without seeing eye or feeling heart.

But a perfect church history calls for more than this. While we respect and admire in Neander the complete blending of the scientific element with the *Christian,* we miss, on the other hand, its union with the *churchly.* By this we mean, first, that he lacks decided *orthodoxy.* In his treatment of the life of Jesus and the Apostolic period, we meet with views respecting the Holy Scriptures, their inspiration and authority, together with doubts respecting the strictly historical character of certain sections of the gospel history, and the genuineness of particular books of the sacred canon (the First Epistle to Timothy, the Second Epistle of Peter, and the Apocalypse), which, though by no means rationalistic, are yet rather too loose and indefinite, and involve, in our judgment, too many and sometimes too serious concessions to modern criticism. Of all his works, his *Leben Jesu* is, perhaps, in this respect, the farthest from satisfying the demands of sound faith, however highly we must esteem the honesty and tender conscientiousness, which usually give rise to his critical scruples and doubts. There is, it is true, in this difficult field, a skepticism more commendable than that hasty and positive dogmatism, which, instead of seriously laboring to untie the Gordian knot, either refuses to see, or carelessly cuts it. But the *full* and *unconditional* reverence for the holy word of God, in which the whole Schleiermacherian school is more or less deficient, requires, wherever science cannot yet clear away the darkness, an humble submission of reason to the obedience of faith, or a present suspension of decisive judgment, in the hope, that farther and deeper research may lead to more satisfactory results.

Again, Neander must be called unchurchly in his views of theology and history, on account of his comparative disregard for the *objective* and *realistic* character of Christianity and the church, and his disposition, throughout his writings, to resolve the whole mystery into something purely inward and ideal. In this respect he appears to us quite too little Catholic, in the real and historical sense of the word. True, he is neither a Gnostic, nor a Baptist, nor a Quaker; though many of his expressions, sundered from their connection, sound very favorable to these hyper-spiritualistic sects. He by no means mistakes the objective forces of history, and can readily appreciate the realistic element in such men as Tertullian, Athanasius, Augustine, Bernard, and even in the popes and schoolmen, up to a certain point. He, in fact, speaks frequently of general directions of mind, which embody themselves in individuals; and the antitheses of idealism and realism, rationalism and supranaturalism, logical intelligence and mystic contemplation, and the various combinations of these tendencies, belong to the standing categories of his treatment of history. But, in the first place, he refers these differences themselves, for the most part, to a merely psychological basis, to the differences of men's constitutions, that is, to a purely subjective ground. His prevailing view is, that the kingdom of God forms itself from individuals, and therefore, in a certain sense, from below upwards; that, as Schleiermacher once said, "the doctrinal system of the church takes its rise from the opinions of individuals."[35] Then, in the next place, it is plain, that Neander himself is of the spiritualistic and idealistic turn, and does not always succeed in avoiding the dangers to which this tendency, in itself needful and legitimate, is exposed. Hence his predilection for the Alexandrian fathers, Clement and Origen. Hence his too favorable representation, as it appears to us, of Gnosticism, especially of Marcion, whose pseudo-Pauline hostility to the Catholic tradition he even makes to be a presage of the Reformation—which, if true, would do the Reformation poor service. Hence his overstrained love of equity towards all heretical and schismatical movements, in which he almost always takes for granted some deep moral and religious interest, even where they clearly rest on the most willful insurrection against lawful authority; the love of justice, with him, though by no means so abused as by that patron of sects, the pietistic Arnold, still often running into injustice to the historical church. Hence his undisguised dislike for all that he comprehends under the phrase, *reintroduction of the legal Jewish ideas* into the Catholic church, including the special priesthood and outward service; this he thinks to be against the freedom advocated by St. Paul and the idea of the universal priesthood (which, however, even under the Old Testament, had place *along with* the special; comp. 1 Pet. 2:9 with Ex. 19:6); though he is forced to concede to this Catholic legalism at least an important office in the training of the Teutonic nations. Hence his indifference to fixed ecclesiastical organization, and his aversion to all restriction to confessions in the Protestant church; this, to him, savors of "bondage to the letter," "mechanism of forms," "symbol-worship." On this latter point we must, indeed, regard him as mainly in the right against those, who

---

[35](Ed.) The editor was unable to identify the Schleiermacher quotation.

would absolutely repristinate some particular confession of the past—
the Form of Concord, perhaps, with its rigid Lutheranism—utterly
regardless of the enlarged wants of the present. There was still more
ground, also, for his zeal against the philosophical tyranny of the Hegelian intellectualists and pantheists, who, in the zenith of their pro-
pensity, aimed to supplant a warm, living Christianity by dry
scholasticism and unfruitful traffic in dialectic forms. Still the theological school now in hand is plainly wanting in a just appreciation
of the import of law and authority in general—a defect, closely connected with the false view taken of the Old Testament in Schleiermacher's theology and philosophy of religion, and with his half-
Gnostic ultra-Rationalism. The freedom, for which Neander so zealously contends, is of quite a latitudinarian sort, running, at times,
into indefiniteness and arbitrariness, and covering Sabellian, Semi-
Arian, Anabaptist, Quakerish, and other dangerous errors with the
mantle of charity. Much as we respect the noble disposition, from
which this springs, we must still never forget the important principle, that true freedom can thrive only in the sphere of authority;
the individual, only in due subordination to the general; and that
genuine catholicity is as rigid against error, as it is liberal towards
the various manifestations of truth.

Neander views Christianity and the church, not, indeed, as necessarily opposed to each other, yet as two separate and more or less
mutually exclusive spheres. In the mind, at least, of the whole ancient Eastern and Western church, these two conceptions virtually
coincide, or, at all events, are as closely related as soul and body; and
the one is always the measure of the other. This is abundantly proved
by the examples of Irenaeus, Tertullian, Cyprian, Ambrose, Augustine, Athanasius, Chrysostom, Anselm, Bernard, etc., even according to Neander's own representations of them. But the very title of
his large work: "General History of the Christian Religion and
Church," seems to involve the idea, to which a one-sided Protestant
view of the world may easily lead, that there is a Christian religion
out of and beside the church. On this point we venture no positive decision; but we think that such a separation can hardly be reconciled
with Paul's doctrine of the church, as the "body of Jesus Christ,"
"the fulness of him, that filleth all in all" [Eph. 1:23]. The future

must reveal, whether Christianity can be upheld, without the divine institution of the church; that is, whether the soul can live without the body; whether it will not, at last, resolve itself into a ghost or Gnostic phantom, as certainly as the body without the soul sinks into a corpse. Meanwhile, we hold to the maxim: *Where Christ is, there also is the church, his body; and where the church is, there also is Christ, her head, and all grace; and what God hath joined together, let not man put asunder.*

With these principal faults of Neander's Church History, which we have comprehended under the term, "unchurchliness," in the wide sense; though, on the other hand, with its above named merits too, are more or less closely connected several other subordinate defects. Neander is preeminently the historian, so to speak, of the *invisible* church, and has, therefore, exhibited the development of Christian *doctrine* and Christian *life,* especially so far as these express themselves in single theologians and pious men, in the most thorough and original way. In this he has, in general, surpassed all his predecessors. On the contrary, in what pertains more to the outward manifestation of the church, to its bodily form, his contemplative, idealistic turn allows him less interest. This appears at once in his sections on the *constitution* of the church, where the subject is treated, even in the first period, in a very unsatisfactory manner, and under the influence of his antipathy to the hierarchical element; which, we may here remark, undeniably made its appearance as early as the second century, in the Epistles of Ignatius, too groundlessly charged by him with interpolation, even in their shorter form. For the worldly and political aspect of church history, with which the department of ecclesiastical polity has chiefly to do; the connection of the church with the state; the play of human passions, which, alas! are perpetually intruding even into the most sacred affairs, the godly man, in his guileless, childlike simplicity and his recluse student life, had, at any rate, no very keen eye. But while he takes little notice of small and low motives, he enters the more carefully into the deeper and nobler springs of actions and events. For the superficial pragmatism of his instructor, Planck, who often derives the most important controversies from the merest accidents and the most corrupt sources, he thus substitutes a far more spiritual and profound pragmatism, which makes the interest of religion the main factor in church history. If he sometimes causes almost to forget, that the kingdom of God is *in* the world; it is only to bring out the more forcibly the great truth of that declaration of Christ, which he has characteristically taken as a motto for each volume of his larger work: "My kingdom is not *of* this world" [John 18:36].

Equally lacking was the excellent Neander in a cultivated sense for the *esthetic* or *artistic* in church history; though this defect, again, appears as the shadow of a virtue, arising from the unworldly character of his mind. Had he lived in the first centuries, he, with Clement of Alexandria, Tertullian, and others, would have looked upon art, so prostituted to the service of heathen idolatry, as a vain show, inconsistent with the humble condition of the church, if not as an actual *pompa diaboli*.[36] This, indeed, is by no means his view. He is not puritanically, from principle, opposed to art. The all-pervading, leavenlike nature of the gospel is one of his favorite thoughts. He advocates even the use of painting "for the glorifying of religion; agreeably to the spirit of Christianity, which should reject nothing purely human, but appropriate, pervade, and sanctify all";[37] and in his account of the image controversies, he approves the middle course between the two extremes of worship of images and war upon them. But a full description of the influence of Christianity upon this sphere of human activity, a history of church sculpture, painting, architecture, music, poetry, as well as of all that belongs to the symbolic show of the medieval Catholic worship, is not to be looked for in his work. In this respect he is far surpassed by the spirited, though much less spiritual Hase, who was the first to interweave the history of Christian art into the general body of church history, with his elegant taste,

---

[36](Ed.) In his treatise *De Spectaculis* Tertullian declared that the public games and theatrical shows of the pagans are idolatrous and belong to the "pomp of the devil" which the Christian renounced in baptism; for in baptism (ch. 3) "we bear public testimony that we have renounced the devil, his pomp, and his angels."

[37](Ed.) Neander, *General History of the Christian Religion and Church*, vol. 3 (Boston, 1851) 198.

in short, but expressive and pointed sketches.[38] But Neander's indifference to the beautiful as such, is fairly balanced, to a great extent, by his merit, in not allowing himself to be repelled, like polite wits and worldlings, by the homely and poor servant-form, in which the divine on earth is often veiled; in discerning the real worth of the heavenly treasure in earthen vessels, of the rich kernel even under a rough shell; or, as he himself says of Tertullian, in "recognizing, and bringing out from beneath its temporal obscurity, the stamp of divinity in real life."[39]

From the same point of view must we judge, finally, Neander's style. His writing moves along with heavy uniformity and wearisome verbosity, without any picturesque alternation of light and shade, without rhetorical elegance or polish, without comprehensive classification; like a noiseless stream over an unbroken plain. Thus far it can by no means be recommended as a model of historical delineation. But, on the other hand, by its perfect naturalness, its contemplative unction, and its calm presentation of the subject in hand, it appeals to sound feeling, and faithfully reflects the finest features of the great man's character, his *simplicity and his humility.* The golden mean here appears to us to lie between the unadorned and uncolored plainness of a Neander and the dazzling brilliancy of a Macaulay.

But, in spite of all these faults, Neander still remains, on the whole, beyond doubt the greatest church historian thus far of the nineteenth century. Great, too, especially in this, that he never suffered his renown to obscure at all his sense of the sinfulness and weakness of every human work in this world. With all his comprehensive knowledge, he justly regarded himself as, among many others, merely a forerunner of a new creative epoch of ever-young Christianity; and towards that time he gladly stretched his vision, with the prophetic gaze of faith and hope, from amidst the errors and confusion around him. "We stand," says he, "on the line between an old world and a

---

[38](Ed.) Karl August von Hase, *Kirchengeschichte* (Leipzig, 1834); trans. (from the 7th German ed.) Charles E. Blumenthal and Conway P. Wing, *A History of the Christian Church* (New York, 1885).

[39](Ed.) Neander, *Antignostikus; or Spirit of Tertullian,* preface.

new, about to be called into being by the ever fresh energy of the
gospel. For the fourth time an epoch in the life of our race is in preparation by means of Christianity. We, therefore, can furnish, *in every
respect, but pioneer work* for the period of the new creation, when life
and science shall be regenerated, and the wonderful works of God
proclaimed with new tongues of fire."[40]

To the school of Schleiermacher and Neander, in the *wide* sense,
belongs the majority of the latest theologians of Germany, who have
become known in the field of church and doctrine history, by larger
or smaller, general or monographic works. . . . From Hagenbach for
instance we have a doctrine history, and, in more popular style for
the general reader, an interesting work on Protestantism, and another on the first three centuries; which, by their simple, clear vivacity, and freedom from technical pedantry, commend themselves
even to English taste.[41] Hundeshagen and Schenkel have likewise bestowed their chief strength upon the nature and history of German
Protestantism; the former, at the same time, touching, with the
soundest discernment, upon many of its weaknesses, and the bad effects of a disproportionate literary activity, from which Germany has
long suffered.[42] But still more distinguished is Ullmann, Professor
in Heidelberg, whom we consider, next to Neander, the most eminent church historian of Schleiermacher's school. His monograph on
Gregory Nazianzen (A.D. 1825), and still more his work on the Reformers before the Reformation (two volumes, 1841–1842), are, for
thorough learning, calm clearness, and classic elegance, real master-

---

[40](Ed.) Neander, *Life of Jesus Christ*, xv.

[41](Ed.) Karl Rudolf Hagenbach, *A Textbook of the History of Doctrines*, trans.
(from the 2nd German ed.) C. W. Buch, revised with additions (from the 4th German ed. and other sources) by Henry B. Smith, 2 vols. (New York, 1861–1862);
also *A History of Christian Doctrines*, trans. (from the 5th German ed.) E. H. Plumtre,
3 vols. (Edinburgh, 1880–1881); *History of the Reformation in Germany and Switzerland Chiefly*, trans. (from the 4th German ed.) E. Moore, 2 vols. (Edinburgh,
1878–1879); *Die christliche Kirche der ersten drei Jahrhunderte* (Leipzig, 1853).

[42](Ed.) Karl Bernhard Hundeshagen, *Der deutsche Protestantismus* (Frankfurt,
1846). Daniel Schenkel, *Das Wesen des Protestantismus aus den Quellen des Reforma-
tionszeitalters*, 3 vols. (Schaffhausen, 1846–1851).

pieces of church historiography. From this mild and amiable author we may, perhaps, still look for a general church history, which, as to form and style, would undoubtedly greatly surpass that of Neander.[43]

Among the historians, who, though not professional theologians, have yet made church history the subject of their study, we cannot omit to mention, in this connection, the celebrated Leopold Ranke, Professor in Berlin, and author of the history of the popes in the sixteenth and seventeenth centuries, and of a German history in the age of the Reformation. He is not a man of system, and seldom rises to general philosophical views; but he has an uncommonly keen eye for details and individuals, and is, in this respect, akin to the school of Schleiermacher, and still more to Dr. Hase. With this he combines fine diplomatic tact and shrewdness; the power to reveal the most secret springs of historical movements, and that, too, in part from original investigations with graphic perspicuity and lively elegance, affording his readers, at the same time, instruction and delightful entertainment. He might be termed, in many respects, the German Macaulay.[44]

Dr. Baur. Pantheistic Rationalism and Modern Gnosticism.

In direct opposition to the Neandrian style of church history stands the new Tübingen school, in close connection with the *Hegelian philosophy*. This philosophy carries out in all directions, and brings into well-proportioned shape the fundamental views of Schelling; though, at the same time, it is, in a high degree, independent, and a wonderful monument of comprehensive knowledge and of the power of human thought. Its original peculiarity, which distinguished it from the systems of Fichte and Schleiermacher, was its objective and so far historical spirit. It was, in a certain sense, a philosophy of restoration, in rigid antagonism to the revolutionary,

---

[43](Ed.) Karl Ullmann, *Gregory of Nazianzum*, trans. G. V. Cox (London, 1851); *Reformers before the Reformation*, trans. R. Menzies, 2 vols. (Edinburgh, 1855).

[44](Ed.) Leopold Ranke, *The Ecclesiastical and Political History of the Popes of Rome during the Sixteenth and Seventeenth Centuries*, trans. S. Austin, 3 vols. (London, 1840); *History of the Reformation in Germany*, trans. S. Austin, 3 vols. (London, 1845–1847).

self-sufficient Illuminationism of the last century. To arbitrary self-will it opposed stern law; to private individual opinion, the general reason of the world and the public opinion of the state. It regarded history, not as the play of capricious chance, but as the product of the necessary, eternal laws of the spirit. Its maxim is: Everything reasonable is actual, and everything actual (all that *truly* exists) is reasonable.[45] It sees, in all ages of history, the agency of higher powers; not, indeed, of the Holy Ghost, in the Biblical sense; yet of a rational world-spirit, which makes use of individual men for the accomplishment of its plans. Hegel acknowledges Christianity as the absolute religion, and ascribes to the ideas of the Incarnation and the Trinity, though in a view very different from that of the church doctrine, a deep philosophical truth; carrying the idea of trinity into his view of the whole universe, the world of matter as well as of mind.

But these general principles were capable, in theology, of leading to wholly opposite views, according as the objective forces, by which Hegel conceived the process of history to be started and ruled, were taken to be real existences or mere abstract conceptions; according as the mind was guided by a living faith in Christianity, or by a purely speculative and scientific interest. Thus arise from the Hegelian philosophy two very different theological schools; a positive and a negative; a churchly and an antichristian. They are related to one another as the Alexandrian fathers, Clement and Origen, who brought the Hellenistic, particularly the Platonic philosophy into the service of Christianity, were related to the Gnostics, who by the same philosophy caricatured the Christian religion, and to the Neoplatonists, who arrayed themselves directly against it. The notorious Strauss, one of the infidel Hegelians, has applied to these parties the political terms, *right* wing, and *left* wing, calling the neutral and intermediate party the *center*.[46] The leaders of the Right are Marheineke, Daub, and Göschel, (the last two, however, having nothing to do with

---

[45](Ed.) This is Hegel's famous dictum: "What is rational is actual and what is actual is rational" (*Philosophy of Right,* preface).

[46](Ed.) See Strauss, *Streitschriften zur Verteidigung meiner Schrift über das Leben Jesu und zur Charakteristik der gegenwärtigen Theologie* (Tübingen, 1837) 3. Heft.

church history); of the Left, Baur, and his disciples, Strauss, Zeller, and Schwegler, all from Württemberg, and all students and afterwards teachers in Tübingen; so that they may be called the Tübingen school.[47] As the Tübingen theologians have paid more attention to historical theology than the older Hegelians, who devoted themselves almost exclusively to systematic divinity, we turn our eye first to them, and more particularly to Baur, on whom they all depend.

Dr. Ferdinand Christian Baur, Professor of Historical Theology in Tübingen, is a man of imposing learning, bold criticism, surprising power of combination, and restless productiveness; but, properly, too philosophical to be a faithful historian, and too historical to be an original philosopher; a pure theorist, moreover, and intellectualist, destitute of all sympathy with the practical religious interests of Christianity and the church. He has founded, since the appearance of his article on the Christ-party in Corinth, a formal historical, or rather unhistorical, school, which in the negation of everything positive, and in destructive criticism upon the former orthodox views of primitive Christianity, has far outstripped Semler and his followers.[48] We might, therefore, have placed it in the fourth period, as a new phase of the Rationalistic mode of treating history. But, in the first place, this would too much interrupt the chronological order; and then again, there is, after all, a considerable scientific difference between the older and the later Rationalism; although, in their practical results, when consistently carried out, they come to the same thing, namely, the destruction of the church

---

[47](Ed.) Philip Konrad Marheineke (1780–1846), professor of systematic theology at Berlin where he was one of Schaff's teachers. Karl Daub (1765–1836), professor of dogmatic theology at Heidelberg. Karl Friedrich Goeschel (1784–1861), German jurist and philosopher, who tried to reconcile Christianity and modern culture as represented by Hegel and Goethe. Eduard Zeller (1814–1908) began his university career in theology at Tübingen in 1840, edited *Theologische Jahrbücher* (1842–1857), but due to the resistance of the orthodox party was forced to transfer to the Department of Philosophy.

[48]"Die Christuspartei in der Korinthischen Gemeinde, der Gegensatz des petrinischen und paulinischen Christenthums in der ältesten Kirche," in *Tübinger Zeitschrift für Theologie*, 1831, No. 4.

and of Christianity. The vulgar Rationalism proceeds from the common human understanding (whence its name, *rationalismus communis* or *vulgaris*), and employs, accordingly, a tolerably popular, but exceedingly dry, spiritless style. The more refined Rationalism deals with the speculative reason, and clothes its ideas in the stately garb of a high-sounding scientific terminology and dexterous logic. The former is deistic, abstractly sundering the divine and the human, so as to allow no real intercommunion of both. The latter is pantheistic, confounding God and the world, and deifying the human spirit. The one is allied to the Ebionistic heresy; the other, to the Gnostic. The first holds fast the ideas of so-called natural religion, God, freedom, and immortality, and endeavors to keep on some sort of terms with the Bible. The last recognizes neither a personal God, nor a personal immortality of man; denies the apostolic authorship of almost all the books of the New Testament; and resolves the most important historical statements of the Bible into mythological conceits or even intentional impositions. Both give themselves out for legitimate products of the Protestant principle of free inquiry and resistance to human authority; but both keep entirely to the negative destructive side of the Reformation; have no concern for its positively religious, evangelical character; and must, in the end, destroy Protestantism itself, as well as Catholicism.

Baur, in virtue of his predominant turn for philosophy, has applied himself, with particular zest, to the most difficult parts of doctrine history. These suit him much better than biographical monographs, which require a lively interest in individual persons. The extent of his productions since 1831 is really astonishing.[49] Besides a small textbook of doctrine history and several treatises in var-

---

[49](Ed.) It is remarkable that none of Baur's works here mentioned are available in English: *Lehrbuch der christlichen Dogmengeschichte* (Stuttgart, 1847); *Die christliche Gnosis oder die christliche Religions-Philosophie in ihrer geschichtlichen Entwicklung* (Tübingen, 1835); *Das Manichäische Religionssystem nach den Quellen neu untersucht und entwickelt* (Tübingen, 1831); *Die christliche Lehre von der Versöhnung in ihrer geschichtlichen Entwicklung von der ältesten Zeit bis auf die neueste* (Tübingen, 1838); *Die christliche Lehre von der Dreieinigkeit und Menschwerdung in ihrer geschichtlichen Entwicklung,* 3 vols. (Tübingen, 1841–1843).

ious journals, we have from him a number of larger works, of which we may mention particularly those on the Gnosis (1835), in which he wrongly and somewhat arbitrarily includes not only the proper Gnosticism of antiquity, but also all attempts at a philosophical apprehension of Christianity; on Manicheism (1831); on the historical development of the doctrine of the Atonement (1838), and of the dogma of the Trinity and Incarnation (three stout volumes, 1841–1843); all characterized by extensive, thorough, and well-digested learning, great philosophical acumen, freshness of combination, and skillful description; forming epochs in their kinds; but too much under the influence of his own false preconceptions, to claim justly the praise of invariable objective fidelity.[50]

The Tübingen school, however, has made most noise with its investigations respecting the history of *primitive Christianity*; seeking to overthrow, in due form, the old views on this subject. This operation was publicly commenced by Dr. David Frederick Strauss— a younger pupil of Baur's, but rather more daring and consistent than his master—in his *Leben Jesu,* which astounded the world in 1835. In this book, he reduces the life of the God-man, with icy, wanton hand, to a dry skeleton of everyday history, and resolves all the gospel accounts of miracles, partly on the ground of pretended contradictions, but chiefly on account of the offensiveness of their supernatural character to the carnal mind, into a mythical picture of the idea of the Messiah, as it grew unconsciously from the imagination of the first Christians; thus sinking the gospels, virtually, to the level of heathen mythology. This, of course, puts an end to the idea of a divine origin

---

[50]True, this school, especially Strauss in his *Leben Jesu,* boasts of freedom from all philosophical or doctrinal prepossession. But, with Strauss, this consists in freedom from all leaning towards the Christian faith, and a full bias towards unbelief, which wholly unfits him for any right apprehension or representation of the life of Jesus. Absolute freedom from prepossession, in an author of any character, is a sheer impossibility and absurdity. The grand requisite for the theologian is not that he have no preconceptions, but that his preconceptions be just, and such as the nature of the case demands. Without being fully possessed, beforehand, with the Christian faith, a man can rightly understand neither the Holy Scriptures nor the history of the church.

of Christianity, and turns its apologetic history of eighteeen hundred years into an air-castle, built on pure illusions, a pleasing dream, a tragi-comedy, entitled: "Much ado about nothing."

The same crafty, sophistical criticism, which Strauss did not hesitate to employ upon the inspired biographies of the Saviour, Baur and several of his younger disciples have applied to the Acts of the Apostles, and to the whole Christian literature of the first and second centuries, gradually constructing an entirely peculiar view of early Christianity. This philosophico-critical construction is most completely exhibited in Baur's *Paulus, der Apostel Jesu Christi* (1845),[51] and Schwegler's *Nachapostolischer Zeitalter* (two volumes, 1846). It makes Christianity proper only a product of the catholic church in the middle of the second century. In the minds of Jesus, of the twelve apostles, and of the first Christian community, Christianity was only a perfected *Judaism,* and hence essentially the same as the Ebionism afterwards condemned as heresy. Paul, the Apostle of the Gentiles—no one knows how he came to be an apostle of Jesus Christ—was the first to emancipate it from the bondage of Jewish particularism, and to apprehend it as a new and peculiar system; and that too, in violent, irreconcilable opposition to the other apostles, particularly to Peter, the leading representative of Jewish Christianity. Of this the Epistle to the Galatians and the well-known collision at Antioch (Gal. 2:11 sqq.) give authentic proof; while the Acts of the Apostles throughout, and especially in its description of the apostolic council at Jerusalem, intentionally conceals the difference. This latter production, falsely attributed to Luke, was not written till towards the middle of the second century; and then, not from a purely historical interest, but with the twofold apologetic object of justifying the Apostle of the Gentiles against the reproaches of the Judaizers, and reconciling the two parties of Christendom. These objects the unknown author accomplished by making Peter, in the first part, come as near as possible to Paul in his sentiments, that is, approach the free, Gentile-Christian position; and in the latter part, on the con-

---

[51](Ed.) *Paul, the Apostle of Jesus Christ,* trans. (from the 2nd German ed.) A. Menzies, 2 vols. (London and Edinburgh, 1875–1876).

trary, assimilating Paul as much as possible to Peter, or, which is the same thing, to the Ebionites and Judaizers. A similar pacific design is ascribed to the epistles of Peter and the later epistles of Paul, which all come from the second century; for, of all the epistles of the New Testament, Baur holds as genuine only those of Paul to the Galatians, Corinthians, and Romans; and even from the Epistle to the Romans he rejects the last two chapters. At length, after a long and severe struggle, the two violent antagonists, Petrinism and Paulinism, or properly, Ebionism and Gnosticism, became reconciled, and gave rise to the orthodox catholic Christianity. The grand agent in completing this mighty change was the fourth gospel; which, however, is, of course, not the work of the apostle John—though the author plainly enough pretends to be that apostle—but of an anonymous writer in the middle of the second century. Thus the most profound and spiritual of all productions comes from an obscure nobody; the most sublime and ideal portrait of the immaculate Redeemer, from an imposter!! And it is not a real history, but a sort of philosophico-religious romance, the offspring of the speculative fancy of the Christians after the time of the apostles!! Here this panlogistic school, with its critical acumen and *a priori* construction, reaches the point, where, in its mockery of all outward historical testimony, its palpable extravagence, and violation of all sound common sense, it confutes itself. "Professing themselves to be wise, they became fools" [Rom. 1:22]. The notion, in itself true and important, of a difference between the Jewish Christianity of Peter and the Gentile Christianity of Paul, is pushed so far, that it becomes a caricature, a Gnostic fable. The process of sound criticism is tasked to its utmost by the Tübingen school. The genuine and reliable testimony of the apostolic and old catholic church is rejected or suspected; and, on the other hand, the self-contradictory, heretical productions of the second century, Ebionistic and Gnostic whims and distortions of history, are made the sources of the knowledge of primitive Christianity! Such a procedure can, of course, amount to nothing but theological romancing, a venturesome traffic in airy hypotheses. And, in fact, the books of Baur and Schwegler form, in this respect, fit counterparts to the pseudo-Clementine Homilies and Recognitions, which charge the apostles James and Peter with a Gnostic Ebionism, and bitterly attack the apostle Paul under the name of Simon Magus; clothing their theory in the dress of a historical romance.

Generally speaking, this whole modern construction of primitive Christianity is, substantially, but a revival, with some modification, of the ancient Gnosticism; and of that, too, mainly in its heathen, pseudo-Pauline form. In truth, Baur and his followers are, in the principles of their philosophy and criticism, the Gnostics of German Protestantism.[52] The only difference is, that they are pure theorists and scholars of the study; while at least the more earnest of their predecessors joined with their fantastic speculations a rigid asceticism—seeking, by an unnatural mortification of the body, to work out the salvation of the soul. It was not, therefore, a mere accident, that Baur, in the very beginning of his theological course, paid so much attention to the Gnostic and Manichean systems. His affinity with the anti-Judaistic and pseudo-Pauline fanatic Marcion is particularly striking. In criticism, he seems to have taken this man for his model, only going beyond him. Marcion retained in his canon at least ten of Paul's epistles and the Gospel of Luke; though he mutilated the latter in a very arbitrary way, to cleanse it of pretended Jewish interpolations. But Baur rejects all the Gospels, the Acts, all the General Epistles, and all but four of Paul's; and then these four he either arbitrarily clips (condemning, for instance, the last two chapters of the Epistle to the Romans, as a later addition by another pen), or wrests, to suit his own preconceived hypotheses. This Tübingen school will, no doubt, meet the fate of the old Gnostic heresies. Its investigations will act with stimulating and fertilizing power upon the church calling forth, especially, a deeper scientific apprehension and defense of the historical Christianity of antiquity; and, for itself, it will dry up like the streams of the desert, and figure hereafter only in the history of human aberrations and heresies.

The fundamental defect of this destructive method is the *entire want of faith,* without which it is impossible duly to understand

---

[52]Had the late Dr. Möhler lived to see the subsequent course of his former colleague and opponent in Tübingen, he would have found in him a strong confirmation of the parallel between Protestantism and Gnosticism which he draws in his able *Symbolik,* 27. (Ed.) *Symbolism,* trans. J. B. Robertson (New York, 1844).

Christianity, its inspired records, and its inward history, as to perceive light and color without eyes. Here this school is on the same footing with the older Rationalism. But it differs from the latter in having a philosophical groundwork. It rests not, like the works of Semler, Henke, Gibbon, etc., on an abstract Deism, which denies the presence of God in history; but upon a logical Pantheism, or a denial of the *personality* of God, which necessarily brings with it an entire misconception of the personality of man. Baur finds fault with Neander for recognizing merely the individual, nothing general, in doctrine history; and claims for himself the merit of having advanced this branch of history from the empiric method to the speculative, and of having found, in the idea of the *spirit,* the motive power of history.[53] What, then, is this "spirit," this "dogma," which, according to his ever recurring high-sounding, but pretty empty terminology, "comes to terms with itself," "unfolds itself in the boundless multiplicity of its predicates, and then gathers itself up again into the unity of self-consciousness?" Is it the personal, living God, the Father of our Lord Jesus Christ? Of this that philosophy has, at best, but the name, making it the vehicle of an entirely different conception. The objective forces, which Baur justly declares to be the factors of history—are they substantial things, living realities? No! They amount to nothing but bare formulas of the logical understanding, abstract categories, Gnostic phantoms. The entire history of doctrines is, according to this school, a mere fruitless process of thinking, which thinks thought itself; a tedious mechanism of dialectic method; the "reeling off of a fine logical thread," which invariably runs out, at last, into Hegelian pantheism. The labor of the most profound and pious minds for centuries upon the mystery of the Incarnation, the Trinity, the Atonement, results merely in the philosophical formula of the identity of thought and being, the finite and the infinite, the subject and the object! Thus withers, beneath

---

[53]Baur, *Lehrbuch der christlichen Dogmengeschichte,* 52, 53. Comp. also the conclusion of his latest work, *Die Epochen der kirchlichen Geschichtsschreibung* [Tübingen, 1852], 247 sqq. (Ed.) The latter work is now available in English in *Ferdinand Christian Baur: On the Writing of Church History,* trans. and ed. Peter C. Hodgson (New York, 1968) 43-257.

the simoom of a purely dialectic process, that glorious garden of the
Lord, the history of the church and her doctrines, with its boundless
wealth of flowers, with its innumerable fruits of love, of faith, of
prayer, of holiness. All becomes a sandy desert of metaphysics, without a green oasis, without a refreshing fountain.[54] This method fails
most, of course, in those parts of church history, where the leading
interest is that of practical religion, as in the apostolic period and the
one immediately following. Here, under the pretense of objective
treatment, it falls into the most wretched subjectivity of a hypercriticism, which has no solid ground, and sets at defiance all the laws
of history. But even the purely doctrinal investigations of Baur, highly
as we are willing to rate their other scientific merits, need complete
revision. For, interested only in speculation, he turns even the church
fathers, the schoolmen of the Middle Ages, Calvin and Schleiermacher, into critics and speculators "upon the arid heath;" sunders their
thinking from its ground in their religious life; and hence frequently
loads them with opinions, of which they never dreamed.

This is true even of his celebrated reply to Möhler's *Symbolik*
(1834), though written before his Gnosticism had fully developed
itself.[55] The Protestantism which he seeks to guard from the ingenious assaults of Möhler, is by no means the faith of the Reformers in

---

[54]Here apply, in their full force, the words of the poet: *Ich sag' es dir: ein Kerl,
der speculirt, / Ist wie ein Thier, auf dürrer Heide / Von einem bösen Geist im Kreis herum
geführt, / Und rings umher liegt eine schöne grüne Weide.* (Ed.) Goethe, *Faust*, I
("Study"): "I say, a chap who speculates on things / Is like a beast upon the arid
heath / by some bad demon driven round and round in rings / While lush, green
pastures all about it lie."

[55](Ed.) Johann Adam Möhler (1796–1838), Roman Catholic historian and
theologian, had taught since 1823 in the Roman Catholic Department of Theology at Tübingen, but, because of his controversy with Baur, moved to Munich in
1835, two years before Schaff began his studies at Tübingen. *Der Gegensatz des
Katholizismus und Protestantismus nach den Principien und Hauptdogmen der beiden Lehr-
begriffe* (Tübingen, 1834; 2nd ed., 1836) was Baur's response to Möhler's *Symbolik
oder Darstellung der dogmatischen Gegensätze der Katholiken und Protestanten nach ihren
öffentlichen Bekenntnisschriften* (Mainz, 1832; rev. eds., 1833, 1834, 1835, 1838).
Schaff also had learned from Möhler's *Patrologie, oder christliche Literärgeschichte*, ed.
F. X. Teitmayr, vol. 1 (Regensburg, 1840).

its purity, but corrupted by elements of modern pantheism and fatalism. Such assistance the true evangelical Christian is compelled to decline; and he often feels tempted to join hands with the pious Catholic, in common opposition to modern skepticism and infidelity. Baur has since gone much farther from the proper ground and limits of history. He justly regards the grand antagonists, Catholicism and Protestantism, as the two poles, around which the entire history of the church now turns. But he looks at Protestantism almost exclusively in its negative aspect. "Protestantism," says he, "is the principle of individual freedom of faith and conscience, in which the person is a law unto himself, in opposition to all the outward authority involved in the Catholic idea of the church." Catholicism, he owns, was indispensable, as the only basis, on which this freedom could arise; and, so far, has great significance and full historical authority; but only for the past. "The Reformation is the grand turning point whence the whole tendency of the idea of the church seems to be, to unravel again the web, which itself had woven. If the development of the church previously moved only forward, it now appears to have suddenly veered, to have turned backwards, and to have bent back into itself. Opposition and protestation, hostility, negation of what exists; this is the spirit, which now animates the Church."[56] Though he immediately adds, that this negation is, on the other hand, a deepening, which will lead to a new affirmation of what is true and permanent; yet, in his system, this is saying very little or nothing. According to the whole texture of his views, as above explained, the history of Protestantism is a progressive dissolution of the church, as such; till, at last, even the Holy Scriptures, on which the Reformers planted themselves in protesting against human additions, are, by a shameless, profane, conceited hypercriticism, snatched from under our feet, and nothing is left us, but our own natural, helpless selves, with that empty notion of likeness to God,

---

[56]*Die Epochen der kirchlichen Geschichtsschreibung*, 257, 255. See p. 260: "Protestantism must itself remain an inexplicable riddle, if, to be what it has become, it could think of itself in any other way than by having its consciousness of itself mediated by papacy and Catholicism." (Ed.) Cf. now *Ferdinand Christian Baur: On the Writing of Church History*, 249, 247-48, 251.

with which the fearful tragedy of the fall began. This is the legitimate and necessary result of this negative Protestantism of the extreme Left.

This extensive literature of modern philosophical and critical antichristianity would be absolutely disheartening, and would awaken the most gloomy anticipations for Protestantism, which embosoms it and even tolerates some of its champions in her chairs of theology, were we not assured, by the cheering testimony of many centuries of history, that God, in his infinite wisdom and love, can bring good out of all evil, and make all the aberrations of the human mind aid the triumph of the truth. Like all previous enemies of Christianity, this most learned, most ingenious, and therefore most dangerous form of ultra, false, infidel Protestantism, which appears in the exegetical and historical productions of the Tübingen school, will also surely miss its aim. Nay, it has already involuntarily given a mighty impulse to the productive energy of the positive, evangelical, churchly theology. As Strauss' *Leben Jesu* has already been philosophically refuted by the counter productions of Tholuck, Neander, Lange, Ebrard, Hoffmann, Lücke, Ullmann, etc.; so also the speculations of Baur, Schwegler, and Zeller on the age of the apostles and the succeeding period have been directly or indirectly assailed with the invincible weapons of thorough learning, and their inward weakness exposed, by the investigations of Dorner, (in his history of Christology), Lechler, (on the apostolic and postapostolic periods), Weitzel, (on the paschal controversies of the first three centuries), Wieseler, (on the chronology of the Acts of the Apostles), Neander, (in the last edition of his history of the planting and training of the Church), Bunsen (on the Ignatian Epistles, and on Hippolytus), Thiersch, (on the formation of the New Testament canon, and on the apostolic Church), and others. But certainly no work has yet appeared, which fully sets forth the whole history of the early church in its organic connection, with steady reference to these modern errors.

Marheineke. Leo. Rothe. Dorner. Thiersch. Recapitulation.

The *right* or *conservative* wing of the Hegelian school sought to reconcile this philosophical system with the faith of the Bible and the church; though it must be confessed, that, in so doing, they often too much spiritualized the articles of faith, and unwittingly did them more or less violence by their logic, resolving them pretty much into unsubstantial notions and metaphysical abstractions. Their case was even worse than that of Origen, in whom Platonism, instead of always bending to Christianity, sometimes gained the mastery over it. The older Hegelians of this class, moreover, have confined their labors almost entirely to the philosophical and systematic branches of theology. Marheineke alone, (died 1847), was, at the same time, a historian. His General Church History of Christianity, (first part, 1806), is the first attempt to construct a history on the basis of the modern speculations, and to set up a more objective method against the rationalistic subjectivism. But the work is very defective, and, at all events, unfinished. Of far more permanent value is his History of the German Reformation, drawn from the sources, and presented in a purely objective way, but without the learned apparatus, and intended more for the general reader. This work, unsurpassable in its kind, is fortunately free from all that heavy dialectic accoutrement, in which his *Dogmatik* is clothed, and is distinguished for its genuine national, old German style and spirit, peculiarly appropriate to the character of its leading hero, the thoroughly German Luther. Marheineke has also won laurels in doctrine history and symbolism, and especially by his extended and on the whole faithful exhibition of the system of Catholicism (3 vols. 1810–13).[57]

As to orthodoxy, this theologian, though a member and advocate of the United Evangelical Church of Prussia, was predominantly of the Lutheran doctrinal stamp. This confession with its closer affinity to catholicism, speculation and mysticism, suited the Hegelian mode of treating history better, than the genius of the Reformed church, which recedes farther from the previous traditions, gives larger scope to subjectivity, and concerns itself more with practice than with theory. With the younger Wiggers, author of a work on ecclesiastical

---

[57](Ed.) None of Marheineke's works are available in English: *Geschichte der deutschen Reformation,* 4 vols. (Berlin, 1816–34); *Das System des Katholicismus in seiner symbolischen Entwicklung,* 3 vols. (Heidelberg, 1810–13); *Universalkirchenhistorie des Christentums* (Erlangen, 1806); *Die Grundlehren der christlichen Dogmatik* (Berlin, 1819; 2nd ed., 1827).

statistics (1842–43); still more with Martensen, a Danish divine, but of purely German education, and a very spirited, original theologian; with Theodore Kliefoth, the excellent author of an extended philosophical introduction to doctrine history; with Kahnis, who has published a work on the history of the doctrine concerning the Holy Ghost (1847), and another on the doctrine of the eucharist (1851); and with the jurist Göschel, only an amateur, however, in theology, a confused compound of heterogeneous elements, Hegel, Göthe, and Christianity—with all these the Hegelian philosophy has become a bridge to strict symbolical Lutheranism.

But on the same ground the method of history, started by Hegel, may be considered as involving also, to some extent, a tendency towards *Catholicism.* By its objective character it is better fitted than the more subjective method of the school of Schleiermacher and Neander, to appreciate and do full justice to the heroes of the Roman church, and especially to the Middle Ages. We have an example of this in F. R. Hasse's monograph on Anselm of Canterbury; a model of purely objective and minute, yet living and clear historical representation, superior to Neander's *Bernard.*[58]

This Catholicizing tendency is still more visible in Heinrich Leo, and assumes with him an almost Romanizing form.[59] Though not a theologian, he has yet, in his Universal History, carefully noticed religion and the church; and we cannot here omit his name. Leo, a man of great originality and native force, but rough, unsparing, and prone to extravagence, altogether threw off, it is true, in later life, the straitjacket of the Hegelian logic and dialectics; but the influence of this philosophy still appears in his making the subject entirely subordinate to the objective powers; the individual, to the general. Since he exchanged his youthful free-thinking, however, which vented itself in his worthless history of the Jewish commonwealth, for posi-

---

[58](Ed.) Friedrich Rudolf Hasse, *Anselm von Canterbury,* 2 vols. (Leipzig, 1842–52); trans. and abridged by W. Turner, *The Life of Anselm, Archbishop of Canterbury* (London, 1850).

[59](Ed.) Heinrich Leo (1799–1878), professor of history at Halle, author of *Lehrbuch der Universalgeschichte,* 6 vols. (Halle, 1840–51).

tive Christianity, he has meant by these objective forces, not dialectic forms and notions, but concrete realities, laws and institutions of the personal, Christian God, which to resist is sin and guilt, which to obey is man's true feedom, honor, and glory. He regards history as proceeding from above; the will of God, not the popular will, and least of all the individual, as its motive power. Hence his favorable view of the Middle Ages, and his unfavorable, nay, one-sided and unjust judgment of the Reformation; though his fault here may well be excused as a reaction against the blind eulogies of that movement. Leo's view of history is thoroughly ethical, churchly, conservative, absolutely antirevolutionary, even to the favoring of despotism. He feels it to be his duty, amidst the distractions and instability of modern Europe, to lay the strongest emphasis on law, the necessity of the principle of authority and the general will. In this respect he goes undoubtedly too far; he overlooks the real wants of the people and gets into conflict with the progressive spirit of the age. Yet in a polemical character so harsh, violent, irritable and uncompromising as Leo, who often falls like a bulldog on what displeases him, we cannot always take single expressions in their strict sense, any more than in the case of Luther, whom he much resembles in temperament, though his wrath is directed towards entirely different enemies.[60] Hence, we are not to understand from his catholicizing tendency, that he would hold the restoration of an antiquated state of things—say of the Middle Ages—as possible, or even desirable; but, with many of the profoundest minds of our time, he doubtless has in his eye a new age, which will embody what is true in the past, and yet, at the same time, stand on peculiar and higher ground.

Anticipations of such an advancement appear, also, in the works of the two professors of theology in Bonn, Dr. R. Rothe, and Dr. J. A. Dorner, whom we consider the most important speculative di-

---

[60]Particularly in his occasional articles in the *Evangelische Kirchenzeitung* of his friend Hengstenberg, who is, like himself, completely anti-democratic, anti-republican, and absolutistic in his views of both church and state, and in this respect wholly at variance with the Anglo-American taste, with which, in other points in his orthodoxy, especially his views of inspiration and his exegesis, he accords better than most other German theologians.

vines of the day. They have confined themselves chiefly, it is true, to the dogmatic and ethical fields (especially Rothe); but they merit the most honorable mention, also, as historians. The philosophical principles of their theology, and, through these, their conceptions of history, have plainly received powerful impulse and direction from the philosophy of Hegel. But, at the same time, they have appropriated all the elements of Schleiermacher's theology. These two ingredients they have compounded with genuine originality, and wrought into a peculiar shape. Rothe's "Theological Ethics" stands forth as a thoroughly original work, and, in fact, as a master-piece of speculative divinity, with which very few works of ancient or modern times can compare.[61] On account of this relation of both Rothe and Dorner to Hegel and Schleiermacher, and their essential agreement in a positively Christian, and yet genuinely speculative theology, we here put the two together; though in many other respects they differ.

Dr. Rothe, in 1837, published the first volume of a work on the beginnings of the Christian church, and its constitution, which, in our view, has not yet received the attention it merits.[62] It consists chiefly of an exceedingly thorough and acute investigation of the origin and development of the episcopal constitution, and (what is closely connected with this) of the Catholic doctrine concerning the historical, visible church, its unity, holiness, catholicity, apostolicity, and exclusiveness. It comes to the conclusion, that the episcopate, as a necessary substitute for the apostolate in maintaining and promoting unity, reaches back even to the days of St. John, and thus has the apostolic sanction; and that the above-named idea of the church arose by an inward necessity in the first centuries, particularly through the influence of Ignatius, Irenaeus, Cyprian and Augustine, and lay at the bottom of the whole conception of Christianity

---

[61](Ed.) Richard Rothe (1799–1860), who spent most of his career at Heidelberg, has so far been strangely neglected by American scholarship. His major work is *Theologische Ethik*, 3 vols. (Wittenberg, 1845–48).

[62]The continuation he has unfortunately been obliged, thus far, to withhold from the public, on account of the almost universal opposition to his view of the relation of church and state. (Ed.) *Die Anfänge der christlichen Kirche und ihrer Verfassung: Beilage über die Echtheit der Ignatianischen Briefe* (Wittenberg, 1837).

in those days. This conclusion, if true, must have a powerful bearing on the final solution of the church question, which is now pressing so heavily on Protestant Christendom. But while Rothe puts the whole weight of antiquity into the scale of Catholicism, where all the church fathers, in their prevailing spirit, belong, he is, in so doing, far from giving up Protestantism. His position, in this respect, he sets forth in language, which we particularly commend to the consideration of our fanatical anti-Catholics: "There is no more effectual way of defending Protestantism, than by just acknowledging, nay, expressly asserting, that, *in the past,* Catholicism *had,* in its essence, full historical reality and authority; that it *contained* deep inward truth, high moral glory and power."[63] He also supposes, however, that the Reformation of the sixteenth century was a shock to the whole institution of the church in its previous form, a serious breach in its unity and catholicity; and, at the same time, he rejects the distinction of a visible and invisible church, as a mere shift of the older Protestant theologians, to save the catholic idea of the church, whose visible, historical reality had disappeared.[64] He, therefore, vindicates Protestantism on the hypothesis, which he unfolds at large in his philosophical introduction, that the church is but a temporary

---

[63](Ed.) Ibid., ix.

[64]"In consequence of the Reformation," says Rothe, p. 103, "the visible church, i. e. the church, properly so called (which is, in fact, essentially the body of Christ, therefore visible), had been lost. For though even the evangelical party did not dispense with an outward religious union, yet it had no longer a *church*; its union was not really *churchly*; because it had to give up the element of catholicity, i.e. universality and unity which is absolutely essential to the church." But the Protestants, Rothe goes on to say, being unwilling to relinquish entirely this old hallowed notion of a church and communion of saints, sought a substitute for it and thus hit upon the idea of an *invisible* church; to this they transferred all those glorious predicates of unity, universality, holiness, and apostolicity, which they denied to the historical and visible Roman Catholic church. This whole Protestant conception of an invisible church, Rothe calls, p. 109, "a mere hypothesis, a pure fiction, a notion involving a contradiction," and in the introduction to his work, he brings forth arguments against it, which are ingenious, and which, in fact, it is not so easy satisfactorily to refute, although there is, as we believe, a very important truth at the bottom of that old Protestant distinction.

vehicle and a transient form of Christianity, through which it passes
into the more perfect form of the kingdom of God, that is, according
to Rothe, an ideal *state,* a theocracy. This result, moreover, is not
fully attained till the end of the historical development; and thus the
institution of the church is still, for a time, even in Protestantism,
of relative authority and necessity along with the state, in its present
imperfect form, until the latter shall become wholly penetrated and
transformed by Christianity. Rothe here starts from Hegel's overstrained idea of the state; idealizing it, however, even far more than
Hegel; considering it, not indeed as it now is, but as it will one day
be, the most suitable form of moral society; and identifying it with
the idea of the kingdom of God itself. This is not the place to go
more minutely into this remarkable theory. But we must here repeat
the observation, previously made respecting Neander, that such a
separation between the kingdom of God and the church seems to us
to have sufficient ground neither in exegesis nor in history; and that
we very much doubt whether Christianity could perpetuate itself
without the church, which, St. Paul tells us, is the body of Christ,
the fulness of him that filleth all in all [Eph. 1:23]. True, we too
believe, that Catholicism in its former condition can never be restored, that Protestantism is preparing the way for a new outward
form of the kingdom of God, and that church and state will, at last,
be united in one theocracy; not, however, by the church merging in
the state, but rather conversely, by the state being taken up and glorified in the church, as art in worship, as science in theosophy, as
nature in grace, as time in eternity. Of the indestructable permanence of the church we are assured by the express promise of our Lord,
that the gates of hell shall not prevail against her [Matt. 16:18]. Even
from her present shattered and apparently ruined condition, therefore, she will rise, phenix-like, in loftier beauty and new power; convert the whole world to Christ; and thenceforth, as his bride, reign
blissfully over the new heavens and new earth forever.

From Dr. Dorner we have a very valuable, (but, in its new, enlarged form, not yet finished), history of the doctrine of the Incarnation of God and the Person of Christ (1845).[65] He here traces the

---

[65](Ed.) See above, p. 26n22.

development of this central doctrine of Christianity, on which the solution of all other theological problems depends, and which is justly, therefore, again claiming the serious attention of our age. He sets forth the history, with exemplary thoroughness, keen penetration, perfect command of the copious material, and in dignified, happy language, though not entirely without a certain scientific pretension and stiffness. At the same time he makes it bear throughout, and triumphantly, against Baur's investigations on the same subject. He is not a whit behind his opponent in speculative talent, while he far excels him in sound comprehension, and writes, in the service not merely of science, but also of the church. Similar in spirit and contents, but not so full and satisfactory, is the work of George Augustus Meier on the history of the doctrine of the Trinity (1844), in part, also, a successful positive refutation of Baur's work on the Trinity and Christology.[66]

In this connection we must mention, finally, a younger theologian, Dr. Henry W. J. Thiersch, one of the most learned opponents of Dr. Baur and the Tübingen school. He has already written several interesting works— Lectures on Catholicism and Protestantism, a kind of conciliatory symbolism (1846); a book on the Formation of the New Testament Canon, against the modern hypercritics and dealers in hypotheses (1845); and a History of the Christian Church in Primitive Times, the first volume of which, embracing the apostolic period, appeared in 1852.[67] Thiersch has no sympathy whatever with the Hegelian philosophy, and as little with Schleiermacher's theology; but fights against both with a zeal, which reminds one of Tertullian's war against Gnosticism. In his doctrinal persuasion he

---

[66](Ed.) George August Meier, *Die Lehre von der Trinität in ihrer historischen Entwicklung* (Hamburg, 1844).

[67](Ed.) Heinrich Wilhelm Josias Thiersch (1817–85) was Schaff's classmate at Tübingen in 1837–38, became professor at Marburg in 1843, the same year he joined the Irvingites, and resigned his professorship in 1850. He remained a member of the Catholic Apostolic church until his death. Among his major works are *Versuch zur Herstellung des historischen Standpuncts für die Kritik der neutestamentlichen Schriften* (Erlangen, 1845); *Vorlesungen über Katholizismus und Protestantismus* (Erlangen, 1846); and *The Church in the Apostolic Age*, trans. T. Carlyle (London, 1852).

was at first decidedly Lutheran, with a strong leaning to an ascetic pietism. But of late he has fallen out with the present state of Protestantism at large, and, in honorable disinterestedness and impatient haste, has resigned his professorship at Marburg and joined the *Irvingites.* Of all Protestant sects, this is the most churchly, catholic, hierarchical, sacramental, and liturgical. It arose in England A. D. 1831, and has of late made some little progress also in Germany and in the United States. It has in view the restoration of the apostolic church, with its peculiar supernatural offices, particularly the apostolate, and with its miraculous powers, as speaking with tongues and prophecy; the collection of all the vital forces of the Catholic and Protestant churches into this community, to save them from the approaching judgment; and preparation for the glorious return of the Lord. Thiersch is related to this so-called "Apostolic Community," as the essentially catholic and orthodox, and yet schismatic Tertullian was to the kindred sect of the Montanists in the second and third centuries.[68] He is the theological representative of Irvingism, and stands mediating between it and Protestantism, especially in Germany. But the proper value of his historical works depends not so much, or not exclusively, on these Irvingite peculiarities and extravagences. It consists, rather, in his clear, elegant, and noble style, which everywhere evinces the classical scholar and worthy son of the celebrated Greek philologian of Munich; in his extensive and thorough acquaintance with patristic literature; in the lovely spirit of deep and warm, though sometimes enthusiastic and visionary piety, which breathes in all his writings; and in his mild, irenic, conciliatory posture towards the great antagonism of Catholicism and Protestantism. Even his latest work, the history of the apostolic Church, is, as he himself says, "not a part of his new activity, as pastor in the Apostolic Community, but a sequel to his former labors as teacher of

---

[68]Compare our articles on Irvingism and the church question in the February, March, May and June numbers of *Der deutsche Kirchenfreund* for 1850, where we have taken particular notice of our esteemed and beloved friend and fellow-student, Thiersch, and of his spirited and suggestive Lectures on Catholicism and Protestantism. (Ed.) Especially important is Schaff's concluding article in the June number, which assesses the validity of Irvingism.

theology."[69] Besides, Irvingism contains many elements of truth, well worthy of the most serious consideration; and it is to be expected, that, through the writings of Thiersch, it will exert some influence on German theology. So Montanism wrought, through Tertullian, on the catholic church, though the system itself shared the inevitable fate of sects, death, without the hope of resurrection. Only the universal, historical church has the promise that the gates of hell shall not prevail against her.

We have now traced the history of our science down to the labors of our contemporaries. It runs parallel with, and reflects, in an interesting manner, the development of the church itself in its different ages. We have seen, how, in the abounding historical literature of Germany, since the appearance of Neander, is mirrored the whole confused diversity of the elements of modern culture; now repelling, now attracting one another, and now striving towards a higher position of union; at one time bound, entirely or in part, in the fetters of a philosophical system; at another, with free, untrammelled spirit, endeavoring to apprehend and do justice to everything, according to its own peculiar nature. We have observed, too, that the most profound and earnest students in this department become more and more convinced of the high practical office of this science, to set forth faithfully and candidly the whole undivided fulness of the life of Jesus Christ, as it has continuously unfolded itself in time; to aid thereby in understanding the present; to animate for the work of the future; and gradually to effect the final, satisfactory solution of the question of all questions, that of *Christ and his church,* in relation as well to the unbelieving world, as to the various parties in Christendom itself, especially to the colossal, all-comprehending antagonism of Catholicism and Protestantism.

Unite, now, the most extensive and thorough learning with the simple piety and tender conscientiousness of a *Neander,* the speculative talent and combining ingenuity of a *Rothe* and a *Dorner,* the lovely mildness and calm clearness of an *Ullmann,* the sober inves-

---

[69](Ed.) Thiersch, *Die Kirche im apostolischen Zeitalter und die Entstehung der neutestamentlichen Schriften* (Frankfurt, 1852) vii.

tigation of a *Gieseler,* the fine diplomatic wisdom of a *Ranke,* the energetic decision of a *Leo,* the vivacity and elegant taste of a *Hase*— unite all these, we say, in one person, free from all slavery to philosophy, yet not disdaining to employ it thankfully in the service of Scriptural truth; pervaded and controlled by living faith and genuine, ardent love; and working, not for himself, nor for a party, but wholly in the spirit and service of the God-man, Jesus Christ, the life-giving sun of history, and for the interests of His bride, the one, Holy, Catholic, Apostolic Church; weaving into a crown of glory for the Saviour all the flowers of sanctified thought, faith, life, and suffering, from every age and clime—and we have, so to speak, the ideal of a Christian church historian in full form before us; an ideal, which, indeed, may never be realized on earth in any one individual, but to which all, who are called to labor in this most interesting and important field of theology, should honestly strive to conform.

PART II
Major Themes—
The Mercersburg Years
(1844-1863)

CHAPTER 2

Toward a New Reformation

EDITORIAL INTRODUCTION

An enlarged version of Schaff's inaugural lecture "The Principle of Protestantism" was published the following year, in 1845, first in German, then in an English translation by his colleague Nevin. To the English edition Nevin added an introduction and, at Schaff's request, his sermon "Catholic Unity," which he had preached at the Triennial Convention of the Dutch and German Reformed churches just a few days after Schaff's arrival in the United States. Schaff himself appended to the published versions of his lecture a summary of his views in the form of 112 "Theses for the Time," which is our opening selection.

The "Theses for the Time" offer a convenient and succinct summary of Schaff's complex and controversial program for the renewal of the contemporary church.[1] The lack of conceptual clarity in his doctrine of the church, as he grappled with such contrasting pairs of adjectives as "visible" and "invisible," "ideal" and "real," rendered all the more explicit his real intention: once again to link organically Christology and ecclesiology. He wanted to affirm that Christ has never been without the church and that Christ's true

---

[1]For a fuller discussion of Schaff's theological program, see my article "The Reformation Goes West: The Notion of Historical Development in the Thought of Philip Schaff," *Journal of Religion* 62 (July 1982): 219-41.

church is not an invisible Platonic castle in the air but the historical, visible church, even though the "ideal" church, the church
without sin and error, will appear only at Christ's second coming.
Having learned from Hegel to regard history as "the self-evolution
of the absolute spirit and hence supremely rational throughout,"[2]
he viewed even the history of Christianity, quaint as it must have
sounded to the ears of his American readers, as the dialectical unfolding of abstract principles, for example, objectivity and subjectivity, authority and freedom, that consistently follows the rhythm
of thesis, antithesis and synthesis. But it was Schelling's ecumenical vision of the course of church history—the distinction of three
ages that in logical and chronological sequence are to be identified
with the apostles Peter, Paul and John—which truly illuminated
for Schaff the history of Christianity and guided all of his efforts on
behalf of Christian unity.

Embedded in this general historical and ecumenical scheme was
Schaff's novel and provocative understanding of the sixteenth-century Reformation and the subsequent history of Protestantism. To
the startled surprise of most of his American fellow Christians he
affirmed both the "Christian" character of the Catholic Middle Ages
and the "catholic" character of the Protestant Reformation, for both
are to be viewed as necessary and hence legitimate stages in the historical development of the Christian church. Schaff then went on
to combine eclectically the orthodox Protestant concentration on
what German Protestants had just learned to call the Reformation's
"material" and "formal" principles—justification by faith alone
and the sole authority of Scripture—with the romantic and idealistic interpretation of the Reformation as the historical break-
through of the principles of subjectivity and freedom.[3] But whereas

---

[2]Schaff, *What is Church History? A Vindication of the Idea of Historical Development,* trans. John W. Nevin (Philadelphia, 1846) 76.

[3]The rationalist theologian K. G. Bretschneider, *Handbuch der Dogmatik der
evangelisch-lutherischen Kirche* (1814, 4th ed. 1838), apparently originated the notion of the two Protestant principles; cf. also Albrecht Ritschl, "Über die beiden
Prinzipien des Protestantismus," *Gesammelte Aufsätze,* ed. O. Ritschl (Freiburg and
Leipzig, 1893) 235-47. Heinrich Bornkamm, *Luther im Spiegel der deutschen Geis-
tesgeschichte* (Heidelberg, 1955) 27-36, provides a good summary of the romantic
and idealistic interpretations of the Reformation.

the idealistic philosophy of history took these principles to be the strength and glory of Protestantism, the romantic movement, as well as the Roman Catholic critics of Protestantism, on the contrary, found in them the vitiating fault and fundamental weakness of the Protestant age in western history. It was obvious that Schaff allied himself polemically with the romantic censure of the Protestant age of "subjectivity" and "freedom" and only occasionally, and then far less assertively, with its idealistic praise. Attacking modern "pseudo-Protestantism," he identified "sectarianism," "rationalism," and "secularization" as its major manifestations. As we already noted, he opposed, broadly speaking, the ethos of the European Enlightenment and the Free-Church tradition of Anglo-American Christianity. They had spawned revolutionary and destructive tendencies in church and state, over against which he welcomed even Roman Catholicism as an ally in a common cause. He welcomed even more fervently such kindred movements as the incipient Lutheran confessionalism and England's Puseyism, but— and this was something that most of Schaff's American opponents overlooked—they were acceptable as allies only as long as they supported his unique fusion of a high-church pietism and the romantic-idealistic theory of historical development. This broad and complex understanding then issued in his firm hope that in his own time the "johannean age" with its final union of the Catholic principle of objectivity and the Protestant principle of subjectivity was close at hand; moreover, it would be achieved right here in the United States. What an unusual expectation this was for a recent immigrant! Its full meaning Schaff would gradualy begin to grasp and then more fully unfold in his book *America*.

Seven years later, in 1852, Schaff published a series of articles in *Der deutsche Kirchenfreund*, which were intended for his American readers as an introduction to the most distinguished living German theologians ("Gallerie der bedeutendsten jetzt lebenden Universitätstheologen Deutschlands"). The concluding article appeared in the September issue, where Schaff set out to pen some general and laudatory remarks about the nature and mission of contemporary German theology. He explained at greater length its five most distinctive features: no other theology is as rich and diverse; none is as lively and relevant; it represents a rebirth of the evangelical faith; rising above the confessional strife of previous centuries, it now stands for the union of the Lutheran and Reformed traditions; it exhibits a new openness toward Roman Catholicism. But when Schaff came to the final point, he deemed its importance so great that he decided to write a separate article, "German Theology and the Church Question." It is this article which is here also included.

Both of these concluding articles are distinguished by two seemingly disparate features: their ecumenical emphasis and polemical thrusts. In few other writings was Schaff as sharply polemical and pugnacious as in these two articles. One needs to remember, however, that they were written at the very time when the crisis caused by the theological views of the two Mercersburg professors was coming to its head in the German Reformed church. Nevin had resigned from the Seminary in 1852. He had published in the *Mercersburg Review* his remarkable series of scholarly, but controversial articles: "Anglican Crisis," "Early Christianity" and "Cyprian" (of which the last two installments appeared in September and November of 1852). He had entered those "five years of dizziness," when he darkly and moodily suspected that the malaise of modern Protestantism would leave only the Roman Catholic church as the contemporary Christian's true home.[4] Additionally, the rampant anti-Catholicism of American Protestantism continued to agitate Schaff. Perhaps most of all, he now also viewed with growing alarm the increasing strength of an exclusive Lutheran confessionalism both in Germany and the United States. As soon as he began to extol the "united" character of contemporary German Protestantism (his fourth point), the discussion, therefore, erupted into bitter and biting criticism of the direction in which American and German Lutherans appeared to be moving.

As to Roman Catholicism, in the years since he had written *The Principle of Protestantism,* he and Nevin had come to accept the essentially Catholic character of early Christianity. Both men had increasingly been influenced by the works of such church historians as August Neander (though Neander was inclined to emphasize more the "evangelical" character of the early church), Johann Adam Möhler, Richard Rothe and Isaac Taylor. Nevin and Schaff were

---

[4]The words are those of one of Nevin's opponents, as quoted in James I. Good, *History of the Reformed Church in the United States in the Nineteenth Century* (New York, 1911) 312.

now eager to assert that the early Catholic church was as truly the church of Christ as was the medieval Catholic church at a later stage. In view of these significant concessions to Roman Catholicism, Schaff faced the challenge of having to explain how Protestantism can still be validated. And he replied: only with the help of the idealistic theory of historical development. Schelling's ecumenical vision of church history in particular was for Schaff the bright "polar star" that in the end alone will be a sure guide for all those who are painfully conscious of the sectarian and rationalistic shortcomings of Protestantism. It will safely lead them toward the goal of an "evangelical catholicism" and thus prevent them from converting to Roman Catholicism. Lutheran confessionalism and Puseyism, bereft of the guidance of the theory of historical development, by contrast, will most surely end at Rome. For as Schaff now heatedly warned: "In short, for all those who view not only biblical but also churchly Christianity as a complete, once and for all finished system and reject the concept of historical development, Rome is the proper, final home, whether they know and admit this or not."[5]

Schaff's two articles (especially when read alongside of Nevin's articles in the *Mercersburg Review*) upset many of his readers. They perceived Schaff to be anti-Lutheran and pro-Catholic and therefore anti-Protestant. One is struck by the fact that most of them apparently hardly noticed the ecumenical implications of his views. The unfavorable reaction persuaded Schaff to hand the editorship of *Der deutsche Kirchenfreund* over to his friend Julius Mann at the end of 1853. But one may surmise that this decision was also prompted by his eagerness to free his hands for the continuing work on his church history and to ready himself for his first return trip to Europe in December of 1853.

In Europe, even in the midst of a busy schedule of travels, lectures, visits and interviews, the "church question" was still uppermost on Schaff's mind. This is vividly shown by the "Letter from Trent" that he addressed to the readers of *Der deutsche Kirchenfreund* (which was, in fact, an article composed later in the form of a letter). The text allows us to catch a lively glimpse of the inveterate traveller, who everywhere eagerly studied whatever was of general,

[5]Schaff, "Gallerie der bedeutendsten jetzt lebenden Universitätstheologen Deutschlands," *Der deutsche Kirchenfreund* 5 (September 1852): 334.

but especially of historical and religious significance. On the evening of an eventful Trinity Sunday, and in the city where in the
sixteenth century the great council of the Roman Catholic church
had met and sealed the division of the western church, he followed
once again, as was his habit, the gospel injunction to retreat "into
your room and shut your door and pray" (Matt. 6:6). He had sometimes, as in 1846, spoken in the spirit and language of romanticism of the Christian world with its many denominations as the
"garden of the Lord," which holds a great variety of flowers, each
adding something to the beauty of the whole.[6] He was still seeking
to find his way through that garden's bewildering variety of flowers—what just recently he had called, changing metaphors, the
maze of "the labyrinth of the church question."[7] But as his sojourn
in Europe drew to its close, he had become determined to set more
narrowly the fences of that Christian garden. More and more often
he looked at Roman Catholicism and even at Puseyism and Lutheran confessionalism, as it were, from across the fence, for he now
accepted as the ecumenical task at hand the narrower, though still
formidable challenge of cultivating the garden of "evangelical"
Protestantism on both sides of the Atlantic Ocean, without giving
up his hope for the ultimate reunion of all of Christendom. This
meaning, too, was implied in the remark at the letter's end that he
would return to his adopted country "probably a better Protestant
and American."

THESES FOR THE TIME*

Introduction

1. Every period of the church and of theology has its particular
problem to solve; and every doctrine, in a measure every book also of
the Bible, has its classic age in which it first comes to be fully understood and appropriated by the consciousness of the Christian world.

---

[6]Schaff, What is Church History?, 121.

[7]Schaff, Der deutsche Kirchenfreund 5 (September 1852): 335.

*The Principle of Protestantism, trans. John W. Nevin (Chambersburg PA, 1845)
177-90.

2. The main question of *our* time concerns the nature of the church itself in relation to the world and to single Christians.

The Church in General

3. The church is the Body of Jesus Christ. This expresses her communion with her Head, and also the relation of her members to one another.

4. In the first respect, she is an institution founded by Christ, proceeding from his loins, and animated by his Spirit, for the glory of God and the salvation of man; through which alone, as its necessary organ, the revelation of God in Christ becomes effective in the history of the world. Hence out of the church, as there is no Christianity, there can be no salvation.

5. In the second respect, she is, like every other body, a living unity of different members; a communion in faith and love, visible as well as invisible, external as well as internal, of the most manifold individualities, gifts, and powers, pervaded with the same Spirit and serving the same end.

6. The definition implies further that as the life of the parents flows forward in the child, so the church also is the depository and continuation of the earthly human life of the Redeemer, in his threefold office of prophet, priest, and king.

7. Hence she possesses, like her Founder, a divine and human, an ideal and a real, a heavenly and an earthly nature; only with this difference, that in her militant stage, freedom from sin and error cannot be predicated of her in the same sense as of Christ; that is, she possesses the principle of holiness and the full truth, mixed however still with sin and error.

8. To the church belong, in the wider sense, all baptized persons, even though they may have fallen back to the world; in the narrower sense, however, such only as believe in Jesus Christ.

9. The relation of the church to the world, with its different spheres of science, art, government, and social life, is neither one of destruction on her part nor one of indifference; but the object of it is that she should transfuse the world with the purifying power of her own divine life, and thus bring it at last to its true and proper perfection.

10. The ultimate scope of history accordingly is this, that Christianity may become completely the same with nature, and the world be formally organized as the kingdom of Christ; which must involve the absolute identity of church and state, theology and philosophy, worship and art, religion and morality; the state of the renovated earth, in which God will be All in all.

11. In relation to single Christians, the church is the mother from which they derive their religious life and to which they owe therefore constant fidelity, gratitude, and obedience; she is the power of the objective and general to which the subjective and single should ever be subordinate.

12. Only in such regular and rational subordination can the individual Christian be truly free; and his personal piety can as little come to perfection apart from an inward and outward communion with the life of the church, as a limb separated from the body or a branch torn from the vine.

13. Christianity in itself is the *absolute* religion, and in this view unsusceptible to improvement.

14. We must not confound with this, however, the *apprehension* and *appropriation* of Christianity in the consciousness of mankind. This is a progressive process of development that will reach its close only with the second coming of the Lord.

15. All historical progress then, in the case of the church, consists, not in going beyond Christianity itself, which could only be to fall back to heathenism and Judaism, but in entering always more and more (materially as well as formally) into the life and doctrine of the Redeemer and in throwing off by this means, always more and more, the elements of sin and error still remaining from the state of nature.

16. It is possible for the church to be in possession of a truth and to live upon it, before it has come to be discerned in her consciousness. So it was, for instance, with the doctrine of the Trinity before the time of Athanasius, with the doctrine of divine grace and human freedom before Augustine, and with the evangelical doctrine of justification during the Middle Ages. Thus the child eats and drinks long before it has the knowledge of food, and walks before it is aware of the fact, much less *how* it walks.

17. The idea, unfolded in comprehensive and profound style particularly by the later German philosophy, that history involves a continual progress toward something better, by means of dialectic contrapositions (*Gegensaetze*), is substantially true and correct.

18. It must not be forgotten, however, in connection with this, that there is a corresponding movement also on the part of evil toward that which is worse. Light and darkness, the wheat and the tares, grow together till their development shall become complete.

19. We must distinguish in the church accordingly between idea and manifestation. As to her idea, or as comprehended in Christ, she is already complete; in the way of manifestation, however, she passes—like every one of her members—outwardly and inwardly, through different stages of life, until the ideal enclosed in Christ shall be fully actualized in humanity and his body appear thus in the ripeness of complete manhood.

20. Such a process of growth is attended necessarily with certain diseases and crises, as well theoretical, in the form of heresies; as practical, in the form of schisms.

21. These diseases are to be referred partly to the remaining force of sin and error in the regenerate themselves, and partly to the unavoidable connection of the church with the still unchristian world, by means of which the corrupt elements of this last are always forcing their way into her communion.

22. They can never overthrow, however, the existence of the church. The church may fall down, sore wounded, divided and torn, without ceasing for this reason to be the Body of Christ. Through her humiliation gleams evermore the unwasting glory of her divine nature.

23. In the wise providence of God, all heresies and schisms serve only to bring the church to a clearer consciousness of her true vocation, a deeper apprehension of her faith, and a purer revelation of the power included in her life.

24. But the presence of disease in the body requires to the same extent a remedial or curative process, that is, a reformation.

25. Protestantism consequently, in the true sense, belongs indispensably to the life of the church; being the reaction simply of her

proper vitality, depressed but not destroyed, in opposition to the
workings of disease in her system.

The Reformation

26. Protestantism runs through the entire history of the church,
and will not cease till she is purged completely from all ungodly elements. So, for instance, Paul protested against Jewish legalism and
pagan licentiousness as found insidiously at work in the first Christian communities; the Catholic Church of the first centuries, against
the heresies and schisms of Ebionitism, Gnosticism, Montanism,
Arianism, Pelagianism, Donatism, etc.

27. The grandest and most widely influential exhibition of Protestantism is presented to us under the formal constitution of a special
church, in the Reformation of the sixteenth century, as originated,
and in its deepest inward, and truly apostolic form, carried out and
consummated by the German nation.

28. It is a jejune and narrow conception of this event, to look
upon it as a restoration simply of the original state of the church, or
a renewal of Augustinianism against the Pelagian system by which
it had been supplanted.

29. Such a view proceeds on the fundamentally erroneous sup-
position that the religious life revealed in the person of Christ primarily, and by derivation from him in his apostles, has been fully
actualized also from the beginning in the general mass of the church.

30. Rather, the Reformation must be viewed as an actual advance of the religious life and consciousness of the church, by means
of a deeper apprehension of God's word, beyond all previous attain-
ments of Christendom.

31. As little is the Reformation to be regarded as a revolutionary
separation from the Catholic Church, holding connection at best
perhaps with some fractionary sect of the Middle Ages, and only
through this and the help of certain desperate historical leaps besides, reaching back to the age of the apostles.

32. This contracted view of Protestantism is not only unhistorical and unchurchly altogether, but conscious or unconscious treason
at the same time to the Lord's promise that he would build his church
upon a rock, and that the gates of hell should not prevail against it

[Matt. 16:18]; as well as to his engagement: "Lo I am with you always even to the end of the world" [Matt. 28:20]; and to the apostolic word: "The church is the pillar and ground of the truth" [1 Tim. 3:15].

33. Rather, the Reformation is the greatest act of the Catholic Church itself, the full ripe fruit of all its better tendencies, particularly of the deep spiritual law conflicts of the Middle Period, which were as a schoolmaster toward the Protestant doctrine of justification.

34. The separation was produced, not by the will of the Reformers, but by the stiff-necked papacy, which like Judaism at the time of Christ, identifying itself in a fleshly way with the idea of the absolute church, refused to admit the onward movement.

35. Thus apprehended, Protestantism has as large an interest in the vast historical treasures of the previous period, as can be claimed rightfully by the Church of Rome. Hence the arguments drawn by Romanists from this quarter, and particularly from the Middle Ages—the proper cradle of the Reformation—have no application against our standpoint.

36. Equally false finally is the view, whether popular or philosophical, by which the Reformation is made to consist in the absolute emancipation of the Christian life subjectively considered from all church authority, and the exaltation of private judgment to the papal throne.

37. This view confounds with the Reformation itself the foul excrescences that revealed themselves along with it in the beginning, and the one-sided character of its development since.

38. On the contrary, it is quite clear from history that the Reformers aimed only at such liberty of faith and conscience and such independence of private judgment, as should involve a humble subjection of the natural will, which they held to be incapable of all good, to God's grace, and of the human reason to God's word. Indeed their opposition to the Roman traditions was itself based on the conviction that they were the product of such reason sundered from the divine word.

39. The material or life principle of Protestantism is the doctrine of justification by grace alone, through the merits of Jesus Christ, by

means of living faith; that is, the personal appropriation of Christ in the totality of the inner man.

40. This does not overthrow good works; rather they are rightly called for and made possible only in this way—with dependence however on faith, as being its necessary fruit, the subjective impression of the life of Christ, in opposition to Pelagianism which places works parallel with faith, or even above it.

41. The formal or knowledge principle of Protestantism is the sufficiency and unerring certainty of the holy Scriptures as the only norm of all-saving knowledge.

42. This does not overthrow the idea of church tradition, but simply makes it dependent on the written word, as the stream is upon the fountain—the necessary, ever-deepening onward flow of the sense of scripture itself, as it is carried forward in the consciousness of the Christian world; contrary to the Romish dogma by which tradition, as the bearer of different contents altogether, is made coordinate with the Bible or even exalted above it.

43. These two principles, rightly apprehended, are only different, mutually supplementary sides of one and the same principle, and their living interpenetration forms the criterion of orthodox Protestantism.

44. Opposition to the Roman Catholic extreme, according to the general law of historical progress, led the Reformers to place the strongest emphasis on justification and faith, scripture and preaching; whence the possibility of a one-sided development in which holiness and love, tradition and sacrament, might not be allowed to come to their full rights.

45. Respect for the Reformation as a divine work in no way forbids the admission that it included some mixture of error and sin; as where God builds a church, the devil erects a chapel by its side.

46. In any view moreover the Reformation must be regarded as still incomplete. It needs yet its concluding act to unite what has fallen asunder, to bring the subjective to a reconciliation with the objective.

47. Puritanism may be considered a sort of second reformation, called for by the reappearance of Romanizing elements in the An-

glican Church, and as such forms the basis to a great extent of American Protestantism, particularly in New England.

48. Its highest recommendation, bearing clearly a divine signature, is presented in its deep practical earnestness as it regards religion, and its zeal for personal piety, by which it has been more successful perhaps than any other section of the church, for a time, in the work of saving individual souls.

49. However, it falls far behind the German Reformation by its revolutionary, unhistorical, and consequently unchurchly character, and carries in itself no protection whatever against an indefinite subdivision of the church into separate atomistic sects. For having no conception at all of a historical development of Christianity, and with its negative attitude of blind irrational zeal toward its own past, it may be said to have armed its children with the same right and the same tendency, too, to treat its own authority with equal independence and contempt.

The Present State of the Church

50. Protestantism has formed the starting point and center of almost all important world movements in the history of the last three centuries, and constitutes now also the main interest of the time.

51. The history of Protestantism in the spheres of religion, science, art, and government, especially since the commencement of the eighteenth century, may be regarded as the development of the principle of subjectivity, the consciousness of *freedom.*

52. In this development, however, it has gradually become estranged to a great extent from its own original nature, and fallen over dialectically into its opposite, according to the general course of history.

53. Its grand maladies at this time are *rationalism* and *sectarism.*

54. Rationalism is one-sided *theoretic religious subjectivism* and its fullest and most perfect exhibition has taken place accordingly in Germany— the land of theory and science—and in the bosom of the Lutheran Church.

55. Sectarism is one-sided *practical religious subjectivism* and has found its classic ground within the territory of the Reformed Church, in the predominantly practical countries, England and America.

56. These two maladies of Protestantism stand in a relation to it similar to that of the papacy to Catholicism in the Middle Ages; that is, they have a conditional historical necessity and an outward connection with the system to which they adhere, but contradict nevertheless and caricature its inmost nature.

57. The secular interests— science, art, government, and social life—have become since the Reformation always more and more dissociated from the church, in whose service they stood though with unfree subjugation in the Middle Ages, and in this separate form are advanced to a high state of perfection.

58. This is a false position, since the idea of the kingdom of God requires that all divinely constituted forms and spheres of life should be brought to serve him in the most intimate alliance with religion, that God may be All in all.

59. The orthodox Protestantism of our day, with all its different character in other respects, is distinguished in common with rationalism and sectarism, particularly in this country, by the quality of one-sided subjectivity; only with the advantage of course of a large amount of personal piety.

60. Its great defect is the want of an adequate conception of the nature of the church and of its relation to the individual Christian on the one hand, and the general life of man on the other.

61. Hence proceeds, first, indifference toward sectarian, or at least denominational divisions, which are at war with the idea of the church as the Body of Christ.

62. Second, a want of respect for history, by which it is affected to fall back immediately and wholly upon the Scriptures without regard to the development of their contents in the life of the church as it has stood from the beginning.

63. Third, an undervaluation of the sacraments as objective institutions of the Lord, independent of individual views and states.

64. Fourth, a disproportionate esteem for the service of preaching, with a corresponding sacrifice in the case of the liturgy, the standing objective part of divine worship, in which the *whole congregation* is called to pour forth its religious life to God.

65. Fifth, a circumscribed conception of the all-pervading leavenlike nature of the gospel, involving an abstract separation of religion from the divinely established order of the world in other spheres.

66. To this must be added in the case of a number of denominations the fancy of their own perfection, an idea that *their* particular traditional style of religion can never be improved into anything better; which is a rejection of the Protestant principle of mobility and progress, and a virtual relapse accordingly into the ground error of the Romish Church.

67. From all this it is clear that the standpoint, and with it the wants of our time, is wholly different from that of the sixteenth century.

68. Our most immediate and most threatening danger is not now from the Church of Rome, but from the in part heterodox and antichristian, in part orthodox and pious, but always one-sided and false subjectivism, by which the rights of the church are wronged in our own midst; which however must itself be considered again as indirectly the most alarming aspect of the danger that does in fact threaten us on the side of Rome, since one extreme serves always to facilitate the triumph of another.

69. The redeeming tendency of the age therefore is not such as looks directly to the emancipation of the individual and subjective from the bonds of authority, as at the time of the Reformation, but it is that rather which regards the claims of the objective in the true idea of the church.

70. Not until Protestantism shall have repented of its own faults and healed its own wounds, may it expect to prevail finally over the Church of Rome.

71. As this duty has been thus far in a great measure neglected, it is to be taken as a divine judgment in the case that popery has been enabled to make such formidable advances lately, especially in England and the United States.

72. Puseyism (with which of course we must not confound the spurious afterbirth of fantastic, hollow-hearted affectation, always to be expected in such a case) may be considered in its original intention and best tendency a well-meant, but insufficient and unsuccessful attempt to correct the ultra-subjectivity of Protestantism.

73. In this view we have reason to rejoice in its appearance, as indicating on the part of the Protestant world a waking consciousness of the malady under which it labors in this direction, and serving also to promote right church feeling.

74. By its reverence for church antiquity it exerts a salutary influence against what may be viewed, as the reigning error of our time, a wild revolutionary zeal for liberty, coupled with a profane scorn of all that is holy in the experience of the past.

75. So also its stress laid upon forms exhibits a wholesome reaction against the irrational hyper-spiritualism so common among even the best Protestants; which the doctrine of the resurrection alone, as taught in the Bible, is enough to prove fallacious.

76. Church forms serve two general purposes: first, they are for the lower stages of religious development conductors over into the life of the spirit; second, they are for the church at large the necessary utterance or corporealization of the spirit, in the view in which Oetinger's remark holds good: "Corporeity is the scope of God's ways."[1]

77. All turns simply on this that the form be answerable to the contents and be actuated by the spirit. A formless spiritualism is no whit better than a spiritless formalism. The only right condition is a sound spirit within a sound body.

78. The grand defect of Puseyism, however, is its unprotestant character in not recognizing the importance of the Reformation and the idea of progress in the life of the church since.

79. It is for this reason only half-historical and half-catholic, since its sympathy and respect for the past life of the church stop short with the sixteenth century.

80. Its view of the church altogether is outward and mechanical, excluding the conception of a living development through the successive periods of its history.

81. This character appears particularly in its theory of episcopal succession, which is only a new form of the old pharisaic Judaism,

---

[1](Ed.) Friedrich Christoph Oetinger, *Biblisches und Emblematisches Wörterbuch, dem Tellerischen Wörterbuch und Anderer falschen Schrifterklärungen entgegen gesetzt* (n.p., 1776) 407.

and moreover makes the apostolicity of the church dependent on a historical inquiry (in the case of which besides no absolute certainty is possible), resting it thus on a wholly precarious human foundation.

82. Puseyism is to be viewed then as nothing more than a simple reaction, which has served to bring to light the evils of ultra pseudo-Protestant individualism, but offers no remedy for it save the perilous alternative of falling back to a standpoint already surmounted in the way of religious progress.

83. The true standpoint, all necessary for the wants of the time, is that of *Protestant Catholicism,* or genuine historical progress.

84. This holds equally remote from unchurchly subjectivity and all Romanizing churchism, though it acknowledges and seeks to unite in itself the truth which lies at the ground of both these extremes.

85. Occupying this conservative historical standpoint, from which the moving of God's Spirit is discerned in all periods of the church, we may not in the first place surrender anything essential of the positive acquisition secured by the Reformation, whether Lutheran or Reformed.

86. Neither may we again absolutely negate the later development of Protestantism, not even rationalism and sectarism themselves, but must appropriate to ourselves rather the element of truth they contain, rejecting only the vast alloy of error from which it is to be extracted.

87. Rationalism and sectarism possess historical right, so far as the principle of subjectivity, individuality, singleness, and independence can be said to be possessed of right; that is, so far as this comes not in contradiction to the principle of objectivity, generality, the church, authority, and law, so far then as it continues subordinate to these forces.

88. Rationalism was a necessary schoolmaster for orthodox theology, destroying its groundless prejudices and compelling it both to accept a more scientific form in general, and also in particular to allow the human, the earthly, the historical, in the theanthropic nature of Christ and the church, to come more fully to its rights.

89. While however the earlier historico-critical rationalism has promoted a right understanding of the natural and historical in

Christianity, this understanding in its case remains still but *half* true, since it has no organ for *ideas,* the inward life of which history after all is but the body.

90. The later speculative rationalism, or pantheistic mythologism, or the "Hegelingians" as they have been deridingly styled (Strauss and his colleagues), which from the Ebionitic standpoint of the old system has swung over to the opposite extreme of docetic Gnostic idealism, fails to apprehend the idea of Christianity in its full truth and vitality, and substitutes for it a phantom or mere shadow, since it has no organ for historical *reality,* the outward life without which after all the idea must perish.

91. As in the first centuries, the theology of the Catholic Church gradually developed itself through scientific struggles with the two ground heresies—Ebionism or christianizing Judaism, and Gnosticism or christianizing heathenism—so now also we are to look for a higher orthodoxy, overmastering inwardly both forms of Protestant rationalism, which shall bring the real and the ideal into the most intimate union and recognize in full as well as the eternal spirit of Christianity as its historical body.

92. The germs of all this are at hand in the later movements and achievements of the believing German theology, and need only a further development to issue at last in a full dogmatical reformation.

93. Separation, where it is characterized by religious life, springs almost always from some real evil in the state of the church, and hence sectarism is to be regarded as a necessary disciplinarian and reformer of the church in its practical life.

94. Almost every sect represents in strong relief some single particular aspect of piety, and contributes to the fuller evolution of individual religious activity.

95. Since however the truths of the gospel form an inseparable unity, and the single member can become complete only along with the whole body of which it is a part, it follows that no sect can ever do justice fully even to the single interest to which it is one-sidedly devoted.

96. Sects then owe it to themselves, as soon as they have fulfilled their historical vocation, to fall back to the general church communion from which they have seceded, as in no other way can their spir-

itual acquisitions be either completed or secured, and they must themselves otherwise stiffen into monumental petrifactions, never to be revisited with the warm life pulse of the one universal church.

97. It is a cheering sign of the time that in the most different Protestant lands, and particularly in the bosom of the Reformed Church, in which religious individualism both in the good and in the bad sense has been most fully developed, it is coming to be felt more and more that the existing divisions of the church are wrong, and with this is waking more and more an earnest longing after a true union of all believers, in no communication whatever with the errors either of Oxford or Rome.

98. Finally, also, the liberation of the secular spheres of life from the church since the Reformation, though not the ultimate normal order, forms—notwithstanding as compared with the previous vassalage of the world to a despotic hierarchy—an advance in the naturalization process of Christianity.

99. The luxuriant separate growth of these interests, as unfolded in the Protestant states, sciences, arts, and social culture, lays the church under obligation to appropriate these advances to herself, and impress upon them a religious character.

100. The signs of the time, then, and the teachings of history point us not backward, but forward to a new era of the church that may be expected to evolve itself gradually from the present process of fermentation, enriched with the entire positive gain of Protestantism.

101. As the movement of history in the church is like that of the sun from east to west, it is possible that America, into whose broad majestic bosom the most various elements of character and education are poured from the Old World, may prove the theater of this unitive reformation.

102. Thus far, if we put out of view the rise of a few insignificant sects and the separation of church and state, which to be sure has very momentous bearings, American church history has produced nothing original, no new *fact* in the history of the church as a whole.

103. Nowhere else however is there at present the same favorable room for further development, since in no country of the Old World

does the church enjoy such entire freedom, or the same power to renovate itself from within according to its own pleasure.

104. The historical progress of the church is always conditioned by the national elements, which form its physical basis.

105. The two leading nationalities, which are continually coming into contact in this country, and flowing into one another with reciprocal action, are the English and the German.

106. The further advancement of the American church, consequently, must proceed mainly from a special combination of German depth and *Gemuetlichkeit* with the force of character and active practical talent, for which the English are distinguished.

107. It would be a rich offering then to the service of this approaching reformation, on the part of the German Churches in America, to transplant hither in proper measure the rich wealth of the better German theology, improving it into such form as our peculiar relations might require.

108. This their proper vocation however they have thus far almost entirely overlooked, seeking their salvation for the most part in a characterless surrender of their own nationality.

109. In view of the particular constituton of a large part of the German immigration, this subjection to the power of a foreign life may be regarded indeed as salutary.

110. But the time has now come, when our churches should again rise out of the ashes of the old German Adam, enriched and refined with the advantages of the English nationality.

111. What we most need now is, theoretically, a thorough, intellectual theology, scientifically free as well as decidedly believing, together with a genuine sense for history; and practically, a determination to hold fast the patrimony of our fathers and to go forward joyfully at the same time in the way in which God's Spirit by providential signs may lead, with a proper humble subordination of all we do for our own denomination to the general interest of the one universal church.

112. The ultimate, sure scope of the church, toward which the inmost wish and most earnest prayer of all her true friends continually tend, is that perfect and glorious unity, the desire of which may

be said to constitute the burden of our Lord's last, memorable, intercessory prayer.

GERMAN THEOLOGY AND THE CHURCH QUESTION*

If we compare the present theological literature of English and American Protestantism with that of the modern Evangelical school of Germany, we meet with a remarkable difference in their conception of *Catholicism*. Of this we have already had occasion to speak, more fully, in our review of Dr. Ullmann's "Reformers before the Reformation," which rests throughout on the assumption that Protestantism can be properly understood and defended only as the legitimate and necessary product of mediaeval Catholicism, and not as an abrupt unhistorical revolution.[2] To unchurch the Catholic Church, to cut her off entirely from the kingdom of God, and to identify her with the kingdom of the Antichrist, as was almost unanimously done by the General Assembly of the Old School Presbyterian Church, during its sessions at Cincinnati, 1845, and which that Church, notwithstanding the well-founded protest of her able and learned Professors at Princeton, has not yet rescinded, would, upon German ground, be absolutely impossible. The Evangelical Theology of Germany is indeed also thoroughly Protestant in principle and spirit, and rests upon that freedom of thought and impartiality of investigation, which we properly owe to the Reformation. But this very freedom and impartiality of research has also lead her to conceive and judge of the Catholic Church in a manner totally different from the old Protestant polemics of the sixteenth and seventeenth centuries. This, however, does by no means necessarily involve an approach towards Rome, but indicates rather a new and advanced position of Protes-

---

*"German Theology and the Church Question," *The Mercersburg Review* 5 (January 1855): 124-44. The original German article, "Die deutsche Theologie und die Kirchenfrage," appeared in *Der deutsche Kirchenfreund* 5 (September 1852): 338-53.

[2](Ed.) See also *Der deutsche Kirchenfreund* 5 (August 1852): 291ff., and *Germany*, 354-58.

tantism itself, which we understand to be the progressive principle of modern church history, whilst Romanizing tendencies are retrograde movements and deadly hostile to a proper conception of progressive development, which underlies all living German theology of the present day, especially its best works on church history.

First of all, the modern investigation of ecclesiastical and profane historians have entirely overthrown the earlier views concerning the *Middle Ages*. It may now be received as an established fact, admitted by all learned judges, that the Roman Catholic Church as such, during that age, was, by no means, the great Apostasy or kingdom of Antichrist, but the bearer of true Christianity, with its sacred canon and saving ordinances, the mother of the Romanic and Germanic nations, and of the whole modern European civilization, and notwithstanding her adherent corruption, carried within herself a vast amount of elevated piety and heroic virtue. The Papacy itself is regarded now by the most distinguished modern church historians, and even by profane historians, such as John von Müller, Leo, Ranke, and Macaulay, as an institution absolutely indispensable for that time, and upon the whole highly beneficial, for the education of the Germanic nations, for the preservation of the unity and security and freedom and independence of the Church, over against the encroachments of the secular power. As the law of Moses was a schoolmaster to Christ, so the new Christian legalism of medieaval Catholicism prepared the way for Evangelical Protestantism . . .

The proper coryphei of the papacy, such as Nicholas, Hildebrand, and Innocent III, heretofore regarded as scarcely anything better than incarnate devils, are now looked upon as heroes and benefactors of humanity. Even Neander, who is well known to have naturally a great antipathy to everything priestly and hierarchical, and who zealously endeavors to place the opposers of the ruling Church in the most advantageous light possible, candidly expresses his profound admiration for the moral character and great merits of these popes. In the same manner has the judgment concerning the other prominent phenomena of the Middle Ages—the crusades, the monastic orders and their founders, religious art, scholasticism, and mysticism—assumed a more favorable form, in proportion as they are brought from the dust of the past to light, and understood in their organic connection with the nature and wants of that period. It is impossible, e. g., to read with attention Neander's Bernard or Hasse's Anselm, without being filled with profound admiration for the spirit, virtue and piety of these men, although they move throughout in the spirit and mould of the Catholic Church, and belong, as is well known, to her most distinguished teachers and saints.

But this altered conception of the Middle Ages involves an enormous concession to Catholicism, and a fatal blow against a bigoted ultra-Protestantism. A Church, which throughout this whole transition period, from ancient to modern times, sent out such a host of self-denying missionaries to heathen nations, who carried the Gospel to the Germans, Scandinavians, Anglo-Saxons, Picts, and Scots and Slavonians—a Church, which had power to excite all Europe to a heroic conflict against the false prophet for the recovery of the holy sepulchre of the Redeemer—a Church, which contended vigorously and successfully against the despotism of worldly potentates, slavery, barbarity, and a thousand other evils of society, which gave wholesome laws to the states, raised the female sex to its present dignity, which interested herself in behalf of the poor and suffering of all classes, which established asylums for misery, and institutions of benevolence in all places, which erected unto the Lord numberless churches, chapels, and those Gothic cathedrals, which even yet command the admiration of the world, which gave the first impulse to a general education of the people, which founded and sheltered almost all those European universities, which even to this day exert an immeasurable influence—a Church which has produced within her bosom such an incalculable number of profound minds, elevated characters and devoted saints:—such a church cannot possibly, in the nature of the case, be the Anti-Christ and synagogue of Satan, notwithstanding the many anti-Christian elements which she may have included within her bosom, and of which no age and no denomination is entirely free. That extreme representation, which the majority of our popular religious papers continue to repeat from week to week, cannot for one moment maintain itself against the results of later Protestant historical research, and must therefore in due time disappear from the consciousness of all educated and unprejudiced minds.

Moreover, not only the Middle Ages, but also the *first six centuries* of the Christian Church, have been thoroughly re-examined, and documents have been brought to light, which for the most part were unknown even by name at the time of the Reformation, when historical study and the publication of ancient works had scarcely begun. Even Luther once calls Tertullian, who lived as late as the end of the second, and beginning of the third centuries, "the oldest teacher which we have since the time of the Apostles," so that for him, the line of the Apostolical Fathers, and the numerous Apologists of the second century did not exist, with the exception of uncertain fragments which he could not but know from the legends of the martyr Ignatius, Polycarp and Clement, "for whom," as he once remarks, "a bad boy forged books."[3] The Reformers were best acquainted with Augustine, and their reverence and love for this profoundly pious as well as spirited and highly gifted father was of immeasurable importance for their theological and moral training and position, as otherwise the Reformation would most probably have assumed a far more radical character. Through the indefatigable diligence and zealous inquiry of modern times, and through the impulse, which more especially Neander has given to historical Monography, we have at present, in the German language, thorough and complete works on Leo, Augustine, Chrysostom, Gregory of Nazianzen, Basil, Athanasius, Origen, Cyprian, Tertullian, Irenaeus, Justin Martyr, and even back to the immediate successors to the Apostles; so that the Nicene and Ante-Nicene Christianity, with the corresponding heresies of Arianism, Gnosticism and Ebionism, etc., are clearly presented to our view, or at least as accessible as the Christianity of the seventeenth century. If we now read impartially from those valuable monographies, or similar and more comprehensive works, such as Rothe's *Anfänge der christlichen Kirche,* Dorner's *Geschichte der Christologie,* Möhler's *Patrologie,* etc., and if we, in connection with these, candidly study only some of the more important productions of patristic theology, such as Chrysostom on the Priest-

---

[3](Ed.) *Luther's Works* (American Edition) 37:108. The editor was unable to identify the second Luther citation.

hood, Augustine's Confessions, Cyprian on the Unity of the Church, Tertullian on the Prescription of the Heretics, Irenaeus against the Gnostics, and the Epistles of Ignatius, we must inevitably receive the impression that the Church of antiquity was in its predominant spirit and tendency far more Catholic than Protestant, and that the Middle Ages are only a natural continuation of the Nicene Christianity. Could Ambrosius, Athanasius, Cyprian, Irenaeus, Ignatius, Clement and Polycarp suddenly arise from their graves and be transferred to Puritan New England, they would scarcely there recognize the Christianity of those venerable Martyrs and Confessors, for which they lived and suffered; but on the contrary, would much sooner discover, not only amongst the Universalists and the Unitarians, but amongst the Baptists and Puritans themselves, distinct traces of a congeniality of spirit with the heretics and schismatics of their own days. We say this, however, without any disrespect whatever, but simply as the impression received from an impartial comparison of historical facts. The most striking difference between the Primitive Church and Protestantism lies in the doctrine of the Rule of Faith, of the Relation of the Scriptures to Tradition, of the Church, her Unity, her Catholicity, her Exclusiveness, and of the Sacraments. Even of the material principle of Protestantism, the doctrine of Justification by Faith *alone,* in *Luther's* sense, the Fathers knew nothing, not even Augustine, and instead of making this the article of the standing and falling Church, they assign rather to the Christology, to the mystery of the Incarnation and to the Holy Trinity, the central position in the Christian system, and the confession or denial of Christ's real humanity is with them, according to 1 John 4, the sure criterion of orthodoxy or heterodoxy.[4] In all these points of doctrine, as well as in

---

[4](Ed.) After citing a lengthy passage from Thiersch, *Versuch zur Herstellung des historischen Standpuncts für die Kritik der neutestamentlichen Schriften,* 280, in which the author recounts in vivid detail his discovery of the theology of the Church Fathers, and that patristic Christianity differed from Eastern Orthodoxy and Roman Catholicism and "still far more from Protestantism," Schaff called attention to the third book of Rothe's *Die Anfänge der christlichen Kirche* and Nevin's articles "Early Christianity" and "Cyprian" in *The Mercersburg Review* 3 (1851) nos. 5-6, and 4 (1852) nos. 1, 3-6. All these authors, Schaff affirmed, prove convincingly "that

the hierarchical constitution, the sacrificial worship, and the ascetic conception of Christian virtue and piety, we clearly discover in the Church Fathers, from Gregory and Leo up to Cyprian, Irenaeus and Ignatius, at least the germs of that systen, which afterwards completed itself in the Roman Catholic Church. This is continually becoming acknowledged the more in proportion as researches are extended in this sphere, and their results produced in a popular form. Without this resemblance, it would be absolutely impossible to account for the fact, that the Roman Catholic Church has canonized the most distinguished and pious of the fathers and cherishes their memory with filial veneration and gratitude to this day. It is only through want of knowledge, or a singular delusion, that any section of Protestantism could ever imagine itself to be a simple restoration of the Nicene or ante-Nicene age.

If however we concede this much, from a mere historical standpoint, it is easy to see what an enormous influence such an admission must have upon the final solution of the *Church Question*. For whoever despises the judgment of History, robs himself at the same time of all foundation and basis. If the fifteen centuries prior to the Reformation are deserving of no confidence, neither are the last three centuries entitled to any respect. "If any one neglect to hear the voice of the Church," saith our Lord, "let him be unto thee as a heathen man and a publican" (Matt. 18:17). In proportion as we undermine and reject the testimony of Church History, in theological and religious questions, do we also open the door to skepticism and nihilism. Herein precisely lies the great ecclesiastical and religious importance of modern church-historical research, even if this should not yet be duly acknowledged by many German theologians. The time will and must come, when the practical conclusions will be drawn from the theory.

---

the views of the Fathers from Ignatius down to Augustine on the nature of the *Church*, which in some respects is the most important and comprehensive point of difference between Romanism and Protestantism, are essentially Catholic, and that the article of the creed, *Credo unam sanctam apostolicam ecclesiam*, with them, did not refer to an invisible abstraction, but to a visible historical reality."

But some will at once ask, of what concern is the testimony of history to me, if I have the *Word of God* in my favor, which is, after all, the only certain Rule of Faith and Life, whilst the greatest schoolmen and Church Fathers, according to their own confession, were themselves sinful men, and liable to err? Very true! But who has made you an infallible *interpreter* of this Word? Has not this Word already existed in the Church before the sixteenth century, and as such been highly honored, read, transcribed, translated and commented upon? Whence then have you the canon, save directly from the faithful collection and transmission of the Catholic Church? Who furnishes you the proof of the genuineness and integrity of the apostolical writings, except the testimonies of the ancient ecclesiastical authors? If already the immediate disciples of the Apostles, if Ignatius, Clement and Polycarp, if the fathers and martyrs of the second and third centuries, have radically misunderstood the New Testament, what guaranty have we then that *you,* in the nineteenth century, understand it properly throughout, wherever you may differ from them? Are you then made of better stuff than the Confessors and Martyrs of the blooming period of the Church? Have you done and suffered more for Christ? You say: the clear letter of Paul and John condemns the Catholic Church as Antichrist, as the Man of Sin, the Beast from the Abyss, as the Babylon destined to be destroyed. But whence do you know that this interpretation is correct? Since you totally reject the infallibility of the Pope, and perhaps also of the Church in general, you will certainly not be so inconsistent and ridiculously presumptuous, as to claim it for yourself or any other Protestant interpreter? Moreover, such an application of the passages in question was wholly unheard of until within the later period of the Middle Ages, when it was invented by certain fanatical sects, to suit their polemical ends. The Church Fathers without exception, even Irenaeus, who through Polycarp stood in close relation to the Apostle John himself, have referred them to Gnosticism and to the World-Empire of *heathen* Rome. At all events, the Reformers could not have used consistently the Revelation of John for any polemical purpose, since Luther and Zwingli denied its Apostolic origin, and Calvin, with all his masterly skill as a commentator, wisely suffered it to remain unexplained. Later Protestant interpreters, such as Hammond and

Grotius, and all modern expounders of Scripture (quite lately the orthodox Hengstenberg, in his Commentary on the Apocalypse, and
even the Puritan Stuart,) have, almost without exception, rejected
the Anti-Roman interpretation, as entirely untenable, and again returned to the explanation of the Church Fathers.

However this may be, there are, at all events, many more *clear*
and *distinct* passages in Scripture, which, according to the unanimous
explanation of Catholic and Protestant commentators, promise to the
Church of Christ an *indestructible continuation and an uninterrupted presence of her divine Head, even to the end of the world.* Of this there cannot
be the least doubt, and therefore must we above all build our theory
of Church History upon *such* declarations, and not upon a very
doubtful interpretation of the darkest passages in the most mysterious book of the Bible—which, not without reason, stands last in
our canon. But if it should appear as the result of the modern thorough and impartial investigations of the greatest Protestant Historians, that the Christian Church, before the Reformation, even back
to the days of the Apostolic Fathers, was not in her predominant spirit
and character Protestant, but essentially Catholic, in most of those
points where the two systems are at war with each other, and that
the protesting sects, from the Ebionites and Gnostics, down to the
Cathari and Albigenses present a confused mixture of contradictory
opinions, and as such cannot possibly constitute the uninterrupted
continuation of the Life of Christ and evangelical truth: it necessarily
follows that such a defense of Protestantism, which rests upon an entire rejection of Catholicism,—as a system of falsehood,—be it Bap-
tistic, Puritanic, Presbyterian or Anglican—stands in direct
contradiction to the testimony of history and those unequivocal say-
ings of Christ and his Apostles, and must therefore be abandoned.

This is the deciding point, to which the controversy between
Protestantism and Catholicism, which has lately arisen with renewed
zeal and energy in Germany, England and the United States, is forced,
and should some German theologians, who have aided in bringing
about this issue, in their predominantly theoretical tendency and scientific self-complacency, concern themselves little about the practical consequences, there are many divines in practical England and
America, who will draw the final conclusions. Examples might

readily be pointed out, which in reality confirm this. It is a remarkable and interesting fact, that German evangelical theology becomes far more practical and serious in its consequences, upon English ground, than in Germany itself. For the Englishman seldom contents himself with naked theories and speculations, but endeavors directly to bring them into practical life, to organize them externally and realize them in some concrete form. This can easily be seen in Methodism, compared with the congenial, but unorganized Pietism. Puseyism exhibits the same tendency, though in an opposite direction; for in it, the idea of the Church has long since emerged from the sphere of theological research, and has beome a solemn practical life-question, which has already driven a considerable number of the Clergy and Laity from the Protestant into the Roman camp. Neither would it greatly surprise us, should we live to see also in America a larger secession of educated men towards Rome, arising partly at least from an earnest but one-sided study of Church history. For here such a step could be more easily accounted for than in Germany, as a necessary reaction against extreme forms of anti-catholic theology. To do this, we need only consider that the Protestant Press of America, with few honorable exceptions, from the city papers, with their ten and twenty thousand subscribers, down to the most obscure country sheets, rests upon this totally anti-scriptural and anti-historical theology; that it contends against the Roman Church with weapons of the blindest fanaticism, and that it suffers itself to make use of such rude and uncharitable misrepresentations, which we should be obliged to stigmatize directly as barefaced lies, could they not be accounted for, on the ground of ignorance and prejudice, and did not the otherwise religious character of these Intelligencers and non-Intelligencers compel us to adopt the latter expedient. He who has ever thoroughly and impartially studied the history of the Church before the Reformation and the classical productions of Roman Divines, such as Bellarmine, Bossuet, Möhler, Wiseman, Balmes and Newman, must possess a more than ordinary amount of patient and stoical tranquillity of mind, if he can behold these caricatures which are circulated from week to week, without being filled with indignation against the conscious or unconscious calumniators, and with an increasing sympathy for the slandered party.[5] Add to this the growing confusion in Protestantism, which notwithstanding its great advantages in many other respects is, precisely in this country, more than in any other, split into numberless denominations and sects, without any human prospect for a consolidation or union, and presents a confused mixture of private opinions and subjective, ever changing notions, which threaten finally to wash away all the solid ground of real supernatural faith and fixed doctrine from under our feet, unless important conservative powers should stay the wild stream. The most trifling cause is considered sufficient to mangle the Body of Christ, and to transgress the Apostle's command: "Forbearing one another in love; endeavoring to keep the unity of the spirit in the bond of peace" [Eph. 4:2-3]. And along with this there is such an abuse made of the Word of God, that it must furnish proof texts for the wildest dreams, as if it were a nose of wax and a book of all sorts of contradictions. If then we have any idea of the Church, its inherent unity and catholicity, of law and authority, and regard Christianity as a supernatural power, to which we must humbly submit, instead of fashioning it according to a rationalistic common sense, and the conceptions of modern times, until it is finally sunk

---

[5](Ed.) Schaff, no doubt, had in mind here Robert Bellarmino (1542–1621), *Disputationes de controversiis christianiae fidei* (4 vols., 1581–93); Jacques Bénigne Bossuet (1627–1704), *An Exposition of the Doctrine of the Catholic Church in Matters of Controversy* (1st American ed., 1808), and *The History of the Variations of the Protestant Churches* (2 vols.; English translation, 1836–42); Johann Adam Möhler, see 58n52 and 60n55, above; Jaime Luciano Balmes (1810–48), *Protestantism and Catholicity Compared in their Effects on the Civilization of Europe* (trans. from the French, 1850) and, of course, John Henry Newman's *Essay on the Development of Christian Doctrine* (1845). When Schaff had his students read and discuss some of these and still other Roman Catholic books during the school year 1851–52, a great deal of unrest and even a minor student rebellion ensued. Especially disturbed by their professor's "Romanizing" reading lists were eight students who had recently arrived from Germany, six of whom then left the Seminary in protest. For this episode, which occurred at a time the Mercersburg controversy seemed to be coming to a head, cf. James I. Good, *History of the Reformed Church in the United States in the Nineteenth Century*, 293-95, and James H. Nichols, *Romanticism in American Theology: Nevin and Schaff at Mercersburg*, 209-10.

to the sphere of Nature and becomes the product of our reason and imagination; we must have an unusually strong confidence in History, and continually look to the past, and with hope to the future, so as not to become disheartened sometimes by the present Babel of Protestant sects. Without such a confidence in God—who, as a Portugese proverb says, writes also on a crooked line, and can call a beautiful creation out of chaos; without the virtue of patient expectation and hope, there is a strong inducement for serious minds, which have become fully conscious of the weight and difficulties of this subject, to cast themselves into the arms of Roman uniformity, if only for the purpose of escaping this eternal fluctuation, and experimenting to acquire a firm foundation and basis, and to enjoy as they hope at least, the feeling of comfortable rest and security.

If therefore Protestantism is to be defended, without surrendering the thoroughly scriptural idea of an indestructible Church, and an uninterrupted indwelling presence of Christ, and without doing violence to the clear testimony of History, prior to the Reformation, it can only be done by conceding, at the same time, a relative title to Catholicism, and allowing it to have been the chief, if not the only bearer of Christianity, down to the sixteenth century, and that it even yet constitutes a vital member of the Body of Christ. Dr. Rothe says in his learned and not sufficiently appreciated work, entitled *Die Anfänge der christlichen Kirche* "There can be no more powerful apology for Protestantism, than the acknowledgement, yea even the positive affirmation of the fact, that in the *past,* Catholicism, according to its substance, has had full historical reality and necessity, deep inward truth, and high moral excellence and power."[6] So we say also: The noblest and most efficient way of defending Protestantism, is not to run down and abuse, but rather to glorify and defend Catholicism, as the bearer of mediaeval Christianity, and as a necessary preparation for Protestantism itself, without which the latter could as little have made its appearance, as Christianity without Judaism, or as liberty without the school of authority and obedience. In the same way we may say, that the honor of the New Testament is not diminished,

---

[6](Ed.) See p. 67, above.

but increased rather and properly guarded, by giving the Old Testament all due credit and importance as a preparatory dispensation of the gospel.

But even this alone is not sufficient. For a Church, which, in spite of the tremendous shock experienced in the sixteenth century, depriving herself of the most vigorous nations, has yet power to revive herself, and replace, at least to a great extent, the lost territory by means of important conquests in the heathen world; which has since been able to reproduce in the sphere of theology a Bellarmine, a Baronio, a Peteau, a Bossuet, a Möhler,—in the sphere of missions and Christian Life a Xavier, a Borromeo, a Filippo of Neri, a Vincens of Paula, a Paschal, a Fenelon, a Sailer; which in later times has attracted talented men so differently constituted, such as Haller, Stolberg, Novalis, Schlegel, Hurter, Florencourt, Newman, Manning, Wilberforce and Brownson; which subsequent to the Revolutionary storm of 1848 has elevated herself with renewed energy, extended her arms towards the North and West, into the very heart of Protestant civilization, and the bulwark of Protestant power, and wherever she goes, throws the Government, Clergy, and Laity into a feverish agitation, and sets a thousand tongues and pens in motion against her—such a Church cannot have her significance in the past *alone,* but must possess even yet an important life-power, a relative necessity for the present, and a significant mission for the future. This is, of course, at once to confess that Protestantism does not describe the entire circumference of the Church even since the time of the Reformation—although it is evidently the chief bearer of modern civilization—but that it is in its own nature onesided, that it suffers from imperfections, as well as its adversary, although of an opposite character, that it, on this account, again stands in need of a Reformation, that it has in Catholicism its necessary complement, and that it can never complete itself without it. The signs of the times also point clearly enough to this issue. Protestantism is just at this time undergoing a thorough examination and sifting in Germany, England, and North America, and it is to be hoped that the sermon of repentance, which is thus delivered unto it, may not be overheard, but that it may reap similar benefits from the progress of its old hereditary enemy, whilst the Roman Church has evidently gained to a great extent, in activity and zeal, by means of the reacting and arousing influence of Protestantism. For wherever they have come into contact, it can easily be seen, that Romanism is in a far more living and hopeful condition, than where it sways the sceptre of undisturbed dominion, e.g., in the spiritually dead Mexico, Brazil, Portugal, and Croatia.

This liberal position towards Rome is, at all events, more generous, far more consistent with the spirit of Christian charity, and much better calculated to gain over the adversary, than that harsh and repulsive fanaticism, which hesitates not even to make common cause with Rationalists, Pantheists, Atheists, Socialists and impure Revolutionary spirits of every possible character, over against Catholicism, as is too frequently the case with many of our religious sheets. Only think of the many Protestant patrons, such miserable apostates and unprincipled slanderers as Maria Monk, Ronge, Leahy (who lately turned out a murderer!), Achilli, etc., have found in our midst![7] "What communion hath Christ with Belial, or light with

---

[7](Ed.) Maria Monk, who claimed to be an escaped nun, fanned anti-catholic prejudices with her sensational *Awful Disclosures of the Hotel Dieu Nunnery of Montreal* (1836), which soon turned out to be a fabrication. Arrested for thievery in a brothel, she died in prison in 1849. Johannes Ronge (1813–87), an excommunicated Roman Catholic priest, was one of the leaders of the German Catholic movement which aimed at establishing a National Catholic church. After its heyday around 1848, the movement soon embraced a shallow rationalistic spirit. Edward Leahy was an Italian Roman Catholic priest turned Protestant missionary, whom Dr. Joseph Berg, Schaff's Mercersburg opponent, had converted and in 1844 had sent to Mercersburg to study theology. Later Leahy stirred up anti-Catholicism with such lectures as "The Unchristian Treatment of Females in the Confessional, by Popish Priests, according to the standard of Popish Theology." After he committed a murder, he was sentenced to life imprisonment in Wisconsin. The Rev. G. G. Achilli brought suit against Newman in Ireland for slander. After a sensational trial, the court found in his favor, which Schaff attributed to anti-catholic Protestant prejudice. In 1853 Achilli immigrated to the United States, where he created again a sensation with his vivid descriptions of the Inquisition and priestly immorality. See Ray Allen Billington, *Protestant Crusade, 1800–1860* (New York, 1938) 99-108; and Schaff's article, "Newman and Achilli," *Der deutsche Kirchenfreund* 5 (August 1852): 314-18, where he pointedly remarks, "The hatred of Rome covers a multitude of sins" (315).

darkness?" [2 Cor. 6:14, 15]. But the main point here is, that this mild and moderate polemic is more in keeping with *truth,* the Word of God, and the testimony of History, than the other, which rests purely on historical suppositions, caricatures and perversions.

But now it may be asked, How can one remain a Protestant any longer, with a good conscience, if he makes such significant concessions to the Catholic Church, regarding her as the only true Church down to the Reformation, and attributing to her even to this day such an important position and mission? Is not that which was once the true Church, always the true Church? How can Christianity be first Catholic, then Protestant, without contradicting itself? Of course, from the standpoint of a mechanical conception of Christianity and History, this difficulty is not easily solved. Just as soon as we conceive of ecclesiastical Christianity as a system, preconcluded from the start, and completed in its outward form, for all time, so soon must we consistently become either Roman Catholic or Ultra-Protestant. There is no middle ground. But far otherwise is it from the standpoint of *historical development,* which underlies all the more important German historical works of modern times, although the thing itself is as old as history, and has a firm foundation in the Bible. The only merit which German theology can claim in this respect is, that it has brought out the idea in a scientific form and applied it to the treatment of history. This conception, it seems to us, affords the only tenable foundation upon which to justify the Reformation and Protestantism, without doing violence to preceding history and destroying the nature of an uninterrupted Church. Hence its vast practical importance for the solution of the Church question. We speak here, of course, only of the *theological and scientific* defense of Protestantism. For the plain practical Christian is not and ought not to be troubled with these historical difficulties; he bases his faith in Protestantism very properly on the Word of God, as he understands it, on his own religious experience, and on the practical fruits of the system which he finds to compare very favorably on the whole with those of the opposite system. But the theologian must battle with the solemn problem of the Church question, as it stares him in the face from the pages of history. To him, it cannot possibly be indifferent what Christianity has been in the different ages of the world, and what relation his own view of it sustains to the great and good men of by-gone days who have suffered all for Christ.

Development is properly identical with history itself; for history is life, and all life involves growth, evolution and progress. Our bodily existence, all our mental faculties, the Christian life, and the sanctification of every individual, constitute such a process of development from the lower to the higher. Why should not the same law hold, when applied to the whole, the communion which is made up of individuals? Any reasonable person will allow a progress in trade, business, in politics, arts, science and civilization; why not also in the Church? Why should she alone, which is a communion of individual believers, and something historical, yea the greatest fact and phenomenon of history, be made an exception to the laws of all organic life and development? The New Testament itself distinctly applies this law to the Church. For Christ compares his kingdom to a mustard seed which groweth into a mighty tree, and to a leaven which gradually leaveneth the whole lump, and the Apostles, especially St. Paul, speak continually of the growth of the body of Christ as well as of individual believers.

Even Roman Catholic Divines, such as Möhler and Newman, must resort to the idea of development in some form—whether this naturally follows from the Roman standpoint of stability or not, is another question—in order to understand and explain the history of their own Church.[8] Much less can a Protestant historian advance a single step, and justify the Reformation, without the torchlight of this idea. It is now determined, as before remarked, that Protestantism in those doctrines differing from Catholicism is not the Christianity of the Schoolmen and Mystics, not the Christianity of the Church Fathers of the Nicene age, not the Christianity of the Apologists, of the Apostolic Fathers, of the Martyrs and Confessors of the second and third centuries, but that all these are substantially more closely related to the Catholic standpoint, although this itself

---

[8](Ed.) Schaff noted that Orestes Brownson (1803–76), the American convert to Roman Catholicism, forcefully opposed Newman's theory of development and he agreed "that the idea of development is not congenial to the genuine spirit of Romanism, but essentially of Protestant growth."

had only gradually developed and perfected itself. This is placed beyond doubt already by the character of the Greek Church, which remains stationary at the point of the Ancient Church, and is evidently far more Catholic than Protestant. The doctrine of the Trinity, of the Divinity of Christ, of the Relation of the two Natures in Christ, of the Atonement, in short all the articles of the Apostolic and Nicene creeds, are here not brought into view; for these are not specifically and exclusively Protestant, but in their origin and substance Catholic, and manifestly inherited from an earlier Catholicism, fully as much so as the canon of Scripture and the doctrine of Inspiration. They constitute the primitive foundation common to all orthodox Churches, in opposition to all heretical sects. If then the Reformation is not a work of Satan, but a divine fact, which we for good reasons believe, it must be viewed and defended as a *new phase* in the progressive development of Protestantism, as an *advance* on the earlier periods of the history of the Church.

This is then the last but safe anchor for a Protestant divine of the German historical school. To this position has, for example, Dr. Nevin been forced, who is thoroughly acquainted with all the forms of English and German Protestantism. The Puritan, Presbyterian, and Anglican historical hypotheses have proved wholly untenable to him, and in his late articles on "Early Christianity" and "Cyprian," in the *Mercersburg Review,* he has produced arguments against them, which none of his many dissatisfied opponents have attempted to refute, and which indeed, in a historical view, so far as the main facts are concerned, can scarcely ever be refuted. Consequently there remains for him nothing except the German theory of development, which, in the mean time, is held in reproach by almost all English theologians. As long as he adheres to this theory an exodus to Rome will be impossible, as it would be a retrogression, and consequently a nullification of the fundamental law of historical development. For this, in the nature of the case, implies progress, an advance from the lower to the higher, and this must hold good when applied to the Church, although in the individual parts of all the divisions of the Church, retrogressive movements and temporary stagnation may occur.

For the purpose, however, of justifying Protestantism satisfactorily, on the ground of the development theory, two important points must be settled. First, it must be proved that it was not a *radical* rupture with the religious life of the early, i.e., the Catholic Church, but that it has *in common with her a primitive Christian and a primitive Church basis,* which we, in our opposition, should never lose sight of. For, in the course of her development, the Church must yet continually remain identical in her nature, and dare not advance beyond herself, without falling into heresy, and thus make the promise of Christ to her of none effect. Thus man from childhood to old age still remains man, and each successive step is but a higher evolution of the idea contained already in the infant. Hence it is of immense importance, that the Reformers without exception retained the Catholic Canon of Scripture, the ancient oecumenical symbols, and especially the Apostle's Creed, and incorporated them in their own confessions, and that they stood in direct opposition to the ultra-Protestant sects of their times. Certain portions of modern Protestantism manifest, indeed, a fearful tendency in their bitter hostility against Rome, to separate themselves from this fundamental basis, and in like proportion sink into the character of heresies and sects. But the main branches of Protestantism will, by no means, surrender this Apostolic symbol, which connects them with the Ancient Church, and never cease to claim an interest in the Christianity before the Reformation, especially in the Patristic literature. Indeed there are evidently manifold strivings to recover numerous treasures, which have been cast overboard, and particularly to reconstruct, enlarge and conform their worship to the Church principle.

Then again it must be proved that Protestantism has its foundation substantially in *Apostolical* Christianity. For the New Testament, the Word of Christ and his inspired organs, is, after all, the final resort in all religious questions, and whatever has no connecting point with it cannot be sustained in the end. The germs of all legitimate stages of progress must already appear in the Apostolic Church, whilst a development beyond Christ himself and his Apostles, in the sense of Rationalists and Free-thinkers of all classes, must naturally assume the character of a degeneration, and a relapse into Heathenism or Judaism. With *such* development we, of course, have not the least sympathy whatever, but abhor it as essential antichristian. But the Reformers, we all know, without exception placed themselves on the Bible as the only infallible rule of Christian faith and practice. Now it would indeed be an inextricable historical riddle, if the close association which Protestantism has from the start formed with the Bible, and if the zeal with which it continually devotes itself to its translation, interpretation and promulgation throughout the world, should rest finally upon a mere delusion. It is, indeed, manifestly impossible for the Bible to contain *all* that the various denominations and sects imagine to find in it—but which, in truth, they force into it, by means of their private interpretation—or it would contradict itself, and cease to be the truth any longer. It cannot possibly contain at once the contrary doctrines of Episcopalianism, Lutheranism, Methodism, the Baptists and Quakers, (if by special indulgence, we should still number the last two with orthodox Protestantism); it cannot, at the same time, teach and condemn the doctrine of Predestination, or both affirm and deny the real presence of Christ in the Eucharist; it cannot at one time declare Baptismal Regeneration, and yet degrade the Sacrament to the level of an empty sign; it cannot enjoin the baptism of Infants, and yet reject it as unchristian; it cannot establish three orders in the Ministry, and then again, but one, or teach no peculiar spiritual office at all, but only a universal Priesthood, and favor whatever other points of difference there may be in Doctrine, Constitution and Cultus, partly essential, partly non-essential, concerning which Protestants have quarreled already for three hundred years, with equally zealous appeal to the Bible, without advancing a single step towards each other. Still justice requires us to allow, that they agree, we will not say in all—as this would evidently be saying too much—but in most of the fundamental articles of the Gospel; for if it were otherwise, we would, according to the incontrovertible maxim, "out of the Church, no salvation," be compelled to deny the possibility of salvation in one or the other of these communions, to which extent even the extreme Puseyites and Old-Lutherans will not venture.

Some such relation then must evidently exist between the Bible and orthodox Protestantism in order to explain intelligently their close connection for three hundred years. In this dilemma, German

Theology again comes to our relief and transfers us, to what appears to us, the only correct point of view.

Modern exegetical investigations, in which sphere, as is well known, it has displayed an extraordinary activity, place it beyond all doubt for us at least, that we must distinguish three stages of development and types of doctrine in the apostolic Church, which of course, in no way, contradict or exclude each other, as the school of Dr. Baur in Tübingen, after the precedence of the ancient Gnostics, maintains, but mutually complete each other, to wit:—*Jewish Christianity*, represented by the Apostles Peter and James, *Gentile Christianity*, represented by the Gentile Apostle Paul and his co-laborers, and *the higher union of both* by John, the beloved disciple, who, surviving all his colleagues, exhibits the third and last period and completion of the Apostolic Church, and looks forward, at the same time, as the Prophet of the New Covenant, through the most distant future, to the new heavens and the new earth, wherein dwelleth righteousness and peace for evermore. If this view be correct, and we find it more and more confirmed the longer we study the New Testament in its proper connection—we have a polar star to guide us through the entire labyrinth of Church History, in her manifold phases and stages of development. According to this view then, the history of the Catholic Church, which stays herself on Peter as her rock and derives her doctrine on justification, faith and good works chiefly from the first two Gospels and from the Epistle of James, corresponds to Apostolic Jewish Christianity, and with it lays stress principally on authority, law and the closest possible connection with the theocracy of the Old Testament. Protestantism, which originally proceeded from a renewed study of the Epistles of Paul, is a onesided enforcing of the Pauline-Gentile Christianity with its spirit of evangelical freedom and independence, over against the Jewish Christian excesses. In its relation to Catholicism it has thus far imitated St. Paul far more in his temporary inimical collision with Peter at Antioch (Gal. 2:11, 19) than in his subsequent friendly co-operation with him, and has frequently given occasion to his antagonist to repeat the warning of Peter against the abuse of the writings of Paul "in which there are some things hard to be understood" (2 Peter 3:16). Then again Protestantism has unfolded thus far almost exclusively the anthropological and soteriological doctrines of Paul, his Epistles to the Galatians and Romans; whilst the later Epistles of the same Apostle, especially his profound doctrine of the Church, as the one, undivided body of Christ, the fullness of him that filleth all in all, have evidently not yet received their full share of attention. As soon as this shall be done, there will be at the same time a certain approximation to the Catholic church-principle, and the way become prepared for the third and last Period of the Christian Church, in which the great truths of Catholicism and evangelical Protestantism, with the exclusion of their mutual errors, may become united in a higher union and harmony, through the renewal and complete appropriation of the spirit of John, especially of his doctrine of the person of Christ, and the living communion of the faithful with Him and with each other. But this union must be preceded by a universal repentance, and we may here appropriate to ourselves the significant words of the great and generous Catholic Divine, Möhler who, after frankly acknowledging the unwarrantable lack of principle in so many priests, bishops and Popes, "whom hell has swallowed up," as the cause of corruption in his Church and of the Reformation in the sixteenth century, adds "This is the point (the consciousness of guilt) at which Catholics and Protestants will in great multitudes one day meet and give each other the hand of friendship. Both, conscious of guilt, must exclaim, We *all* have erred—it is the Church only—as an institution of Christ—which cannot err; we *all* have sinned—the Church alone is spotless on earth. This open confession of mutual guilt will be followed by the festival of reconciliation."[9]

Herewith we bring the series of essays on German Theology to a close. We have rendered it high praise, and joined bright hopes with it. But we would not be so misunderstood, as though we were blind to its manifold wants and imperfections; we have rather distinctly stated the contrary, and intimated that its principal practical task has by no means yet been accomplished. We know also full well that salvation comes not from theology, science or learning, under any form, as many German closet-scholars imagine, but from *life,* from those

---

[9](Ed.) Möhler, *Symbolik,* 6th ed. (Mainz, 1843) 353.

divine-human powers, those aged yet ever youthful *supernatural facts,* which alone have founded and which alone can renew and complete the Church. But if the evangelical theology of Germany, in connection with the other instruments of the age, should, in the hands of a merciful God, serve the purpose of preparing the way, from the Protestant side, through the inward, quiet, yet deeply working "power of thought," for such a reconciliation between Catholicism and Protestantism, and aid in bringing to an end the great schism of the sixteenth century by a greater and more difficult act of reunion: it would truly deserve the praise and gratitude of all true friends of the kingdom of God, which is a kingdom of love, harmony and peace. For what can be more grand and glorious than to heal the bleeding wounds of the body of Christ, and to labor for the realization of the last prayer of our Eternal High Priest: "Neither pray I for these alone, but for them also which shall believe on me through their word: that they all may be one; as thou, Father, art in me, and I in thee, that they also may be one in us: that the world may believe that thou hast sent me!" [John 17:20-21].

LETTER FROM TRENT*

Who has not heard of Trent and of the Council of Trent? . . . There the holy fathers of the Roman Catholic Church met for almost 20 years, 1545 to 1563, though with many interruptions. There they settled their account with the Reformation and condemned as heresy the principles of Protestantism, to be sure, mostly in a distorted and exaggerated form. There they completed unalterably the doctrinal system of the papacy, exclusive of the decision regarding the complete sinlessness of the Mother of the Lord, which was reserved for the pontificate of Pius IX and the war-threatened year of 1854. To this day every Roman Catholic priest must take an oath on the *Professio Fidei Tridentinae* which will form an insurmountable wall of separation between the Roman and evangelical Churches as long as

---

*"Reisebilder für den Kirchenfreund: Trient," *Der deutsche Kirchenfreund* 8 (October 1855): 321-27. (Editor's translation.)

that Church holds fast to the principle of infallibility and irreform-
ability, according to which it can never revoke anything that was once
established solemnly as an article of faith.[10] This, to be sure, confers
upon it a rock-like character, an unshakeable firmness, tenacity,
consistency and immutability of which no Protestant community can
and should boast. But is there not also a rock-like obstinacy and im-
penitence? And is not Rome's greatest error precisely this that it never
admits an error?

I therefore felt not a little curiosity to set foot on this classical soil
of more recent church history and opened my eyes wide when we first
saw from a beautiful eminence its towers, and descending between
vineyards and mulberry trees approached its walls. We came from
the lovely Lago di Garda through the romantic Sacca valley in a comfortable carriage with a kind-hearted German-Tyrolean coachman. It
was a bright morning in June when nature is still decked out in the
festive bridal gown of hope. My company consisted of a brave German merchant from Trieste who with wife and in-laws was journey-
ing home for a visit, an amusing Hungarian, and an exceedingly dull
Englishman who put our patience to an extreme test. To be sure, he
was returning directly from an excursion to Constantinople, but instead of satisfying our curiosity about the oriental war and the prospects of the Turkish empire he was utterly determined to learn from
us in a few hours Italian, French, and German, all-the-while un-
mercifully tearing at these languages and inflicting bloody injuries
upon each word. . . .

Most of all I was interested in what I saw of the churches and the
ecclesiastical life in Trent. For this I had a very good opportunity since
it happened to be Trinity Sunday (June 11, 1854). The waiter in the
inn was unable to tell me when and where divine services were held.
And so I went first to the cathedral, a magnificent, venerable building, which was begun in 1048 and completed at the beginning of
the fifteenth century, in a large square adorned with beautiful foun-

---

[10](Ed.) The Profession of the Tridentine Faith (1564) included in its twelve
articles the Nicene Creed, a summary of the Roman Catholic doctrines as settled
at the Council of Trent, and the requirement of an oath of obedience to the Pope.
The text is in Schaff, *Creeds of Christendom*, 6th ed. (1931) 2:207-10.

tains. It has two cupolas, two fierce-looking lions at the entrance (like the parish church at Bozen, without doubt in remembrance of Christ, the lion of the tribe of Judah, the guardian of the sanctuary), and its interior is embellished with imposing pillars, strange, ascending staircases, a few old tombs, and half-faded frescoes. On my way there I found posted at the street-corners play-bills with the announcement that this evening (on holy Trinity Sunday!) "Il barbiere de Seviglia," an opera by Rossini, was to be performed. Also posted was the notice of a menagerie which was open all day—clear evidence that a Sabbath in the English and American sense is unknown in Trent as in the Roman Catholic Church in general and on the European continent. By the way, I should add that I noticed very little noise and commotion in the streets, which may have to do with the town's stagnation.

I arrived at the cathedral just in time for the sermon. It was delivered in Italian by a Capuchin, with a crucifix next to him, and was not related to the day's significance but dealt with prayer. Neither was it a textual interpretation nor did it reveal spiritual depth or rhetorical gifts, but it contained rather good, practical Christian thoughts and edified me. He lifted up in particular the thought that one should pray not so much with one's lips but above all with the heart, in sincere humility and fervent confidence in the power of the cross (here he bowed before the crucifix) and the *infinito amore di Deo*.[11] Regarding the answering of a prayer which seemingly was rejected, he pointed out quite appropriately the example of Monica when her son Augustine departed for Italy, which was against the immediate meaning of her petition but led to his conversion, that is, in the end precisely to the fulfillment of her heart's deepest desire. Between the two parts of this service, following an Italian custom, the preacher sat down and asked for an offering with the remark that giving of alms and charity is the sister of prayer. The number of auditors was considerable, men and women separated by a curtain which was raised during the mass. I could observe in the faces neither much intelligence nor particular devotion. Many slept, among them also one of

---

[11](Ed.) "the infinite love of God."

the four red-clad canons next to whom I sat; he kept nodding, while the others listened indifferently.

The sermon at 11 o'clock was followed by a silent mass simultaneously at three altars. Again I saw quite clearly that the service at the altar, the offering of the unbloody sacrifice in remembrance and application of the eternal sacrifice on the cross, is the central and essential element of the Roman Catholic cultus. As is well-known, Claus Harms said in one of his Ninety-five Theses: "The Catholic Church is a glorious church, for it builds itself up on the sacrament; the Reformed Church is a glorious church, for it builds itself up on the Word; but more glorious than both is the Lutheran Church, for it builds itself up simultaneously on the sacrament and the Word."[12] It can be conceded that the latter in its purest representatives aims at such a combination; but whether it really achieves it and has in its cultus a specific advantage over the Reformed Church (especially if one includes the Anglican Church) we will leave here undecided. One of the officiating priests, a handsome young man, appeared especially absorbed in the mystery of the cross. Many onlookers had their prayer-books, the mass with an Italian translation, and participated with real devotion, especially the women, among whom indeed everywhere the religious feeling asserts itself much more generally and with greater liveliness, though not as deeply and energetically as among the race of men who are colder, more reflective, and more independent-minded.

Among these devout Roman Catholics there knelt a lonely Protestant near the altar-step, unknown to and unnoticed by those around him. He was absorbed in the unfathomable mystery of Christ's reconciling death. He thanked God for sending his son, and for the gift of his infallible Word, for the simple evangelical faith which justifies, sanctifies and saves, and for the high privilege of direct access to the throne of his grace and of personal communion with Christ,

---

[12](Ed.) Claus Harms (1778–1855), pastor at Kiel and a leader in the resurgence of Lutheran confessionalism, created in 1817, the tercentennial of the Reformation, a sensation with the publication of his Ninety-five Theses (Luther's and his own). Schaff is quoting Theses 92-94, from *Das sind die 95 Thesen oder Streitsätze Dr. Martin Luthers, teuren Andenkens* (Kiel, 1817).

the all-sufficient and ever-present savior. He prayed for humility and love, the illumination of the spirit, sanctification of the heart, and blessing for his vocation in the kingdom of God. He offered inter-cessory prayers for his distant family, his friends and colleagues, for his denomination, for the whole evangelical Church, the Roman Catholic Church, and the Greek Church, for the pouring out of the spirit of God and the spreading of the life of Christ over all those who call themselves Christians, yea, even to the ends of the earth, and for the ultimate union of all believers into one flock under the care of him, the one shepherd. And where human feelings and words were insufficient, there the Spirit of God interceded for him "with sighs too deep for words" [Rom. 8:26] and gave testimony to his spirit that the sacrifice of his prayer is acceptable to God for Christ's sake and that in the crucified and risen one we have forgiveness of sins, adoption as God's children, and inheritance of eternal life.

In the afternoon I heard a well-intentioned but very ordinary and tearfully delivered German sermon about the mystery of the trinity in the former Jesuit church, now the seminary church.

Then I walked to Santa Maria Maggiore, a small, plain church, but equipped with an excellent organ, and made above all memo-rable by the fact that here the famous council was held. One can hardly believe that it could comfortably accommodate the many bishops and their theologians. A crowded assembly attented the religious in-struction of the young which was given from the pulpit and con-cluded with the singing of a few psalms. After the crowd dispersed, I inspected the painting which portrays the members of the Council of Trent, among them 7 cardinals, 3 patriarchs, 33 archbishops, and 235 bishops. The cardinals in red and the papal legates in particular stand out. The president sits underneath the pulpit, the doctors of theology toward the door, the imperial commissioners in the center. The painting has more historical-theological than artistic value, however, it is well executed. It hangs on the left wall of the chancel and is veiled, but the custodian will show and explain it to every stranger for a tip. In the small square in front of the church there stands a pillar of red marble with a statue of the virgin Mary which the town had caused to be erected in 1845 during the tri-centennial celebration commemorating this council. It bears on one side the in-

scription: *Te Tridentini honorant supplices, uti sibi praesidio sies* (probably a mistake for *sis*); on the second side: *Ecclesia columna et
fundamentum veritatis*; on the third: *Sentiant omnes tuum juvamen, ut fiat
unum ovile et unus pastor.*[13] With the last wish I agree sincerely but
expect its fulfillment directly from Christ, the great head of the congregation, whose words are Yea and Amen.

Toward evening I visited once more the cathedral and was present,
not without edification, at the singing of the psalms and the benediction.

That was Trinity Sunday at Trent. I had gathered enough material for meditations of several hours' duration during a lonely walk
along the banks of the Etsch and in my living quarters. Before my
mind's eye there passed the history of the Roman Catholic and Protestant Churches, their unity and diversity, attraction and repulsion,
fellowship and hostility, and their future prospects until the glorious
return of the Lord. I made a comparison between Trent and the towns
of the Reformation: Geneva, Zurich, Wittenberg, between the sermons I heard there[14] and the evangelical testimonies which probably
on the same day were delivered from the pulpits of the Luther-town
on the sandy banks of the Elbe by the spirit-filled and unctuous Su-
perintendent-General Sander, the successor of the venerable Heubner, or by his learned and ingenious colleague Schmieder.[15] Again I

---

[13](Ed.) "The Tridentine Suppliants honor you, so that you may be their protection" (Schaff was wrong: "sies" is a not uncommon substitute for "sis"). "The
church is the pillar and foundation of truth." "May all experience your help, so
that there may be one sheepfold and one shepherd."

[14](Ed.) "There" (instead of "here") makes clear that Schaff's "Letter from
Trent" was an article written later (though, no doubt, based on his notes) for the
benefit of the readers of *Der deutsche Kirchenfreund*.

[15](Ed.) When by royal decree in 1817 the University of Wittenberg was absorbed into the University of Halle, in its place a seminary was established for the
further training of selected ministerial candidates after the conclusion of their university studies. Heinrich Leonard Heubner (1780–1853) since 1832, Heinrich
Eduard Schmieder (1794–1893) since 1839, and Immanuel Friedrich Emil Sander
(1797–1859) since 1854 were directors of the seminary at Wittenberg, distinguished evangelical preachers, and church officials. Sander assisted at Schaff's ordination in 1843.

felt the full impact of the church question, as it now weighs upon the old and new world, and I found its only solution in the question of Christ—for Christ is the beginning, the middle, and the end of all.

The following day I wrote a letter to an intimate friend in America which I concluded approximately with the words:[16] "Let us always joyfully acknowledge and thank God for the glorious gifts and powers which he has given the Roman Catholic Church and for the countless good things which he for many centuries has done, and still does, through it to the world. But we will also never forget that we are called to freedom and the apostle admonishes us: 'Stand fast in the freedom through which Christ has set us free . . . and do not submit again to a yoke of slavery' [Gal. 5:1]. I will probably return a better Protestant and American, but full of grateful respect and love for good old Europe and full of the most pleasant memories of my present visit."

---

[16](Ed.) The friend was William Julius Mann.

CHAPTER 3

What Is Church History?

EDITORIAL INTRODUCTION

Schaff had dedicated the original German version of his *History of the Apostolic Church* (1853) to the memory of August Neander. The "Preface," here included, shows how closely he followed in his great Berlin teacher's footsteps. Like Neander Schaff desired to write church history in a spirit of liberality and catholicity and for the spiritual edification of his readers as "a living witness of the divine power of Christianity; as a school of Christian experience; a voice, sounding through the ages, of instruction, of doctrine and of reproof, for all who are disposed to listen."[1] And like Neander he offered a conservative rebuttal to the Tübingen School's rival interpretation of apostolic Christianity. The book displayed to great advantage the erudition and literary skill of the young scholar, even though the work was drawn not so much from an independent and thorough study of the historical sources as of the secondary literature. Twice more Schaff discussed the history of the apostolic church, though the basic point of view, that of the Neander School, remained unchanged. In the first volume of his *History of the Christian Church* of 1859, which now covered the first three centuries, he limited the discussion of apostolic Christianity to just 140 pages.

---

[1] August Neander, *General History of the Christian Religion and Church*, trans. J. Terry, vol. 1, 2nd ed. (Boston, 1851) preface to 1st edition.

It is further noteworthy that in 1853 Schaff's analysis of the four aspects of the apostolic church—moral and religious life, government, worship and (coming last) doctrine—had reflected Schleiermacher's and Neander's understanding of Christianity as "life" rather than "doctrine," as a new "moral creation" rather than an (Hegelian) "idea." In his second attempt of 1859, however, he had heeded Baur's criticism of Neander's similar arrangement and first discussed the apostolic literature and theology.[2] In his third and final survey of apostolic Christianity, published once again as a separate volume in 1882, he reverted to his earlier sequence of topics. And though he finally also offered an extended discussion of the Tübingen School's textual criticism of the New Testament writings, he rejected even then all of its more radical findings.[3]

He prefaced the *History of the Apostolic Church* of 1853 with a remarkable "General Introduction to Church History." His earlier publication *What is Church History? A Vindication of the Idea of Historical Development* (1846) was a spirited first draft, so to say, that had now ripened into a mature, thoughtful presentation.[4] Here too he stood, at least formally, somewhere between Neander and Baur. For Neander had dispensed entirely with an introduction to his church history, while Baur, at about the same time that Schaff's book appeared, published his programmatic and brilliant introduction to the study of church history as a separate volume, *Die Epochen der kirchlichen Geschichtsschreibung* (1852), before he went on to write *Das Christentum und die christliche Kirche der drei ersten Jahrhunderte* (1853).

Our earlier selection from "General Introduction to Church History" set forth the formative influences that had shaped Schaff's

---

[2]*Ferdinand Christian Baur: On the Writing of Church History,* ed. and trans. Peter C. Hodgson, 256.

[3]See Schaff, *History of the Christian Church,* vol. 1 (1882), "The Critical Reconstruction of the Apostolic Church," 205-17.

[4]It should be noted that Schaff (without acknowledging his dependence) drew not only upon Theodor Kliefoth's article series "Die neuere Kirchengeschichtsschreibung in der deutsch-evangelischen Kirche," as already noted (see above, 14), but also, interestingly enough, upon the Roman Catholic Johann Adam Möhler's "Einleitung in die Kirchengeschichte," *Gesammelte Schriften und Aufsätze,* ed. I. Döllinger (Regensburg, 1840) 2:261-90.

position as a church historian.[5] That selection was taken from the final chapter, which offered an extensive survey of the history of the writing of church history—the first such survey available in English. Here we add selections taken from the preceding chapter "Church History," which in logical progression followed upon the first two chapters, "History" and "The Church." We should first note Schaff's characteristic conviction that constituted one of the most distinctive features of his position as a church historian: to define the nature of the church is to define the task of the church historian. Schaff believed that the study of church history is the study of the church itself, or conversely, that only those who know the universal history of the church can also be expected to perceive the true nature of the universal church. But to the question, What then is the object of church history?, Schaff characteristically replied by embracing eclectically three different concepts of the church: it is the "kingdom of God" in its course through history (as in pietism and with Neander), the organic growth of the church as the "Body of Christ" (as in romanticism), and the dialectic development of the "Idea" of the church (as in the philosophy of idealism). He was aware, though, of a necessary circle of cognition at this point, for he readily admitted that the relation between the concept of the church, however defined, and church history "is one of reciprocal light and confirmation."[6]

One should further note that Schaff employed a combination of "empiricism" and "speculation," that is, of critical attention to the historical detail and a philosophical approach to history centered on "ideas." This methodology explains that he could present side by side an "empirical" and "philosophical" survey of the history of Christianity. Together they offer a remarkable historical and ecumenical scheme for understanding the total sweep of church history, which was to guide Schaff to the end of his life. It is true

---

[5]For a fuller discussion of Schaff's position as a church historian, see David W. Lotz, "Philip Schaff and the Idea of Church History," in *A Century of Church History: The Legacy of Philip Schaff*, ed. Henry W. Bowden (Carbondale and Edwardsville, 1988) 1-35, and my own essay "Church History in Context: The Case of Philip Schaff," in *Our Common History as Christians*, ed. John Deschner et al. (New York, 1975) 217-60.

[6]Schaff, *What is Church History?*, 37.

that this grand scheme allowed Schaff to explain the two major historical types of Christianity, medieval Catholicism and Reformation Protestantism, as necessary and sequential stages in the
development of the church. But it also needs to be emphasized that
the idealistic dialectics of his scheme prevented him from doing even
minimal justice to the history of the Eastern Orthodox churches,
of modern Roman Catholicism and of the post-Reformation
churches of Anglo-American Christianity. Indeed, Schaff echoed
the ignorance and even arrogance that western Christians have ha-
bitually shown toward Eastern Orthodoxy: he called it, for instance, "a mummy in the posture of prayer."[7] And despite his better
intentions and occasionally laudatory remarks, he also continued to
mirror the common Protestant lack of appreciation of the history
of post-Reformation Roman Catholicism. Only his attitude toward
the denominations of English-speaking Protestantism would
quickly and dramatically change from the traditional parochial rejection representative of continental European Protestants to the full
appreciation characteristic of his later career.

Schaff offered the fullest elaboration of the laws that he had
found to rule the development of the church in its course through
history in *What is Church History?*, once again drawing eclectically
upon pietistic, romantic and dialectic categories and notions. Because they remained characteristic features of his interpretation of
church history throughout his career, they deserve brief enumeration: (1) The development of the church is "partly external and
partly internal," as Christ himself taught his disciples in the twin-
parables of the mustard seed and the leaven (Mt. 13: 31-33); these
parables served as the classical biblical text for the pietistic, and
Schaff's own, interpretation of the history of Christianity. (2) As a
living organism, the church changes as it passes through the various stages of growth, each stage being necessary at its own time,
while yet the church always retains its self-same identity; in short,
continuity-with-change is the law of church history. (3) Every stage
of growth has "its own corresponding disease," for "(w)here God
builds a temple, the devil is sure to have a chapel alongside." (4)
But in God's overriding providence, these diseases in the life of the

---

[7]Schaff, *Das Princip des Protestantismus,* 76 (cf. *The Principle of Protestantism* [repr.
1964] 128), and David S. Schaff, *Life of Schaff,* 199.

church turn out to be "the negative conditions precisely of her progress." (5) The church advances to a higher stage only through the negation, conservation and elevation of the previous stage, which, as Schaff informed his American readers, is the triple meaning of the German word *aufheben*. (6) That the development of the church occurs only "by means of dialectic opposites and extremes" is an insight "indispensable to a right understanding of Church History," both of the whole and of each period. (7) The truth, however, lies never "in the extremes, but in the middle," which was one of the ruling conceptions not only of the *Vermittlungstheologie* but of Schaff's whole career. (8) Three kinds of movements—restoration, revolution or reformation—may initiate a new historical period, but only reformatory movements assure true progress, because they alone simultaneously preserve the best traditions of the past and innovatively shape the future. (9) From Hegel's philosophy of history Schaff borrowed the notion that great religious individuals always lead reformations: "History proceeds aristocratically." (10) The development of the church, "though full of turns, moves always forward." (11) This development, in its geographical course, proceeds in general "like that of the sun, from east to west," until the Gospel finally "shall return, with the millenium and the coming of the Lord in his glory, to the point from which it started on its circuit round the globe"—traces of the adventism of Württemberg's pietism.[8] These were the novel ideas that animated and guided Schaff's interpretation of the history of the universal church. It is obvious that Schaff plucked the golden apple of the belief in progress—a gloriously optimistic and triumphalist view of church history—from the tree of the romantic-idealistic philosophy of history, though, to be sure, this tree had been nurtured also in the soil of the pietistic doctrine of divine providence.

This rich understanding both of the historical process and of the nature of church history as a scholarly discipline was obviously of great practical and ecumenical significance and usefulness. Church history, so Schaff informed his readers, is "the key to the present condition of Christendom and the guide to succesful labor in her cause."[9] For it "aims to sketch forth from the old founda-

---

[8] For the preceding quotations, see Schaff, *What is Church History?*, 88-114.

[9] Schaff, *History of the Christian Church*, vol. 1, new ed. (1869) 15.

tions of the church the plan for its new superstructure."[10] He was
convinced that for the pressing contemporary task of restoring the
unity of the church none is professionally better qualified than the
church historian, whose "duty and privilege" it is, after all, "to
trace the image of Christ in the various physiognomies of his disciples, and to act as a mediator between the different branches of
his kingdom."[11] A deeply felt ecumenism characterized Schaff's
whole career as the historian and ambassador of the universal church.

Certainly, these were challenging new concepts, interpretations and methodologies for most of Schaff's American readers.
Schaff had soon discovered that an anti-historical bias set Americans apart, for they are, as he wrote, "disposed rather to make than
to contemplate history."[12] And if most American Protestants might
not go as far as did Thomas Campbell when he called church history "the rubbish of ages," still they tended to leap-frog across the
centuries by appealing directly to the Bibel and their own religious
experience as the sole two poles around which the Christian life
fixedly revolved.[13] How pleased Schaff must have been to note the
sad lament of Princeton's Joseph Addison Alexander in 1847: "Our
national tendency, so far as we have any, is to slight the past and
overrate the present," and then the proposed remedy: "To coun-
teract this tendency we need some influence *ab extra,* some infusion
of strange blood into our veins."[14] That influence *ab extra,* Schaff
affirmed, had already taken hold of Nevin. He also noted the inaugural lecture, "Nature and Worth of the Science of Church History," which the "Puritan divine" Henry B. Smith had delivered
at Union Theological Seminary in 1851. Schaff pronounced it "excellent," for to his pleasant surprise he found it committed to
Neander's conception of the nature and task of church history.[15] But
more than anyone else, it was Schaff himself who in those years rep-

---

[10]Schaff, *History of the Apostolic Church,* 94.

[11]Schaff, *History of the Christian Church,* vol. 1, 3rd ed. (1890) 26.

[12]Schaff, *History of the Apostolic Church,* 131.

[13]Thomas Campbell, "Declaration and Address" (1809), in *Historical Documents Advocating Christian Union,* ed. Charles A. Young (Chicago, 1904) 115.

[14]Schaff, *History of the Apostolic Church,* 132n.

[15]Ibid., 131n.3.

resented a direct infusion of the historical consciousness of German culture into the bloodstream of American Protestantism.

PREFACE,
*History of the Apostolic Church**

To present from original sources, in a faithful, clear and life-like picture, the history of the Church of Jesus Christ, the God-man and Saviour of the world; to reproduce, with ardent love of truth and with genuine catholicity, her inward and outward experience, her conflicts and triumphs, her sufferings and joys, her thoughts, her words and her deeds; and to hold up to the present age this panorama of eighteen centuries as the most complete apology for Christianity, full of encouragement and warning, of precept and example:—this is a task well worthy of the best energies of a long life, and offering in itself the amplest reward, but at the same time so vast and comprehensive, that it cannot be accomplished to any satisfaction, except by the cooperation of all varieties of talent. The individual must feel sufficiently fortunate and honored, if he succeed in furnishing a few blocks for a gigantic edifice, which, in the nature of the case, cannot be finished, till the church shall have reached the goal of her militant stage. For science grows with experience and with it alone becomes complete. . . .

I prefer, for several reasons, to publish this volume as a separate work on the Apostolic Church, with a full General Introduction, which contains the outlines of a philosophy of Church History, and will supply, I hope, a defect in this department of our literature. It is my wish and intention, however, if God spares my life and strength, to bring the history down to the present time; and thus, so far as lies within my humble abilities, to give from reliable sources, under the guidance of our Lord's twin parables of the mustard-seed and leaven [Matt. 13:31-33], a complete, true, and graphic account of the development of Christ's kingdom on earth, for the theoretical and

---

*History of the Apostolic Church, with a General Introduction to Church History, trans. Edward D. Yeomans (New York, 1853) iii, v-vi.

practical benefit especially of ministers and students of theology. As regards compass, I propose to steer midway between the synoptical brevity of a mere compend and the voluminous fullness of a work which seeks to exhaust its subject and is designed simply for the professional scholar. Each of the nine periods, according to the scheme proposed in the General Introduction, §17, will probably require a moderate volume.[1]

With these remarks, I send the book forth to the public, fully conscious of its many imperfections, yet not without hope, that under the blessing of Almighty God it may accomplish some good, so long as its time may last. With modest claims and the most peaceful intentions, polemical and uncompromising only towards rationalism and infidelity, whether of German or English origin, but conservative, conciliatory, and respectful towards the various forms of positive Christianity, and reaching the hand of fellowship to all who love the Lord Jesus in sincerity and in truth, it sails into the ocean of a deeply distracted, yet most interesting and hopeful age, where amid powerful fermentations and keen birth-throes a new era of church history seems to be preparing. Whatever the future may bring, we know, that the Church of Christ is built upon a rock, against which even the gates of hell shall never prevail [Matt. 16:18]; that she must go on conquering and to conquer, until the whole world shall bow to the peaceful sceptre of the cross; and that all obstructions and persecutions, all heresies and schisms, all wickedness and corruption of men, will only tend at last, in the hands of infinite wisdom and mercy, to bring out her glorious attributes of unity, catholicity, and holiness in brighter colors and with more triumphant power. May the

---

[1](Ed.) Schaff distinguished three ages in the history of the Christian Church (see below, pp. 136-45) and in each age again three periods: Ancient Christianity: the apostolic church, to the reign of Constantine, to Gregory I; Medieval Christianity: to Gregory VII, to Boniface VIII, to 1517; Modern Christianity: sixteenth-century Reformation, seventeenth-century Orthodoxy, to the present. This periodization is still maintained, and each period indeed treated in a separate volume, in the final edition of his *History of the Christian Church* (1882–92), except that the Protestant Reformation is given two volumes, one each for the reform movements in Lutheran Germany and in Schaff's native Switzerland.

great Head of the Church use this representation of her history as an humble instrument to promote his own glory, to serve the cause of truth, unity and peace, and to strengthen the faith of His people in the divine character, immovable foundation and ultimate triumph of the kingdom of God!

Philip Schaff

Mercersburg, Pa., September, 1853

GENERAL INTRODUCTION TO CHURCH HISTORY*

Definition of Church History

We are now prepared to define *church history*. It is simply the progressive execution of the scheme of the divine kingdom in the actual life of humanity; the outward and inward development of Christianity; the extension of the church over the whole earth, and the infusion of the spirit of Christ into all the spheres of human existence, the family, the state, science, art, and morality, making them all organs and expressions of this spirit, for the glory of God, and for the elevation of man to his proper perfection and happiness. It is the sum of all the utterances and deeds, experiences and fortunes, all the sufferings, the conflicts, and the victories of Christianity, as well as of all the divine manifestations in and through it.

As we have distinguished two factors, a divine and a human, in general history; so we must view church history as the joint product of Christ and of his people, or regenerate humanity. On the part of Christ, it may be called the evolution of his own life in the world, a perpetual repetition, or unbroken continuation, as it were, of his incarnation, his words and deeds, his death and his resurrection, in the hearts of individuals and of nations. On the part of men, church history is the external and internal unfolding of the life of believers collectively, who live and move and have their being in Christ. But as

---

*History of the Apostolic Church, with a General Introduction to Church History, 16-17, 33-35, 38-50.

these are not perfect saints this side of the grave, as they still remain more or less under the influence of sin and error, and as, moreover, the church militant is associated with the ungodly world, which intrudes into it in manifold ways, there appear, of course, in church history all kinds of sinful passions, perversions and caricatures of divine truth, heresies and schisms. We find all these in fact even in the age of the New Testament. For in proportion as the kingdom of light asserts itself, the kingdom of darkness also rouses to greater activity, and whets its weapons on Christianity itself. Judas not only stood in the sacred circle of the apostles but wanders, like Ahasuerus, through the ecclesiastical sanctuary of all centuries. It is in opposition to the highest manifestations of the Spirit of God, that the most dangerous and hateful forms of human and diabolical perversion arise.

But, in the first place, church history shows that this opposition, and that all errors and divisions, even though they may have a long and almost universal prevalence, must, in the end, serve only to awaken the church to her real work, to call forth her deepest energies, to furnish the occasion for higher developments, and thus to glorify the name of God and his Son Jesus Christ. All tribulation, too, and persecutions are for the church, what they are for the individual Christian, only a powerful refining fire, in which she is to be gradually purged from all her dross, till at last, adorned as a bride at the side of her heavenly spouse, upon the renovated earth, she shall celebrate the resurrection morning as her last and most glorious pentecost.

In the next place, however, this dark side of church history is only, as it were, its earthly and temporary outwork. Its inmost and permanent substance, its heart's blood, is the divine love and wisdom itself, of which it is the manifestation. Church history first of all presents to us Christ, as he moves through all time, living and working in his people, cleansing them from all foreign elements, and conquering the world and Satan. It is the repository of the manifold attestations and seals of his Holy Spirit in that bright cloud of witnesses, who have denied themselves even unto death; who have battled faithfully against all ungodliness within and without; who have preached the gospel of peace to every creature; who have bathed in the depths of the divine life and everlasting truth, and have brought forth and unfolded the treasures of revelation for the instruction, edification, and comfort of their contemporaries and posterity; who, with many tears and prayers, willingly bearing their master's cross, but also rejoicing in faith and hope, and triumphing over death and the grave, have passed into the upper sanctuary, to rest forever from their labors.

Method of Writing Church History

We come now to consider the way of arranging and presenting the material of church history.

1. As to the *external* method, or the disposition of the matter, it is best to combine the two modes of dividing, by *time,* and by *subjects.* The *chronological* method, which has hitherto been in much favor, has its advantages, but is very external and mechanical, when carried out by itself, especially in the form of Annals. It degrades history to a mere chronicle, and interrupts the flow of events, so that things, which should go together, are sundered, and not unfrequently a heterogeneous mass is crowded into one section, because it belongs in one chronological division. This is the case, to some extent, even with the division into *centuries,* adopted by the celebrated *Mosheim,* and others.[2] For though we may attribute to each century a peculiar spirit, yet the epochs of history by no means coincide with the beginnings and ends of centuries. The apostolic period commences with the year 30; the age of Constantine, A. D. 311; that of Hildebrand, A. D. 1049; that of the Reformation, A. D. 1517. The divisions ought never to be arbitrarily made, upon a preconceived scheme; they should grow out of the history itself. But it is equally inconvenient to ar-

---

[2](Ed.) Johann Lorenz von Mosheim (1693–1755), German church historian, whose major work, *Institutiones historiae ecclesiasticae antiquae et recentioris* (Helmstedt, 1755) was twice translated into English: by Archibald Maclaine, *An Ecclesiastical History,* 2 vols. (London, 1675, and later editions); and by James Murdoch, *Institutes of Ecclesiastical History,* 3 vols. (New Haven, 1832, and later editions). Schaff was surprised to discover that this book "gained, in England and North America, an authority even greater than in Germany, being used to this day . . . as a textbook in most seminaries of theology" (*History of the Apostolic Church* [1853] 74).

range rigidly and exclusively by *subjects,* distributing the material under certain heads, as missions, doctrine, government, etc., and following out each single head, irrespective of the others, from the beginning to the present time. This would make history a number of independent, parallel lines. It would afford no view of the inward connection and mutual influence of the different departments, no complete general view of any one period.

In view of these disadvantages on either side, the best way will be so to combine the two methods, as to have the benefit of both. While we follow the course of time, we may make our division of it depend upon the character and succession of events, and pursue those things, which naturally belong together, to their relative goal, whether this goal coincide with the end of a year or century, or not. Thus, by dividing the entire history into periods, which correspond to the stages of the development itself, we meet the chronological demand, while, by arranging the material, within these periods, under particular sections or heads, as many as each period may need, we conform to the order of things.

2. The *internal* method of the historian is that of *genetic development,* i. e. the natural reproduction of the history itself, or the representation of it exactly as it has occurred. This method differs, on the one hand, from simple *narration,* which arranges facts and names in a mere outward juxtaposition, without rising to general views and a philosophical survey; and, on the other hand, from *a priori construction,* which adjusts the history to a preconceived scheme, and for the spirit of a past age substitutes that of the writer himself.[3] The historian must give himself up entirely to his object; in the first place, accurately and conscientiously investigating the facts; then identifying himself, in spirit, with the different men and times, which have produced the facts; and then so presenting the facts, instinct with their proper spirit and life, that the whole process of development shall be repeated before the eyes of the reader, and the actors stand

---

[3]Against such historians the couple of the poet holds good: "Was sie den Geist der Zeiten heissen, / Das ist der Herren *eigner* Geist." (Ed.) Goethe, *Faust,* I ("Night"): "And what the spirit of the time men call, / is merely their own spirit after all."

forth in living forms. History is neither all body, nor all soul, but an inseparable union of both; therefore both the body and the soul, the fact and the idea, in their mutual vital relation, must be recognized and brought into view. The older historians have done invaluable service in the accumulation of material, but their works generally lack the character of impartial criticism and living freedom. Historians of the modern school penetrate more to the marrow of history, discover the hidden springs of its life, and lay all open to our view. The two methods do not of necessity absolutely exclude each other, though they call for different kinds of talent; but each completes the other, and only by the intimate union of the two can the entire fulness of the history be presented.

Truth and fidelity are, therefore, the highest aim of the historian. As a fallible man, he can never, indeed, perfectly attain it; yet he is bound to keep it always before his eyes. He must divest himself of all prejudice, of all party interest, so as to present the truth, the whole truth, and nothing but the truth. Not, as some have unreasonably demanded, that he should lay aside his own mental agency, his character, nay, even his religion, and become a mere *tabula rasa* ["blank tablet"]. For, in the first place, this is an absolute impossibility. A man can know nothing, without the exercise of his own thought and judgment; and it is plain, that those very persons, who make the greatest boast of their philosophical freedom from all prepossession, as *Strauss,* for instance, in his notorious "Leben Jesu," are most under the domain of preconceived opinions and principles, with which they seek to master history, instead of sitting, as modest learners, at her feet. Then again, the very first condition of all right knowledge is a pre-existing sympathy with the object to be known. He who would know truth, must himself stand in the truth; only the philosopher can understand philosophy; only the poet, poetry; only the pious man, religion. So also the church historian, to do justice to his subject, must live and move in Christianity. And as Christianity is the centre of the world's life, and is truth itself, it throws the clearest light on all other history. Nor can it be said, that, according to the same rule, only a heathen can understand heathenism; only a Jew, Judaism, only a rationalist, rationalism. For it is from above that we survey what is below, and not the reverse. It is only by means of truth that we can comprehend error; whereas error understands not even itself. *Verum index sui et falsi.*[4] Paganism, as opposed to Christianity, it a false religion; and whatever of truth it may contain, such as its longing after redemption, is found complete in Christianity. The same is true of sects in their relation to the Biblical truth in the church. And as to Judaism, it is but a direct preparation for Christianity, which is its completion; and hence the Christian can obtain clearer views of Judaism than the Jew, just as the man is able to understand the child, while the child can have no proper apprehension of himself. Hence Augustine, with perfect propriety, says: *Novum Testamentum in Vetere latet, Vetus in Novo patet.*[5]

The object, then, after which the historian must always strive, though he may never, in this life, fully attain it, is truth itself, which can be found only in Christ. In him are hid all the treasures of wisdom and knowledge, and he is the soul of church history. This truth is, at the same time, inseparable from justice; it allows no partiality, no violation of the *suum cuique* ["to each his own"]. Such impartiality, however, as springs from a self-denying, tender sensibility to truth, and from a spirit of comprehensive love to the Lord, and to all his followers, of whatever name, time, or nation, is totaly different from that colorless neutrality and indifferentism, which treats all religions, churches, and sects with equal interest, or rather want of interest, and is, in reality, a hidden enmity to the truth and moral earnestness of Christianity.

General Character of the Three Ages of Church History

Our division can be justified, in detail, only by the history itself. It may be proper here, however, in some degree, to verify the main division into three ages by a preliminary survey of their general character.

1. The *Ancient* church, from her foundation to the close of the sixth century, has her local theatre in the countries immediately

---

[4](Ed.) "The truth is the touchstone of itself and of falsehood."

[5](Ed.) "The New Testament is concealed in the Old, the Old is revealed in the New." Augustine, *Quaestionum in Heptateuchum* 2.83.

around the Mediterranean Sea; viz., Western Asia (particularly Palestine and Asia Minor), Southern Europe (Greece, Italy, Southern Gaul), and Northern Africa (Egypt, Numidia, etc.) Thus was she planted in the very centre of the old world and its heathen culture. Emanating from the bosom of the Jewish nation, Christianity, even in the days of the apostles, incorporated itself into the Grecian and Roman nationality; and this national substratum reaches through the whole first age. Hence we have good reason to style this the age of the *Graeco-Roman,* or, which is here the same thing, the *Eastern and Western Universal* church. For the Grecian mind, at that time, ruled not only in Greece proper, but also in all the East, and in Egypt; nay, in such cities as Alexandria and Antioch it was, in its later character, even more active and vigorous, and therefore more important for church history, than in the mother country. Western Asia and Egypt, since the conquest of Alexander the Great, had lost their former character, and become Grecian in language and culture. Even the Jewish nationality, stiff as it was, could not withstand this foreign pressure; as the writings of Philo and Josephus abundantly prove. Hence the oldest Christian literature is predominantly Greek. So, on the other hand, the Roman mind held sway not only over Italy, but over the whole Western portion of the empire.

Christianity, at first, had to sustain a mighty conflict with Judaism and heathenism; and with the latter, too, in its most cultivated and powerful form. Hence, together with the history of the spread of the church, an important place belongs also to the history of its persecution, partly by the Roman sword, and partly by Grecian science and art. But in this conflict, the church, by her moral power in life and in death, on the one hand, and by her new view of the world on the other, comes off triumphant. She appropriates the classic language and culture, fills them with Christian contents, and produces the imposing literature of the fathers, which has had a fertilizing influence on all subsequent periods. The Eastern or Greek church, as the main channel of the development, occupies the foreground. In this age she gives birth to her greatest heroes, as Clement of Alexandria, Origen, Athanasius, Basil, Gregory of Nazianzen, and Gregory of Nyssa, Eusebius and Chrysostom. At this time she displays her highest power, and unfolds her fairest blossoms, especially in the field of theology proper. With great depth of speculation and dialectic skill, she establishes the fundamental doctrines of the divinity of Christ and the Holy Ghost, and of the Trinity; whence her complacency in the title of the *orthodox* church. The Latin church, also, enters the field, but moves more slowly and steadily, and exhibits a more practical spirit; bearing the impress of the old Roman national character, as distinct from the scientific and artistic turn of the Greek genius. For theology and general culture she, at first, depends altogether on the Greek church; but in government and religious life she pursues a path of her own. It is a remarkable fact, that the Romanized Punic nationality comes into view before the Roman proper. The North-African church, in the second period and part of the third, displays far more activity than the Italian. Through Tertullian she lays the foundation for a Latin theology. Through Cyprian she takes a prominent part in the development of the episcopal hierarchy. And finally, in St. Augustine, she furnishes the most pious, profound, and spirited of all the fathers; one who took the lead in the doctrinal controversies of his time; directed theological investigation in the most important practical questions, in anthropology, and the doctrines of sin and grace; and, by his writings, exerted the greatest influence upon the whole Middle Age, and even upon the Reformation of the sixteenth century.

The first age forms, in dogma, polity, and worship, the foundation for all subsequent centuries; the common ground, out of which the main branches of the church have since sprung. In this age, too, the church presents, even outwardly and visibly, an imposing unity, joined, at the same time, with great freedom and diversity; and she commands our admiration by her power to overcome, with the moral heroism of martyrdom and with the weapons of the Spirit and the truth, not only Judaism and Paganism without, but also the most dangerous errors and schisms within.

2. The church of the *Middle Ages,* though, in one view, the product and legitimate succession of the primitive church, is yet, both externally and internally, very different. In the first place, the territorial field changes. It moves west and north into the heart of Europe, to Italy, Spain, France, Britain, Germany, Scandinavia, Russia. The one universal church splits into two great halves. The Eastern

church, separated from the Western, gradually loses her vitality; a part of it stiffening into dead formalism; a part yielding to a new enemy from without, Mohammedanism, before which also the North-African church, after having first been conquered by the Arian Vandals at the death of Augustine (A.D. 430), is forced to give way. This loss in the East, however, is amply compensated by a gain in the West. The Latin church receives into her bosom an entirely new national element, barbarian, indeed, at first, but possessed of most valuable endowments and vast native force. The *Germanic* hordes, pouring from the north like a flood upon the rotten empire of Rome, ruthlessly destroyed her political institutions and literary treasures, but, at the same time, found upon the ruins a succession of new states full of energy and promise. The church rescues from the rubbish the Roman language and the remains of ancient culture, together with her own literature; from Rome as her centre she Christianizes and civilizes these rude tribes; and thus brings on the Middle Ages, in which the pope represents the supreme spiritual power; the German emperor, the highest temporal; and the church rules all social relations and popular movements of the West. This is, therefore, the age of *Romano-Germanic Catholicism*. Here we meet the colossal phenomena of the papacy, in league or conflict with the German imperial power; the monastic orders, the scholastic and mystic divinity, the Gothic architecture and other arts, vying with each other in adorning the worship of the church.

But in this activity the church gradually loses sight of her apostolical foundation, and becomes, like Judaism in the hands of the Pharisees, encumbered with all sorts of human additions and impurities, which made "the word of God of none effect" (Mark 7:13). The papacy becomes an intellectual and spiritual despotism; the school divinity degenerates into empty forms and useless subtleties; and the whole religious life assumes a legal, Pelagian character, in which outward good works are substituted for an inward living faith in the only Saviour. Against this oppression of the hierarchy with its human ordinances, the deeper life of the church, the spirit of evangelical freedom, reacts.

3. Thus, after due preparation, not only outside of the medieval Catholicism, but still more, in its very bosom, comes the *Reformation*

of the sixteenth century, which gives the stream of church history an entirely different direction, and opens a new age, in the progress of which we ourselves have our place. The *Modern* church has its birthplace in *Germany* and *Switzerland,* where the Reformation broke out in two simultaneous movements, and was inwardly matured. This gives it, in a national point of view, a predominantly Germanic character. It spreads, however, with rapid triumph, into the Scandinavian North, into France, the Netherlands, England, Scotland, and finally, by emigration, into North America. And this latter country, gradually rising into view from the beginning of the seventeenth century, filling up with both the good and the evil of the old world, particularly of Great Britain and Germany, and representing, in unbounded freedom and endless diversity, the various tendencies of Protestantism, together with the renovated life of Roman Catholicism, promises to become even the main theatre of the church history of the future.

As, in the second age, the Greek and Latin churches fell asunder, so, in the beginning of the third age, the Latin church itself divides into the Roman and the Protestant, the latter separating again into the Lutheran and Reformed branches. As, in the Middle Ages, the Roman Catholic church was the spring of all great movements, while the Greek church, which now, indeed, seems to have a new future before her in the vast empire of Russia, had stagnated at an earlier stage; so Protestantism is plainly the centre of life for modern history. The Roman church herself, though numerically the stronger branch, owes her activity mainly to the impulse she receives, directly or indirectly, from the Protestant. This third grand division of the history may, therefore, be fitly termed as to its leading characteristic, the age of the *Evangelical Protestant* church.

Character of the Three Ages (continued)

The most general mutual relation and difference of these three ages may be best described by means of the comprehensive philosophical distinction of *objectivity* and *subjectivity*.

The first age presents the immediate union of *objectivity* and *subjectivity*; that is, the two great moral principles, on which the individual human life, as well as all history, turns, the *authority* of the general and the *freedom* of the individual, appear tolerably balanced, but still only in their first stage, without any clear definition of their relative limits. In the primitive church we meet a highly productive activity and diversity of Christian life and Christian science, and a multitude of deformities, also, of dangerous heresies and divisions. But over all these individual and national tendencies, views, and characters, the mind of the universal church holds sway, separating the false element with infallible instinct, and, in ecumenical councils, settling doctrines and promulgating ecclesiastical laws, to which individual Christians and nations submit. The prevailing tendency of this early Christianity, however, in doctrine, government, worship, and practical piety, is essentially Catholic, and prepares the way for that system, which reached its full proportions in the Middle Ages.

Afterwards, these two principles of objectivity and subjectivity, the outward and the inward, the general and the individual, authority and freedom, appear, each in turn, in disproportionate prominence. And in the nature of the case, the principle of *objectivity* first prevails. In the Catholic church of the Middle Ages Christianity appears chiefly as law, as a pedagogical institution, a power from without, controlling the whole life of nations and individuals. Hence this may be termed the age of *Christian legalism,* of *church authority.* Personal freedom is here, to a great extent, lost in slavish subjection to fixed, traditional rules and forms. The individual subject is of account, only as the organ and medium of the general spirit of the church. All secular powers, the state, science, art, are under the guardianship of the hierarchy, and must everywhere serve its ends. This is emphatically the era of grand universal enterprises, of colossal works, whose completion required the co-operation of nations and centuries; the age of the supreme outward sovereignty of the visible church. Such a well ordered and imposing system of authority was necessary for the training of the Romanic and Germanic nations, to raise them from barbarism to the consciousness and rational use of freedom. Parental discipline must precede independence; children must first be governed, before they can govern themselves; the law is still, as in the days of Moses, a schoolmaster to bring men to Christ. This consciousness of independence awoke, even before the close of the Middle Ages. The more the dominion of Rome degenerated from a patriarchal government into a tyranny over conscience and all free thought, the more powerfully was the national and subjective spirit caused to shake off the ignominious yoke.

All this agitation of awakened freedom was at last concentrated in a decisive historical movement, and assumed a positive, religious character in the Reformation of the sixteenth century. Here begins the age of *subjectivity* and *individuality*;—a name which may be given it both in praise and in censure. It is the characteristic feature of Protestantism, and its great merit, that it views religion as a *personal* concern, which every man, as an individual, and for himself, has to settle with God, and with his own conscience. It breaks down the walls of partition between Christ and the believer, and teaches every one to go to the fountain of the divine word, without the medium of human traditions, and to converse, not through interceding saints and priests, but directly, with his Saviour, individually appropriating Christ's merit by a living faith, and rejoicing in his own personal salvation, while he ascribes all the glory of it to the divine mercy alone. Evangelical Protestantism, in its genuine form, moves throughout in the element of that freedom, into which Christ has brought us, and naturally calls forth vast individual activity in literary culture, social improvement, and practical piety. What Germany, Switzerland, Holland, England, Scotland and the United States have accomplished during the last three centuries in religion, literature, and politics, is all more or less connected with the memorable Reformation of the sixteenth century. We ourselves are all involved in its development. Our present Protestant theology and piety breathe in its atmosphere. The Puritanism of the seventeenth century, the Pietism and Methodism of the eighteenth, and most of the religious movements of our day are but continued vibrations of the Reformation; essentially the same Protestant principle of religious subjectivity, variously modified and applied.

But, on the other hand, what thus constitutes the strength of Protestantism, may be called also its weakness. Every right principle is liable to abuse. Every truth may be caricatured, and turned into dangerous error, by being carried to an extreme, and placed in a hostile attitude towards other truths equally important and necessary. Thus, together with its evangelical religious life, the Protestant movement includes also revolutionary and destructive elements, and dangerous tendencies to licentiousness and dissolution in church and state. True, the Reformers themselves aimed to free the Christian world only from the oppressive authority of human ordinances, and not by any means from the authority of God. On the contrary, they sought to make reason obedient to the word of God, and the natural will subject to his grace. They wanted no licentiousness, but a freedom pervaded by faith, and ruled by the Holy Scriptures. Nay, so many churchly and Catholic elements did they retain, that much of our present Protestantism must be considered an apostasy from the position of Luther, Melanchthon, and Calvin. But, as history, by reason of human sinfulness, which is always attended with error, proceeds only by opposites and extremes, the Protestant subjectivity gradually degenerated, to a fearful extent, into the corresponding extreme of division, arbitrary judgment, and contempt for every sort of authority. This has been the case especially since the middle of the last century, theoretically in *Rationalism*, practically in *Sectarianism*.

Rationalism has grown, indeed, into a learned and scientific system chiefly among the Germans, a predominantly theoretic and thinking people, and in the Lutheran church, which has been styled the church of theologians. But, in substance, it exists also in other European countries, and in North America, under various forms, as Arminianism, Deism, Unitarianism, Universalism, Indifferentism, and downright infidelity; and it infects, to some extent, the theology even of the orthodox denominations. It places private judgment, as is well known, not only above the pope and the church, but also above the Bible itself, receiving only so much of the word of God, as can be grasped by the natural understanding or reason (*ratio*, whence *rationalism*).

The system of sect and denomination has sprung more from the bosom of the Reformed church, the church of congregational life, and owes its form to the practical English character, which has a tendency to organize every new principle into a party, and to substitute sects for mere schools. In North America, under the banner of full religious freedom, it has reached its height; but, in its essence, it belongs properly to Protestant Christianity as a whole. All our Protestantism is sadly wanting in unity, at least in outward, visible unity, which is as necessary a fruit of inward unity, as works are of faith. The sects, indeed, do not commonly reject the Bible. On the contrary, they stiffly adhere to it, in their own way. But they rely on it in opposition to all history, and in the conceit, that they alone are in possession of its true sense. Thus their appealing to the Bible, after all, practically amounts, in the end, to rationalism; since, by the Bible, they always mean *their own sense* of it, and thus, in fact, follow merely their private judgment.

Finally the principle of false subjectivity reveals itself in the fact, that, since the Reformation, the various departments of the world's activity, science, art, politics, and social life, have gradually separated from the church, and pursue their own independent course. In this widespread rationalism, in this frittering of the church into innumerable party interests, and in her consequent weakness in relation to all the spheres of human life, and especially in relation to the state, we see the operation of a bad, diseased subjectivity, which forms just the opposite pole to the stiff, petrified, and burdensome objectivity of degenerate Catholicism.

But against these evils the deeper life of the church, which can never be extinguished, again reacts. In opposition to Rationalism there arises victoriously a new evangelical theology, which aims to satisfy the demands of science as well as of faith. And, on the other hand, against the sect system there comes up a more and more painful sense of its evils, which calls for a longing for church union. This practical want presses the question of the nature and form of the church prominently into the foreground. The deeper, though by no means the prevailing and popular tendency of the time is thus towards objectivity; not, indeed, towards that of the Middle Ages, or even of the Romanism of our day—for history can no more flow backwards, than a stream up hill,—but to an objectivity enriched with all the experience and diversified energies of the age of subjectivity, to a *higher union of Protestantism and Catholicism* in their pure forms, freed from their respective errors and infirmities. These yearnings of the present, when properly matured, will doubtless issue in a reformation far more glorious, than any the church has yet seen. And then will open a new age, in which human activity, in all its branches, shall freely come back into league with the church; science and art join to glorify the name of God; and all nations and dominions, according to the word of prophecy, be given to the saints of the Most High.

We may find a parallel to this development of the Christian church in the history of the Jewish theocracy, which is everywhere typical of the experience of Christ's people. The age of the Primitive church corresponds to the Patriarchal age, which already contained, in embryo, the two succeeding periods. Medieval Catholicism may be compared to the Mosaic period, when law and authority and the organization of the Jewish commonwealth were fully developed. And the Modern, or Evangelical Protestant church is not without resemblance to the age of the Old Testament prophets, in whom the evangelical element, the Messianic hope predominated, and who stood, to a certain extent, in a hostile attitude towards the unfaithful hierarchy, and towards the dead formalism and ceremonialism of the people. Law and prophecy, the two poles of the Old Testament religion, after having been separately developed, appeared, at last, united, and, as it were, incarnate, in the person of John the Baptist immediately before the first advent of Christ. Perhaps in this point also the analogy will hold; and then we might indulge the hope, that a union, or at least a friendly approach of the two greatest principles of church history, and of the pious portions of the two most hostile sections of Christendom, will precede the second coming of our Lord, and the perfection of his kingdom, when there shall be one fold and one shepherd. Such private speculations, however, must not be too much trusted, and by no means permitted to influence the representation of facts. Philosophy, instead of presuming to dictate the course of history, and to accomodate it to a preconceived theory, must be made to depend upon it, and must draw her wisdom from its teachings.

Uses of Church History

1. It is in the knowledge of her history, that the church has a sense of her own development; and this knowledge, therefore, has an *intrinsic* value. On this we must lay stress, in opposition to a contracted utilitarian view, in which church history is cultivated only for certain party interests, and thus degraded to a mere tool for tem-

porary purposes. The present is the result of the past, and cannot possibly be fully understood without a thorough knowledge of the past. The church cannot properly comprehend herself, without a clear view of her origin and growth. Her past deeds, sufferings, and fortunes belong to the substance of her life. They are constituent elements of her being, which requires the gradual course of time for its evolution. We wait no outward impulse to engage our interest in the history of the kingdom of God. Faith itself, in its nature prompts every one to this investigation, according to his inward calling and outward opportunity. Continually striving after a clearer apprehension of its object, it takes the deepest interest in the ways of God, the words and deeds of his servants, the innumerable witnesses of the past. If man, as man, according to the old saying: *homo sum, nihil humani a me alienum puto,* is prompted and bound to take an interest in everything properly human; the Christian also, as a Christian, should cultivate the liveliest sympathy with the deeds and fortunes of all his brethren in the faith, with whom he is joined in one body.[6] Theology, apprehended and cultivated in the right spirit, is in no deparment a mere theoretical matter, but divine worship. Church history, therefore, deserves to be studied for its own sake, as an essential part of that knowledge of the Triune God, which is life eternal (John 17:3).

From this high, intrinsic, and abiding worth of church history arise its practical utility and necessity for particular purposes and callings, especially for the teachers and leaders of the Christian community. This science, like all human knowledge and action, should be made subservient to the glory of God and the advancement of his kingdom.

2. Thus, the knowledge of church history is also one of the most powerful *helps to successful action in the service of the kingdom of God.* The present is not only the product of the past, but the fertile soil of the future, which he, who would cultivate, must understand. But the

---

[6](Ed.) "I am man: nothing human is alien to me." Terence, *Heauton Timoroumenos* 1.77, as quoted in Latin by Cicero, *De Officiis* 1.30. Schaff's paraphrase, *Christianus sum: Christiani nihil a me alienum puto* ("I am a Christian: nothing Christian is alien to me"), became the motto of each volume of the final edition of his *History of the Christian Church.*

present can be thoroughly understood only by an accurate acquaintance with the past. No one, for example, is prepared to govern a state *well,* and to advance its interests, who has not made himself familiar with its wants and its history. Ignorance can produce but a bungling work, which must soon again fall to pieces. History is, next to the word of God, the richest source of wisdom and experience. Her treasures are inexhaustible. Whence the emphemeral character of so many productions in church and in state? Their authors were ignorant and regardless of history. That tree only defies the storm, whose roots strike deep. And that work only can stand, which is built on the solid foundation of the past.

3. Again church history is the best and most complete *defence of Christianity,* and is, therefore, pre-eminently fitted to strengthen faith, and to minister abundant comfort and edification. It is a continuous commentary on the promise of our Lord: "Lo, I am with you always, even unto the end of the world" [Matt. 28:20]. The Saviour moves along, with the fullness of his grace, through all the centuries of Christianity, revealing himself in the most diverse personalities, and making them organs of his Spirit, his will, his truth, and his peace. The apostles and martyrs, the apologists and church fathers, the schoolmen and mystics, the reformers, and all those countless witnesses, whose names are indelibly traced on the pages of church history, form one choir, sending up an eternal anthem of praise to the Redeemer, and most emphatically declaring, that the gospel is no fable, no fancy, but power and life, peace and joy; in short, all that man can wish, of good or glory. Such examples, bearing the actual impress of the life of the Godman, and, as it were, embodying Christ, speak far more forcibly, than any intellectual demonstration or abstract theory.

So, also, church history furnishes the strongest evidence of the indestructibility of Christianity. To the words of the Lord: "On this rock I will build my church, and the gates of hell shall not prevail against it" [Matt. 16:18], every century responds Yea! and Amen! There is no power on or under the earth, which has not sworn hostility to the band of the redeemed, and has done its utmost to annihilate the infant community. But the church has vanquished them all. Stiff-necked and blinded Judaism laid its hand upon the Anointed of the Lord and his servants. But the Saviour has risen from the dead; his followers have beheld with adoration his wonderful judgments upon Jerusalem; the chosen people are scattered, without a shepherd, and without a sanctuary, through all nations and times, a perpetual living witness to the truth of the divine threatenings; and "this generation shall not pass away" till the Lord come again in his glory. Greece applied all her art and philosophy to confute the doctrine of the cross, and make it ridiculous in the eyes of the cultivated world. But her wisdom was turned into foolishness, or made a bridge to Christianity. Rome, proud mistress of the world, devised the most inhuman torments, to torture Christians to death, and root out their name from the earth. But tender virgins faced eternity more firmly than tried soldiers or Stoic philosophers; and after two centuries of the most bloody persecution, lo, the Roman emperor himself casts his crown at the feet of the despised Nazarene, and receives baptism in His name. The crescent of Islam thought to outshine the sun of Christianity, and moved, blood-red, along the horizon of the Eastern and African churches, passing over even into Spain and France. But the messengers of the Lord have driven back the false prophet, and his kingdom is now a mouldering corpse. Heresies and schisms of all sorts arose in the bosom of the church itself, even in its earliest history, and seemed, for a long time, to have displaced the pure doctrine of the gospel. But the truth has always broken for itself a new path, and forced the hosts of error to submission. The Middle Ages loaded the simple doctrine of salvation with so many human additions that it could scarcely be discerned, and was made almost "of none effect" (Mark 7:13). But the inward energy of the church powerfully worked its way through the superincumbent mass; placed the candle of the pure word again on its candlestick; and set conscience free from the fetters of the hierarchy. Deists, materialists, and atheists, in the seventeenth and eighteenth centuries, poured contempt upon the Bible; nay, the heroes of the French Revolution, in their mad fanaticism, even set aside the God of Christians, and, in the midst of scenes of the most frightful cruelty, placed the goddess of Reason on the throne of the world. But they soon had to undo their own folly. The Lord in heaven laughed, and had them in derision. Napoleon, the greatest potentate and captain of modern times, proposed to substitute for the universal dominion of Christianity, the universal dominion of his own sword, and to degrade the church into an instrument for his own political ends. But the Lord of the church hurled him from his throne; and the giant, who had thrown all Europe out of joint, must die of a broken heart, a prisoner on a lonely rock of the ocean. In the bosom of Protestantism had arisen, within the last and present century, a Rationalism, which, wielding all the powers of learning and philosophy, had gradually advanced to the denial of a personal God, and of immortality, and has turned the history of the Saviour into a book of myths. But it has been promptly met by a believing theology, which has triumphantly driven its objections from the field; while division has broken out in the camp of the enemy itself, and one system of unbelief is found actively refuting another. Indifferentism and spiritual death have spread, in the train of Rationalism, over whole sections of the church. But the Christian life already celebrates its own resurrection. Banished from one land, it flourishes with fresh vigor in another, and pushes its activity even to the uttermost parts of the heathen world. The mightiest empires, the most perfect systems of human wisdom, have perished; while the simple faith of the Galilean fisherman shows itself to-day as powerful as ever; regenerating the most hardened sinners; imparting strength to do good, joy in affliction, and triumph in death. The Lord of hosts has ever been a wall round about his Zion. The gates of hell, through eighteen centuries, have not prevailed against the church; as little will they prevail against her in time to come. To have weathered so many storms, coming forth only purer and stronger from them all, she must, indeed, be made of indestructible material. Church history, studied with a truth-loving spirit, places this beyond a doubt. It is, therefore, next to the word of God, the richest and most edifying book of devotion, forbidding despair, even when thick darkness rests upon the present, and the walls of Zion are beset with foes.

4. Finally, church history, in proportion as it strengthens our faith in the divine origin and indestructible nature of Christianity, must also exert a wholesome *moral influence* on our character and conduct, and thus prove a help to *practical piety*. It is morality in the form of facts; divine philosophy taught by examples; a preaching of Christ

and his gospel from the annals of his kingdom. Its shining examples of godly men powerfully challenge our imitation; that we, like them, may consecrate our thought and life to the honor of the Lord and the welfare of man, and may leave a lasting, hallowed influence behind us, when we die. The study of history is especially fitted to free our minds from all prejudice, narrowness, party and sectarian feeling, and to fill us with a truly catholic spirit; with that love, which joyfully accords due praise to the most diverse forms of the Christian life, adores the wonderful wisdom of the heavenly gardener in the variegated splendor of the garden of the Lord, and feels itself vitally united with the pious of all ages and nations; with that love, which must be poured out copiously upon the church, before her present mournful divisions can be healed, the precious promise of one fold and one shepherd be accomplished, and the prayer of our great High Priest be fulfilled: "That they all may be one; as thou, Father, art in me, and I in thee, that they also may be one in us; that the world may believe that thou hast sent me" [John 17:21].

Here, of course, all depends on the spirit, in which church history is studied. Like every other science, and like the Bible itself, it may be, and often has been, scandalously perverted to the service of bad ends. This will sufficiently appear from the history of our science, to which we shall devote the last chapter of the General Introduction.[7]

---

[7]On the subject of this section, compare the third division of our tract: *What is Church History?*, 144ff.

CHAPTER 4

Religion in America

EDITORIAL INTRODUCTION

When Schaff later stated that German church historians, "with all their extensive and varied knowledge, have but a very superficial acquaintance with the religious world of the English tongue . . . and cannot duly appreciate its vast present and future importance for the kingdom of God"; when he reproached German scholars for being "much better at home with the most remote sources of Greek and Roman antiquity than with modern English—to say nothing of American— literature"; and when he later warned his German readers "against the ridiculous caricatures of American Christianity which abound in European works"—then, we may safely assume, he was also describing the scope and limitations of his own knowledge of the political, social and religious life of the United States at the time of his departure for the new world.[1] Less than ten years later, when he returned to Germany and lectured in Berlin and at the *Kirchentag* in Frankfurt on the land he had adopted as his own, he gave ample proof of how much he had learned in the meantime. Indeed, he had been as ardent and perceptive a student of the strange new world of American society, politics and religion as he had been in those earlier ten years of the exciting new world of Ger-

---

[1] Schaff, *History of the Apostolic Church,* 124; "Impressions of England," *The Mercersburg Review* 9 (April 1858): 329; *America,* ed. P. Miller, 104n.

man scholarship. These lectures, which were published in Germany in 1854 and already the following year in an English translation in the United States under the title *America: A Sketch of its Political, Social, and Religious Character,* offered a remarkably perceptive and well-informed discussion of the various forces, but especially the religious forces, that were shaping the character of the new American civilization.

There is no doubt that even today a perusal of Schaff's *America* is highly rewarding. As Perry Miller put it succinctly, the book is "an astute reading of the American destiny" and "a document of primary importance" for anyone interested in "the history of that mysterious process called 'Americanization'."[2] Schaff's *America* deserves, therefore, to be ranked alongside of the other outstanding interpretations of America which European immigrants and visitors had published just a few years earlier: Alexis de Tocqueville, *Democracy in America* (1835–40), Francis Grund, *The Americans in Their Moral, Social, and Political Relations* (1837), and Harriet Martineau, *Society in America* (1837). Even more inviting, however, is a comparison with Robert Baird's *Religion in America* (1843), of which an edited German translation, with an introduction by August Neander, appeared in Berlin in 1845 (the year after Schaff's departure for the United States). Originally written for Europeans, the final edition, now revised for American readers, was published in 1856. The differences between Schaff's and Baird's accounts reflected mostly the different backgrounds of their authors: the Puritan-Pietist orientation of the American Baird and the new theology and philosophy of history of the German-trained Schaff. Nevertheless, they had in common many themes and together were to provide the interpretative categories for the next century for all those who tried to see the religious life of America whole. It is true, however, that the "use of data and interpretational themes is more comprehensive" in Baird's work than in Schaff's.[3] Since Schaff rarely ever referred to Baird's book in his published writings, it will be

---

[2]Ibid., xxvii.

[3]Robert Baird, *Religion in America.* ed. Henry W. Bowden (New York, 1970) xiii. See also the perceptive comments on Baird and Schaff in Brauer, "Changing Perspectives on Religion in America," in *Reinterpretation in American Church History,* ed. Jerald C. Brauer (Chicago, 1968) 2-4.

difficult to decide how much he had learned from it and when it had first come to his attention. Later Schaff was to succeed Baird as the official interpreter of American Christianity in the international meetings of the Evangelical Alliance. His report, "Christianity in America," was read in his absence at the Berlin meeting of the Evangelical Alliance in 1857. At the Basel meeting in 1879 he again presented a paper, "Christianity in the United States of America." These papers were continuing attempts, together with his German lectures of 1865 on the Civil War, to keep European Christians informed of the progress and prospects of Christianity in the United States.[4] Even though these publications show that his views on religion in America evolved in some respects in response to new developments, it nevertheless remains true that Schaff had already set down firmly and lastingly all the basic themes of his understanding of the unique character of American Christianity and of America's unique role in the progress of the kingdom of God in *America*.

In 1854, Schaff's German audience, it appears, was mostly interested in America's oldest and then newest products, the primeval forest (that is, the "western frontier") and the Mormon church.[5] But Schaff gave his audience, and he gives today's readers, immeasurably more. The story of this new nation, then barely fifty years old, was so exciting to him because he could tell it as a confirmation of his bold assertion that the United States is "emphatically a land of the future" and that it "has already turned over a new leaf in the history of the world and of the church and will assuredly write it full of great deeds."[6] He singled out for special consideration the dominant influence of evangelical Protestantism, the separation of church and state, the so-called voluntary system in religion, the denominational diversity and— because of and not despite these new and unique arrangements—the creation of a Christian nation. He was by no means blind to several serious flaws in the social fabric of the American republic, such as slavery, ma-

---

[4]One should also mention Schaff's article "Nordamerika," *Real-Encyclopädie für protestantische Theologie und Kirche*, 2nd ed., vol. 10 (1882) 631-42.

[5]Schaff, *America*, ed. P. Miller, 198.

[6]Ibid., 16-17.

terialism, religious sectarianism and political radicalism. But he never doubted that because of the cultural, ethnic and religious pluralism of this new democracy, the great challenge and true destiny of the American republic lie in unifying all the one-sided opposites of the political, social and religious life of the human race. On this vast continent all the cultural, ethnic and ecclesiastical traditions inherited from Europe's past have been thrown together seemingly in the same kind of primeval chaos that preceded God's original creation. Hence it was precisely the ecclesiastical and religious ferment of American Christianity out of which would gradually arise "something wholly new," "a beautiful creation," a "church cosmos." I should add that expectations of this kind (and not just the steady, guiding light of the theory of historical development) helped to prevent Schaff from sharing Nevin's "dizziness."[7] What Roman Catholicism was for some of those Protestants who were caught up in the romantic currents of these years, namely, the alluring "safe retreat of totality," the one true "mediation" of all the opposite or diverse forces of modern culture and religion—that America had become for Schaff.[8] This young immigrant scholar had soon come to realize that neither will anyone of the existing churches ever become dominant in the United States nor will sectarian anarchy prevail. Instead, the grand synthesis of an "evangelical catholicism," as the ripe fruit of a new reformation, will find its providential locale in the United States. These ecumenical views prompted Perry Miller to claim that Schaff's *America* "is in many respects a more profound, a more accurate work than Tocqueville's overrated one."[9] One needs to add, however, that Schaff never offered a specific, detailed blueprint of the concrete ecclesiastical arrangement that would embody the "evangelical catholicism" he so fervently hoped and worked for.

One particular aspect of American society and religion surprised and deeply impressed Schaff and his German audiences. Schaff

---

[7]See p. 78, above.

[8]Oskar Walzel, *German Romanticism*, trans. Alma Elise Lussky (New York, 1932) 98.

[9]Perry Miller, "From the Covenant to the Revival," *The Shaping of American Religion*, vol. 1 of *Religion in American Life*, ed. J. W. Smith and A. L. Jamison (Princeton NJ, 1961) 367.

had discovered that those revolutionary and unique features in the American situation that seemed to most Europeans to threaten social and religious chaos—freedom of religion, separation of church and state, religious voluntaryism, denominational diversity—had in fact had the opposite effect of assuring political and social stability and even the still growing strength and missionary outreach of the forces and institutions of evangelical and orthodox Protestantism. Those liberal, even radical arrangements that Europeans feared most in the American experiment with democracy had actually turned out to be precisely the most effective means for insuring the achievement of conservative ends, namely, a Christian nation (even if it was not a Christian state, which was the end sought by the Prussian High-Orthodoxy). Only a paradoxical statement can, therefore, do justice to the American situation: Americans, Schaff claimed, are "at once liberal and conservative."[10] As Perry Miller perceptively remarked, Schaff's interpretation of the role of religion in America testifies "to the varying connotations of such smashing words as 'liberal' and 'conservative'" and thus can help to illuminate even today "the problems of the dialogue between Europe and America."[11] Schaff had found "freedom" and "order" to be intimately conjoined in the political, social and religious life of this new nation. And it was precisely this combination that powerfully appealed to the liberal and conservative instincts of his own personality as well as to the republicanism of his native Switzerland and the political conservatism of the Berlin circles in which he had formerly moved. A curious retention of the theocratic ideology of the Prussian High-Orthodoxy, however, should be noted. He disavowed the notion that separation of church and state, though historically fully justified in the American situation and certainly preferable to the European state churches, was the final goal of history. Instead, that goal is a theocracy. For in the end Christ and his church, he firmly believed, will triumph over the state and all the other spheres of human culture.

A perceptive reader of Schaff's *America* will also note how quickly and nearly completely this recent immigrant had been "Americanized." Today we might point out especially Schaff's easy embrace

---

[10]Schaff, *America*, ed. P. Miller, 47.

[11]Ibid., xxvii.

of the Eurocentric racism and millenial messianism so deeply in-
grained in nineteenth-century American society and religion. The
Anglo-Saxon and the German, he would always believe, formed the
basis of the American national character; together they were destined to execute the designs of divine providence for the further
progress of Christ's church and the human race. Elsewhere Schaff
acknowledged that "Even the tribes of Africa and Asia are largely
represented amongst us and call our country their home" (one notes
the possesive pronoun!). He did not want to speculate what was to
be "the ultimate fate of the red man, the negro and the Chinese,
who are separated from us by insurmountable differences of race."
The evidence was already conclusive, however, that "all the civilized nations of Europe, especially those of Germanic origin, have
contributed and will contribute to our stock."[12] Furthermore, for
him, too, the new republic was the "redeemer nation," and he soon
echoed loudly the millenialism so characteristic of American Protestantism—for instance, Jonathan Edwards' belief that "the Lat-
ter-Day Glory is probably to begin in America."[13] He shared, and
in his writings reinforced, what Arthur Schlesinger, Jr. has called
the "delusion of a sacred mission and a sanctified destiny" for the
United States, which is rooted in the belief, as indeed it was for
Schaff too, that the kingdom of God is "both imminent in time
and immanent in America."[14] The all too obvious flaws in the national character, Schaff was sure, were but the growing pains of a
youthful giant sowing his wild oats. When in the Civil War the
nation experienced a veritable "baptism of blood" and a subsequent regeneration, it then entered, according to Schaff, "upon the

---

[12]Schaff, *American Nationality* (Chambersburg PA, 1856) 8.

[13]See Ernest Lee Tuveson, *Redeemer Nation: The Idea of America's Millenial Role*
(Chicago, 1968), and Jonathan Edwards, *Some Thoughts Concerning the Revival in
New England,* pt. 2, §2 (section heading in some editions).

[14]Arthur Schlesinger, Jr., "America: Experiment or Destiny?," *American Historical Review* 82 (June 1977): 516-17. In the discussion following Schaff's address
at the Frankfurt *Kirchentag,* a Professor Stern somberly remarked that he could find
no biblical warrant for the speaker's millenial hope for the church in America
(*Amerika,* 2nd ed., 318).

age of manly vigor and independence," with even brighter prospects for its future.[15]

Finally, one should note the progress that *America* represented over against *The Principle of Protestantism* in Schaff's discussion of the denominational diversity and shape of American Christianity. In his first American publication it was that section, deriding the sectarian character of American Christianity, that Charles Hodge had found to be "more marred by false principles and false views of facts and of their historical relations, than any other in the book."[16] Schaff had in fact merely mirrored Israel Daniel Rupp's compilation of denominational histories published in 1844, *He Pasa Ecclesia: An Original History of the Religious Denominations at Present Existing in the United States,* writing with palpable indignation that this book "gives an account of not less than forty-one Protestant sects, but is notwithstanding by no means complete."[17] Ten years later he no longer reflected what he had earlier taken to be the sad spectacle of sectarian anarchy but insisted, like Robert Baird's *Religion in America,* on the unity underlying the denominational diversity of America's evangelical Protestantism. Furthermore, as already noted, from his narrow European perspective Schaff had initially acknowledged as historically legitimate churches only the Roman Catholic church and the two great churches of the sixteenth-century Reformation, Lutheran and Reformed (Anglicanism he viewed as a Reformed variant, and of the "sects" he occasionally classified Methodism as belonging to "orthodox" Protestantism). In *America,* he rejected the European "church-sect" distinction, and he now recognized as legitimate Christian bodies all the major denominations, from Congregationalists to Quakers, of what he called the "orthodox and evangelical Protestantism" of the United States.[18] In Part II he dis-

---

[15]*Der Bürgerkrieg und das christliche Leben in Nord Amerika* (Berlin, 1866) 25 and 16 (cf. "Dr. Schaff's Lectures on America Delivered in Europe, 1865," *The Christian Intelligencer* 37 [1866] 10:1 and 9:3).

[16]Charles Hodge, "Schaff's Protestantism," *Princeton Review* 17 (October 1845): 630.

[17]Schaff, *Das Princip des Protestantismus,* 95n.1 (cf. *The Principle of Protestantism* [repr. 1964] 149n.)

[18]Schaff, *America,* ed. P. Miller, 105.

cussed with sympathy and understanding each of these denominations as well as the Roman Catholic church, even though he retained the heading "Churches and Sects," but he judged only the Mormons to be a "sect," and un-American to boot.

Schaff's two Berlin lectures—"Importance, Political System, National Character, Culture, and Religion of the United States" and "The Churches and Sects"—were first published in Germany in *Deutsche Zeitschrift für christliche Wissenschaft und christliches Leben* (1854) and in the United States in *Der deutsche Kirchenfreund* (1854), though the second lecture there only in an abridged version. In the original German text of *Amerika* (1854) Schaff added a separate section, more than 100 pages long, on the German-American churches, which he had written while vacationing among his beloved Swiss mountains. This section is especially noteworthy because it offered an extended discussion of the Mercersburg movement and Schaff's most balanced, public appraisal of his colleague Nevin's work and current travail of mind and heart.[19] In the English translation this third section was reduced to twenty-four pages and again made a part of the second lecture, though Schaff now added the address "Germany and America," which he had delivered at the Frankfurt *Kirchentag*. The second German edition of 1858 included this address as well, and also the report Schaff prepared for the Berlin conference of the Evangelical Alliance in 1857.[20] The selections here included are especially relevant for understanding Schaff's interpretation of the American religious scene and his grand vision of religion's role in shaping the American destiny. The selections are taken from both Berlin lectures and the address at the Frankfurt *Kirchentag* as printed in the original American edition.*

---

[19]Schaff, *Amerika*, 2nd ed., 242-59. A "free translation" (actually an abridged version) of this section can be found in Theodore Appel, *The Life and Work of John Williamson Nevin* (Philadelphia, 1889) 411-17.

[20]English translation, "Christianity in America," *The Mercersburg Review* 9 (October 1857): 493-539.

*America: A Sketch of the Political, Social, and Religious Character of the United States of America, trans. Edward D. Yeomans (New York, 1855) 86-98; 101-103, 115-25; 256-64, 266-67.

RELIGION AND THE CHURCH

I come now to the point most important in my own view, and, doubtless, most interesting to this assembly. But want of time obliges me to confine myself to some general remarks, which may, at least, help to pilot you through the mazes of American church history.

It is a vast advantage to that country itself, and one may say to the whole world, that the United States were first settled in great part from religious motives; that the first emigrants left the homes of their fathers for faith and conscience' sake, and thus at the outset stamped upon their new home the impress of positive Christianity, which now exerts a wholesome influence even on those later emigrants, who have no religion at all.

The ecclesiastical character of America, however, is certainly very different from that of the Old World. Two points in particular require notice.

The first is this. While in Europe ecclesiastical institutions appear in historical connection with Catholicism, and even in evangelical countries, most of the city and village churches, the universities, and religious foundations, point to a mediaeval origin; in North America, on the contrary, every thing had a Protestant beginning, and the Catholic Church has come in afterwards as one sect among the others, and has always remained subordinate. In Europe, Protestantism has, so to speak, fallen heir to Catholicism; in America, Catholicism under the wing of Protestant toleration and freedom of conscience, has found an adopted home, and is everywhere surrounded by purely Protestant institutions. True, the colony of Maryland, planted by the Catholic Lord Baltimore, was one of the earliest settlements of North America. But, in the first place, even this was by no means specifically Roman. It was founded expressly on the thoroughly anti-Roman, and essentially Protestant, principles of religious toleration. And then, again, it never had any specific influence on the character of the country; for even the prominent position of the city of Baltimore, as the American metropolis of the Roman Church, is of much later date. Far more important and influential were the settlements of the Puritans in New England, the Episcopalians in Virginia, the Quakers in Pennsylvania, the Dutch in New

York, in the course of the seventeenth century, the Presbyterians from
Scotland and North Ireland, and the German Lutherans and Reformed from the Palatinate, in the first half of the eighteenth. These
have given the country its spirit and character. Its past course and
present condition are unquestionably due mainly to the influence of
Protestant principles. The Roman church has attained social and political importance in the eastern and western States only within the
last twenty years, chiefly in consequence of the vast Irish emigration;
but it will never be able to control the doctrines of the New World,
though it should increase a hundred fold.

Another peculiarity in the ecclesiastical condition of North
America, connected with the Protestant origin and character of the
country, is the separation of church and state. The infidel reproach,
that had it not been for the power of the state, Christianity would
have long ago died out; and the argument of Roman controversial-
ists, that Protestantism could not stand without the support of princes
and civil governments, both are practically refuted and utterly annihilated in the United States. The president and governors, the congress at Washington, and the state legislatures, have as such nothing
to do with the church, and are by the Constitution expressly forbidden to interfere in its affairs. State officers have no other rights in the
church than their personal rights as members of particular denominations. The church, indeed, everywhere enjoys the protection of the
laws for its property, and the exercise of its functions; but it manages
its own affairs independently, and has also to depend for its resources
entirely on voluntary contributions. As the state commits itself to no
particular form of Christianity, there is of course also no civil req-
uisition of baptism, confirmation, and communion. Religion is left
to the free will of each individual, and the church has none but moral
means of influencing the world.

This separation was by no means a sudden, abrupt event, occasioned, say, by the Revolution. The first settlers, indeed, had certainly no idea of such a thing; they proceeded rather on Old Testament
theocratic principles, like Calvin, John Knox, the Scottish Presbyterians, and the English Puritans of the seventeenth century; regarding state and church as the two arms of one and the same divine will.
In the colony of Massachusetts, the Puritans, in fact, founded a rigid

Calvinistic state-church system. They made the civil franchise depend on membership in the church; and punished not only blasphemy and open infidelity, but even every departure from the publicly acknowledged code of Christian faith and practice as a political offense. In Boston, in the seventeenth century, even the Quakers, who certainly acted there in a very fanatical and grossly indecent way, were formally persecuted, publicly scourged, imprisoned, and banished; and, in Salem, of the same State, witches were burnt as accomplices of the devil. The last traces of this state-church system in New England were not obliterated till long after the American Revolution, and even to this day most of the States have laws for the observance of the Sabbath, monogamy, and other specifically Christian institutions. Thus the separation of the temporal and spiritual powers is by no means absolute. While New England had Congregationalism for its established religion, New York also had at first the Dutch Reformed, and afterwards the English Episcopal church, and Virginia, and some other Southern States, also the English Episcopal, for their establishments. With these the other forms of Christianity were tolerated either not at all, or under serious restrictions, as formerly the Dissenters were in England.

But on the other hand, there prevailed in other North American colonies from their foundation, therefore long before the Revolution of 1776, entire freedom of faith and conscience; as in Rhode Island, founded by the Baptist, Roger Williams, who was banished from Massachusetts for heresy, and thus set by bitter experience against religious intolerance; in Pennsylvania, which the Quaker, William Penn, originally designed as an asylum for his brethren in faith, but to which he soon invited also German Reformed and Lutherans from the Palatinate, guaranteeing equal rights to all, and leaving each to the guidance of the "inward light"; and, finally, in Maryland, founded by Lord Baltimore on the same basis of universal religious toleration.

After the American Revolution this posture of the State gradually became general. First, the legislature of Virginia, after the colony had separated from the mother-country, annulled the rights and privileges of the Episcopal establishment, and placed all the dissenting bodies on a perfectly equal footing with it in the eye of the law.[1] Her example was followed by the other colonies, which had established churches. When Congress was organized at the close of the war, an article was placed in the Constitution, forbidding the enactment of laws about religion;[2] and similar prohibitions are found in the constitutions of the several States.

We would by no means vindicate this separation of church and state as the perfect and final relation between the two. The kingdom of Christ is to penetrate and transform like leaven all the relations of individual and national life. We much prefer this separation, however, to the territorial system and a police guardianship of the church, the Bride of the God-man, the free-born daughter of heaven; and we regard it as adapted to the present wants of America, and favorable to her religious interests. For it is by no means to be thought, that the separation of church and state there is a renunciation of Christianity by the nation; like the separation of the state and the school from the church, and the civil equality of Atheism with Christianity, which some members of the abortive Frankfurt Parliament were for introducing into Germany.[3] It is not an annihilation of one factor, but only an amicable separation of the two in their spheres of outward operation; and thus equally the church's declaration of independence towards the state, and an emancipation of the state from bondage to a particular confession. The nation, therefore, is still Christian, though it refuses to be governed in this deepest concern of the mind and heart by the temporal power. In fact, under such circumstances, Christianity, as the free expression of personal conviction and of the national character, has even greater power over the

---

[1] The result is owing to the combined influence of the oppressed dissenters, the liberal amongst the Episcopalians, and the infidels of the school of Jefferson, who was then almighty in the political circles of Virginia.

[2] "Congress shall make no law respecting an establishment of religion, or prohibiting the free exercise thereof."

[3] (Ed.) The National Assembly at Frankfurt, which was convened in 1848 in response to the revolutionary uprisings of that same year, attempted the unification of Germany and the introduction of a liberal national constitution. In the end both attempts failed.

mind, than when enjoined by civil laws and upheld by police regulations.

This appears practically in the strict observance of the Sabbath, the countless churches and religious schools, the zealous support of Bible and Tract societies, of domestic and foreign missions, the numerous revivals, the general attendance on divine worship, and the custom of family devotion—all expressions of the general Christian character of the people, in which the Americans are already in advance of most of the old Christian nations of Europe.

In fact, even the state, as such, to some extent officially recognizes Christianity. Congress appoints chaplains (mostly from the Episcopal, sometimes from the Presbyterian and the Methodist clergy) for itself, the army, and the navy. It opens every day's session with prayer, and holds public worship on the Sabbath in the Senate Chamber at Washington. The laws of the several states also contain strict prohibitions of blasphemy, atheism, Sabbath-breaking, polygamy, and other gross violations of general Christian morality.

Thus the separation is not fully carried out in practice, on account of the influence of Christianity on the popular mind. It is even quite possible that the two powers may still come into collision. The tolerance of the Americans has its limits and counterpoise in that religious fanaticism, to which they are much inclined. This may be seen in the expulsion of the Mormons, who so grossly offended the religious and moral sense of the people. Great political difficulties may arise, especially from the growth of the Roman church, which has been latterly aiming everywhere at political influence, and thus rousing the jealousy and opposition of the great Protestant majority. The Puritanic Americans see in Catholicism an ecclesiastical despotism, from which they fear also political despotism, so that its sway in the United States must be the death of Republican freedom. Thus the Catholic question has already come to be regarded by many as at the same time a political question, involving the existence of the Republic; and a religious war between Catholics and Protestants, though in the highest degree improbable, is still by no means an absolute impossibility; as, in fact, slight skirmishes have already occurred in the street fight between the two parties in Philadelphia in 1844, and the violent demolition of a Roman convent at Charlestown, Mass.

The secret political party of the "Know-Nothings," which is just sweeping over the States with the rapidity of the whirlwind, but which, for this very reason, cannot last long in this particular form, is mainly directed against the influence of Romanism.

If, however, the great question of the relation of church and state be not by any means fully solved even in the United States, still the two powers are there at all events much more distant than in any other country.

The natural result of this arrangement is a general prevalence of freedom of conscience and religious faith, and of the voluntary principle, as it is called: that is, the promotion of every religious work by the free-will offerings of the people. The state, except in the few cases mentioned above, does nothing towards building churches, supporting ministers, founding theological seminaries, or aiding indigent students in preparation for the ministry. No taxes are laid for these objects; no one is compelled to contribute a farthing to them. What is done for them is far, indeed, from being always done from the purest motives—love to God and to religion—often from a certain sense of honor, and for all sorts of selfish by-ends; yet always from free impulses, without any outward coercion.

This duly considered, it is truly wonderful, what a multitude of churches, ministers, colleges, theological seminaries, and benevolent institutions are there founded and maintained entirely by free-will offerings. In Berlin there are hardly forty churches for a population of four hundred and fifty thousand, of whom, in spite of all the union of church and state, only some thirty thousand attend public worship. In New York, to a population of six hundred thousand, there are over two hundred and fifty well-attended churches, some of them quite costly and splendid, especially on Broadway and Fifth Avenue.[4] In the city of Brooklyn, across the East River, the number of churches is still larger in proportion to the population, and in the

---

[4]In 1854 there were in New York city forty-eight Episcopal churches, forty-eight Presbyterian, thirty-five Methodist, nineteen Reformed Dutch, twenty-nine Baptist, eight Congregational, five Lutheran, and twenty-four Roman Catholic; besides the church edifices of several smaller denominations and sects, which must swell the number to nearly 300.

country towns and villages, especially in New England, the houses of worship average one to every thousand, or frequently even five hundred, souls. If these are not Gothic cathedrals, they are yet mostly decent, comfortable buildings, answering all the purposes of the congregation often even far better than the most imposing works of architecture. In every new city district, in every new settlement, one of the first things thought of is the building of a temple to the Lord, where the neighboring population may be regularly fed with the bread of life and encouraged to labor, order, obedience, and every good work. Suppose the state, in Germany, should suddenly withdraw its support from church and university, how many preachers and professors would be breadless, and how many auditories closed!

The voluntary system unquestionably has its great blemishes. It is connected with all sorts of petty drudgery, vexations, and troubles, unknown in well endowed Established Churches. Ministers and teachers, especially among the recent German emigrants in America, who have been accustomed to State provision for religion and education, have very much to suffer from the free system. They very often have to make begging tours for the erection of a church, and submit to innumerable other inconveniences for the good cause, till a congregation is brought into a proper course, and its members become practised in free giving.

But, on the other hand, the voluntary system calls forth a mass of individual activity and interest among the laity in ecclesaiastical affairs, in the founding of new churches and congregations, colleges and seminaries, in home and foreign missions, and in the promotion of all forms of Christian philanthropy. We may here apply in a good sense our Lord's word: "Where the treasure is, there the heart will be also" [Matt. 6:19]. The man, who, without coercion, brings his regular offering for the maintenance of the church and the minister, has commonly much more interest in both, and in their prosperity he sees with pleasure the fruit of his own labor. The same is true of seminaries. All the congregations and synods are interested in the theological teacher, whom they support, and who trains ministers of the Word for them, while in Europe the people give themselves little or no trouble about theological faculties.

It is commonly thought that this state of things necessarily involves an unworthy dependence of the minister on his congregation. But this is not usually the case. The Americans expect a minister to do his duty, and they most esteem that one who fearlessly and impartially declares the whole counsel of God, and presents the depravity of man and the threatenings of the Divine Word as faithfully as he does the comforting promises. Cases of ministers employed for a certain time, as hired servants, occur indeed occasionally in independent German rationalistic congregations, and perhaps among the Universalists, but not in a regular synod. A pious congregation well knows that by such a degradation of the holy office, which preaches reconciliation, and binds and looses in the name of Christ, it would degrade itself; and a minister, in any respectable church connection, would not be allowed to accept a call on such terms, even were he willing.

Favored by the general freedom of faith, all Christian denominations and sects, except the Oriental, have settled in the United States, on equal footing in the eye of the law; here attracting each other, there repelling; rivalling in both the good and the bad sense; and mutually contending through innumerable religious publications. They thus present a motley sampler of all church history, and the results it has thus far attained. A detailed description of these at present is forbidden, both by want of time and by the proportion of the discourse. Suffice it to say, in general, that the whole present distracted condition of the church in America, pleasing and promising as it may be, in one view, must yet be regarded on the whole as unsatisfactory, and as only a state of transition to something higher and better.

America seems destined to be the Phenix [sic] grave not only of all European nationalities, as we have said above, but also of all European churches and sects, of Protestantism and Romanism. I cannot think, that any one of the present confessions and sects, the Roman, or the Episcopal, or the Congregational, or the Presbyterian, or the Lutheran, or the German or Dutch Reformed, or the Methodist, or the Baptist communion, will ever become exclusively dominant there; but rather that out of the mutual conflict of all something wholly new will gradually arise.

At all events, whatever may become of the American denominations and sects of the present day, the kingdom of Jesus Christ must at last triumph in the New World, as elsewhere, over all foes, old and new. Of this we have the pledge in the mass of individual Christianity in America; but above all, in the promise of the Lord, who is with his people always to the end of the world, and who has founded his church upon a rock, against which the gates of hell shall never prevail. And his words are yea and amen.

With this prospect we finish this outline miniature of life in the United States. You see from it, that all the powers of Europe, good and bad, are there fermenting together under new and peculiar conditions. All is yet in a chaotic transition state; but organizing energies are already present, and the spirit of God broods over them, to speak in time the almighty word: "Let there be light!" and to call forth from the chaos a beautiful creation.

Perhaps in the view of many of my respected hearers, I have drawn too favorable a picture. But I beg to remind them, first, that the dark side, which, indeed, I have not concealed, has been only too often presented in disproportion and caricature by European tourists or distant observers; and, secondly, that it would be very ungrateful and dishonorable for me to disparage my new fatherland behind its back, to uncover its nakedness with unsparing hand, and neglect its virtues and its glorious prospects.

THE CHURCHES AND SECTS

"Westward the star of empire takes its way."[5] This verse of a celebrated English philosopher is a characteristic watch-word of the American's restless reachings into the future. It flatters his vanity, it spurs his ambition, it rouses his energy, it constantly excites and strengthens in him the impression that his nation is one day to be

---

[5](Ed.) Schaff preferred John Quincy Adams's wording in *Oration at Plymouth* (1802) to George Berkeley's original statement: "Westward the course of empire takes its way" (*On the Prospect of Planting Arts and Learning in America* [1752], stanza 6).

the greatest of the earth, to attain the perfection of church as well as state, and then to react with regenerating power on Europe, and from California to convert China and Japan. These are, to be sure, extravagant notions, favored no less by ignorance of the state of Europe than by American vanity.

Yet this verse has truth. It expresses the general law of the geographical march of history both secular and sacred. Thus far civilization and Christianity have followed in the main the course of the sun from East to West. The East, the land of the morning, is not only the cradle of mankind and of civilization, but also the birthplace of the church. Around the venerable countries of Palestine, Syria, Asia Minor, now desolate, and groaning under the yoke of the false prophet, cluster the earliest and holiest associations of Christendom. Hence Christendom now, at this critical moment, looks out upon them from Europe and America with the intensest interest, and in hope of an approaching regeneration of the Eastern churches. From Asia Christianity spread to Greece and to Rome; and thence flowed the conversion and civilization of the Romanic and Germanic tribes. But as early as the close of the Middle Ages Paris still further West became a model of a higher culture, and a chief seat of the scholastic and mystic theology, and of reformatory efforts in the church, which gradually and steadily spread, and struck deepest root in Germanic soil.

In the sixteenth century, Germany and Switzerland, became the starting-place of another grand movement of history, in which we now have our place, and whose end cannot yet be seen. Germany, lying geographically in the center of Europe, was commissioned in the age of the Reformation to furnish the heart's blood for the modern history of the world and the church, to bring out from the inexhaustible mines of the word and the spirit principles and ideas, which should embody themselves as institutions and become flesh and blood in other lands.

From Germany and Switzerland the great Reformation passed to the west of Europe, visiting especially that remarkable Anglo-Saxon island, which has since risen to the dominion of the sea and of commerce, and at the same time to the vast duty of spreading Christianity and European culture in all its colonies. From England and

Scotland the northern half of the western hemisphere has been, and in our own day the still newer world of Australia is being, colonized and prepared for political and religious independence. The history of England and North America for the last three centuries is utterly unintelligible without the Reformation. It is at bottom a continuation of the movement, which, starting from Wittenberg, Zurich, and Geneva, spread into the Germanic countries North and West, and has given the Anglo-Saxon race especially the most powerful impulse towards the fulfillment of its mission for the world.

In North America all sections and interests of European Protestantism are now more or less fully represented. There they all find a free asylum and room for unrestrained development. There the Roman Church also finds the same freedom. There all confessions and sects come into contact, and into a conflict, the result of which must greatly affect the future fortunes of all Christendom. America will also in time take a very active part in the Christianizing of China and Japan, and a lively interest in all great missionary operations. However unfavorable our judgment, therefore, of its present ecclesiastical condition—and I confess my own dissatisfaction with it—we have every year less room to deny or, save from sheer prejudice, to overlook its great prospective importance.

From this point I will now endeavor to present, first, a general ecclesiastcal view of North America, and then a sketch of each of the most prominent confessions and sects.

America is the classic land of sects, where in perfect freedom from civil disqualification, they can develop themselves without restraint. This fact is connected indeed with the above-mentioned predominance of the Reformed type of religion. For in the Reformed church the Protestant features, and with them the subjective, individualizing principle, are most prominent. But in the term *sect-system* we refer at the same time to the whole ecclesiastical condition of the country. For there the distinction of church and sect properly disappears; at least the distinction of established church and dissenting bodies, as it is commonly understood in England and Germany. In America, there is, in fact, no national or established church; there-

fore no dissenter. There all religious associations, which do not out-
rage the general Christian sentiment and the public morality (as the
Mormons, who, for their conduct, were driven from Ohio and Illinois), enjoy the same protection and the same rights. The distinction
between confessions or denominations (as the word is there) and sects
is therefore likewise entirely arbitrary, unless perhaps the acknowledgment or rejection of the ecumenical or old Catholic symbols be
made the test; though this would not strictly apply even in Germany.

Favored by the general freedom of conscience, the representatives
of all the forms of Christianity in the Old World, except the Greek—
for we here leave out of view the isolated Russian colony in the
Northwest of America—have gradually planted themselves in the vast
field of the United States by emigration from all European countries,
and are receiving reinforcements every year. There is the Roman with
his Tridentinum and pompous mass; the Episcopal Anglican with his
Thirty-nine Articles and Book of Common Prayer; the Scotch Presbyterian with his Westminster Confession, and his presbyteries and
synods; the Congregationalist, or Puritan in the stricter sense, also
with the Westminster Confession, but with his congregational independence; the Baptist, with his immersion and anti-paedobap-
tism; the Quaker, with his inward light; the Methodist, with his call
to repentance and conversion, and his artificial machinery; the Lutheran, now with all his symbols, from the Augustana to the Form
of Concord, now with the first only, and now with none of them; the
German Reformed and Reformed Dutch, with the Heidelberg Catechism and the Presbyterian Synodal church polity; the Unionist,
either with the consensus of both confessions, or indifferently rejecting all symbols; the Moravian community, with its silent educational and missionary operations; and a multitude of smaller sects
besides, mostly of European origin, but some of American. In short,
all the English and Scotch churches and sects, and all branches of
German and Netherland Protestantism, are there represented. Each
one alone is, of course, weaker than its mother church in Europe, except the Puritanic, which has attained its chief historical importance
only in New England. But they are all there, not rarely half a dozen
in a single country town, each with its own church or chapel; and,

where they have any real vitality at all, they grow there proportionally much faster than in Europe. Some, as the Presbyterian, the Methodist, the German Protestant, and the Roman Catholic, have even almost doubled their numbers within the last ten or twenty years.

This confusion of denominations and sects makes very different impressions on the observer from different theological and religious points of view. If he makes all of individual Christianity, and regards the conversion of men as the whole work of the church, he will readily receive a very favorable impression of the religious state of things in America. It is not to be denied, that by the great number of churches and sects this work is promoted; since they multiply the agencies, spur each other on, vie with each other, striving to outdo one another in zeal and success. We might refer to the separation of Paul and Barnabas, by which one stream of apostolic missionary labor was divided into two, and fructified a greater number of fields with its living waters. There are in America probably more awakened souls, and more individual effort and self-sacrifice for religious purposes, proportionally, than in any other country in the world, Scotland alone perhaps excepted. This is attributable, at least in part, to the unrestricted freedom with which all Christian energies may there put themselves forth; and to the fact, that no sect can rely on the favor of the State, but that each is thrown upon its own resources, and has therefore to apply all its energies to keep pace with its neighbors and prevent itself from being swallowed up.

The charge that the sect system necessarily plays into the hands of infidelity on one side and Romanism on the other has hitherto at least not proved true, though such a result is very naturally suggested. There is in America far less open unbelief and skepticism, than in Europe; and Romanism is extremely unpopular. Whether things will continue so is a very different question.

But on closer inspection the sect system is seen to have also its weaknesses and its shady side. It brings all sorts of impure motives into play, and encourages the use of unfair, or at least questionable means for the promotion of its ends. It nourishes party spirit and passion, envy, selfishness, and bigotry. It changes the peaceful kingdom of God into a battle-field, where brother fights brother, not, of course, with sword and bayonet, yet with loveless harshness and all manner of detraction, and too often subordinates the interests of the church universal to those of his own party. It tears to pieces the beautiful body of Jesus Christ, and continually throws in among its members the fire-brands of jealousy and discord, instead of making them work together harmoniously for the same high and holy end. It should not be forgotten, that Christianity aims not merely to save individual souls, and then leave them to themselves, but to unite them with God and therefore also with one another. It is essentially love, and tends towards association; and the church is and ought to become more and more the one body of Jesus Christ, the fullness of Him who filleth all in all. If, therefore, the observer start with the conception of the church as an organic communion of saints, making unity and universality its indispensable marks, and duly weighing the many exhortations of Holy Scripture to keep the unity of the Spirit in the bond of peace; he cannot possibly be satisfied with the sect system, but must ever come out against it with the warnings of Paul against the divisions and parties in the Corinthian church. A friend very near to me, and a thoughtful, deeply earnest theologian, has keenly assailed and exposed the sect system as the proper American Antichrist.[6] The noblest and most pious minds in America most deeply disapprove and deplore at least the sect *spirit*; and fortunately too, this spirit recedes in proportion as the genuine spirit of Christianity, the uniting and co-operative spirit of brotherly love and peace, makes itself felt. In the American Bible and Tract Societies, and Sunday School Union, the various evangelical denominations work hand in hand and get along right well together, although their Catholicity is more of a negative character, not reconciling, but concealing the confessional differences, and although their charity is at an end as soon as the Romish church is mentioned, as if she was simply an enemy of Christ. Several of the most prominent churches maintain a friendly inter-delegation; and even in those which do not, or which make it a mere form, all the true children of God, when they see one another

---

[6](Ed.) Schaff is referring to his Mercersburg colleague John Williamson Nevin, *Antichrist, or the Spirit of Sect and Schism* (New York, 1848).

face to face, exchange the hand of fellowship in spite of all the jealousy and controversy between their respective communions.

Sectarianism, moreover—and this I might especially commend to the attention of German divines—is by no means a specifically American malady, as often represented; it is deeply seated in Protestantism itself, and is so far a matter of general Protestant interest. Suppose that in Prussia church and state should be suddenly severed; the same state of things would at once arise here. The parties now in conflict within the Established Church, would embody themselves in as many independent churches and sects, and you would have an Old Lutheran Church, a New Lutheran Church, a Reformed Church, a United Church—and that again divided into a union positively resting on the symbols, and a union acknowledging only the Scriptures—perhaps, also, a Schleiermacherian Church, and who knows how many spiritualistic and rationalistic sects and independent single congregations besides. America in fact draws all its life originally from Europe. It is not a land of *new* sects; for those which have originated there, as the Mormons, are the most insignificant, and have done nothing at all to determine the religious character of the people. It is only the rendezvous of all European churches and sects, which existed long before, either as establishments or as dissenting bodies. England and Scotland have almost as many different religious bodies as the United States, with the single difference that in the former countries one (the Episcopal in England, the Presbyterian in Scotland) enjoys the privilege of state patronage, while in America all stand on the same footing.

In forming our judgment of the American sect system, therefore, we are led back to the general question, whether Protestantism constitutionally involves a tendency towards denominationalism and sectarianism, wherever it is not hindered by the secular power. This we cannot so very easily deny. Protestantism is Christianity in the form of free subjectivity; of course not an unregenerate subjectivity, resting on natural reason—for this is the essence of rationalism—but a regenerate subjectivity, based on and submitting to the Word of God. It is thus distinguished from Catholicism, which takes Christianity in an entirely objective sense, as a new law, and as absolute authority. And to harmonize perfectly these two opposite yet correlative principles, is the highest, but also the most difficult, problem of history.

Accordingly it is the great work and the divine mission of Protestantism, to place each individual soul in immediate union with Christ and his Word; to complete in each one the work of redemption, to build in each one a temple of God, a spiritual church; and to unfold and sanctify all the energies of the individual. But, through the sinfulness of human nature, the principle of subjectivity and freedom may run out into selfish isolation, endless division, confusion, and licentiousness; just as the principle of objectivity, disproportionately applied, leads to stagnation and petrifaction; the principle of authority, to despotism in the rulers and slavery in the ruled. In North America, the most radically Protestant land, the constitutional infirmities of Protestantism, in religious and political life, are most fully developed, together with its energy and restless activity; just as the natural diseases of Catholicism appear most distinctly in the exclusively Roman countries of southern Europe.

Now in this unrestrained development and splitting up of Christian interests, most palpable in America, the Roman Catholic sees symptoms of an approaching dissolution of Protestantism and the negative preparation for its return into the bosom of the only saving church. But such a relapse to a position already transcended in church history, such an annulling of the whole history of the last three centuries, is, according to all historical analogy, impossible. How inconceivable, that in this age of the general circulation of literature, the Book of all books can again be taken away from the people, and all the liberties, hard won by the Reformation, obliterated! Catholicism can, indeed, draw over to itself as it has lately done in Germany, England, and America, individuals, tired of the Protestant confusion and uncertainty, having no patience with the present, and no faith in the future, longing for a comfortable pillow of the absolute, tangible authority. But Protestantism in the mass can never be swallowed up by it; or if it should be, it would soon break out again with increased violence, and shake the Roman structure still more deeply than it did in the sixteenth century.

We believe, indeed, by all means, that the present divided condition of Protestantism is only a temporary transition state, but that it will produce something far more grand and glorious, than Catholicism ever presented in its best days. Protestantism after all still contains the most vigorous energies and the greatest activity of the church. It represents the progressive principle of history. It is Christianity in motion. Hence more may be expected from it than from the comparative stagnation of the Roman or Greek Catholicism. Converted regenerate individuals, these subjective Protestant heart-churches, are the living stones for the true Evangelical Catholic Church, which is to combine and perfect in itself all that is true and good and beautiful in the past. But this requires the previous fulfillment of the mission of Protestantism, the transforming of each individual man into a temple of God. Out of the most confused chaos God will bring the most beautiful order; out of the deepest discords, the noblest harmony; out of the most thoroughly developed Protestantism, the most harmonious and at the same time the freest Catholicism. What wild controversy has already raged, what violent passion has been kindled among theologians, about the doctrine of the Eucharist! And yet this sacrament is the feast of the holiest and deepest love, the symbol of the closest fellowship of Christ and the church. The one, holy, universal, apostolic church is an article not only of faith, but also of hope, to be fully accomplished only with the glorious return of Christ.

In America are found, in some degree, as a preparation, for this great end, all the data for the problem of the most comprehensive union. For there, not only the Lutheran and Reformed confessions, but also the English and all the European sections and forms of the church are found in mutual attrition and in ferment. But, of course, Europe likewise, especially Germany and England, must have its part in the work; nay, must make the beginning. For Europe still stands at the head of Christian civilization, and is ever producing from her prolific womb new ideas and movements, which, through the growing facility, and frequency of inter-communication, the swelling emigration, and the exportation of elements of literature and culture of every kind, at once make themselves felt in America, perpetuate themselves there in modified forms, and come into immediate contact and conflict, so as to bury themselves in each other, and rise again as the powers of a new age in the history of the world and the church.

Therefore have I called America, even in respect to religion and the church, the Phenix-grave [*sic*] of Europe.

THE SIGNIFICANCE OF NORTH AMERICA
FOR THE FUTURE DEVELOPMENT
OF THE KINGDOM OF GOD

The United States of North America—whose citizens are called *Americans* in an emphatic sense— because the bearers of the historical life and progress of the whole Western Hemisphere—are a wonder in the annals of the human race. Their development, in its rapidity and gigantic proportions, far outstrip all former experience, and their significance for the future mocks the boldest calculation. Though not an hundred years old, they have become already, by natural force of expansion, one of the mightiest empires of the civilized world, with the control of one entire continent and two oceans, and spread, in the most peaceful manner, the meshes of their influence over Europe, Asia and Africa. And yet their history up to this time is only a faint prelude of what is to come, and the Americans of the twentieth century will look upon the present age of their country, with feelings akin to those with which modern Europeans regard the exodus of the threshold of the Middle Ages. The "Young Giant," has not yet, so to speak, sown all his wild oats, and along with many heroic deeds, commits also some wanton and extravagant pranks, which prove, however, the exuberant vigor of his youthful powers. Providence, who creates nothing in vain, has there made physical preparations on the grandest scale, and formed an immeasurable territory, containing the most fruitful soil, the most valuable mineral treasures and the most favorable means of commercial intercourse, as a tempting asylum for all European nations, churches and sects, who, there freed from the fetters of antiquated institutions, amid circumstances and conditions altogether new, and with renovated energies, swarm, and jostle each other, and yet, in an incredibly short space of time, are moulded by the process into one powerful nationality. Whilst Europe had first to work her way up out of heathen-barbarism, America, without earning it, has appropriated the civilization and church-history of two thousand years, as an inheritance, and already put out at the highest rate of interest for the benefit of after generations.

For these Americans have not the least desire to rest on the laurels of the past and comfortably enjoy the present; they are full of ambition and national pride, and firmly resolved to soar above the Old World. They are a people of the boldest enterprise and untiring progress—Restlessness and Agitation personified. Even when seated, they push themselves to and fro on their rocking chairs; they live in a state of perpetual excitement in their business, their politics and their religion, and remind one of the storm-lashed sea, which here

Seethes and bubbles and hisses and roars,
As when fire with water is commixed and contending
— it never will rest, nor from travail be free,
Like a sea that is laboring the birth of a sea.[7]

They are excellently characterized by the expressions, "Help yourself" and "Go ahead," which are never out of their mouths. It is also a very significant fact, that they have invented the magnetic telegraph, or at least perfected it, and are far advanced in the useful arts. For there the car of the world's history moves swifter on the pinions of steam and electricity, and "the days become shortened."

The grandest destiny is evidently reserved for such a people. We can and must, it is true, find fault with many things in them and their institutions—slavery, the lust of conquest, the worship of Mammon, the rage for speculation, political and religious fanaticism and party-spirit, boundless temerity, boasting, quackery, and—to use the American word for it—humbug, as well as other weaknesses and dangers, that are moreover wanting to no country in Europe. But we must not overlook the healthy, vital energies, that continually react against these diseases: the moral, yea Puritanical earnestness of the American character, its patriotism and noble love of liberty in connection with deep-rooted reverence for the law of God and authority, its clear, practical understanding, its talent for organization, its inclination for improvement in every sphere, its fresh

---

[7](Ed.) From Schiller's ballad "Der Taucher" ("The Diver"), stanza 6.

enthusiasm for great plans and schemes of moral reform, and its willingness to make sacrifices for the promotion of God's kingdom and every good work. The acquisition of riches is to them only a help toward higher spiritual and moral ends; the grain derived from the inexhaustible physical resources of their glorious country only the material ground-work toward the furtherance of civilization. They wrestle with the most colossal projects. The deepest meaning and aim of their political institutions are to actualize the idea of *universal* sovereignty, the education of every individual for intellectual and moral self-government and thus for true freedom. They wish to make culture, which in Europe is everywhere aristocratic and confined to a comparatively small portion of society, the common property of the people, and train up if possible every youth as a gentleman and every girl as a lady; and in the six States of New England at least, they have attained this object in a higher degree than any country in the Old World, England and Scotland not even excepted.

In short, if anywhere in the wide world a new page of universal history has been unfolded and a new fountain opened, fraught with incalculable curses or blessings for future generations, it is the Republic of the United States with her starspangled banner. Either humanity has no earthly future and everything is tending to destruction, or this future lies—I say not exclusively, but mainly—in America, according to the victorious march of history, with the sun from east to west.

But America has also equally as great a prospective significance and mission for the internal and external development of *the kingdom of God*. The history of the world is only the vestibule to the history of the church, the voice of one crying in the wilderness, preparing the way for Him, who shall come. All political events and revolutions, all discoveries and inventions, all advances in art and science; in fine, all that belongs to the kingdom of the Father and is under the guidance of his general providence, must serve the Son and spread abroad his name, until the whole world is filled with his glory, and all nations walk in the light of eternal truth and love. For the Father draws all men to the Son, and "they shall honor the Son, even as they honor the Father" [John 5:23].

American church-history is still in the storm-and-pressure-period. Its roots, with all their living fibres, are in Europe, especially in England. It draws its life from the past, most of all from the conquests of the Reformation of the sixteenth century, and the principles then established exert there an enormous power, and find the freest scope of action and influence upon the entire national life. Meanwhile it is all merely the labor of preparation, the heaping up of materials and plans, the chaotic fermentation that precedes the act of creation. But the prolegomena are laid out on the most comprehensive scale; the cosmos lies in the chaos, as man in embryo, and He who in the beginning said: "Let there be light!" lives and rules with his Divine Spirit, brooding over the ecclesiastical *Thohuvavohu* of the New World [Gen. 1:2-3].

The history of the kingdom of God in America has already entered upon the dawn of a new era, and will unfold itself, under circumstances and conditions altogether peculiar, not indeed beyond Christ—for He is Alpha and Omega of church-history, and before Him the Americans bow with the deepest reverence as before the highest and holiest name in the universe--but beyond all that has hitherto existed in the ecclesiasticism of Europe. I can only touch briefly upon the new circumstances and conditions, which aid *the internal progress* of the church. To these belong the Protestant, or rather Puritan starting-point of North American Christianity, its complete deliverance from Mediaeval Catholic and feudal institutions, its independence of the State, the universal religious freedom and liberty of conscience, and the meeting of all European confessions and sects on the basis of the voluntary system and political equality. In America the most interesting experiments in church-history are now made. There the idea is, to found a church, which, without any direct support from the government, and having for this very reason a stronger hold on the sympathies of the people, shall be the expression of all their untrammeled convictions, the bearer and guardian of their highest spiritual and moral interests. There the idea is, to actualize the genuine Protestant principle of a congregation, independent and yet bound to an organic whole, in a far greater degree than has heretofore been the case in the Old World; and to make each Christian a priest and a king in the service of the universal High Priest and King of Kings. There the idea is, to settle the conflict between the greatest diversity and essential unity, between freedom and authority in religion. There the whole controversy between Romanism and Protestantism has been taken up anew, and is rapidly drawing towards a most earnest, perhaps even a bloody issue. For North America is a land thoroughly Protestant, almost to an extreme, since Protestantism embraces not merely the large majority of the population, but is the source, at the same time, of all its social and political principles; in fine, is interwoven most intimately with the entire national life, and goes hand in hand with all the nobler struggles after freedom and ideas of progress. The public opinion, formed under the influence of Puritanism, regards Romanism, whether justly or unjustly, as the veritable Antichrist, Intolerance and Persecution personified, a system of the most terrible spiritual despotism, which, if successfully established, would also annihilate all political freedom and arrest the progress of history. Hence the more this church grows—although its growth does not keep pace with the immigration from Ireland, Germany and France, so that in fact much more material is lost than gained by the transition to America—the more do national jealousy and hatred, which have already found vent in manifold riotous proceedings, increase also. Here it will be seen, whether the Papacy, under conditions and circumstances like these, can maintain herself unaltered, or whether she will rush to ruin, or undergo a fundamental change.

In North America, moreover, the fate of the Reformation is to be decided. There Protestantism, along with its enormous vital energies, its devotion to liberty, its ability to make sacrifices and its bold enterprising spirit, exhibits also its faults and weaknesses much more plainly than in Europe, where its free development is still checked by the fetters of ecclesiastical and civil forms and regulations, the growth of ages. There it will be seen, whether it, as its enemies prophecy, being left to its centrifugal and unchurchly tendencies, will at last break up into atoms, and prepare a greater triumph for Catholicism than even the victory over the Old Roman and Germanic heathenism; or whether, as we believe and hope, following its positive Christian principles, with the Word of God in hand and heart, it will come together, consolidate, concentrate itself, and out of the phoenix-ashes of all Christian denominations and sects, rise glorified, as the truly universal, evangelical Catholic Bride of the Lord, adorned with the fairest flowers of the church-history of all centuries.

Not only upon the internal development of the Church but also upon the *external spread* of the Gospel, in all heathen lands, America from its geographical position and by its rapidly increasing commerce, must exert an incalculable influence. The Sandwich Islands, that halfway station upon the route over the Pacific Ocean, have, by Puritan missionaries of New England, been already won over to the Gospel, and will soon become an integral part of the great Anglo-Saxon Republic. The ports of Japan have been lately opened to American trade, and the various Missionary, Bible and Tract Societies, with their fresh, energetic powers, will certainly follow up this advantage at the earliest favorable opportunity. The railroad and canal, soon to be made over the Isthmus of Panama, indicates that the whole commerce between Europe and Further Asia, as well as the Missionary operations, for which it has thus providentially furnished a path, will, in a short time, take up their march through America, as the real centre of the world. Already a direct line of steam ships between San Francisco and Canton has been projected, and through this channel, Christianizing and civilizing influences beyond number will stream towards China, and already these Divine preparations are met, without their knowledge or wish, by the inhabitants of the "Celestial Empire" crowding by the thousands into California, who, lured thither by the gold and the high wages of labor, will yet find there and carry back to their native land, where just now events occur that will fill the whole world with astonishment, something infinitely better than all the treasure of the Sacramento, the precious pearl of the Gospel. For the colossus of three hundred and sixty millions, after a long stagnation, amid dim forebodings of what should come, has at last set itself in motion, and rolls, like a tremendous avalanche of nations, toward a speedy political revolution which, in the end, must certainly pave the way for a much more important one, in the sphere of the spirit.

Similar stars of hope for the approaching triumph of the peaceful kingdom of Christ have risen above the African horizon. In the negro colony of Liberia, founded by American philanthropists, we not only see the first step toward the solution of the fearful riddle of negro slavery, but the dawn also of a new day for the dark night of Africa, which will be yet conquered for the Gospel and civilization by her own sons and daughters, exported as rude heathen and now returning as Christian men and women.

But finally, North America will also take part in Inner Missions among the nominal Christians of the Old World, in order to restore the candlestick of the pure Word of God, where it has been obscured, or thrust aside, by various human ordinances and inventions. . . .

Such a mighty mission appears to lie before the church-history of the country, of which we speak; not indeed as isolated from the rest of the world, but in connection with the other Christian nations, who are brought nearer every year, the barriers of space and time being broken down. To such a mission even the rude beginnings of their labor point, and thus much, according to human view, is at all events certain, that North America, along with England and Germany, furnishes the most important contributions toward solving the vast problems touching Christ and his Church, which now press upon Christendom with a mighty weight, and which will yet be determined to the honor of the God-man and Saviour of the world, and His Bride. . . .

I do not say all this in vain-glorious laudation of America, still less of the Americans, who, as men and Christians, are not one whit better than their European forefathers. Their vast mission and significance in the future history of the Church and the world can just as little be ascribed to any special merit on their part, as the choice of the people of Israel, who, in spite of their stubbornness and ingratitude, were called to be the bearers of the Law and the Prophets, and the stock from whence the Saviour of the world should spring. There is the hidden purpose of God, alike in both cases, and each time bound to a corresponding measure of enormous responsibility.

And just as little do I wish to depreciate Europe and the Europeans by the above remarks. For America is indeed the daughter of Europe and operates with European forces, of which a fuller stream flows thither every year. And the signs of the times appear to indicate, that, as the powers of darkness deepen and concentrate, so likewise all the positive elements of Christendom, in all parts of the world, should draw nearer, and become more closely joined together, so that they may achieve a more certain victory in the last decisive conflict. America and Europe ought to understand more clearly, prize more highly, and seek to know and love each other more fully in the common service of the one Lord, to whom all the parts of the globe belong, and must at last submit in free, blessed obedience.

PART III
Major Projects— The New York Years (1863–1893)

CHAPTER 5

A Christology "from Below"

EDITORIAL INTRODUCTION

In the April 1848 issue of the *Methodist Quarterly Review* Schaff reviewed August Neander's *Life of Christ*.[1] Eloquent even as he was still trying to master the English language, he referred only briefly to Neander's book but offered a lengthy discussion of what had provoked it, *The Life of Jesus Critically Examined* by David Friedrich Strauss. From his student days at Tübingen he recollected vividly the "immense sensation this production made throughout Germany!" After a spirited review of the fatal flaws in Strauss's work, he concluded happily, however, that Strauss already belongs to a bygone age, never to be revived again, "except it be among transcendental Unitarians and Universalists in the new world." In Germany, "his palmy days are for ever gone." Still, Schaff admitted that the orthodox system of Christianity is "a human system which requires constant reformation." Opposed to all "blind traditionalists," he therefore declared it to be the great mission of German theology "to restore the old faith, but in a new form, which shall make a real progress toward the ultimate reconciliation, and free, intelligent agreement, of the human mind with divine truth." This mission, however, has not yet been fulfilled. Even Neander's *Life*

---

[1]"Neander's Life of Christ," *Methodist Quarterly Review* 30 (April 1848): 248-68.

of Christ is still flawed by unnecessary concessions to the rationalistic point of view, but they may be excused, Schaff declared, as
merely "some wounds" that the great church historian brought
away from his honorable battle with this latest and most dangerous
form of German unbelief.

This article is noteworthy because it contained in a nutshell,
and with a remarkable degree of accuracy, Schaff's theological program for a Life of Christ, or a Christology "from below." He was
to execute this program several years later, after the agitation over
the "church question" of the Mercersburg years had finally sub-
sided and he began to pursue more practical concerns. Then he also
took up the apologetic project of a Christology that would "restore
the old faith, but in a new form." The article further makes clear
that Schaff's christological program itself, as well as its later execution, in all essentials was that of Germany's *Vermittlungstheologie.*
The article's predictive value fell far short in only one crucial respect: Strauss's "palmy days" were far from over. Strauss, after all,
had "probably set in motion the greatest and most intense theological debate in the nineteenth century."[2] The reverberations of
that debate in the new world during Schaff's lifetime were to be but
slight and indeed largely confined to New England's Unitarians and
Transcendentalists, for to the evangelical Protestants Strauss's book
was at first "about as intimidating as a Hindu preaching in Sanscrit
from atop Plymouth Rock."[3] Nevertheless, this debate continued
to overshadow Schaff's own christological efforts. Strauss's dark
shadow was even lengthened when Ernest Renan published his no
less sensational *Vie de Jésus* (1863), turning Christ's life into a "legend," as Strauss had turned it into a "myth." Renan's work, however, Schaff believed, was of slight scholarly substance, even if it
was suffused by the charm and inventive ingenuity of a great French

---

[2]Holte, *Die Vermittlungstheologie: Ihre theologischen Grundbegriffe kritisch untersucht,* 72.

[3]Herbert Hovenkamp, *Science and Religion in America, 1800–1860* (Philadel-
phia, 1978) 73. For the American reactions to Strauss's book, see also Jerry Wayne
Brown, *The Rise of Biblical Criticism in America, 1800–1870: The New England
Scholars* (Middletown CT, 1969) chs. 9 and 10, and Henry A. Pochmann, *German
Culture in America, 1600–1900* (Madison, 1957) 111-12 and passim.

novelist, and he disposed of it with the curt remark that "a refutation of Strauss is also a refutation of Renan."[4]

The mediating theologians had self-consciously placed themselves at a most appropriate moment in the historical development of the doctrine of the person of Christ.[5] According to Isaak August Dorner's historical scheme, which was, not surprisingly, informed by the familiar three-step dialectic of German idealism, the *union* of the two natures of Christ was first worked out in the period until 381; then the *divine* nature was emphasized at the expense of the human nature until about 1700 (only Luther's Christology was held to be an exception); next, during the eighteenth century, the *human* nature was lifted up at the expense of the divine. In the nineteenth century Protestant theology now faced the peculiar challenge of mediating between supernaturalism and rationalism by combining in a living (and presumably final) synthesis the appropriate emphases on both the divine and the human in Christ.

Two approaches to this task suggested themselves to the mediating theologians. A more historical approach was pursued by Karl Ullmann, whose popular *The Sinlessness of Christ* (1828, 7th ed., 1863) interpreted Christ, following in Schleiermacher's footsteps, as the archetype and ideal of humanity and then ingeniously set out to emphasize the sinless humanity of Christ as a proof of his divinity. The more speculative approach of such theologians as Isaak August Dorner, Karl Liebner, Julius Müller and Richard Rothe, by contrast, inclined toward the philosophy of identity of German idealism and then emphasised the idea of the God-man, which made possible also a more direct attachment to the orthodox christological tradition of the church. In either case, though, these theologians appeared to have gained the advantage of keeping their christological projects at some distance, even if it was not an entirely safe distance, from the seemingly treacherous terrain to which the Tübingen School's historical criticism of the New Testament had transferred Christ's question to his followers: "Who do you say that I am?" (Matt. 16:13).

---

[4]Schaff, *The Person of Christ*, 2nd ed. (London, 1880) 130.

[5]For the following see Holte, *Die Vermittlungstheologie*, chs. 3 and 5; Emanuel Hirsch, *Geschichte der neueren evangelischen Theologie*, vol. 5, ch. 52; and Colin Brown, *Jesus in European Protestant Thought, 1778–1860* (Durham NC, 1985) ch. 14.

When Schaff and Nevin finally also addressed the "question of Christ," their differences, one notes with interest, resembled closely those that separated Ullmann and the more speculative mediating theologians. James H. Nichols has shown that Nevin developed his christological position in dialogue with Dorner, Liebner and Müller; Ullmann is not even mentioned.[6] Surprisingly, Nichols entirely ignored Schaff's contributions to the christological debate. One can, perhaps, justify this omission on the ground that Schaff showed no originality of thought (unlike Nevin) though great apologetic fervor and skill in his own christological work. Indeed, Schaff wrote apologetically for the benefit of "doubters" and polemically against all those infidel assaults that tried to destroy faith in the divine-human Savior. As he embraced Ullmann's approach to the christological task, he was deeply conscious of the immensity of the challenge of describing the moral character of Christ, for "Who can empty the ocean into a bucket?"[7] He was convinced that in this sceptical age a Christology "from below" was called for that will clearly focus on Christ's humanity and demonstrate its perfection as the most persuasive argument for sustaining belief in Christ's divinity. *The Person of Christ* was to be Schaff's most popular book. With considerable literary skill he developed the notion that Christ, though sinless, "passed through all the stages of human life from infancy to manhood, and represented each in its ideal form, that he might redeem and sanctify them all, and be a perpetual model for imitation." Betraying the philistinism of the Victorian age, he portrayed Jesus as "the model infant, the model boy, the model youth, and the model man."[8] He wanted to prove beyond any reasonable doubt that Christ's character was the "greatest moral miracle" in history. He then concluded that for this Christ not to have performed the miracles the New Testament records, or not to affirm of him the miracles of Virgin Birth and Resurrection, would be more incomprehensible than the miracles themselves were alleged to be. The book's value was further enhanced by a section ex-

---

[6]Nichols, *Romanticims in American Theology: Nevin and Schaff at Mercersburg*, ch. 6, "The Second Adam and the New Humanity."

[7]Schaff, *History of the Christian Church*, vol. 1 (1882; rev. ed., 1890) 106.

[8]Schaff, *Person of Christ*, 10.

amining and refuting "false theories" about Christ's life and an "Appendix" of more than 100 pages, which presented "impartial testimonies of the character of Christ" taken from the whole history of the West. Our selections are the "Introduction" and the "Conclusion" of this book.

The book itself was an elaboration of a lecture, "The Moral Character of Christ," which Schaff had delivered in 1861 and subsequently published. He again addressed the "question of Christ" in 1871, in a German essay, *Die Christusfrage,* of which an English translation, "Christ His Own Best Witness," was included in *Christ and Christianity* (1885). Schaff's last word in this matter was the chapter on the founder of Christianity in the final edition of the first volume of his *History of the Christian Church* (1882; rev. ed., 1890). Again he affirmed the basic principle of his Christology: "There is no conflict between the historical Jesus of Nazareth and the ideal Christ of Faith."[9] The biblical record, as Schaff read it, established the divinity of Christ as "an article of faith," which as such was above logical and mathematical demonstration. Nevertheless, the divinity of Christ, he firmly believed, forces itself "irresistibly upon the reflecting mind and historical inquirer."[10] Two other publications should also be mentioned: a lengthy survey of the history of christology, "Christ in Theology,"[11] which, in a sense, was a condensed and compact version of the more than 2000 pages of Dorner's *History of the Development of the Doctrine of the Person of Christ,* and the article "Christology," a contribution to the *Religious Encyclopedia* (later *Schaff-Herzog Encyclopedia*). In these contributions he also discussed and, like Dorner, found wanting another nineteenth-century christological option, the kenotic theory, for the same reason that he had detected deficiencies in the duophysic formula of the Chalcedonian creed: both neglected the human and historical side of Christ, the God-man. Though Schaff believed that christological speculations will continue because the mystery of the Christian affirmation that "God was in Christ" is inexhaustible, he did give a passing nod of approval to Dorner's own theory of a grad-

---

[9]Schaff, *History of the Christian Church,* 1:101.

[10]Ibid., 1:107-108.

[11]Schaff, *Christ and Christianity,* 45-123.

ual incarnation of the divine Logos. For the present, this theory seemed to be the most successful attempt at combining the "old faith" with the modern demand of establishing "the historical realness of Christ's humanity."[12] Among American contemporaries, he found a position similar to Ullmann's and his own expressed in the tenth chapter of Horace Bushnell's *Nature and the Supernatural*. However, he faulted Bushnell for having established only that Christ was "more than man, and cannot be classified with man," and so, "(h)aving carried the reader over the great difficulty," he left him to draw his own conclusions regarding the full measure of Christ's divinity.[13]

Strauss's rejoinder to Ullmann's position that the doctrine of the sinlessness of Christ signifies "the death of all true humanity" carried no weight either with Ullmann or with Schaff.[14] Schaff himself broke no new ground in his rejoinder to Strauss's claim that we must substitute for the Christ of dogma the Christ of myth, an ordinary human being, though a genius, to whom after his death the disciples attached the high-flung notions of Christian supernaturalism. Repeating familiar arguments, he pointed out alleged flaws in Strauss's position: the *a priori* rejection of miracles denies the living, personal God, in whose hands, according to Schaff, the laws of nature are not "iron chains" but "elastic cords" which he can stretch as he sees fit;[15] the late dating of the gospels to make time for the myth-forming process is contradicted by the early date of the pauline letters; the alleged contradictions between the gospels are nothing but differences complementary in nature; the claim that myth creates the hero, poetry history, is untenable, for innumerable historical examples prove the reverse relationship: "Facts give rise to songs";[16] Strauss's retention of the idea of the God-man by making the whole human race to be the incarnation of the divine is the poor substitute of a metaphysical abstraction for the living reality of the historical Jesus; it contradicts as well the testimony

---

[12]Ibid., 69.

[13]Schaff, *Person of Christ*, 161n.49.

[14]Quoted by Holte, *Die Vermittlungstheologie*, 123.

[15]Schaff, *Person of Christ*, 100.

[16]Ibid., 124.

of all of history that a great individual always is at the head of a new epoch.

Occasionally Schaff also addressed the larger question of the relationship of Christian faith and modern criticism. He did so, for instance, at the conclusion of the final edition of *Apostolic Christianity, A. D. 1-100,* which was vol. 1 of his *History of the Christian Church* (1882; rev. ed., 1890), in a section "Concluding Reflections—Faith and Criticism," most of which is here also included. This section makes it clear that to the end of his life Schaff held to that position which he had enunciated as as a high-school student at Stuttgart in that first shocked reaction to Strauss's book: the traditional supernaturalism of Christian dogma is securely anchored in the Christian's personal experience of Christ's saving presence, all assaults of the modern intellect against this position notwithstanding. With this anchor firmly in hand, Schaff never wavered in upholding the traditional tenets of Christian supernaturalism. Christ's ascension and his sitting at the right hand of power were to him "facts and no empty figures of speech, or mere visions of the disciples"; heaven was as real to him as "earth or hades," though he granted that "we do not know its locality nor the nature of the spiritual bodies."[17] And though his irenic ecumenism allowed for great differences among Christians, he drew the line when it came to the fundamental Christian dogmas, as his reaction to a debate at a ministers' conference in Europe showed: "The supernatural Conception, the Atoning Death, the Resurrection and Ascension of the Lord are most certainly not *dubia* in which *libertas* must prevail, but *necessaria* in which all ministers of the gospel should unite; they are the foundation stones on which rests the whole Christian church."[18] The supernatural foundation of Christianity was attested and confirmed by the history of the Christian church, which in turn continously exhibited the presence of the divine-human head of the church. In the end, the "question of Christ" and the "question of the church" were one, for they mutually determined each other. During the early years at Mercersburg Schaff had written that it is "the perfect understanding of John's conception of Christ. . . . and

---

[17]Schaff, *Christ and Christianity,* 89.

[18]*Evangelische Zeugnisse aus den deutschen Kirchen in Amerika,* ed. P. Schaff, 3 (1865): 337.

the diffusion of his spirit of love" which will usher in the final age of "evangelical catholicism" in the history of the church. [19]

To the last, he held fast to the Johannine authorship of the fourth gospel. In response to those who attacked it, as did Baur and Strauss, he could at times use almost violent language: "And as He can no more be crucified in person, He is crucified in the Gospels by the modern Scribes and Pharisees and Sadducees." Still, he was, he claimed, "as confident as I am of my own existence that the Gospel of John will come triumphant out of this fiery ordeal."[20] But it was not easy, for three years before his death he wrote his friend Frédéric Godet: "I have worried my brain over the Synoptic and Johannean problem." Yet once again he concluded that the denial of the Johannine authorship would turn "the most exalted product of the human mind" into a lie.[21] As a true disciple of Neander, Schaff never strayed from affirming the identity of the Johannine Logos and the Synoptic Jesus. To be sure, his interpretation of the history and literature of the apostolic church—and therewith his whole ecumenical scheme of church history—would have collapsed, had he agreed with the Tübingen School's criticism of the historicity of the Gospel of John and of its author, who was to Schaff "the apostle of incarnation and of love," precisely what all mediating theologians held to be the essence of Christianity.[22]

But was Baur not right when he asserted: "The question whether the origin of Christianity is to be comprehended purely historically or as a miracle is in fact wholly identical with the critical question regarding the relationship of the Johannine Gospel to the Synoptics"? Baur was convinced that the inability of viewing first-century Christianity as purely historical is "therefore chiefly to be attributed to the one-sided preference which Schleiermacher's theology awakened and propagated for the Johannine Gospel."[23]

---

[19]Schaff, *History of the Apostolic Church,* 678.

[20]*A Commentary on the Holy Scriptures by John Peter Lange,* ed. P. Schaff, 25 vols. (New York and Edinburgh, 1868–80) vol. 3 of the New Testament (John) x.

[21]David S. Schaff, *Life of Schaff,* 422.

[22]Schaff, *History of the Apostolic Church,* 648.

[23]Ferdinand Christian Baur, *Die Tübinger Schule und ihre Stellung zur Gegenwart,* 2nd ed. (Tübingen, 1860) 33n.1.

According to Albert Schweitzer, New Testament studies in the nineteenth century confronted three great alternatives: either purely mythical or purely historical, either the Gospel of John or the Synoptic Gospels, either eschatological or non-eschatological.[24] Schaff's orthodox supernaturalism prompted him to reject, or not to consider, all three of these alternatives. Moreover, his Life of Christ bears out Albert Schweitzer's other well-known obervation that "it was not only each epoch that found its reflection in Jesus; each individual created Him in accordance with his own character. There is no historical task which so reveals a man's true self as the writing of a Life of Jesus."[25]

THE PERSON OF CHRIST:
THE PERFECTION OF HIS HUMANITY
AS A PROOF OF HIS DIVINITY*

Introductory

When the angel of the Lord appeared to Moses in the burning bush, he was commanded to put off his shoes from his feet; for the place whereon he stood was holy ground. With what reverence and awe, then, should we approach the contemplation of the great reality—God manifest in the flesh—of which the vision of Moses was but a significant type and shadow!

The life and character of Jesus Christ is the holy of holies in the history of the world. Eighteen centuries have passed away since he appeared, in the fulness of time, on this earth to redeem a fallen race from sin and death, and to open a never-ceasing fountain of righteousness and life. The ages before him anxiously awaited his coming, as the fulfilment of the desire of all nations; the ages after him proclaim his glory, and ever extend his dominion. The noblest and

---

[24]Albert Schweitzer, *The Quest of the Historical Jesus*, trans. William Montgomery (New York, 1959) 238.

[25]Ibid., 4.

*The Person of Christ: The Perfection of His Humanity Viewed as a Proof of His Divinity, 2nd ed. (London, 1880) 1-9, 138-44.

best of men under every clime hold him not only in the purest affection and the profoundest gratitude, but in divine adoration and worship. His name is above every name that may be named in heaven or
on earth, and the only one whereby sinners can be saved. He is the
Author of the new creation; the Way, the Truth, and the Life; the
Prophet, Priest, and King of regenerate humanity. He is Immanuel,
God with us; the Eternal Word become flesh; very God and very man
in one undivided person, the Saviour of the world.

Thus he stands out to the faith of the entire Christian church—
Greek, Latin, and Evangelical—in every civilised country on the
globe. Much as the various confessions and denominations differ in
doctrines and usages, they are agreed in their love and adoration of
Jesus. They lay down their arms when they approach the manger of
Bethlehem where he was born, or the cross of Calvary where he died
for our sins that we might live for ever in heaven. He is the divine
harmony of all human sects and creeds, the common life-centre of all
true Christians; where their hearts meet with their affections, prayers, and hopes, in spite of the discord of their heads. The doctrines
and institutions, the sciences and arts of Christendom, bear witness
to the indelible impression he made upon the world; countless
churches and cathedrals are as many monuments of gratitude to his
holy name; hymns and prayers are daily and hourly ascending to his
praise from public and private sanctuaries in all parts of the globe.
His power is now greater, his kingdom larger, than ever; and it will
continue to spread, until all nations shall bow before him and kiss
his sceptre of righteousness and peace.

Blessed is he who from the heart can believe that Jesus is the Son
of God, and the fountain of salvation. True faith is an act of God
wrought in the soul by the Holy Spirit, who reveals Christ to us in
his true character, as Christ has revealed the Father. Faith, with its
justifying, sanctifying, and saving power, is independent of science
and learning, and may be kindled even in the heart of a little child.
It is the peculiar glory of the Redeemer and his religion to be coex-
tensive with humanity itself, without distinction of sex, age, nation,
and race. His saving grace flows and overflows to all and for all, on
the simple condition of faith.

This fact, however, does not supersede the necessity of thought and argument. Revelation, although above nature and above reason, is not against nature or against reason. On the contrary, nature and the supernatural, as has been well said by a distinguished New England divine, "constitute together the one system of God."[1] Christianity satisfies the deepest intellectual as well as moral wants of man, who is created in the image and for the glory of God. It is the revelation of truth as well as of life. Faith and knowledge are not antagonistic, but complementary forces; not enemies, but inseparable twin sisters. Faith precedes knowledge, but just as necessarily it leads to knowledge; while true knowledge, on the other hand, is always rooted and grounded in faith, and tends to confirm and to strengthen it. Thus we find the two combined in the famous confession of Peter, when he says, in the name of all the other apostles, "We *believe* and we *know* that thou art the Christ" [John 6:69]. So intimately are both connected, that we may also reverse the famous maxim of Augustine, Anselm, and Schleiermacher, "Faith precedes knowledge,"[2] and say "Knowledge precedes faith."[3] For how can we

---

[1] See Dr. Horace Bushnell's able work on *Nature and the Supernatural,* 1858. The same idea is expressed by Dr. John W. Nevin, in *The Mystical Presence,* Philadelphia, 1846, p. 199, in these words: "Nature and Revelation, the world and Christianity, as springing from the same Divine Mind, are not two different systems joined together in a merely outward way. They form a single whole, harmonious with itself in all its parts. The sense of the one, then, is necessarily included and comprehended in the sense of the other. The mystery of the new creation must involve, in the end, the mystery of the old; and the key that serves to unlock the meaning of the first must serve to unlock the innermost secret of the last."

[2] *Fides praecedit intellectum.* Or, more fully, in the language of Anselm of Canterbury, adopted by Schleiermacher as the motto of his *Dogmatics: Neque enim quaero intelligere ut credam, sed credo ut intelligam. Nam qui non crediderit, non experietur, et qui expertus non fuerit, non intelliget.* (Ed.) "For I do not seek to understand in order to believe, but I believe in order to understand" (*Proslogion,* ch. 1). "For he who will not believe will not gain experience, and he who has not had experience will not understand" (*Epistola de Incarnatione Verbi,* ch. 1).

[3] *Intellectus praecedit fidem.* This was Abelard's maxim, which, without the restriction of the opposite maxim, must lead to rationalism and scepticism. (Ed.) These words, often wrongly attributed to Abelard, nevertheless characterize his position.

believe in any object without at least some general historical knowledge of its existence and character? Faith even in its first form, as a
submission to the authority of God and an assent to the truth of his
revelation, is an exercise of the mind and reason as well as of the heart
and the will. Hence faith has been defined as implying three things,—
knowledge, assent, and trust or confidence. An idiot or a madman
cannot believe. Our religion demands a rational, intelligent faith; and
this just in proportion to its strength and fervour, aims at an ever-
deepening insight into its own sacred contents and object.

As living faith in Christ is the soul of all sound practical Christianity and piety, so the true doctrine of Christ is the soul and centre
of all sound Christian theology. St. John makes the denial of the incarnation of the Son of God the criterion of Anti-Christ, and consequently the belief in this truth the test of Christianity. The
incarnation of the eternal Logos, and the divine glory shining through
the veil of Christ's humanity, is the grand theme of his Gospel, which
he wrote with the pen of an angel from the very heart of Christ, as
his favourite disciple and bosom friend. The Apostles' Creed, starting as it does from the confession of Peter, makes the article on Christ
most prominent, and assigns to it the central position between the
preceding article on God the Father, and the succeeding article on
the Holy Ghost. The development of ancient Catholic theology commenced and culminated with the triumphant defence of the true divinity, and the true humanity of Christ, against the opposite heresies
of Judaising Ebionism, which denied the former, and paganising
Gnosticism, which resolved the latter into a shadowy phantom.
Evangelical theology is essentially Christological, or controlled
throughout by the proper idea of Christ as the God-Man and Saviour.
This is emphatically the article of the standing or falling Church. In
this, the two most prominent ideas of the Reformation—the doctrine of the supremacy of the Scriptures, and the doctrine of justification by grace through faith—meet, and are vitally united. Christ's
word, the only unerring and efficient guide of truth; Christ's work,
the only unfailing and sufficient source of peace; Christ all in all--
this is the principle of genuine Protestantism.

In the construction of the true doctrine of Christ's person, we
may, with St. John in the prologue to his Gospel, begin from above

with his eternal Godhead, and proceed, through the creation and the preparatory revelation of the Old Testament economy, till we reach the incarnation and his truly human life for the redemption of the race. Or, with the other Evangelists, we may begin from below with his birth from the Virgin Mary, and rise, through the successive stages of his earthly life, his discourses and miracles to his assumption into that divine glory which he had before the foundation of the world. The result reached in both cases is the same; namely, that Christ unites in his person the whole fulness of the Godhead, and the whole fulness of sinless mankind.

The older theologians, both Catholic and Evangelical, proved the divinity of the Savior in a direct way from the *miracles* performed by him; from the *prophecies* and *types* fulfilled in him; from the divine *names* which he bears; from the divine *attributes* which are predicated of him; from the divine *works* which he performed; and from the divine *honours* which he claims, and which are fully accorded to him by his apostles and the whole Christian Church to this day.

But the divinity of Christ may also be proved by the opposite process—the contemplation of the singular perfection of his humanity, which rises by almost universal consent, even of unbelievers, so far above every human greatness known before or since, that it can only be rationally explained on the ground of such an essential union with the Godhead as he claimed himself, and as his inspired apostles ascribed to him. The more deeply we penetrate the veil of his flesh, the more clearly we behold the glory of the Only-Begotten of the Father shining, through the same, full of grace and of truth.[4]

Modern theology owes this new homage to the Saviour. The powerful and subtle attacks of the latest phases of infidelity upon the credibility of the gospel history call for a more vigorous defence than was ever made before, and have already led, by way of reaction, to new triumphs of the old faith of the Church in her divine Head.

---

[4](Ed.) Quoting in German, Schaff here refers the reader to the two German authors on whom his own argument mainly depends: Karl Ullmann, *The Sinlessness of Jesus: An Evidence for Christianity*, trans. from the 6th German ed. (Edinburgh and London, 1858), and Dorner, *History of the Development of the Doctrine of the Person of Christ*, 5 vols.

Our humanitarian, philanthropic, and yet sceptical age is more open to this argument, which proceeds from the humanity to the divinity, than to the old dogmatic method of demonstration which follows the opposite process. With Thomas, the representative of honest and earnest scepticism among the apostles, many noble and inquiring minds refuse to believe in the divinity of the Lord unless supported by convincing arguments of reason: they desire to put the finger into the print of his nails, and to thrust the hand into his side, before they exclaim, in humble adoration: "My Lord and my God!" [John 20:28]. They cannot easily be brought to believe in miracles on abstract reasoning or on historical evidence. But, if they once could see the great moral miracle of Christ's person and character, they would have no difficulty with his miraculous works. For a superhuman being must of necessity do superhuman deeds. The contrary would be unnatural, and the greatest miracle. The character of the tree accounts for the character of the fruit. We believe in the miracles of Christ because we believe in his perfection as the divine Man and the central miracle of the moral universe.

It is from this point of view that we shall endeavour to analyse and exhibit the *human character* of Christ. We propose to take up the man, Jesus of Nazareth, as he appears on the simple, unsophisticated record of the honest fishermen of Galilee, and as he lives in the faith of Christendom; and we shall find him in all the stages of his life, both as a private individual and as a public character, so far elevated above the reach of successful rivalry, and so singularly perfect, that this very perfection, in the midst of an imperfect and sinful world, constitutes an irresistible proof of his divinity.

A full discussion of the subject would require us to consider Christ in his official as well as personal character; and to describe him as a teacher, a reformer, a worker of miracles, and the founder of a spiritual kingdom universal in extent and perpetual in time. From every point of view, we should be irresistibly driven to the same result. But our present purpose confines us to the consideration of his personal character; and this alone, we think, is sufficient for the conclusion.

Infidels, it is true, are seldom converted by argument; for the springs of unbelief are in the heart and will rather than in the head.

But honest and truth-loving inquirers, like Nathanael and Thomas, will never refuse, on proper evidence, to receive the truth.

Blessed are they that seek the truth; for they shall find it.

Conclusion

Nebicula est; transibit— "It is a little cloud; it will pass away."[5] This was said by Athanasius of Julian the Apostate, who, after a short reign of active hostility to Christianity, perished with a confession of utter failure. The same may be applied to all the recent attempts to undermine the faith of humanity in the person of its divine Lord and Saviour. The clouds, great and small, pass away; the sun continues to shine: darkness has its hour; the light is eternal. No argument against the existence or attack upon the character of the sun will drive the king of day from the sky, or prevent him from blessing the earth. And the eye of man, with its sun-like nature, will ever turn to the sun, and drink the rays of light as they emanate from the face of Jesus, the "Light of the World." "God, who commanded the light to shine out of darkness, hath shined in our hearts to give the light of the knowledge of the glory of God in the face of Jesus Christ" (2 Cor. 4: 4).

With its last and ablest efforts, infidelity seems to have exhausted its scientific resources. It could only repeat itself hereafter. Its different theories have been tried, and found wanting. One has in turn refuted and superseded the other, even during the lifetime of their champions. They explain nothing in the end: on the contrary, they only substitute an unnatural prodigy for a supernatural miracle, an inextricable enigma for a revealed mystery. They equally tend to undermine all faith in God's providence, in history, and ultimately in every principle of truth and virtue; and they deprive a poor and fallen humanity, in a world of sin, temptation, and sorrow, of its only hope and comfort in life and in death.

Dr. Strauss, the most learned of the infidel biographers of Jesus, seems to have had a passing feeling of the disastrous tendency of his

---

[5](Ed.) Rufinus, *Historiae Ecclesiasticae Libri XI* (a translation from the Greek of Eusebius of Caesarea's *History of the Christian Church*, continued down to the death of Theodosius the Great) 10:35.

work of destruction, and the awful responsibility he assumed. "The results of our inquiry," he says in the closing chapter of his large "Life of Jesus," "have apparently annihilated the greatest and most important part of that which the Christian has been wont to believe concerning his Jesus; have uprooted all the encouragements which he has derived from his faith, and deprived him of all his consolations. The boundless stores of truth and life which for eighteen hundred years have been the aliment of humanity seem irretrievably devastated, the most sublime levelled with the dust, God divested of his grace, man of his dignity, and the tie between heaven and earth broken. Piety turns away with horror from so fearful an act of desecration, and, strong in the impregnable self-evidence of its faith, boldly pronounces that— let an audacious criticism attempt what it will— all that the Scriptures declare and the Church believes of Christ will still subsist as eternal truth; nor need one iota of it be renounced."[6] Strauss makes then an attempt, it is true, at a philosophical reconstruction of what he vainly imagines to have annihilated as an historical fact by his sophistical criticism. He professes to admit the abstract truth of the orthodox Christology, or the union of the divine and human, but perverts it into a purely intellectual and pantheistic meaning. He refuses divine attributes and honours to the glorious Head of the race, but applies them to a decapitated humanity. He thus substitutes, from pantheistic prejudice, a metaphysical abstraction for a living reality; a mere notion for an historical fact; a progress in philosophy and mechanical arts for the moral victory over sin and death; a pantheistic hero-worship, or self-adoration of a fallen race, for the worship of the only true and living God; the gift of a stone for the nourishing bread; a gospel of despair and final annihilation for the gospel of hope and eternal life.[7]

---

[6]See his large *Leben Jesu,* Schlussabhandlung ("Concluding Dissertation"), vol. II, page 663 (4th ed., 1840).

[7](Ed.) After quoting a lengthy passage in English in his own translation from Strauss's *Leben Jesu,* 2:710, in which Strauss affirms the union of the divine and human in the whole human race but not in an individual, that is, Jesus Christ, the God-Man of the Christian dogma, Schaff responded as follows: "But the idea of

Humanity scorns such a miserable substitute, which has yet to give the first proof of any power for good, and which is not likely ever to convert or improve a single individual. Humanity must have a living Head, a real Lord, and Saviour from sin and death. With renewed faith and stronger confidence, it will return from the dreary desolations of a heartless infidelity, and the vain conceits of a philosophy falsely so called, to the historical Christ, the promised Messiah, the God incarnate, and will exclaim with Peter: "Lord, where shall we go but to thee? Thou alone hast the words of eternal life, and we believe and are sure that thou art the Son of God!" [John 6:68-69].

Yes! He still lives, the divine Man and incarnate God, on the ever-fresh and self-authenticating records of the Gospels, in the unbroken history of eighteen centuries, and in the hearts and lives of the wisest and best of our race; and there he will live for ever. His person and work are the book of life, which will never grow old. Christianity lives and will continue to live with him, because he lives, the same yesterday, to-day, and for ever.

Jesus Christ is the most sacred, the most glorious, the most certain of all facts; arrayed in a beauty and majesty which throws the "starry heavens above us and the moral law within us" into obscurity, and fills us truly with ever-growing reverence and awe.[8] He

---

the union of the human and divine is no more contradictory in an individual than in the race. What is true in idea or principle must also actualise itself, or be capable of actualisation, in a concrete living fact. History teaches, moreover, that every age, every great movement, and every nation, have their representative heads, who comprehend and act out of the life of the respective whole. This analogy points us to a general representative head of the entire race—Adam in the natural, and Christ in the spiritual order. The divine humanity of Strauss is like a stream without a fountain, or like a body without a head, a metaphysical abstraction and idle delusion. The historical Jesus of Nazareth is the ideal Christ. In his last book, on *The Old and New Faith* [*Der alte und der neue Glaube, Ein Bekenntnis*, 1872], Strauss renounces all deceptive accommodations and restraints, and leaves no middle ground between hopeless atheism and positive historical Christianity."

[8](Ed.) Immanuel Kant, *Critique of Pure Reason* (1781) conclusion: "Two things fill the mind with ever-increasing wonder and awe, the more often and the more intensely the mind of thought is drawn to them: The starry heavens above me and the moral law within me."

shines forth with the self-evidencing light of the noonday sun. He is too great, too pure, too perfect, to have been invented by any sinful and erring man. His character and claims are confirmed by the sublimest doctrine, the purest ethics, the mightiest miracles, the grandest spiritual kingdom, and are daily and hourly exhibited in the virtues and graces of all who yield to the regenerating and sanctifying power of his spirit and example. The historical Christ meets and satisfies all moral and religious aspirations. The soul, if left to its noblest impulses and aspirations, instinctively turns to him, as the needle to the magnet, as the flower to the sun, as the panting heart for the fresh fountain. We are made for him, and "our heart is without rest until it rests in him."[9] He commands our assent, he wins our affections and adoration. We cannot look upon him without spiritual benefit. We cannot think of him without being elevated above all that is low and mean, and encouraged to all that is good and noble. The very hem of his garment is healing to the touch. One hour spent in his communion outweighs all the pleasures of sin. He is the most precious gift of a merciful God to a fallen world. In him are the treasures of wisdom, in him the fountain of pardon and peace, in him the only hope and comfort in this world and that which is to come. Mankind could better afford to lose the literature of Greece and Rome, of Germany and France, of England and America, than the story of Jesus of Nazareth. Without him, history is a dreary waste, a labyrinth of facts without meaning, connection and aim: with him, it is a beautiful, harmonious revelation of God, the unfolding of a plan of infinite wisdom and love; all ancient history converges to his coming, all modern history receives from him its higher life and inspiration. He is the glory of the past, the life of the present, the hope of the future. We cannot even understand ourselves without him. According to an old Jewish proverb: "The secret of man is the secret of the Messiah." Christ is the great central Light of history, and, at the same time, the Light of every soul: he alone can solve the mystery of our being, and fulfil our intellectual desires after truth, our moral aspirations after goodness and holiness, and the longing of our feelings after peace and happiness.

---

[9](Ed.) Augustine, *Confessions* 1.1.

Not for all the wealth and wisdom of this world would I weaken the faith of the humblest Christian in his divine Lord and Saviour; but if, by the grace of God, I could convert a single sceptic to a child-like faith in him who lived and died for me and for all, I would feel that I had not lived in vain.

FAITH AND CRITICISM*

There is no necessary conflict between faith and criticism any more than between revelation and reason or between faith and philosophy. God is the author of both, and he cannot contradict himself. There is an uncritical faith and a faithless criticism, as there is a genuine philosophy and a philosophy falsely so called; but this is no argument either against faith or criticism; for the best gifts are liable to abuse and perversion; and the noblest works of art may be caricatured. The apostle of faith directs us to "prove all things," and to "hold fast that which is good" [1 Thess. 5:21]. We believe in order to understand, and true faith is the mother of knowledge. A rational faith in Christianity, as the best and final religion which God gave to mankind, owes it to itself to examine the foundation on which it rests; and it is urged by an irresistible impulse to vindicate the truth against every form of error. Christianity needs no apology. Conscious of its supernatural strength, it can boldly meet every foe and convert him into an ally.

Looking back upon the history of the apostolic age, it appears to us as a vast battlefield of opposite tendencies and schools. Every inch of ground is disputed and has to be reconquered; every fact, as well as every doctrine of revelation, is called in question; every hypothesis is tried; all the resources of learning, acumen, and ingenuity are arrayed against the citadel of the Christian faith. The citadel is impregnable, and victory is certain, but not to those who ignorantly or superciliously underrate the strength of the besieging army. In the sixteenth century the contest was between Roman Catholicism and

---

*Apostolic Christianity, A.D. 1–100, vol. 1 of History of the Christian Church, rev. ed. (New York, 1890) 853-60, 862-63.

Evangelical Protestantism; in the nineteenth century the question is Christianity or infidelity. Then both parties believed in the inspiration of the New Testament and the extent of the canon, differing only in the interpretation; now inspiration is denied, and the apostolicity of all but four or five books is assailed. Then the Word of God, with or without tradition, was the final arbiter of religious controversies; now human reason is the ultimate tribunal.

We live in an age of discovery, invention, research, and doubt. Scepticism is well nigh omnipresent in the thinking world. It impregnates the atmosphere. We can no more ignore it than the ancient Fathers could ignore the Gnostic speculations of their day. Nothing is taken for granted; nothing believed on mere authority; everything must be supported by adequate proof, everything explained in its natural growth from the seed to the fruit. Roman Catholics believe in an infallible oracle in the Vatican; but whatever the oracle may decree, the earth moves and will continue to move around the sun. Protestants, having safely crossed the Red Sea, cannot go back to the fleshpots of the land of bondage, but must look forward to the land of promise. In the night, says a proverb, all cattle are black, but the day light reveals the different colors. . . .

We must believe in the Holy Spirit who lives and moves in the Church and is the invisible power behind the written and printed word.

The form in which the authentic records of Christianity have come down to us, with their variations and difficulties, is a constant stimulus to study and research and calls into exercise all the intellectual and moral faculties of men. Every one must strive after the best understanding of the truth with a faithful use of his opportunities and privileges, which are multiplying with every generation.

The New Testament is a revelation of spiritual and eternal truth to faith, and faith is the work of the Holy Spirit, though rooted in the deepest wants and aspirations of man. It has to fight its way through an unbelieving world, and the conflict waxes hotter and hotter as the victory comes nearer. For the last half century the apostolic writings have been passing through the purgatory of the most scorching criticism to which a book can be subjected. The opposition is itself a powerful testimony to their vitality and importance. . . .

The critical and historical rationalism which was born and matured in this century in the land of Luther, and has spread in Switzerland, France, Holland, England, Scotland and America, surpasses in depth and breadth of learning, as well as in earnestness of spirit, all older forms of infidelity and heresy. It is not superficial and frivolous, as the rationalism of the eighteenth century; it is not indifferent to truth, but intensely interested in ascertaining the real facts, and tracing the origin and development of Christianity, as a great historical phenomenon. But it arrogantly claims to be the criticism *par excellence,* as the Gnosticism of the ancient church pretended to have the monopoly of knowledge. There is a historical, conservative, and constructive criticism, as well as an unhistorical, radical, and destructive criticism; the former must win the fight as sure as God's truth will outlast all error. So there is a believing and Christian Gnosticism as well as an unbelieving and anti-(or pseudo-)Christian Gnosticism.

The negative criticism of the present generation has concentrated its forces upon the life of Christ and the apostolic age, and spent an astonishing amount of patient research upon the minutest details of its history. And its labors have not been in vain; on the contrary, it has done a vast amount of good as well as evil. Its strength lies in the investigation of the human and literary aspect of the Bible; its weakness in the ignoring of its divine and spiritual character. It forms thus the very antipode of the older orthodoxy, which so overstrained the theory of inspiration as to reduce the human agency to the mechanism of the pen. We must look at both aspects. The Bible is the Word of God and the word of holy men of old. It is a revelation of man, as well as of God. It reveals man in all his phases of development— innocence, fall, redemption—in all the varieties of character, from heavenly purity to satanic wickedness, with all his virtues and vices, in all his states of experience, and is an ever-flowing spring of inspiration to the poet, the artist, the historian, and divine. It reflects and perpetuates the mystery of the incarnation. It is the word of him who proclaimed himself the Son of Man, as well as the Son of God. *"Men* spake from God, being moved by the *Holy Spirit*" [2 Pet. 1:21]. Here all is divine and all is human.

No doubt the New Testament is the result of a gradual growth and conflict of different forces, which were included in the original idea of Christianity and were drawn out as it passed from Christ to his disciples, from the Jews to the Gentiles, from Jerusalem to Antioch and Rome, and as it matured in the mind of the leading apostles. No doubt the Gospels and Epistles were written by certain men, at a certain time, in a certain place, under certain surroundings, and for definite ends; and all these questions are legitimate objects of inquiry and eminently deserving of ever-renewed investigation. Many obscure points have been cleared up, thanks, in part, to these very critics, who intended to destroy, and helped to build up.

The literary history of the apostolic age, like its missionary progress, was guided by a special providence. Christ only finished a part of his work while on earth. He pointed his disciples to greater works, which they would accomplish in his name and by his power, after his resurrection. He promised them his unbroken presence, and the gift of the Holy Spirit, who, as the other advocate, should lead them into the whole truth and open to them the understanding of all his words. The Acts of the Apostles are a history of the Holy Spirit, or of the post-resurrection work of Christ in establishing his kingdom on earth. Filled with that Spirit, the apostles and evangelists went forth into a hostile world and converted it to Christ by their living word, and they continue their conquering march by their written word.

Unbelieving criticism sees only the outside surface of the greatest movement in history, and is blind to the spiritual forces working from within or refuses to acknowledge them as truly divine. In like manner, the materialistic and atheistic scientists of the age conceive of nature's laws without a lawgiver; of a creature without a creator; and stop with the effect, without rising to the cause, which alone affords a rational explanation of the effect.

And here we touch upon the deepest spring of all forms of rationalism, and upon the gulf which inseparably divides it from supernaturalism. It is the opposition to the supernatural and the miraculous. It denies God in nature and God in history, and, in its ultimate consequences, it denies the very existence of God. Deism and atheism have no place for a miracle; but belief in the existence of an Almighty Maker of all things visible and invisible, as the ultimate and all-sufficient cause of all phenomena in nature and in history, implies the possibility of miracle at any time; not, indeed, as a violation of his own laws, but as a manifestation of his lawgiving and creative power over and above (not against) the regular order of events. The reality of the miracle, in any particular case, then, becomes a matter of historical investigation. It cannot be disposed of by a simple denial from *a priori* philosophical prejudice; but must be fairly examined, and, if sufficiently corroborated by external and internal evidence, it must be admitted.

Now, the miracles of Christ cannot be separated from his person and his teachings. His words are as marvelous as his deeds; both form a harmonious whole, and they stand or fall together. His person is the great miracle, and his miracles are simply his natural works. He is as much elevated above other men as his words and deeds are above ordinary words and deeds. He is separated from all mortals by his absolute freedom from sin. He, himself, claims superhuman origin and supernatural powers; and to deny them is to make him a liar and impostor. It is impossible to maintain his human perfection, which all respectable rationalists admit and even emphasize, and yet to refuse his testimony concerning himself. The Christ of Strauss and Renan is the most contradictory of all characters; the most incredible of all enigmas. There is no possible scientific mediation between a purely humanitarian conception of Christ, no matter how high he may be raised in the scale of beings, and the faith in Christ as the Son of God, whom Christendom has adored from the beginning and still adores as the Lord and Saviour of the world.

Nor can we eliminate the supernatural element from the Apostolic Church without destroying its very life and resolving it into a gigantic illusion. What becomes of Paul if we deny his conversion, and how shall we account for his conversion without the Resurrection and Ascension? The greatest of modern sceptics paused at the problem, and felt almost forced to admit an actual miracle, as the only rational solution of that conversion. [10] The Holy Spirit was the inspiring and propelling power of the apostolic age, and made the fishers of Galilee fishers of men.

A Christian, who has experienced the power of the gospel in his heart, can have no difficulty with the supernatural. He is as sure of the regenerating and converting agency of the Spirit of God and the saving efficacy of Christ as he is of his own natural existence. He has tasted the medicine and has been healed. He may say with the man who was born b blind and made to see: "One thing I do know, that, whereas I was blind, now I see" [John 9:25]. This is a short creed; but stronger than any argument. The fortress of personal experience is impregnable; the logic of stubborn facts is more cogent than the logic of reason. Every genuine conversion from sin to holiness is a psychological miracle, as much so as the conversion of Saul of Tarsus. . . .

Strong as the external evidence is, the internal evidence of the truth and credibility of the apostolic writings is still stronger, and may be felt to this day by the unlearned as well as the scholar. They widely differ in style and spirit from all postapostolic productions, and occupy a conspicuous isolation even among the best of books. This position they have occupied for eighteen centuries among the

---

[10](Ed.) Schaff had in mind Ferdinand Christian Baur. In the second German edition of *The Church History of the First Three Centuries* (English trans. Allan Menzies; London and Edinburgh, 1878) which was published in the year of his death (1860), Baur had offered what Schaff repeatedly publicized as "remarkable concessions." He had termed Paul's conversion "a miracle" (47); furthermore, he had declared that the transformation of the disciples from despair to faith could be explained only by "the miracle of the resurrection" (42). Schaff's response characteristically combined edification and scholarship. Honoring the honesty of "this greatest of modern sceptics," he expressed the pious hope that his former Tübingen teacher "was saved at last from 'the eternal night' of despair which is the legitimate end of scepticism. One of his last words, I am told, was the sigh 'Lord, grant me a peaceful end' " (*Person of Christ*, 171n.84). Perhaps even more significant for Schaff was Baur's admission of the miracle of Paul's conversion. This Schaff held to be "fatal to his whole anti-supernaturalistic theory of history. *Si falsus in uno, falsus in omnibus* [If mistaken in one case, then mistaken in all cases]. If we admit the miracle in one case, the door is opened for all other miracles which rest on equally strong evidence" (*History of the Christian Church* [1882; rev. ed. 1890] 1:315).

most civilized nations of the globe; and from this position they are not likely to be deposed.

We must interpret persons and events not only by themselves, but also in the light of subsequent history. "By their fruits ye shall know them" [Matt. 7:16]. Christianity can stand this test better than any other religion, and better than any system of philosophy.

Taking our position at the close of the apostolic age, and looking back to its fountainhead and forward to succeeding generations, we cannot but be amazed at the magnitude of the effects produced by the brief public ministry of Jesus of Nazareth, which sends its blessings through centuries as an unbroken and ever-expanding river of life. There is absolutely nothing like it in the annals of the race. The Roman empire embraced, at the birth of Christ, over one hundred millions of men, conquered by force, and, after having persecuted his religion for three hundred years, it died away without the possibility of a resurrection. The Christian church now numbers four hundred millions, conquered by the love of Christ, and is constantly increasing. The first century is the life and light of history and the turning point of the ages. If ever God revealed himself to man, if ever heaven appeared on earth, it was in the person and work of Jesus of Nazareth. He is, beyond any shadow of doubt, and by the reluctant consent of sceptics and infidels, the wisest of the wise, the purest of the pure, and the mightiest of the mighty. His Cross has become the tree of life to all nations; his teaching is still the highest standard of religious truth; his example the unsurpassed ideal of holiness; the Gospels and Epistles of his Galilean disciples are still the book of books, more powerful than all the classics of human wisdom and genius. No book has attracted so much attention, provoked so much opposition, outlived so many persecutions, called forth so much reference and gratitude, inspired so many noble thoughts and deeds, administered so much comfort and peace from the cradle to the grave to all classes and conditions of men. It is more than a book; it is an institution, an all-pervading omnipotent force, a converting, sanctifying, transforming agency; it rules from the pulpit and the chair; it presides at the family altar; it is the sacred ark of every household, the written conscience of every Christian man, the pillar of cloud by day, the pillar of light by night in the pilgrimage of life. Mankind is bad enough, and human life dark enough with it; but how much worse and how much darker would they be without it? Christianity might live without the letter of the New Testament, but not without the facts and truths which it records and teaches. Were it possible to banish them from the world, the sun of our civilization would be extinguished, and mankind left to midnight darkness, with the dreary prospect of a dreamless and endless Nirvana.

But no power on earth or in hell can extinguish that sun. There it shines on the horizon, the king of day, obscured at times by clouds great or small, but breaking through again and again, and shedding light and life from east to west, until the darkest corners of the globe shall be illuminated. The past is secure; God will take care of the future.

MAGNA EST VERITAS ET PRAEVALEBIT.[11]

---

[11](Ed.) "The Truth is great and will prevail."

CHAPTER 6

The Internationalization of Theology

EDITORIAL INTRODUCTION

Schaff's background and personality, his theological orientation and German-American career, together with the increasing ease of transatlantic commerce and communication in the second half of the nineteenth century, predestined him for the mission of an international mediator between the churches and Christian scholars on both sides of the Atlantic. He believed this mission to be a divine assignment, which was, consequently, at the very heart of his professional self-understanding. Indeed, whatever there was that was useful and good in his career, he wrote, "it lies chiefly in this direction." It is true that he had at first "a very imperfect conception of such a mission."[1] But as its full implications and possibilities gradually unfolded themselves in his professional life, this mission was ultimately to give a unique cast to his whole career. In the end, the claim is justified that in his long career he contributed more than any one else in the nineteenth century (to use his own words) "toward the mutual understanding and appreciation of European and American divines, and toward the great cause of Christian union."[2]

---

[1]Schaff, "Autobiographical Reminiscences," 14-15.

[2]Ibid., 15.

At Mercersburg he at first attempted to establish a distinctive school of German-American theology but was quick to realize that this effort was too narrowly conceived. Using mostly his native German and addressing primarily the German-American churches (Lutheran, Reformed and United), the outstanding monuments of this early effort were the publications of the first few years of his American career. More truly representative of his future efforts were the two books he published in the 1850s, *Amerika* and *Germany*, of which the latter, according to Methodist Bishop John Fletscher Hurst, "gave to multitudes of us our first passion to cross the water, and go by a straight path to the feet of Tholuck, Jacobi, Dorner, Twesten, Nitzsch, Rothe, and other coryphaei of the later German theology."[3] In the preface to *Amerika* Schaff established the guidelines he would follow in building bridges between the Old World and the New. He readily acknowledged that Germany and the United States had each its own work to do. Hence he considered it "altogether unhistorical and unnatural to transfer the institutions of the one country abruptly to the other." But he also maintained that "each may learn very much from the other," provided that they "first become better acquainted with each other, and drop their mutual prejudices." Europe and America should be linked together, as he never tired of insisting, "not only by steamships and commerce, but by the far closer bond of intellectual and religious intercourse." For only then will they learn "to understand, esteem, love, and advance each other," as they join hands in the great cause "of extending the kingdom of God and Christian civilization thoughout the length and breadth of the world."[4]

Schaff conceived his mission to be in particular a combination of German brain and American practicality, thus bringing together the "thinkers" and "doers" of contemporary Christianity in the cause of Christ. Charles Hodge's flippant rejoinder that this is "a division of labor with which we ought to be content, especially if our working does not depend upon our understanding their

---

[3]John Fletcher Hurst, "Dr. Schaff as Uniting Teutonic and Anglo-Saxon Scholarship," *Papers of the American Society of Church History* 6 (1894): 11.

[4]Schaff, *America*, ed. P. Miller, 17-18.

thinking," did nothing but highlight Schaff's own hopes and goals.[5] Quite naturally, a special place and effort belonged, therefore, in Schaff's career to the continuing interchange and interaction with German Christians, but he was to build bridges as well to the Christian churches in other European countries. At Mercersburg he had initially championed, though with certain reservations, the Oxford Movement or Puseyism. Later his closest contacts were with members of the Broad-Church party in the Church of England and with the leading evangelical churchmen of the other English denominations and the Presbyterian churches in Scotland, as well as with the evangelical leaders of continental Protestantism. In the end it could be truly said that Schaff was the major force in the internationalization of the theology of nineteenth-century evangelical Protestantism both in Europe and in the United States.

But obstacles remained. How much closer, he wrote in 1885, Germany and America have come over the last twenty years, and he gave as an instance the ease with which he could now buy German books ("though with a Government tax of twenty-five per cent which is a disgrace to a liberal Republic").[6] German scholars, he also remarked, have "of late" begun to pay some attention to English and American theology, but only "as far as it is brought to their knowledge by occasional presents of books, by foreign students, and by review articles, and as far as their very limited acquaintance with the English enables them to do." He then sadly added: "The regular importation of English and American books of a theological character has not yet even begun on the Continent. In this regard we are far ahead."[7] The lament that it was mostly a one-way flow of scholarly information and exchange was still to be echoed almost a century later: "In Germany *Americana non leguntur.*"[8]

---

[5]Charles Hodge, "Schaff's Protestantism," *Princeton Review* 17 (October 1845): 635.

[6]Schaff, "Sketches of German universities and their theological faculties," *The Independent* (24 September 1885): 1222.

[7]Ibid. (27 August 1885): 1094.

[8]Ernst Benz, *Evolution and Christian Hope,* trans. Heinz G. Frank (Garden City NY, 1966) 143. Benz referred to the European neglect of nineteenth-century

The mission of a modern-day Martin Bucer Schaff fulfilled in ways too numerous to be listed here one by one. It must suffice to select in his career three projects that are representative of his efforts to enhance the international and interdenominational character of theology in the cause of Christian unity and of the extension of Christian civilization throughout the world: the Evangelical Alliance, the American edition of Lange's *Commentary on the Holy Scriptures,* and the *Schaff-Herzog Encyclopedia.*

The *Evangelical Alliance* had been formally organized in London in 1848, and national branches had soon been established in other European countries and in the United States. Because of the controversial issue of slavery, however, the American branch had quickly faded from the scene. After the Civil War it was revived at a preliminary meeting in Schaff's home in 1865 and formally organized as the Evangelical Alliance of the United States in New York City on January 30, 1867. In the meantime, international conferences of the Evangelical Alliance had been held in London (1851), Paris (1855), Berlin (1857) and Geneva (1861). Meeting again at Amsterdam in 1867, the Evangelical Alliance accepted an invitation of the American branch to hold the next international conference in New York City in 1869, which was soon changed to 1870 upon the request of the British branch.

As originally conceived the Evangelical Alliance was to unite the forces of evangelical Protestantism in the cause of Christian unity and religious liberty, at the same time doing battle with modern unbelief, Roman Catholicism and "romanizing" movements such as Puseyism. As we already noted, in the strength of his cherished ideal of "evangelical catholicism" as initially shaped by the Prussian High-Orthodoxy, Schaff at first, and even as late as 1853, fiercely opposed the Evangelical Alliance as a narrowly Protestant, misguided ecumenical effort.[9] But his attitude changed dramatically during his first trip to Europe, when he again drew closer to old mentors and friends such as Kapff, Tholuck, Krummacher and

---

American theology, but he added that even the cooperation of European and American theologians in the work of the World Council of Churches has not yet eliminated those two continental American prejudices: "One does not read American literature," and "There is no independent American theology."

[9]See p. xlix n82, above.

W. Hoffmann, all of whom had attended the meetings of the Evangelical Alliance, Krummacher and Tholuck even from the very beginning. [10] He began his life-long association with the Evangelical Alliance when he sent his paper "Christianity in America" to the Berlin conference of that organization in 1857. Though he received a special invitation to attend the Amsterdam meeting ten years later, the New York conference, which was finally convened in 1873, was the first Evangelical Alliance meeting at which he was present.

Certainly, the success of the New York conference must be attributed to Schaff more than to any other individual. During his trip to Europe in 1869 his tireless efforts appeared to have assured the success of that conference. But then came the outbreak of the Franco-Prussian war; it abruptly forced another postponement, to Schaff's great disappointment: "So much precious time, strength and care apparently wasted! But when God speaks, man must be silent." [11] Rescheduled for October 2-12, 1873—three years after the Vatican Council, which invited constant comparisons on Schaff's part, all favorable to the efforts of the Evangelical Alliance—Schaff crossed the Atlantic Ocean two more times, in 1872 and even as late as the summer of 1873, in order to secure the desired participation of Europeans in the New York meeting. Additionally, in 1871 he joined an Evangelical Alliance delegation to Europe, and was elected its spokesman, for the purpose of petitioning the Czar of Russia on behalf of religious liberty for the Baltic Lutherans.

As the New York conference was about to begin, Schaff noted in his diary: "Now begins the most busy and perhaps the most important week in my life, where I must be literally *servus servorum Dei* and a universal *pontifex,* i.e., bridge maker between a variety of conflicting national, sectional, sectarian and personal interests." On the eve of the last day of the conference, he had reason to record that the conference "surpassed the most sanguine expectations." For the Spirit of God was present, he wrote, and "subdued all ex-

---

[10]See Heinrich Hermelink, *Das Christentum in der Menschheitsgeschichte von der Französischen Revolution bis zur Gegenwart,* vol. 2 (Tübingen and Stuttgart, 1953) 199. Hermelink offers a brief summary of the history and significance of the German branch of the Evangelical Alliance. See also art. "Allianz, Evangelische," *Realencyklopädie für protestantische Theologie und Kirche,* 3rd ed., 1:376-81.

[11]Diary, 8 August 1870.

plosive elements and antagonistic interests, national (French and German), sectional (North and South), sectarian and personal, and has made it a grand and imposing exhibition of Christian unity." His labors of four years, he felt, had been abundantly rewarded, and he concluded: "Thus ends the most important chapter in my life—too rich to be noted here. God be praised. I have never felt more thankful and more humble."[12] As was noted in the official report, the New York conference of 1873, the first international Christian conference on American soil, "made American institutions more favorably known to representative men from abroad" and assured that "(t)he two hemispheres met in Christ and parted with mutual esteem and renewed zeal for the prosecution of the work of their common Lord and Saviour."[13]

Lange's *Commentary on the Holy Scriptures: Critical, Doctrinal, and Homiletical* was, no doubt, the major editorial project of Schaff's career. It was also his most important contribution to the field of biblical studies. Under the general editorship of Johann Peter Lange (1802-84), who himself ranged far and wide, contributing commentaries from Genesis to Malachi, from Matthew to Revelation, the German edition (1857-76) was the work of twenty scholars (eighteen Germans, one Swiss, one Dutch). The American edition occupied Schaff's attention for more than twenty years, from the initial correspondence with Lange in 1858 to the publication of the last volume on the Apocrypha of the Old Testament, the one addition to the German work. In this project Schaff had the collaboration of fifty scholars (forty-seven Americans, three British). Even more translators and collaborators are listed in some of the individual volumes of the Old Testament section, and some volumes of the New Testament section drew upon the work of the translators of the rival Edinburgh edition of Lange's Commentary, which the American edition soon elbowed out of the way. In view of the magnitude of this composite work the indefatigable editor could write near the end of his labors in 1878: "It is doubtful whether any editor or publisher would have ventured on a commentary of twenty-four [twenty-five, if the commentary on the Old Testament apoc-

---

[12]Diary, 28 September and 12 October 1873.

[13]*Sixth Annual Report of the Evangelical Alliance. 1874, Evangelical Alliance Document* 9:7.

rypha is included] large and closely printed volumes, could he have foreseen the difficulties and risks connected with it." However, this massive effort, as Schaff added with justified satisfaction, "has proved successful beyond all expectations."[14] Indeed, a reprint was published as recently as 1960. In its own time, it was the first comprehensive and complete English-language Bible Commentary.

Schaff's contributions to biblical scholarship—as exegete, organizer, editor and ecumenist—have, regrettably, so far been a largely neglected part of his legacy. But it must not be forgotten that his appointment at Mercersburg was to a chair in both church history and biblical literature and that at Union Theological Seminary he taught Hebrew (1873) and biblical literature (1874-87) before he assumed the chair for church history. Moreover, he was one of the founding members of the Society of Biblical Literature and Exegesis, which held its organizing meeting in his study at Bible House in 1880.[15] His remarkable contributions to the Revision of the English Bible will be separately considered. Among his various publications in the field of biblical studies—mostly Bible Dictionaries, Bible Helps and some commentaries—his *Companion to the Greek Testament and the English Version* (1883) stands out, alongside of Lange's Commentary.

Unfortunately, Schaff's own exegetical contributions to the American edition of Lange's Commentary were that of a scholar burdened with too many projects, often concurrently demanding his attention. He edited *Matthew* and *John,* though even then only with the help of younger colleagues. He also completed the first three chapters of *Luke,* but then, "owing to pressing engagements, and a proposed voyage to Europe during the summer," he left the

---

[14]*A Commentary on the Holy Scriptures by John Peter Lange,* ed. P. Schaff, 25 vols. (New York and Edinburgh, 1868–80), vol. 11 of the Old Testament (Isaiah) preface. Hereafter cited as *Lange's Commentary.*

[15]The Society's "Memorial Resolution" of 1894 made "grateful mention, also, of the kind office of Dr. Schaff, at the very inception of the Society. His name stands on the first page of our book of records, the first name found there; and we shall always hold it in affectionate remembrance." Quoted by Ernest W. Saunders, *Searching the Scriptures: A History of the Society of Biblical Literature, 1880–1980* (Chico CA, 1982) 10.

rest to Charles C. Starbuck.[16] And with only the first six chapters
of *Romans* completed, he once again had to confess that "a multiplicity of engagements, and a due regard for my health, compelled
me to entrust the remaining chapters, together with my whole apparatus, including notes in manuscript and a printed essay on the
ninth chapter," to Matthew B. Riddle, another young friend and
colleague.[17] It was already significant, however, that Schaff had left
his own manuscript on the Gospel of Matthew boxed up behind at
Mercersburg so that he could fully devote himself to the American
edition of Lange's Commentary. Thus he had signalled his own
strength, which was not in exegesis itself but in the transmission
of his enormous erudition and in his editorial and executive ability
of organizing and administering a vast project that employed so
large a team of international and interdenominational scholars.
Aided by a phenomenal memory and a seemingly inexhaustible font
of physical and mental energy, Schaff excelled in the biblical field
as elsewhere in the assimilation of vast amounts of materials and
facts, but as an exegete he clearly lacked the creative power of pen-
etrating and explaining, with the help of keen insights and innovative ideas or hypotheses, the meaning of the biblical texts. His
particular strength was the complete mastery of the minutiae of
textual or "lower" criticism and of the relevant literature, both past
and present, which was equally characteristic of all the volumes of
the American edition of Lange's Commentary. One should note,
for instance, the impressive list of commentaries in Greek, Latin,
German, English and French, which Schaff consulted for the Gospel of John.

It should further be noted that the American edition of Lange's
Commentary was by no means a slavish translation but an adaptation intended to further improve the German original by shaping
it to meet the interests of the more practically minded British and
American readers. At least this is how Schaff conceived of his role
as a mediator between European and American scholarship. To this
end he established a list of guiding principles, and with his own
commentary on Matthew, which was the first volume to be published, he set a model to be emulated by his collaborators. Espe-

---

[16]*Lange's Commentary,* vol. 2 of the New Testament (Luke) vii.

[17]Ibid., vol. 5 of the New Testament (Romans) vi.

cially bothersome were the ponderous and often opaque syntax and style in some of the German volumes, so that, as Schaff tactfully remarked, "the difficult labor of translation" had from time to time to be "supplemented by the delicate task of explanation."[18] The editor of *1 Corinthians*, Daniel W. Poor, judging this work "a comparative failure" if literally translated, even went so far as to introduce "such modifications of method and style as seemed necessary to give the Commentary the widest circulation," mischievously retaining, however, a few of those ponderous German sentences "as specimens here and there to show what a German scholar is capable of in this direction."[19] More significant was the addition of American and English commentaries, for, as Schaff noted plaintively, they are "sublimely ignord by continental commentators, as if exegesis had never crossed the English Channel, much less the Atlantic Ocean."[20] In the end the American edition offered an overabundance of riches, "critical, doctrinal, and homiletical;" it was, in Schaff's words, "a thesaurus of biblical learning and piety from all ages and sections of the Christian Church."[21] As the British Baptist Charles Spurgeon put it admiringly: "For homiletical purposes these volumes are so many hills of gold."[22] With biblical studies flourishing in Germany, Schaff's novel and pioneering effort at scholarship by team-work, both international and interdenominational, brought the rich harvest of German scholarship to American shores at a time when there was great demand for it, and by concentrating the attention of his many collaborators on German biblical scholarship he must also "rightly be assigned a major role in fostering both the development and style of biblical criticism" in America.[23]

It is equally characteristic of Schaff's efforts that the American edition of Lange's Commentary also looms large as a pioneering

---

[18]Ibid.

[19]Ibid., vol. 6 of the New Testament (1 and 2 Corinthians) i.

[20]Ibid., vol. 5 of the New Testament (Romans) vi.

[21]Ibid., vol 10 of the New Testament (Revelation) preface.

[22]Quoted by Schaff, *Theological Propaedeutic,* 238.

[23]Jerry Dean Campbell, "Biblical Criticism in America 1858–1892: The Emergence of the Historical Critic" (Ph.D. diss., University of Denver, 1982) 72.

ecumenical effort. In the preface to vol. 8 of the New Testament section (Thessalonians to Hebrews), Schaff proudly pointed out that the authors and translators represented five countries (Germany, Switzerland, Holland, Scotland, USA) and seven denominations (Lutheran, Swiss and Dutch Reformed, Presbyterian, Protestant Episcopal, Congregational, Baptist). He then advised the reader, on the eve of the Vatican Council, that, apart from minor differences of doctrine and polity, "in all essential articles of faith, he will find a striking degree of unity—a unity more spiritual and free, and for this very reason more deep and real than the *consensus patrum*, so called, by which the Roman Church would fain prevent or obstruct all further progress in working the inexhaustible mines of revealed truth." In Lange's Commentary, so said Schaff, "the hill of Zion, where the discords of human creeds are solved in the divine harmony of 'one Lord, one faith, one baptism, one God and Father of all,'" had once again risen far above "all sectarian steeples."[24]

But if Lange's Commentary was an expression of the consensus of the biblical scholarship of evangelical Protestantism both in Europe and America in the years immediately preceding and following the Civil War, this very accomplishment also constituted the reason for its far less favorable evaluation in the history of biblical exegesis. Indeed, the German standard surveys of the history of biblical scholarship by Hans-Joachim Kraus and Werner Kümmel do not even mention Lange's Commentary, nor do recent discussions of the rise of biblical criticism in the United States.[25] The truth

---

[24]*Lange's Commentary*, vol. 8 of the New Testament (Thessalonians to Hebrews) v.

[25]See Hans-Joachim Kraus, *Geschichte der historich-kritischen Erforschung des Alten Testaments* (Neukirchen, 1956); Werner Georg Kümmel, *Das Neue Testament: Geschichte der Erforschung seiner Probleme* (Freiburg and Munich, 1958); and also the following recent American studies: Ira V. Brown, "The Higher Criticism Comes to America, 1880–1900," *Journal of the Presbyterian Historical Society* 38 (December 1960): 193-212, and Jerry Wayne Brown, *The Rise of Biblical Criticism in America, 1800–1870: The New England Scholars* (Middletown CT, 1969). It is surprising that even self-consciously evangelical historians have so far ignored the American edition of Lange's Commentary, e.g., Mark A. Knoll, *Between Faith and Criticism: Evangelicals, Scholarship, and the Bible in America* (San Francisco, 1987). Jerry Dean Campbell's recent doctoral dissertation (see n.23 above) offers an extended, appreciative discussion of the role Schaff's edition of Lange's Commentary played in

is that this massive commentary (both German and English) consistently skirted the whole issue of the "higher" or historical-literary criticism of the Bible. In thoroughly traditionalist ways it dealt, for instance, with the increasingly controversial questions of the authorship of the *Pentateuch, Jesaiah, John* and the Pauline letters—only Paul's authorship of *Hebrews* was timidly questioned, "at least as to its form" by the American editor A. C. Kendrick.[26] It is true that the American edition of Genesis appeared early, in 1868. But when the last volume, *Numbers* and *Deuteronomy,* was published eleven years later, Julius Wellhausen's theories had become widely known, and the heresy trial of his Scottish follower, W. Robertson Smith, was under way. Even though Schaff had asked the American editor to add a "special Appendix" in reference to these revolutionary, new views, such an appendix did not materialize. In a brief and sweeping remark, the American editor Samuel T. Lowrie simply rejected all efforts "to explain the origin and composition of the books of the Bible, except that which ascribes to them a divine and supernatural origin."[27]

Schaff himself expected the ultimate result of these controversies to be "a clearer insight into the human growth of the Bible as a literary production," which in the end can only strengthen "our faith in the divine Scriptures."[28] But how reluctant, if not to say timid and uninformed, he himself appeared in exploring the human side of the Bible's story. Typical of Schaff's (and the whole Commentary's) precritical, supernaturalistic point of view, which, moreover, perceived no literary problem with the biblical texts since they all are to be taken at face value as faithfully and accurately rep-

---

"the emergence of the historical critic" in America, but by failing to distinguish between the "lower" and "higher" criticism Campbell overstates his case and comes close to Merle Curti's mistaken claim that Schaff's edition of Lange's Commentary was one of the "important agencies for the transmission of the higher criticism" (*The Growth of American Thought,* 2nd ed. [New York, 1951] 541). A valuable but so far neglected contribution is by Thomas J. Goliber, "Philip Schaff (1819–1893): A Study in Conservative Biblical Criticism" (Ph. D. diss., Kent State University, 1976).

[26]*Lange's Commentary,* vol. 8 of the New Testament (Hebrews) iii.

[27]Ibid., vol. 3 of the Old Testament (Numbers and Deuteronomy) 3.

[28]Ibid., "Preface by the American Editor," vi.

resenting what actually happened, was his discussion of the resurrection of Lazarus (John 11). He rejected all theories that deny the miracle, for they all "owe their origin to a disbelief in the supernatural." Then, confronting the remaining alternative of "historic truth, or dishonest fiction," he averred that the "historic truth is abundantly attested by the simplicity, vivacity and circumstantiality of the narrative, the four days in the tomb (vers. 39), and the good sense and moral honesty—to say the very least—of Lazarus and his sisters, the Evangelist and Christ Himself."[29] This is what Herbert Hovenkamp recently called the "essentially positivistic stance" that evangelical biblical scholars in the United States at that time maintained. For them "nothing existed between historical and non-historical—no myths, symbols, epics, or poetic expressions." "American orthodoxy," he concluded in words that apply to Schaff's exegesis and Lange's Commentary as well, "was a long way from seeing the need to be rescued from its facts."[30]

Ironically, the conservative views expressed throughout in the Schaff-Lange Commentary strengthened the orthodox ranks of those who would soon put Charles A. Briggs and Henry P. Smith on trial for heresy. Then Schaff supported these fellow-scholars in upholding the principle of free scholarly inquiry within the broadly drawn boundaries of the evangelical camp, just as long as biblical scholars practiced a "believing criticism" (and not the "rationalistic" or "pantheistic" sort of a Baur and a Strauss). Schaff called this particular attempt to mediate between the old faith and the new criticism "the liberal and progressive evangelical orthodoxy."[31] It was a position superficial and untenable and bound to break up, as indeed it did, when not too many years later a more consequent historical-critical approach to the Scriptures and an emerging fundamentalism—a "progressive liberalism" and an "evangelical orthodoxy"—began to confront each other in American Protestantism.[32] The battle between the evangelical exegesis represented

---

[29]Ibid., vol. 3 of the New Testament (John) 339.

[30]Hovenkamp, *Science and Religion in America, 1800–1860,* 73, 78.

[31]Schaff, *Theological Propaedeutic,* 228.

[32]It is symptomatic that two of the contributors to the Lange Commentary were later tried for heresy: besides Charles A. Briggs (Ezra, 1876) Crawford Howell Toy

by Lange and Schaff and their collaborators and the historical-literary criticism of such scholars as Baur, Strauss and Wellhausen did in the end not issue, as Schaff had hoped, "in one of the most brilliant victories of faith over unbelief, of Christian truth over anti-Christian error," though Schaff was more nearly correct in claiming that the "intellectual and spiritual conflict" of those years represented "one of the most important and interesting chapters in history."[33] As it turned out, the Lange-Schaff effort itself soon proved to be no more than a minor footnote in the history of biblical scholarship, calling attention to a superannuated position.

Permanently useful was to be another editorial project, the *Schaff-Herzog Encyclopedia,* the translation and adaptation of the great German encyclopedia initiated by Johann Jakob Herzog, which Schaff considered to be "a depository of the positive Evangelical Union-Theology of Germany."[34] The preface in the first volume of the *New Schaff-Herzog Encyclopedia of Religious Knowledge* (12 vols., 1908-14) offers a detailed review of the history of this publication venture, both in Germany and the United States. The idea of a translation of what soon came to be known as the German "Herzog" occurred first to John Henry Augustus Bromberger, Schaff's fellow-worker on the Liturgical Committee of the German Reformed church, who published two volumes before the Civil War. But as the American edition of Lange's Commentary had replaced the earlier Edinburgh edition, so here, too, the resourceful Schaff took over and then guided this project to its successful conclusion. What would later be simply called "Schaff-Herzog" appeared in three vols., 1882-84, and was revised in 1887, when Schaff noted with satisfaction that the American edition had actually increased the demand for the German edition and the honoraria of the German contributors. A third edition, published during Schaff's life-

---

(1 and 2 Samuel, 1877), who was dismissed from the faculty of the Southern Baptist Seminary at Louisville in 1879; and that still another of Schaff's collaborators, Talbot Wilson Chambers (Zechariah, 1874), the conservative minister at the Collegiate Reformed (Dutch) Church in New York, was among those who attacked Briggs in the early 1890s.

[33]See below, p. 243.

[34]Schaff, *Germany: Its Universities, Theology, and Religion* (Philadelphia, 1857) 250.

time in 1891, incorporated as vol. 4 an *Encyclopedia of Living Divines and Christian Workers of all Denominations in Europe and America,* which Schaff had edited and published separately in 1887.

The American edition was once again a condensed and free translation of the original but also added a large number of articles on topics of particular interest to English and American readers. The supplemental volume of biographies was particularly welcome as a special means for building bridges between the Old World and the New. Schaff himself not only contributed articles to the German "Herzog" but even managed to get an article on Jonathan Edwards and his school included in the first German edition. The article's author was Calvin Ellis Stowe of Andover Seminary, whom Herzog preferred over Edwards Amasa Park because of German familiarity with Mrs. Stowe's *Uncle Tom's Cabin.* To Schaff's dismay, the second edition retained this article unchanged and therefore still referred to Leonard Woods and Lyman Beecher, dead already for several years, as "living" divines.

The actual beginning of the American edition was beset by severe difficulties that tested Schaff's mettle but also revealed his stamina in persevering in a worthy cause, even to the point of taking financial risks. Faced with increasing costs, Scranton & Co. of Hartford, the original publisher, terminated the contract at the last moment, forcing Schaff to search for another publisher "in the heat of the summer" in 1882. After knocking in vain at several doors, Funk & Wagnalls finally agreed to publish the encyclopedia at their own risk. The project initially entailed upon Schaff "a heavy pecuniary loss," for out of his own pocket he paid his three editorial assistants a regular monthly salary, all fees to the special contributors ("at a rate of $5 per page"), the printers' bill for extra corrections ("over a thousand dollars per volume"), room rent, clerical expenses and incidentals. In the end he lamented: "The Encyclopedia has cost me about three times more money than I anticipated." He had no regrets, however. Indeed, he was sure that this work would be increasingly appreciated "as sectarian prejudices pass away."[35]

Schaff also demonstrated once again his remarkable talent for attracting and employing younger men, for he was able to carry

---

[35]Schaff, "Autobiographical Reminiscences," 107-108.

through this editorial project only with the help of Samuel M. Jackson, one of his former students, and Clemens Peterson (from Denmark), who were soon joined by Schaff's son David. Jackson and Peterson had already earlier entered Schaff's life, when for two years in Schaff's study and under his supervision they had toiled to help Schaff prepare A *Dictionary of the Bible* (1880). Jackson (1851-1912), a man of independent means, continued to be associated with the legacy of Schaff's lifework, not only as the editor-in-chief of the *New Schaff-Herzog Encyclopedia of Religious Knowledge* but also in the prominent role of long-time secretary of the American Society of Church History. Schaff, always practical and with his customary foresight, stipulated in his Will that his copyright to the encyclopedia "with its privileges and duties" be made over to his son David (who later withdrew in order to devote himself to his academic duties) and Jackson, who showed himself fully worthy of this trust. Schaff correctly observed that "A good Encyclopaedia, if kept abreast of the times, becomes an institution." He then added prophetically: "Individuals die, but institutions live on."[36]

Our selections begin with Schaff's report on his European trip in 1869, a document that is representative of his tireless international efforts on behalf of the Evangelical Alliance. The design and characteristics of Schaff's edition of *Lange's Commentary* and the *Schaff-Herzog Encyclopedia* are next described in brief excerpts that are taken from the prefaces Schaff wrote for both works.

DR. SCHAFF'S REPORT
OF HIS MISSION TO EUROPE*

It is now very evident that the postponement was wise and necessary, and that a Conference in 1869, as far as European attendance is concerned, would have been an utter failure. I know but one gentleman from the Continent of Europe who *perhaps* would have attended this year. The European Conferences required in every case at least two years of preparation; the American Conference, which on

---

[36]Ibid., 109.

*"The Report of the Rev. Dr. Philip Schaff, of his Mission to Europe in Behalf of the Alliance," *Evangelical Alliance Document* 3 (1870): 21-23, 26-29, 31-33.

account of the intervening ocean involves much more labor and expense than any of its predecessors, can hardly be matured in less time.
The first preliminary step was the sending of an agent to Europe to
arrange proper terms of co-operation with the foreign branches of the
Alliance, especially the British, and to make sure of a sufficient number of such guests as would give the proposed conference an evangelical ecumenical character and weight.

This delicate and responsible agency was intrusted to my hands,
in April last, by the Executive Committee of the American Alliance.
I accepted it, not without diffidence, in view of the discouraging aspect of the whole cause, and with the impaired state of my health at
the time; yet with a clear sense of duty as enjoying, through my
training, personal connections, and public labors, special facilities
for a work of mediation between evangelical Christians of different
denominations and countries.

It is with feelings of sincere joy and gratitude to God that I am
enabled to report the complete success of my mission to make provisional arrangements in Europe for a General Conference of the
Evangelical Alliance to be held in September, 1870, in the city of
New York. Every successive step has strengthened my conviction that
the hand of the great Head of the Church is in this movement, and
that He intends to make the approaching General Conference a means
of rich blessing to Protestant Christendom of America and Europe.

Great Britain

Two days after my arrival in Europe, the annual meeting of the
COUNCIL of the British Organization of the Evangelical Alliance was
held in London, May 6, 1869, and very fully attended. It proved to
be the most important meeting held since the first organization of
the Alliance in 1846. The proposed General Conference, and the relation of the newly-organized American Branch to the British, were
the absorbing topics of deliberation, and created an unusual interest,
which was heightened by the war panic then prevailing in England
in consequence of Senator Sumner's speech on the Alabama question,
and Prof. Goldwin Smith's letter of alarm.[1] Upon the result of my

negotiations with the British brethren, the success or failure of my mission in behalf of the New York Conference, and even the continuance of the American Branch of the Alliance, was made to depend. Had I failed there, I was instructed not to take one further step. I presented a frank and respectful statement of the history and position of the American Alliance, the apparent failure and present crisis of the project of the New York Conference, and the serious misunderstanding which had previously arisen as to the delicate questions of authority and expense. I insisted upon the complete independence of the several branches of the Alliance, which we regarded as co-ordinate bodies with equal rights and duties. After a very animated and full discussion, the difficulties were completely removed, and the most satisfactory terms of fraternal co-operation on a basis of perfect equality were unanimously and enthusiastically adopted. The British Council disclaimed distinctly any supremacy of jurisdiction, or any authority whatever over the sister Alliances, pledged its hearty co-operation in the projected conference, and nobly offered, what I did not ask, to assume the payment of the expenses of their own delegation. This relieves us at once of nearly one-third of the burden of responsibility, and will enable us to increase the Continental delegation. The English *Te Deum* ("Praise God from whom all blessings flow"), with which the meeting closed, was the spontaneous outburst of a solemn feeling of gratitude to God for the happy result in such a great and good cause.

I cannot speak too highly of the manly frankness and Christian courtesy of the officers and members of the British Council. Since that meeting I have been in friendly consultation and correspondence with the Secretaries, and it affords me sincere pleasure to say that their

---

[1](Ed.) In a Senate speech 18 April 1869, "Claims on England—Individual and National," Senator Sumner demanded such enormous payments for damages caused by the battleship *Alabama* during the Civil War that Great Britain might have had to cede Canada to the United States. Goldwin Smith (1824–1910), British historian and publicist, who joined Cornell University as professor of English and Constitutional History in 1868, opposed Sumner in a speech at Ithaca, New York, which was published as "The Relations Between America and England. A Reply to the Late Speech of Mr. Sumner" (Ithaca NY; London, 1869).

co-operation has been most cordial, and was never disturbed by the slightest misunderstanding.

On the evening of the same day, the ANNUAL SOIRÉE of the Evangelical Alliance was held at Freemason's Hall, and was addressed by the Earl of Chichester (who presided), the Rev. James Davis, the Rev. Newman Hall, Wm. McArthur, M. P., in a spirit most friendly to the United States, and contrasting favorably with the warlike tone of many newspapers in that period of transient international excitement. Dr. Robinson, of the American chapel in Paris, and myself, spoke in behalf of the American Alliance. . . . [2]

I spent about six weeks in Great Britain in prosecution of my work. I addressed a number of religious anniversaries, special alliance meetings, and social circles, in behalf of the approaching Conference. I appeared before the Annual Meeting of the CONGREGATIONAL UNION OF ENGLAND AND WALES, which received me most kindly, and unanimously adopted a resolution in favor of the object of my mission. I witnessed the opening sessions of the two GENERAL ASSEMBLIES of the ESTABLISHED and FREE CHURCHES OF SCOTLAND, and was most courteously received by the Moderators and prominent members, and assured of their cordial sympathy with this movement, which will probably be given in a more formal manner at their next May meetings. In the meantime formal action was taken by a spirited Conference of representative men of the various churches of Scotland, held in May, in the Bible House at Edinburgh, and animated by the *perfervidum ingenium Scotorum.* [3] I approached the WESLEYAN CONFERENCE of last summer by letter, which was answered "by a vote of thanks, the Conference at the same time expressing its entire sympathy with the object of the meeting."

I had personal interviews with many of the dignitaries and leading divines of the Church of England. . . . and with distinguished

---

[2](Ed.) Charles Seymour Robinson (1829–99), Presbyterian clergyman and hymnologist, was in charge of the American Chapel in Paris (1868–1870); later he pastored a congregation in New York city, which during his ministry became the Madison Avenue Presbyterian Church.

[3](Ed.) "The torrid temperament of the Scots."

Congregationalists, Presbyterians, Wesleyans, Baptists, too numerous to mention.

I addressed to a large number of eminent persons letters of invitation, enclosing copies of the Provisional Programme.

From most of these gentlemen I received expressions of interest and sympathy with the objects of the proposed Conference, and from many of them the promise to attend it in person; while others declined on the ground of advanced age or official duties which detained them at home, and a few made objections to the doctrinal basis of the Alliance, or confessed a want of confidence in all efforts for promoting Christian Unity in the present distracted state of the Church. . . .

Germany

If our Convocation is to command the respect of the leaders of theological thought, and to make more than a passing impression upon Europe as well as America, it must draw largely upon the learned resources of the land of the Reformation which has fought the severest battles against Popery in the sixteenth century, and against infidelity in the nineteenth, and which for the last fifty years has done the mining operations, so to speak, in theology as well as in philology and philosophy. It is true several of the brightest stars in that rare constellation of Christian scholars, who in our age have done such eminent service in the interpretation of the Bible and in every department of Church History, and who, with few exceptions, would have taken a deep interest in our Alliance Conference, are no more among the living. Neander, Nitzch, Olshausen, Stier, Krummacher, Ullmann, Niedner, Rothe, Hengstenberg, have been called to their rest; but Tholuck, Müller, Lange, Twesten, Wichern, and others hoary with age and honors, still remain on the scene of conflict, and a noble band of younger men are rising up to continue their work.

German professors cannot be so easily moved to cross the ocean as English scholars. With all the advantages of long personal friendship, I found it at first a difficult task, and had to take more than one refusal from men who smiled at me skeptically in view of the apparent impossibility of an ecumenical conference in far-distant America, but who now look upon the enterprise with growing favor and faith.

One of the great objections urged is the want of time, which is dearer than gold. The usual vacation is not long enough for a voyage. But this difficulty was removed by the express promise made to me by Herr von Mühler, the Minister of Worship and Public Instruction in Prussia, and Herr von Golther, who occupies the same position in the cabinet of the King of Würtemberg, to grant three months, or even longer leave of absence, to such professors of the Universities as may desire to attend our Council.

I visited most of the Universities in Germany, conversed freely with a large number of professors, pastors, and prominent laymen, and arranged Alliance meetings in Berlin, Halle, Leipzig, Erlangen, Stuttgart, Bonn, Elberfeld, Barmen, Bremen, etc. I shall only speak of two or three.

The Conference held in Berlin, June 21, where the officers of the German Branch of the Evangelical Alliance reside, and where its organ, the *New Evangelical Church Gazette* is edited by Prof. Messner, was of decisive importance for Germany. It was attended by General Superintendent and first Court Chaplain Dr. Hoffmann, who presided, Prof. Drs. Dorner, Semisch, Messner, Kleinert, Piper, Cassel, Court Chaplain Kögel, Count Bernstorf, Dr. Erbkam, banker Lösche, and a number of professors and pastors of the capital of Prussia, about sixty in all. Our embassador, the Hon. George Bancroft, who is admirably qualified to represent our country in the metropolis of continental science and learning, was likewise present, and declared the meeting to be one of the most interesting he had ever attended. The Evangelical Alliance was discussed under all its aspects, and pronounced by one of the speakers to be "the greatest idea of the century." A new General Conference, it was said, was loudly called for by the exigencies of the times, and would probably far surpass in importance the one held at Berlin in 1857, with the special approbation of King Frederick William IV, who, on that occasion, uttered his last public testimony in favor of evangelical truth and Christian union. A paper expressing unqualified sympathy with the movement was unanimously adopted and Dr. Hoffman, Dr. Dorner, Prof. Messner, and Count Bernstorf positively promised to attend in person, and nearly all expressed a desire to do so, if their duties and circumstances would allow.

Almost simultaneously with this meeting, the Methodist General Conference of Germany and Switzerland, then in session at Berlin, of its own accord, passed a resolution of sympathy with the Evangelical Alliance, which affords a platform for personal Christian intercourse high above the rivalries of State churchism and dissent.

The favorable action of the 15th GERMAN CHURCH DIET, held in Stuttgart, in the first days of September last, is of the greatest importance, and commits the heart of evangelical Germany to our cause. This body is a twin-sister of the Evangelical Alliance, animated by the same spirit, aiming at the same end, but confined to the German Churches (Lutheran, Reformed, United Evangelical, and Moravian), as far as they still hold the faith of the Reformation. With it is connected a Congress for Inner Missions, so called, which embraces the various movements of home evangelization and Christian philanthropy, under the lead of Dr. Wichern.[4] The last meeting of the Diet was one of unusual interest, and characterized by delightful Christian harmony; many of the ablest and best men took part in its deliberations on some of the exciting topics of the day—such as the relation of Christianity to common-school education; the labor question (*Arbeiterfrage*); the ways and means to win back to Christianity the alienated masses of the population, especially in large cities. This body, which embraced many of the greatest and best men from all parts of Germany, I addressed on the subject of my mission. The result was a cordial response by the President, to which the crowded assembly assented by raising their hands.

Another large Alliance meeting must be noticed here, which was held at Barmen, October 3, because it introduced a new feature at the suggestion of the Rev. Dr. Fabri, director of the Mission-house in that city. After expressing their full sympathy with our cause, the clergy and laymen of the Wupperthal present adopted a request to

---

[4](Ed.) Johann Hinrich Wichern (1808–81), founder of the Inner Mission, awakened the social conscience of German Protestantism to the plight of the poor and destitute. Wichern did not attend the New York Conference in 1873.

the Executive Committee of the American Alliance, that they might arrange, in connection with or immediately after the Alliance Conference, an *International Conference on the subject of Immigration,* to take into special consideration the social, moral, and religious aspects of the immense emigration from Germany and other parts of Europe to the United States, and to suggest ways and means for the better promotion of the spiritual welfare of the emigrants to this country. With this end in view, Colonel Herrmann, the President of the Langenberg Society for sending evangelical ministers to the German churches in America, was elected delegate to the New York Conference.[5]

This important suggestion was repeated in an Alliance Conference which I held at Bremen, October 8, a day before I sailed, and is cordially approved by Dr. Wichern and others, who take an active religious interest in the German diaspora. It is for the Executive Committee to decide whether this subject shall be made part of the programme, or left to be assigned to a special Conference to be arranged with the aid of the German ministers of New York and vicinity.

Of the four or five German divines to whom I was authorized to extend a special invitation, with the request to prepare a leading paper, and the offer to pay their expenses, all have accepted with the exception of Prof. Dr. Lange, of Bonn, who pleads his official duties and labors on his long Commentary, as obstacles to so long an absence, but who is with us by his whole heart, and wishes us most abundant success.

The Rev. Prof. Dr. Tholuck of Halle, although seventy years of age and in very feeble health, has promised to attend, and to speak

---

[5](Ed.) The Langenberg Society—officially known as "Evangelische Gesellschaft für die protestantischen Deutschen in Nordamerika in Langenberg, Elberfeld, und Barmen" ["Evangelical Society for the Protestant Germans in North America at Langenberg, Elberfeld, and Barmen"]—was founded in 1837 as an outgrowth of the Lower Rhenish Awakening and was interdenominational in character, supporting all German-language churches in the United States. Its two most distinguished emissaries were Schaff himself and August Rauschenbusch, who became a Baptist and was the father of Walter Rauschenbusch. The projected international conference on immigration did not materialize, neither did the Society's president attend the New York Conference.

on the revival and prospects of evangelical theology and religion in Germany, with which he is so largely identified. Prof. Dr. Dorner, of Berlin, has assumed a paper on the Theology of the Reformation in conflict with modern Romanism, which no living scholar is better qualified to discuss from the depths of theological learning. General Superintendent Dr. Hoffmann, of Berlin, who wields a commanding influence at the Court and in the councils of the Evangelical Church of Prussia, will show the harmony of Revelation and Science, with special reference to the recent questions of the origin and antiquity of Man. The Rev. Dr. Wichern, of Hamburg and Berlin, who has done more than any living man to make the Gospel a vital, working power among the masses in Germany, will give us the results of his life-long experience on Inner Missions and works of Christian philanthropy.

For these gentlemen, who stand in the front rank of theological science and practical religion in Germany, it will be a considerable sacrifice to venture across the ocean, and some doubt may be entertained whether their pressing engagements or their feeble health (as in the case of Dr. Tholuck, who is a mere shadow as to his body, but still remarkably fresh and elastic in spirit) will allow them to redeem their promise. But two or three of them may be relied upon, and all will give us their hearty co-operation to the full extent of their ability[6].

. . .

I should not forget to mention that there is, in Germany, a high Lutheran school of learned divines, orthodox but exclusive, and somewhat resembling the High Church party in the Anglican communion: as Dr. Delitzch, Luthardt, Kahnis, Philippi, Harless, Hofmann, Thomasius, Kliefoth, Uhlhorn, who are opposed to an organic union with the Reformed Church, and who, for this reason, cannot

---

[6](Ed.) In the end, only twelve German delegates were present in New York in 1873, compared to seventy-five delegates from Great Britain. It gave Schaff special pleasure that his Tübingen teacher Isaac August Dorner was a member of the German delegation. Leopold Witte, who later distinguished himself as the biographer of Tholuck, read the absent Tholuck's paper on "Evangelical Theology in Germany." Schaff's friend, the court preacher Wilhelm Hoffman, died unexpectedly in August of 1873.

be expected to co-operate with us. But the more liberal among them told me expressly that, if it was not for their antagonism to the Prussian Church-state union, they would gladly attend such an Alliance Conference, since it aims simply at a closer personal union of individual believers, without interfering with the confessional conscience.

With the exception of this school, we may say that the best Christian men in all parts of Germany, who hold the faith of the Reformation Churches, are in cordial sympathy with the objects of our Alliance Conference, and will follow it with their best wishes and prayers for its success. . . .

Concluding Reflections

This report gives a very imperfect idea of the interest which is likely to attach to the approaching Conference in New York. It was simply impossible for me to see or correspond with all the friends of the Evangelical Alliance, and I may have omitted the names of many important men who will gladly lend us efficient co-operation. But enough has been said to prove that we have abundant material at our disposal for one of the most imposing and interesting religious assemblies ever held in this or any other country. The character and weight of such an assembly does not depend upon the number, but the quality of its members. From our own country we can, without much difficulty, secure the attendance of the most distinguished men of all States and denominations. From Europe we may see one or two hundred delegates; we shall welcome them cordially, and, if necessary, we can accommodate even five hundred or a thousand of them. But if we get only twenty or thirty truly representative men from Great Britain, Germany, France, Holland, and Switzerland, with the acknowledged weight of their names, and with the matured results of their life-long study and experience, they will carry the influence of the meeting to every country and church in the old world. No building in this city will be large enough to accommodate the multitudes anxious to see and hear them.

The strength of the Evangelical Alliance must not be measured by the extent of the organizations bearing that name. A distinguished scholar of Germany expressed the sentiments of many when he wrote to me, "I am no regular member of the Alliance, but my whole heart belonged to the cause from the beginning."

I am by no means prepared to pronounce the Evangelical Alliance "the greatest idea of the century," but it certainly represents a great idea. It is in harmony with the last sacerdotal prayer of our Lord for perfect unity, with the heart and soul of Christianity as a religion of love to God and to man, with the nature of the Christian Church as a communion of saints, with modern inventions and improvements in binding together the ends of the earth for commercial and social intercourse, and with the deeper movements in the churches towards greater unity and fellowship for its own sake as well as for a more effectual testimony against the common foe. Aiming simply at a closer union of individual believers, and disclaiming the intention of effecting an organic union in doctrine, government, and worship, or interfering with the internal affairs of the different denominations the Alliance can expect the sympathy and co-operation of those who recognize Christian brethren everywhere, but who are opposed to schemes of ecclesiastical union or confederation. Protestant Christians must learn to esteem and love one another in spite of the distinctive peculiarities of the different denominations to which they severally belong, and must wish each other God's speed in fulfilling the specific mission which Providence has assigned them in a world where there is abundant room and work for all. This seems to be the evangelical Protestant conception of free unity in diversity, as distinct from a compulsory union or an outward uniformity.

It is certainly desirable to have an organization or a number of co-operative organizations for the special work of defending and promoting the interest of the Christian Union. One of the most efficient means to this end is to arrange, from time to time, a General Conference of Christians from all countries. This requires a vast amount of labor, and this labor can be best performed by the existing organizations of the Evangelical Alliance.

The Conference in New York will be the sixth since the formation of the Alliance in 1846; the first having been held in London, the second in Paris [1855], the third in Berlin [1857], the fourth in Geneva [1861], the fifth in Amsterdam [1867]. It will be the first held in America, and the first of a truly intercontinental as well as international and interdenominational character. The signs of the times are very favorable. The two great Presbyterian bodies of the United States, moved unquestionably by the Spirit of God, who alone can allay the bitterness of a thirty years' theological war, have just completed an organic union, from which we may expect the happiest effect upon other denominations and the interests of Christ's kingdom. The papal ecumenical Council, to be held at the close of this year, will be an important event for good or for evil, and calls for a Protestant answer. The Evangelical Alliance is no negative anti-popery society, its first object being to promote Christian unity for its own sake, but it can and ought to defend the interests of Protestantism whenever they are seriously threatened, and stand up for religious liberty wherever the rights of conscience are denied. The approaching Conference will give an equally clear sound against the infidelity of the age, and every tendency which, under the specious name of liberty, undermines the divine honor of Christ, the authority of God's Word, and the interests of vital religion.

To bring Europe and America together in Christ for closer union and fellowship, for a better mutual understanding, for a united testimony against unbelief and false belief, for the promotion of peace and good will of the great Master—this is the object of the New York Conference. Europe will bring us the benefit of her long experience and wisdom, and will be rejuvenated in turn by the fresh, vigorous and hopeful Christianity of America. The foreign delegates will learn more here, in the few days of the Conference, on the working of our voluntary, self-supporting, and self-governing principle than they could in years, and will distribute their impressions through a hundred channels all over the world.

Let us not listen to the common-place objection, that it will be a debating society and end in mere words, while the Roman Council will settle dogmas and speak with infallible authority. Is there no moral and spiritual power deeper and mightier in its effects than legislation and compulsion? Are there no burning words of burning ideas that produce burning actions? The Reformers operated with living words and set the world a fire. The Apostles and Christ himself spoke words of truth and power, and they will kindle life immortal wherever they are heard, to the end of time.

There never was a greater and worthier opportunity to show American liberality and hospitality to the honor of Christ and in the promotion of his cause throughout the world. The eyes of Europe are now upon us, and will hold us responsible for the success or failure of the free Evangelical Catholic Council of 1870.

A vast amount of energy, enthusiasm, and discretion is necessary on the part of those who shall be entrusted with the final preparations. So far the Evangelical Alliance of America has had to live on faith; let faith now be followed by good works. Large and liberal contributions are necessary to meet the expenses of such an assembly.

But, let us not forget that all the money and learning and wisdom of Europe and America combined cannot insure the success of the approaching meeting. Everything depends, first and last, upon the Spirit and blessing of Almighty God, and this can be secured only by the fervent prayers of His people.

Philip Schaff
New York, November 4, 1869.

THE AMERICAN EDITION OF LANGE'S
*Commentary on the Holy Scriptures**

The Bible

The Bible is a book of life, written for the instruction and edification of all ages and nations. No man who has felt its divine beauty and power, would exchange this one volume for all the literature of the world. Eternity alone can unfold the extent of its influence for good. The Bible, like the person and work of our Saviour, is theanthropic in its character and aim. The eternal personal Word of God "was made flesh" [John 1:14], and the whole fullness of the Godhead and of sinless manhood were united in one person forever. So

---

*"Preface to the American Edition," *A Commentary on the Holy Scriptures by John Peter Lange,* ed. Philip Schaff, vol. 1 of the New Testament (Matthew), (New York and Edinburgh, 1864) v-viii, xii-xiii, xvi-xviii.

the spoken word of God may be said to have become flesh in the Bible. It is therefore all divine, and yet all human, from beginning to end. Through the veil of the letter we behold the glory of the eternal truth of God. The divine and human in the Bible sustain a similar relation to each other, as in the person of Christ: they are unmixed, yet inseparably united, and constitute but one life, which kindles life in the heart of the believer.

Viewed merely as a human or literary production, the Bible is a marvelous book, and without a rival. All the libraries of theology, philosophy, history, antiquities, poetry, law and policy would not furnish material enough for so rich a treasure of the choicest gems of human genius, wisdom, and experience. It embraces works of about forty authors, representing the extremes of society, from the throne of the king to the boat of the fisherman; it was written during a long period of sixteen centuries, on the banks of the Nile, in the desert of Arabia, in the land of promise, in Asia Minor, in classical Greece, and in imperial Rome; it commences with the creation and ends with the final glorification, after describing all the intervening stages in the revelation of God and the spiritual development of man; it uses all forms of literary composition; it rises to the highest heights and descends to the lowest depths of humanity; it measures all states and conditions of life; it is acquainted with every grief and every woe; it touches every chord of sympathy; it contains the spiritual biography of every human heart; it is suited to every class of society, and can be read with the same interest and profit by the king and the beggar, by the philosopher and the child; it is as universal as the race, and reaches beyond the limits of time into the boundless regions of eternity. Even this matchless combination of human excellencies points to its divine character and origin, as the absolute perfection of Christ's humanity is an evidence of His divinity.

But the Bible is first and last a book of religion. It presents the only true, universal, and absolute religion of God, both in its preparatory process or growth under the dispensation of the law and the promise, and in its completion under the dispensation of the gospel, a religion which is intended ultimately to absorb all the other religions of the world. It speaks to us as immortal beings on the highest, noblest, and most important themes which can challenge our attention, and with an authority that is absolutely irresistible and over-whelming. It can instruct, edify, warn, terrify, appease, cheer and encourage as no other book. It seizes man in the hidden depths of his intellectual and moral constitution, and goes to the quick of the soul, to that mysterious point where it is connected with the unseen world and with the great Father of spirits. It acts like an all-penetrating and all-transforming leaven upon every faculty of the mind and every emotion of the heart. It enriches the memory; it elevates the reason; it enlivens the imagination; it directs the judgment; it moves the af-fections; it controls the passions; it quickens the conscience; it strengthens the will; it kindles the sacred flame of faith, hope, and charity; it purifies, ennobles, sanctifies the whole man, and brings him into living union with God. It can not only enlighten, reform, and improve, but regenerate and create anew, and produce effects which lie far beyond the power of human genius. It has light for the blind, strength for the weak, food for the hungry, drink for the thirsty; it has a counsel in precept or example for every relation in life, and comfort for every sorrow, a balm for every wound. Of all the books in the world, the Bible is the only one of which we never tire, but which we admire and love more and more in proportion as we use it. Like a diamond, it casts its lustre in every direction; like a torch, the more it is shaken, the more it shines; like a healing herb, the harder it is pressed, the sweeter is its fragrance.

What an unspeakable blessing, that this inexhaustible treasure of divine truth and comfort is now accessible, without material al-teration, to almost every nation on earth in its own tongue, and in Protestant countries at least, even to the humblest man and woman that can read! Nevertheless we welcome every new attempt to open the meaning of this book of books, which is plain enough to a child, and yet deep enough for the profoundest philosopher and the most comprehensive scholar.

Epochs of Exegesis

The Bible—and this is one of the many arguments for its divine character—has given rise to a greater number of discourses, essays, and commentaries, than any other book or class of books; and yet it is now as far from being exhausted as ever. The strongest and noblest minds, fathers, schoolmen, reformers, and modern critics and scholars of every nation of Christendom, have labored in these mines and brought forth precious ore, and yet they are as rich as ever, and hold out the same inducements of plentiful reward to new miners. The long line of commentators will never break off until faith shall be turned into vision, and the church militant transformed into the church triumphant in heaven.

Biblical exegesis, like every other branch of theological science, has its creative epochs and classical periods, followed by periods of comparative rest, when the results gained by the productive labor of the preceding generation are quietly digested and appropriated to the life of the church.

There are especially three such classical periods: the patristic, the reformatory, and the modern. The exegesis of the fathers, with the great names of Chrysostom and Theodoret of the Greek, and Jerome and Augustine of the Latin Church, is essentially Catholic; the exegesis of the reformers, as laid down in the immortal biblical works of Luther and Melanchthon, Zwingli and Oecolampadius, Calvin and Beza, is Protestant; the modern exegesis of Germany, England, and America, may be called, in its best form and ruling spirit, Evangelical Catholic. . . . The modern Anglo-German exegesis is less dogmatical, confessional, and polemical than either of its predecessors, but more critical, free, and liberal, more thorough and accurate in all that pertains to philological and antiquarian research; and while it thankfully makes use of the labors of the fathers and reformers, it seems to open the avenue for new developments in the ever-expanding and deepening history of Christ's kingdom on earth.

The patristic exegesis is, to a large extent, the result of a victorious conflict of ancient Christianity with Ebionism, Gnosticism, Arianism, Pelagianism, and other radical heresies, which roused and stimulated the fathers to a vigorous investigation and defence of the truth as laid down in the Scriptures and believed by the Church. The exegesis of the reformers bears on every page the marks of the gigantic war with Romanism and its traditions of men. So the modern evangelical theology of Germany has grown up amidst the changing fortunes of more than thirty years' war of Christianity with Rationalism and Pantheism. The future historian will represent this intellectual and spiritual conflict, which is not yet concluded, as one of the most important and interesting chapters in history, and as one of the most brilliant victories of faith over unbelief, of Christian truth over anti-Christian error. The German mind has never, since the Reformation, developed a more intense and persevering activity, both for and against the gospel, than in this period, and if it should fully overcome the modern and most powerful attacks upon Christianity, it will achieve as important a work as the Reformation of the sixteenth century. Former generations have studied the Bible with as much and perhaps more zeal, earnestness, and singleness of purpose, than the present. But never before has it been subjected to such thorough and extensive critical, philological, historical, and antiquarian, as well as theological investigation and research. Never before has the critical apparatus been so ample or so easy of access, the most ancient manuscripts of the Bible having been newly discovered, as the Codex Sinaiticus, Vaticanus, Alexandrinus, Ephraemi Syri, and the discoveries and researches of travellers, antiquarians, historians, and chronologers being made tributary to the science of the Book of books. No age has been so productive in commentaries on almost every part of the sacred canon, but more particularly on the Gospels, the Life of Christ, and the Epistles of the New Testament. It is very difficult to keep up with the progress of the German press in this department. One commentary follows another in rapid succession, and the best of them are constantly reappearing in new and improved editions, which render the old ones useless for critical purposes. Still the intense productivity of this period must sooner or later be exhausted, and give way to the more quiet activity of reproduction and application.

The time has now arrived for the preparation of a comprehensive theological commentary which shall satisfy all the theoretical and practical demands of the evangelical ministry of the present generation; and serve as a complete exegetical library for constant reference: a commentary learned, yet popular, orthodox and sound, yet unsectarian, liberal and truly catholic in spirit and aim; combining with the original research the most valuable results of the exegetical labors of the past and the present, and making them available for the practical use of ministers and the general good of the church. Such a commentary can be successfully wrought out only at such a fruitful period of Biblical research as the present, and by an association of experienced divines equally distinguished for ripe scholarship and sound piety, and fully competent to act as mediators between the severe science of the professorial chair and the practical duties of the pastoral office.

Lange's Commentary

Such a commentary is the *Bibelwerk* of Dr. Lange, assisted by a number of distinguished evangelical divines and pulpit orators of Germany, Switzerland, and Holland. . . .

Dr. Lange's theology is essentially biblical and evangelical catholic, and inspired by a fresh and refreshing enthusiasm for truth in all its types and aspects. It is more positive and decided than that of Neander or Tholuck, and yet more liberal and conciliatory than the orthodoxy of Hengstenberg, which is often harsh and repulsive.[7] Lange is one of the most uncompromising opponents of German rationalism and scepticism, and makes no concessions to the modern attacks on the gospel history. But he always states his views with moderation, and in a Christian and amiable spirit; and he endeavors to spiritualize and idealize doctrines and facts, and thus to make them more plausible to enlightened reason. His orthodoxy, it is true, is not the fixed, exclusive orthodoxy either of the old Lutheran, or of the old Calvinistic Confession, but it belongs to that recent evangelical type which arose in conflict with modern infidelity, and going back to the Reformation and the still higher and purer fountain of primitive Christianity, as it came from the hands of Christ and his inspired apostles, aims to unite the true elements of the Reformed and Lutheran confessions, and on this firm historical basis to promote catholic unity and harmony among the conflicting branches of Christ's Church. It is evangelical catholic, churchly, yet unsectarian, conservative, yet progressive; it is the truly living theology of the age.

---

[7](Ed.) Here Schaff is also describing his own position over against his former teachers at Halle and Berlin.

It is this very theology which, for the last ten or twenty years, has been transplanted in multiplying translations to the soil of other Protestant countries, which has made a deep and lasting impression on the French, Dutch, and especially in the English and American mind. It is this theology which is now undergoing a process of naturalization and amalgamation in the United States, which will here be united with the religious fervor, the sound, strong common sense, and free, practical energy of the Anglo-American race, and which in this modified form has a wider field of usefulness before it in this new world than even in its European fatherland.

There are standard commentaries on special portions of the Scriptures, which excel all others, either in a philosophical or theological or practical point of view, either in brevity and condensation or in fulness of detail, either in orthodoxy of doctrine and soundness of judgment or in expository skill and fertility of adaptation, or in some other particular aspect. But, upon the whole, the Biblical work of Dr. Lange and his associates is the richest, the soundest, and the most useful general commentary which Germany ever produced, and far better adapted than any other to meet the wants of the various evangelical denominations of the English tongue. This is not only my individual opinion, but the deliberate judgment of some of the best Biblical and German scholars of America whom I have had occasion to consult on the subject.

The Anglo-American Edition

A work of such sterling value cannot be long confined to the land of its birth. America, as it is made up of descendants from all countries, nations, and churches of Europe (*e pluribus unum*), is set upon appropriating all important literary treasures of the old world, especially those which promise to promote the moral and religious welfare of the race.

Soon after the appearance of the first volume of Dr. Lange's Commentary, I formed, at the solicitation of a few esteemed friends, and with the full consent of Dr. Lange himself, an association for an American edition, and in September, 1860, I made the necessary ar-

rangements with my friend, Mr. Charles Scribner, as publisher.[8] The
secession of the slave States, and the consequent outbreak of the civil
war in 1861, paralyzed the book trade, and indefinitely suspended
the enterprise. But in 1863 it was resumed at the suggestion of the
publisher and with the consent of Mr. T. Clark, of Edinburgh, who
in the mean time (since 1861) had commenced to publish translations of parts of Lange's Commentary in his "Foreign Theological
Library."[9] I moved to New York for the purpose of devoting myself
more fully to this work amid the literary facilities of the city, completed the first volume, and made arrangements with leading Biblical and German scholars of different evangelical denominations for
the translation of the other volumes. . . .

Principles of the American Edition

The character of the proposed Anglo-American edition of Lange's
Bibelwerk, and its relation to the original, may be seen from the following general principles and rules on which it will be prepared and

---

[8]I may be permitted to state that I went into this enterprise at first with considerable reluctance, partly from a sense of its vast labor and responsibility, partly
because it involved in all probability the abandonment of an original, though much
shorter commentary (German and English) which I had been preparing for the last
twenty years, and of which a few specimens appeared in the *Kirchenfreund* (1848–
53) and in the *Mercersburg Review.* But the task seemed to devolve on me naturally
and providentially, and I gradually became so interested in it that I am willing to
sacrifice for it other cherished literary projects. Dr. Lange himself, in forwarding
to me an early copy of the first volume, wished me to take part in the original
work, and encouraged me afterward to assume the editorial supervision of the English translation, giving me every liberty as regards additions and improvements.
I made, however, no use of my old notes on Matthew, leaving all my exegetical
manuscripts boxed up with my library at Mercersburg. I did not wish to mix two
works which differ in plan and extent, and adapted my additions to the general
character and plan of Lange's work and the wants of the English reader.

(Ed.) Charles Scribner (1821–71), who had founded his publishing house in
1846, from the outset was interested in theological and philosophical publications
by leading evangelical Protestant authorities. Among British authors, for instance, he also published Dean Stanley, Professor Jowett, and Gladstone.

[9](Ed.) Sir Thomas Clark (1823–98) was a partner in the Edinburgh publishing
house of T. & T. Clark, 1846–86.

to which all contributors must conform, to insure unity and symmetry.

1. The Biblical Commentary of Dr. Lange and his associates must be faithfully and freely translated into idiomatic English, without omission or alteration.

2. The translator is authorized to make, within reasonable limits, such additions, original or selected, as will increase the value and interest of the work, and adapt it more fully to the wants of the English and American student. But he must carefully distinguish these additions from the original text by brackets and the initials of his name, or the mark *Tr.*

3. The authorized English version of 1611, according to the present standard edition of the American Bible Society, must be made the basis, instead of giving a new translation, which, in this case, would have to be a translation of a translation. But wherever the text can be more clearly or accurately rendered, according to the present state of textual criticism and biblical learning, or where the translation and the commentary of the German original require it, the improvements should be inserted into the text (in brackets, with or without the Greek, as the writer may deem best in each case) and justified in the Critical Notes below the text, with such references to older and recent English and other versions as seem to be necessary or desirable

4. The various readings are not to be put in foot-notes, as in the original, but to follow immediately after the text in small type, in numerical order, and with references to the verses to which they belong.

5. The three parts of the commentary are to be called: I. EXEGETICAL AND CRITICAL; II. DOCTRINAL AND ETHICAL; III. HOMILETICAL AND PRACTICAL.

6. The EXEGETICAL NOTES are not to be numbered consecutively, as in the original, but marked by the figure indicating the verse to which they belong; an arrangement which facilitates the reference, and better accords with usage.

7. Within these limits each contributor has full liberty, and assumes the entire literary responsibility of his part of the work.

If these general principles are faithfully carried out, the American edition will be not only a complete translation, but an enlarged adaptation and improvement of the original work, giving it an Anglo-German character, and a wider field of usefulness.

The typographical arrangement will be closely conformed to the original, as upon the whole the best in a work of such dimensions. A page of the translation contains even more than a page of the original, and while the size of volumes will be enlarged, their number will be lessened.

THE SCHAFF-HERZOG ENGYCLOPEDIA*

The object of the RELIGIOUS ENCYCLOPAEDIA is to give, in alphabetical order, a summary of the most important information on all branches and topics of theological learning,—exegetical, historical, biographical, doctrinal, and practical,—for the use of ministers, students, and intelligent laymen of all denominations. It will be completed in three volumes.

The ENCYCLOPAEDIA was suggested by the *Real-Encyklopädie für protestantische Theologie und Kirche,* edited by Drs. J. J. Herzog, G. L. Plitt, and A. Hauck (Leipzig, 1877sqq.).[10] This work, with which I have been familiar from its start, as one of the contributors,[11] is uni-

---

A Religious Encyclopedia . . . Based on the Real-Encyclopädie of Herzog, Plitt, and Hauck, vol. 1 (New York, 1882) iii-iv.

[10](Ed.) Johann Jakob Herzog (1805–82), Swiss Reformed theologian, who since 1854 taught Reformed theology at Erlangen, upon Tholuck's recommendation prepared the 1st edition of the *Realencyclopädie* (1853–68). For the 2nd edition (1877–88) he was joined by Gustav Leopold Plitt (1836–80), Lutheran church historian at Erlangen, and after Plitt's death by Albert Hauck (1845–1918), Protestant church historian at Leipzig and author of the monumental *Kirchengeschichte Deutschlands,* 4 vols. (Leipzig, 1886–1905), who after Herzog's death was the sole editor of the 3rd edition of the *Realencyclopädie* (1896–1909).

[11](Ed.) To the second edition Schaff contributed the following articles: "Channing," "Hare, Julius Charles," "Methodismus in Amerika," "Nordamerika, Vereinigte Staaten," "Robinson, Eduard," "Savanarola," "Tertullianus," and "Westminster-Synode."

versally acknowledged to be an invaluable thesaurus of solid information in all departments of biblical and ecclesiastical learning, under the responsible names of a large number of eminent German and other European scholars. The first edition, edited by Dr. Herzog alone, was begun in 1854, and completed in 1868, in twenty-two volumes. The second edition, thoroughly revised and partly rewritten, is now in course of publication, and will be completed in not less than fifteen volumes. A mere translation of this *opus magnum* would not answer the wants of the English and American reader. While many articles are very long, and of comparatively little interest outside of Germany, the department of English and American church history and biography is, naturally, too limited. For instance, the art. *Brüder des gemeinsamen Lebens* ["Brethren of the Common Life"] has 82 pages; *Eherecht* ["Marriage Law"], 35; *Gnosis*, 43, *Jerusalem*, 37; *Liturgie*, 36; *Luther*, 36; *Mandäer*, 17; *Mani*, 36; *Melanchthon*, 54. These articles are all very good; but a proportionate treatment of important English and American topics which are barely mentioned or altogether omitted, would require a much more voluminous encyclopaedia than the original. In the present work few articles exceed four pages; but the reader is throughout referred to books where fuller information can be obtained.

My esteemed friend Dr. Herzog, and his editorial colleagues,— the late Dr. Plitt, who died Sept. 10, 1880, and Professor A. Hauck, who has taken his place, as also the publisher, Mr. H. Rost,[12] who issued the German edition of my *Church History*—have kindly given me full liberty to make such use of their work in English as I may deem best. It is needless to say that I would not have undertaken the task without a previous honorable understanding with the German editors and publisher.

This ENCYCLOPAEDIA, therefore, is not a translation, but a condensed reproduction and adaptation of all the important German articles, with necessary additions, especially in the literature, and with

---

[12](Ed.) Heinrich Rost was the head of the publishing house of J. C. Hinrichs in Leipzig, having succeeded his late father Christian Friedrich Adolf Rost who had carried on the work of the founder Johann Conrad Hinrichs, retaining the original name.

a large number of new articles by the editors and special contributors. More than one-third of the work is original. Every article is credited to its author, except the majority of editorial articles, which were unsigned. An apology may be due the German authors for abridging their contributions, but we have studied to give all the essential facts. Dissenting opinions, or material additions, are included in brackets. The bibliography has been largely increased throughout, especially by English and American works. Living celebrities are excluded. Denominational articles have been assigned to scholars who represent their denomination in a liberal Christian spirit. On important topics of controversy both sides are given a hearing. It has been the desire of the editors to allow a wide latitude of opinion within the limits of evangelical Christianity.

All important encylopaedias besides that of Dr. Herzog and a large number of books in different languages, have been carefully consulted, but never used without due acknowledgment. The assistant editors have devoted their whole time and strength to the work, in my library, and under my direction.[13]

I have been fortunate enough in securing the hearty cooperation of a number of eminent American and English scholars of different denominations and schools of thought, who can speak with authority on the topics assigned them, and will largely increase the original value of this ENCYCLOPAEDIA.

Philip Schaff
New York, September, 1882.

---

[13](Ed.) Clemens Petersen (for a short term) and Samuel Macauley Jackson (1851–1912) became assistant editors in 1880, and the following year were joined by David S. Schaff (1852–1941), Schaff's son and biographer.

CHAPTER 7

The Revision of the English Bible

EDITORIAL INTRODUCTION

The great Bible translations of the sixteenth-century Reformation in Germany and England had entered into the very fabric of the culture of both nations. But with the tremendous strides biblical scholarship had made in the nineteenth century, many felt more and more strongly the need for revising the venerable Luther Bible and King James Version by updating their language and by bringing them into closer conformity with the best biblical texts that had by then become available. A revision of the Luther Bible was officially authorized in 1857 and completed in 1883 with the publication of the so-called *Probebibel.* In England the Convocation of Canterbury of the Church of England authorized in 1870 the first revision in 260 years of the King James Version, at the same time establishing two Companies for the task, one for each of the two Testaments. Rules specified that the revision was to follow a conservative approach: alterations were to reflect the best available biblical texts, but the language of the Authorized Version of 1611 was to be retained as far as possible. The original rules also stipulated that the two Companies should feel free to invite the cooperation of eminent scholars, "to whatever nation or religious body they may belong." Even more significant for the future course of the revision was the resolution passed by the Convocation of Canterbury on July 7, 1870, "to invite the cooperation of some American divines."[1] The "American divine," who more than anyone else would help to assure the successful completion of this international and interdenominational venture, was Philip Schaff. It was probably the most distinguished project of his career.[2]

As the American editor of Lange's *Commentary on the Holy Scriptures,* Schaff was well prepared for this new task. He was in hearty sympathy with the conservative aims of the revision, and he could later claim that the commentaries which he had edited in Lange's Bible Commentary had anticipated many of the alterations of the Revised Version of 1881: Matthew—"about one half"; John—"two thirds to three fourths"; Romans—"more than two thirds."[3]

While the Lange project would continue to occupy him for another decade, his preparations for the New York Conference of the Evanglical Alliance, as already mentioned, had come to an abrupt halt on August 5, 1870. It is remarkable that only two weeks later, August 18, the indefatigable Schaff eagerly and firmly committed himself to the new project of the Bible Revision. Dr. Angus, an English delegate to the Evangelical Alliance conference, had arrived early, but as he also represented the British Revision Committee, he had approached Schaff in New York as the American scholar best qualified to initiate and support a joint revision of the

---

[1]*Documentary History of the American Committee on Revision,* ed. P. Schaff (New York, 1885) 11.

[2]The documentary evidence for the work of the American Bible Revision Committee is conveniently gathered in *Documentary History of the American Committee on Revision,* of which only 100 copies were privately printed. However, an abridged version was published by Timothy Dwight, *Historical Account of the American Committee of Revision of the Authorized English Version of the Bible* (New York, 1885). Presumably because he had at hand so much documentary evidence, chapter 14, "The Revision of the English Bible, 1870–1885," in David S. Schaff's biography of his father is especially helpful, as is C. J. Cadoux, "The Revised Version and After," in *The Bible in Its Ancient and English Versions,* ed. H. Wheeler Robinson (Oxford, 1940) 235-74.

[3]Schaff, *A Companion to the Greek Testament and the English Version,* 4th ed. (New York, 1892) 353n. 1. According to Matthew B. Riddle, *The Story of the Revised New Testament: American Standard Edition* (Philadelphia, 1908) 13, the Lange Commentary "had anticipated the larger proportion of the changes finally accepted by the Revisers."

English Bible. In his written response to Dr. Angus Schaff at once outlined a preliminary program for an American Committee of Revision. In due time, he would become the President of the American Committee and a member of its New Testament Company.

As he cooperated with German scholars in the American edition of Lange's Bible Commentary, so he would now at the same time cooperate with British scholars in the revision of the English Bible, and he would do so by organising a team of American scholars, many of whom he engaged in both of these projects. Indeed, one-third of his collaborators in the American edition of Lange became fellow-revisers, which was one-half of the membership of the American Revision Committee.[4] In 1873 he and Dorner, a delegate to the New York conference of the Evangelical Alliance, attended a meeting of the American Bible Revision Committee and even tried, though unsuccesfully, to initiate cooperation at least by correspondence between the Anglo-American revision and its German counterpart. One should note that several of Schaff's former teachers, Twesten, Tholuck, Kapff and Dorner, participated in the German revision.[5]

All the friends of the Revision had in common the love of the Bible as the inspired record of the divine Word (to which Schaff sang his beautiful paean in the first volume of the American edition of Lange's *Commentary*).[6] But Schaff truly surpassed all other revisers in the strength and depth of his passionate concern for the unity of the church. He was fearful of the threat of "sectarian" Bible revisions, or even the isolated efforts of individual scholars, and therefore bent all his efforts on achieving a revision that would appear, so he wrote Dean Stanley, with a "sort of ecumenical authority" and, consequently, would be another bond of union and a common source of life for the churches of English-speaking Prot-

---

[4]See Campbell, "Biblical Criticism in America 1858–1892: The Emergence of the Historical Critic," 140, who also mentions that seven out of the eight founding members of the Society of Biblical Literature participated in the Lange Commentary or the Bible Revision (251). Some of these same men were also active in the Evangelical Alliance.

[5]See *Documentary History*, 83, and Schaff, *History of the Christian Church*, vol. 6 (New York, 1888) 366.

[6]See above, pp. 239-41.

estantism.[7] He was pleased that the British Committee also included non-Anglicans: the Old Testament Company three
Presbyterians, two Baptists and one Congregationalist, besides
eighteen Anglicans; the New Testament Company three Presbyterians and one Baptist, Congregationalist, Methodist and Unitarian, besides seventeen Anglicans. In organising the American
Companies, not only Biblical scholarship and proximity to New
York but interdenominational representation were Schaff's guiding principles. In the end, nine denominations were represented on
the American Committee: Episcopal, Congregationalist, Presbyterian, Lutheran, Reformed, Methodist, Baptist, Unitarian and
Quaker.[8] Such an auspicious scholarly and ecumenical beginning
later appeared to Schaff "almost in the light of a moral miracle."[9]
The biblical and ecumenical motifs, above all, added to all his labors for the Bible revision the pathos of a holy enthusiasm.

Hardly less significant, however, was Schaff's executive ability
in organising and supervising large scholarly projects that were both
interdenominational and international in scope. Herein he was
greatly aided by his extensive travels and his eagerness to seek out
fellow-scholars wherever he went. He had first displayed his executive talent in his succesful chairmanship of the Liturgical Committee of the German Reformed church (1852-57). During the New
York years of his career this talent came to full fruition, for as soon
as he entered the wider world of evangelical Protestantism he recognized the remarkable potential of the committee as a working tool
in the pursuit of scholarly and practical goals. Gifted as he was in
mediating between ideas and people, he was soon equally adept at
utilizing the committee as a potent instrument for the achievement
of cherished ecumenical and evangelical ends. His ecumenical fervor and executive ability, however, were to be severely tested at three
different occasions in the course of the Bible revision.

At least at the outset sectarian strife could not be avoided. In
England it was the inclusion of the "sects" generally in the Revi-

---

[7]*Documentary History,* 37 (letter, 7 February 1871).

[8]For a full list of the members of the British and American Committees, see
Schaff, *A Companion to the Greek Testament,* 571-77, and Cadoux, "The Revised
Version and After," 242-47.

[9]Schaff, *A Companion to the Greek Testament,* 381.

sion Committee, and especially of the Unitarian Dr. G. Vance Smith in the New Testament Company and his participation in the Committee's opening eucharistic service at Westminster Abbey, that prompted the Dean of Chichester, Dr. Burgon, the redoubtable leader of the opposition to the Revision and spokesman for the high-church party, to cry out with indignation: "What else is this but to offer a deliberate insult to the Majesty of Heaven in the Divine Person of Him who is alike Object of the everlasting Gospel and its author?"[10] In America the question of the participation of episcopal bishops in the work of revision caused similar difficulties, even delaying the beginning of the actual work of the Revision Committee until October 4, 1872. These difficulties reflected the obvious differences between the United States, where the Protestant Episcopal church was one denomination among others, and England, where, for instance, the presiding officer of each of the two companies of the Revision Committee quite naturally was an Anglican bishop. The Protestant Epicopal church, which had declined an official participation in the American Revision through its presiding bishop, Dr. Horatio Potter of New York, could therefore in any event not have been given a privileged position in the work of Revision. As a matter of fact, a broad-minded bishop like Charles P. McIlvaine of the diocese of Ohio thought it most appropriate that Schaff, a non-Episcopalian, had been elected the President of the American Committee.[11] However, Bishop Wilberforce informed Schaff that for the cooperation of the two Committees to begin the Protestant Episcopal church must be represented "distinctly and acceptably" on the American Committee. Schaff was informed that "The presence of two Bishops or so would at once give the home-public of Church-people the needed

---

[10]Quoted in ibid., 294n. Canon Westcott had proposed, and Dean Stanley had arranged, the common eucharistic service. Later one of the revisers, Professor Hort, wrote: "What one goes back to is that marvellous Communion in Henry VII's Chapel. Its quiet and solemnity . . . is never to be forgotten. It is, one can hardly doubt, the beginning of a new period in Church history." See *A History of the Ecumenical Movement: 1517–1948*, ed. Ruth Rouse and Stephen Charles Neill (Philadelphia, 1954) 337.

[11]*Documentary History*, 60.

confidence."[12] A time-consuming scramble was on for Schaff to invite in personal correspondence several bishops, all of whom, for various reasons, sent their regrets, except, finally, for Bishop Alfred Lee of Delaware. His membership in the New Testament Company made possible the inauguration of the work of the American Committee. As Dean Stanley privately told Schaff to his great relief in London during the summer of 1872: "One bishop is quite enough."[13]

An even more formidable hurdle presented itself as soon as the crucial question of the mode of cooperation between the two Committees arose. The American revisers had readily accepted the principles of revision laid down by the British Committee. Both Committees had agreed to exchange the revised text of each biblical book and to consider each other's proposed alterations. Remaining differences, as the constitution of the American Committee proposed, were to be ironed out at a final conference of both Committees, preferrably in London. However, as work progressed, the implementation of joint responsibility for the revision—accepted in principle by both sides but found difficult to carry out in praxis because of the Atlantic Ocean—became increasingly urgent for the American revisers. At stake were the sensitive questions of scholarly self-esteem, the Committee's standing with the American public and financial support. After having at first carried the additional burden of securing financial backing for the Revision almost by himself, Schaff had finally, in the spring of 1875, succeeded in establishing a Financial Committee of dedicated laymen for the support of the American Committee. Though the members of the American Committee did not receive any renumeration for their labors, they still had to have at least their travelling expenses and other incidental Committee expenses covered. While the University Presses paid all the expenses of the British Committee, the American Committee, following a hallowed American tradition, instead relied entirely upon voluntary contributions.[14] These contributions

---

[12]Ibid., 59.

[13]Ibid., 70.

[14]The University Presses paid $100,000 for the expenses of the British Committee; the American Committee raised $44,761.60, not all of which they spent (Dwight, *Historical Account of the American Committee of Revision,* 70).

would hardly be substantial, however, if the American Committee
was perceived to be inferior to the British Committee, that is, if
the British Committee were to recognize the Americans merely as
"advisers" but not as "fellow-revisers."

Early in 1875 the American Committee instructed Schaff to take
up the "unsettled question of our precise status as to the authorship
of the joint revision" with the British Committee.[15] In the summer
of 1875 he entered into personal negotiations with the British
Committee in the historic Jerusalem Chamber in Westminster Abbey, where both Companies, meeting separately, did their work.
At stake was the ecumenical character of the Bible Revision, for
Schaff knew, of course, that each Committee was quite capable of
carrying through successfully its own revision. In separate presen-
tations to both Companies (June 15 and July 8), he argued persua-
sively that scholarly justice, national honor and securing the
American copyright (there was as yet no international copyright)
demanded a joint authorship. And he prevailed. The British Committee agreed, and so did later the American revisers, that each
Committee admit two members from the other Committee. Schaff
considered those strenuous negotiations, which had secured a joint
revision, one of the high points of his life.[16]

Yet another difficulty presented itself almost at once. The University Presses, which as copyright owners had to approve the 1875
resolution, made acceptance of the joint authorship dependent upon
the payment of $25,000 for the American copyright. Then, in the
summer of 1876, they abruptly terminated the cooperation of the
British Committee with the Americans, after the American Committee had found this financial condition unacceptable and, moreover, an unwarranted intrusion of a legal question (copyright) into
a moral question (joint responsibility). At the end of December,
while on his way to Palestine, Schaff visited London for the fourth
time for personal negotiations with the British on behalf of a joint
Bible revision. And once more his efforts prevailed, even though
the agreement was finalized in his absence the following summer.
It was now stipulated that American alterations, which the British

---

[15]*Documentary History,* 85.

[16]David S. Schaff, *Life of Schaff,* 169. For the text of Schaff's "Plea" to the
British Committee, see *Documentary History,* 89-93.

Committee had been unable to accept, would be published as an
Appendix to the Revised Version for fourteen years; then the
Americans would be free to publish a Revised Version incorporating their own alterations. Schaff later offered the opinion that "upon
the whole" this was the best compromise "that could be made in
justice to all the parties concerned."[17] And he viewed the proposed
American edition not as a "rival Revision" but merely as "an
American recension of one and the same Revision," for the American alterations "will no more affect the unity of the Revision than
the differences of English and American spelling now affect the unity
of the English language."[18] In May of 1881, amidst great public
excitement and expectations, the revised New Testament was published in both countries. The Old Testament, together with the
New Testament, "being the Version set forth A.D. 1611 compared
with the most ancient authorities and revised," was published four
years later.

It is no doubt true that the Revision of 1881–1885 marked "a
milestone in the history of the English Bible."[19] Schaff, ever the
optimist, expected the Revised Version to gain the speedy and wide
acceptance of the churches and the public at large. Yet he soon discovered, as he later wrote, that both the German *Probebibel* and the
Anglo-American Bible Revision had to pass "through the same
purgatory of hostile criticism both from conservative and progressive quarters." There was one interesting difference, though. In
Germany interest in the revision was confined to scholars, "and
German scholars, however independent and bold in theory, are very
conservative and timid in practical matters," while in the United
States, "where theology moves in close contact with the life of the
churches, revision challenges the attention of the laity which claims

---

[17]Schaff in Alexander Roberts, *Companion to the Revised Version of the New Testament. With Supplement, By a Member of the American Committee of Revision* (London
and New York, 1881) 172.

[18]Ibid., 205. Schaff's "Supplement" and Riddle, *The Story of the Revised New
Testament: The American Edition,* offer a full discussion of the distinctive features of
the American Appendix.

[19]*The Cambridge History of the Bible: The West from the Reformation to the Present
Day,* ed. S. L. Greenslade (Cambridge, 1963) 372.

the fruits of theological progress."[20] In the English-speaking world books, pamphlets and numerous articles in journals and newspapers soon argued heatedly and learnedly for and against the Revised Version. Dean Burgon, who temperamentally was "so conservative as to be the ideal Oxonian defender of lost causes," spoke out most loudly and even brilliantly in favor of the *textus receptus* and the hallowed Elizabethan idiom of the King James Version.[21] On the American side, Charles A. Briggs, to Schaff's great disappointment, trenchantly criticized the Old Testament revision because of its complete neglect of the insights offered by the "higher criticism"; he mildly criticized the New Testament revision because of its often pedantic and overrefined scholarship.[22] A consensus soon developed that the Revised Version was "useful for study" but the King James Version better for "devotional purposes." As Charles Spurgeon, the popular English preacher, put it for the New Testament: the revision was "strong in Greek, weak in English."[23] Schaff knew that the revision would be viewed as either "too radical" or "too conservative," but he added hopefully, ever the mediator: "it will be found to occupy the sound medium between the two extremes."[24] He offered his most detailed and explicit explanation and defense of the Revision in his *Companion to the Greek Testament and English Version* (1883, 4th ed. 1892), which some considered his "best book" and which was highly regarded also by

---

[20]Schaff, *History of the Christian Church*, 6:367. According to Schaff, German alterations for the New Testament numbered only 200, as compared with 36,000 in the Anglo-American Revision. A further revision of the *Probebibel* was published in 1892.

[21]F. F. Bruce, *The English Bible* (New York, 1961) 148. For Dr. Burgon's criticism, see his *The Revision Revised* (London, 1883).

[22]Charles A. Briggs, "The Revised English Version of the Old Testament," *The Presbyterian Review* 6 (July 1885): 486-533.

[23]Riddle, *The Story of the Revised New Testament*, 72. Spurgeon is quoted by Geddes MacGregor, *The Bible in the Making* (Philadelphia and New York, 1959) 212.

[24]Schaff in *Anglo-American Bible Revision. By Members of the American Revision Committee*, ed. P. Schaff (New York, 1879) 20.

German scholars.[25] The texts here included are taken from this book and an "Introduction" (1873) Schaff had earlier written for *The Revision of the English Version of the New Testament*, whose authors were the English revisers J. B. Lightfoot, R. C. Trench and C. J. Ellicott. Publicist and spokesman for the Bible Revision, Schaff also travelled widely, in the summer of 1878 to the Midwest and even to San Francisco, and kept his pen busy writing articles for journals and newspapers.

When the members of the American Revision Committee looked back at their work in 1885, they also praised the "great service" their President had rendered, his "untiring energy and constant devotion to the interests of the work, from its inception to its close," and they publicly declared: "It was owing to him, more than to any other, that the work was undertaken in this country, and to him likewise is largely due the success with which the means for carrying it forward have been secured."[26] Schaff himself felt fully compensated for all the time and labor he and the others had expended upon the Bible revision because of two accomplishments that remind us once more of the biblical and ecumenical mainsprings of his work. He celebrated the publication of the Revised New Testament as "a republication of the Gospel" and the joint revision as "the noblest monument of Christian union and co-operation in this nineteenth century."[27] To Timothy Dwight he wrote in 1892: "It is impossible that a work to which a hundred scholars of various denominations of England and America have unselfishly devoted so much time and strength can be lost. Whether the Revised Version may or may not replace the King James's Version, it will remain a noble monument of Christian scholarship and co-operation, which in its single devotion to Christ and to truth rises above the dividing

---

[25]For an appreciative German review, see Oscar von Gebhardt, *Theologische Literaturzeitung* (8 March 1890). Having noted the claim that this was his "best book," Schaff added: "But I hope that this is not true. At all events, the Church History and the Creeds of Christendom cost me a great deal more labor" ("Autobiographical Reminiscences," 106).

[26]Dwight, *Historical Account of the American Committee of Revision*, 56.

[27]Roberts, *Companion to the Revised Version of the English New Testament. With Supplement*, 175, 206.

lines of schools and sects."[28] Only four months before his death he attended a meeting of the surviving members of the New Testament Company, who had gathered in New Haven to begin preparing the American Revised Version published finally in 1901.[29] Schaff wanted the Bible to be kept alive by revising it every fifty years. The Revised Standard Version, more succesful in gaining public acceptance than the Revised Version Schaff had helped to prepare, was in fact published about fifty years after the American Edition of 1901.[30] We conclude the introduction to this important chapter in Schaff's life with words that seem especially appropriate: "This brings us to the end of a story which has no end, for the task of revision will never be completed."[31]

THE REVISION OF THE ENGLISH VERSION OF HOLY SCRIPTURES*

The British Revision Committee

The present organized effort to revise the Authorized English Version of the Holy Scriptures originated, after long previous dis-

---

[28]*The Semi-Centennial of Philip Schaff* (privately printed, 1893) 47.

[29]See Matthew B. Riddle, one of the surviving members of the American Revision Committee who began work on the American Standard Edition: "As Dr. Schaff had been so successful in soliciting funds for the expenses prior to 1881, both companies instinctively looked to him for leadership in the new enterprise" (*The Story of the Revised New Testament*, 55). When the publishing firm of Thomas Nelson and Sons acquired the copyright for the American Standard Edition in 1897, it agreed to pay in full the incidental expenses of the Committee. Unauthorized Bible Versions incorporating the American Appendix had already been published in 1881 and, without prior consultation with the American revisers, by the English University Presses in 1898.

[30]For a brief account of the relationship of the Revised Version (1881–1885) and the American Standard Edition (1901) to the Revised Standard Version (1946–1951), see the preface to the Revised Standard Version.

[31]Allen Wikgren, "The English Bible," In *The Interpreter's Bible*, vol. 1 (New York and Nashville, 1952) 101.

*Introduction to J. B. Lightfoot, R. C. Trench, and C. J. Ellicott, *The Revision of the English Version of the New Testament* (New York, 1873) ix, xv-xvii, xx-xxiv.

cussions, in the Convocation of Canterbury. This body, at its session May 6, 1870, took the following action, proposed by a committee which consisted of eight bishops, the late Dean Alford, Dean Stanley, and several other dignitaries:[1]

1. That it is desirable that a revision of the Authorized Version of the Holy Scriptures be undertaken.
2. That the revision be so conducted as to comprise both marginal renderings and such emendations as it may be found necessary to insert in the text of the Authorized Version.
3. That in the above resolutions we do not contemplate any new translation of the Bible, or any alteration of the language, except where, in the judgment of the most competent scholars, such change is necessary.
4. That it is desirable that Convocation should nominate a body of its own members to undertake the work of revision, who shall be at liberty to invite the co-operation of any eminent for scholarship, to whatever nation or religious body they may belong.

The report was accepted unanimously by the Upper House and by a great majority of the Lower House. A committee was also appointed, consisting of eight bishops and eight presbyters, to take the necessary steps for carrying out the resolutions.

American Cooperation

The British Committee is fully competent, without foreign aid, to do justice to the work committed to its care. Yet, in view of its practical aim to furnish a revision not for scholars, but for the churches, it is of great importance to secure, at the outset, the sympathy and co-operation of Biblical scholars in the United States, where the Authorized Version is as widely used and as highly respected as in Great Britain. Rival revisions would only add new fuel to sectarian divisions already too numerous among Protestants. Let us hold fast by all means to the strongest bond of interdenominational and international union which we have in a common Bible. The new re-

---

[1](Ed.) Henry Alford (1810–71), biblical scholar who was well acquainted with German biblical scholarship, since 1857 dean of Canterbury.

vision, when completed, should appear with the imprimatur of the united Biblical scholarship of English-speaking Christendom.

In August, 1870, Dr. Joseph Angus, President of Regent's Park College, London, and one of the British revisers, arrived in New York, with a letter from Bishop Ellicott, chairman of the New Testament Company, authorizing him to open negotiations for the formation of an American Committee of Revision.[2] At his request, I prepared a draft of rules for co-operation, and a list of names of Biblical scholars who would probably best represent the different denominations and literary institutions in this movement. The suggestions were submitted to the British Committee and substantially approved. Then followed an interesting official correspondence, conducted, on behalf of the British Committee, by the Bishop of Winchester, the Dean of Westminster, the Bishop of Gloucester and Bristol, and Dr. Angus. I was empowered by the British Committee, to select and invite scholars from non-Episcopal Churches; the nomination of members from the American Episcopal Church was, for obvious reasons, placed in the hands of some of its Bishops; but, as they declined to take action, I was requested to fill out the list. . . .

In the delicate task of selection, reference was had, first of all, to ability, experience, and reputation in Biblical learning and criticism; next, to denominational connection and standing, so as to have a fair representation of the leading Churches and theological institutions; and last, to local convenience, in order to secure regular attendance. Some distinguished scholars were necessarily omitted, but may be added hereafter by the committee itself. . . .

The American companies will hold their first meeting for active work October 4, 1872. The result of their deliberations will in due time be forwarded to the British Committee for consideration before the second revision.

When the whole work shall be completed, it will go to the English-speaking churches for their adoption or rejection. By its own

---

[2](Ed.) Joseph Angus (1816–1902), Baptist minister and biblical scholar. Charles John Ellicott (1819–1905), professor of divinity at King's College, London, and at Cambridge, since 1863 bishop of Gloucester and Bristol.

merits it will stand or fall. We firmly believe that it will gradually take the place of the Authorized Version.

Character of the English Version. The Work Proposed

In presenting briefly my own views on the subject of revision, I have no authority to speak in behalf of the American revisers, who have not yet fairly begun their work; but I apprehend no material difficulty with the British Committee. I have reason to believe that there is a general disposition among us to retain the idiom, grammar, and vocabulary of the Authorized Version so far as is consistent with faithfulness to the Greek and Hebrew Scriptures, and with justice to the present stage of the English language.

The popular English Bible is the greatest blessing which the Reformation of the sixteenth century bestowed upon the Anglo-Saxon race. It is, upon the whole, the best translation ever made, not excepting even Jerome's Vulgate and Luther's Version. It is not the production of a single mind, but of a large number of wise and good men, representing three generations in the most eventful and productive period of modern church history. It is 'the pure well of English undefiled.'[3] It has formed the style and taste of the English classics. It has a hold upon the popular heart which it can never lose. Its vocabulary and phrases, its happy blending of Saxon force and Latin dignity, its uniform chasteness, earnestness, and solemnity, its thoroughly idiomatic tone, its rhythmic flow, its more than poetic beauty and harmony, have secured the admiration of scholars and the affection of whole churches and nations in which it is used. . . .

The power and influence of this version can not be estimated. Being from the very start a truly national work for the British Isles, it has gradually assumed, with the English language itself, an almost cosmopolitan character and importance, and is now used more than any translation in all parts of the globe. The British and Foreign Bible Society, or the American Bible Society, probably send forth more copies of the English Scriptures than are printed in all other lan-

---

[3](Ed.) Edmund Spenser, *The Faerie Queene* 4.2.32, praised Chaucer as the "well of English undefyled"—an expression, slightly enlarged, which Schaff (and others before him?) liked to apply to the King James Version.

guages combined. Eternity alone can reveal how many millions have been made wise unto salvation through the instrumentality of this version.

To substitute a new popular *version* for such a work would be almost a sacrilege, certainly an ungrateful task and inevitable failure.

But this is not at all the question. The present movement contemplates no new version, but simply a scholarly and conscientious *revision*, in the spirit, and, as far as possible, in the very language, of the old. The object is to make a good translation still better, more accurate and self-consistent, and to bring it up to the present standard of Biblical scholarship.

The abstract *right* of revision can not be disputed. It is the duty of the Church, especially the Protestant, to give the Bible to the people in the best possible form, and to adapt existing translations, from time to time, to the progress in Scripture learning and the inevitable changes of a living language. Without this right and duty, King James's Version of 1611 would not exist at all, for it is itself the result of several revisions, going back—through the Bishops' Bible (1568), The Geneva Bible (1557, completed 1560), Cranmer's Bible (1539), Matthew's (or Rogers's) Bible (1537), Coverdale's Bible (1535 and 1537)—to the New Testament (with parts of the Old Testament) of Tyndale (1525-1535), who is the real author, as well as martyr, of the English Version, and, in the former respect, the English Luther.

The *need* and *desirableness* of a new revision are now almost generally admitted, at least by those who are best acquainted with the Bible in its original languages. The most ardent admirers of King James's Version do not claim for it perfection and infallibility. It has a very considerable number of errors, defects, and obscurities. It was the best translation which could be made in the beginning of the seventeenth century, but it can be greatly improved with the enlarged facilities of the present age.

The only debatable question, then, is as to the proper *time* and best *mode* of undertaking this important and desirable work. A few years ago many of the most judicious friends of revision would have said that the pear is not ripe yet, although fast ripening; but the recent movement in Great Britain settles the question. It combines all the needful scholarship, ability, authority, and co-operation. It presents the most favorable juncture which can be desired, and it must be turned to the best account. The greatest difficulty was in our sectarian divisions: it has been removed by the Spirit of God, who alone can so move the hearts of men as to bring Churchmen and Dissenters, Episcopalians, Presbyterians, Independents, Methodists, Baptists, and others, together in brotherly harmony and co-operation. To miss the glorious opportunity now is indefinitely to postpone the great work, or to risk the multiplication of sectarian versions—as there are already a Baptist and a Unitarian New Testament.[4] Let us by all means have an oecumenical revision now when we can have it, which shall be a new and stronger bond of union among the many branches of Anglo-Saxon Christendom, and make the good old Bible clearer and dearer to the people.

PUBLICATION, RECEPTION, CRITICISM, AND PROSPECT[*]

Tuesday, the 17th of May and Friday, the 20th of May, of the year 1881, deserve to be remembered as the publication days of the Revised English New Testament—the first in England, the second in the United States. They form an epoch in the history of the Bible, and furnish a valuable testimony to its absolute sovereignty among literary productions. In those days the Gospel was republished to the whole English-reading world with the aid of all the modern facilities which the print-press and the telegraph could afford. The eagerness of the public to secure the Revision, and the rapidity and extent of its sale, surpassed all expectations, and are without a parallel in the history of the book trade. In the year 30 of our era the Great Teacher addressed twelve disciples and a few thousand hearers on the hills of Galilee and in the temple court at Jerusalem, while the Greek and

---

[4](Ed.) Baptist: the Bible Union New Testament of 1865 (final revision of earlier revisions). Unitarian: Schaff was probably referring to G. R. Noyes's version published by the American Unitarian Association in 1869.

[*]*A Companion to the Greek Testament and the English Version*, 4th ed. rev. (New York and London, 1891) 403-406, 411-17.

Roman world outside of Palestine were ignorant of His very existence; in the year 1881, He addressed the same words of truth and life in a fresh version to millions of readers in both hemispheres. Who will doubt that the New Testament has a stronger hold upon mankind now than ever before, and is beyond all comparison the most popular book among the two most civilized nations of the earth? . . .

It is probably not too much to say that within less than one year three million copies of the book, in all editions, were actually bought and more or less read in Great Britain and America.

This estimate does not include the immense circulation through the periodical papers of the United States, which published the Revised New Testament in whole or in part, and did for two or three weeks the work of as many Bible Societies. Two daily papers in Chicago (*The Tribune* and *The Times*) had the book telegraphed to them from New York, and sent it to their readers two days after publication, at a distance of nine hundred and seventy-eight miles.[5]

Such facts stand isolated and alone in the whole history of literature, and furnish the best answer to the attacks and sneers of modern infidelity, which would fain make the world believe that the Bible is antiquated. All the ancient and modern classics together, if they were reissued in improved editions and translations, could not awaken such an interest and enthusiasm. England and America have honored themselves by thus honoring the Bible, and proved its inseparable connection with true freedom and progress. . . .

The Revisers, familiar with the history of previous revisions from Jerome's Vulgate down to King James's Version, were prepared for

---

[5]*The Tribune* employed for the purpose ninety-two compositors and five correctors and the whole work was completed in twelve hours. *The Times* boastfully says of its own issue: "Such a publication as this is entirely without precedent. It indicates on the one hand the wide-spread desire to see the Revised Version, and on the other the ability of *The Times* to supply the public with what is wanted. The Four Gospels, the Acts of the Apostles, and the Epistle to the Romans were telegraphed from New York. This portion of the New Testament contains about one hundred and eighteen thousand words, and constitutes by manyfold the largest dispatch ever sent over the wires. The remainder of the work was printed from the copies of the Revised Testament received here last night." See *The Tribune* and *The Times,* of Chicago, for May 22, 1881.

a great deal of opposition, though hopeful of ultimate success. They well knew that their work was imperfect, and that it is impossible to please all. They themselves had to sacrifice their individual preferences to the will of the majority. A product of so many minds and intended for so many churches must necessarily be a compromise, but for this very reason is more likely to satisfy the general wants and demands.

The extraordinary interest of the Anglo-American public in the Revision showed itself at once in the number and diversity of criticisms. Never was any book, within so short a time, so much discussed, reviewed, praised, and condemned by the press, from the pulpit, in private circles, and public meetings. In the language of a British scholar, "there never was a time when the attention of so great a variety of well-qualified critics has been concentrated on the problem of the relation between the Greek text and the English version, and the best way of representing the one by the other."[6]

The first and the prevailing impression was one of disappointment and disapproval, especially in England. The expectations of the public were unreasonable and conflicting. Many were in hopes that the revision would supersede commentaries, and clear up all the difficulties; instead of that, they found the same obscurities, and a perplexing number of marginal notes, raising as many questions of reading or rendering. The liberals looked for more, the conservatives for fewer, departures from the old version. Some wanted the language modernized, others preferred even the antiquated words and phrases, including the "whiches" and the "devils." A few would prefer a more literal rendering; but a much greater number of critics, including some warm friends and even members of the Committee, charge the Revision with sacrificing grace and ease, poetry and rhythm, to pedantic fidelity. The same objection is made by literary critics who care more for classical English than the homely Hebraistic Greek of the Apostles and Evangelists. The only point in which the adverse critics agree is opposition to the new version as wholly unfit to displace the old.

---

[6]From "The Church Quarterly Review," London, January, 1883, p. 345 ["The Revised Version and Its Critics," 30:343-68].

The strongest condemnation and the most formidable assaults have come from conservative admirers of the received Greek text and the Authorized Version. Most of them had previously resisted all attempts at revision as a sort of sacrilege, and found their worst fears realized. They were amazed and shocked at the havoc made with their favorite notions and pet texts. How many sacred associations, they said, are ruthlessly disturbed! How many edifying sermons spoiled! Even the Lord's Prayer has been tampered with, and a discord thrown into the daily devotions. The inspired text is changed and unsettled, the faith of the people in God's holy Word is undermined, and aid and comfort given to the enemy of all religion. We need not be surprised at such talk, for to the great mass of English readers King James's Version is virtually the inspired Word of God. So for Roman Catholics, the Vulgate of Jerome, with all its blunders, occupies the place of the original, and the voice of the infallible Church or Pope is to them the very voice of God. Religious prejudices are the deepest of all prejudices, and religious conservatism is the most conservative of conservatisms. It may take a whole generation to emancipate the mass of the people from the tyranny of ignorance and prejudice. In all this opposition we should not forget that its extent and intensity reveal a praiseworthy attachment to the Bible. In no other nation would a new version have met with so many and earnest protests as among the English and the Americans, for the simple reason that there is not among any other people the same degree of interest in the book.

In the meantime, however, the Revision has been steadily gaining ground among scholars and thoughtful laymen who take the trouble to compare the rival versions with the Greek original. This, of course, is the only proper test. With a few conspicuous exceptions, the verdict of competent judges has been favorable, and the force of the exceptions is broken by the intemperance and bitterness of the opposition. Whatever be the defects of the Revision, it must in all fairness be admitted that it is the most faithful and accurate version ever made for popular use, and that it brings the English reader far nearer to the spirit and words of Christ and his Apostles than any other version. This is its chief merit, and it alone is sufficient compensation for all the labor and expense devoted to it. An able writer from the Church of England, after reviewing the short history and large literature of the Revision during the first eighteen months, emphatically declares his "unshaken conviction that, after all reasonable deductions have been made, the Revisers have earned the deep respect and gratitude of all who can appreciate the importance of supplying the English reader with an exact interpretation of the Word of God."[7]

Upon the whole, the Revision is more popular in America than in England, although it is more an English work. Many ministers (especially among Congregationalists and Baptists, who are not hampered by church authority) use it already in the pulpit, either alone or alongside of the old version. The rising generation is familiarized with it in Sunday schools, Bible classes, and through popular comments. Religious periodicals present from week to week the international lessons in both versions in parallel columns; and the comparison of the two is found stimulating and profitable. Even opponents use the Revision, and admit its value as a commentary.

It would be premature to predict the course of the Convocation of Canterbury. No one can tell whether, when, and how it will act. Three ways are open—to reject, to recommit, to adopt. The Convocation is not likely to disown and destroy her own child. A revision of the Revision, by recommitment to the old, or by the appointment of a new, Committee, is surrounded by almost as many difficulties as the original movement. If the adverse critics could agree among themselves about a limited number of changes backward or forward, it would be an easy matter for the old Committee to reconvene and vote on these specific changes; but there is no such agreement. A new Committee (which would have to be composed, like the old, of scholars of all theological schools and denominations), to do justice to themselves and to the work, would have to go through the whole laborious and expensive process of ten or more years, and could at best only produce another compromise between conflicting principles and opinions. The adoption of the Revision as it is will be strongly opposed by an able and influential party. But it would be sufficient, and perhaps the wisest course (we speak with becoming

---

[7](Ed.) Ibid., 345.

modesty, as an outsider), if Convocation would authorize the *optional* use of the Revised Version, and leave the ultimate result to the future, as in the case of King James's Version, which gradually and slowly superseded, by its own merits, the Bishops' Bible and the Geneva Bible.

Acknowledged inconsistencies and other minor blemishes ought to be corrected by the Revisers themselves. But the English Companies have disbanded, and are not likely to meet again.

The non-episcopal denominations are more free to use the Revision, even without special legislation. They had no share in King James's Version, though strongly attached to it by long habit; they are not bound by canons and rubrics, and an obligatory liturgy. Some may formally authorize the Revision, others will leave its use to the option of pastors and congregations. It will certainly be used more and more in public and private as the highest standard of accuracy and fidelity, until it shall be superseded by a better one at some future generation. It would be well to revise the Bible every fifty years, and thus to renew its youth, that the people might read it with increased interest.

The Anglo-American Revision is not the best possible, but the best existing version, and as good as the present generation of scholars hailing from different churches and countries can produce. If we cannot have the very best, let us prefer the better to the good.

CHAPTER 8

Creed Revision

EDITORIAL INTRODUCTION

Schaff firmly believed that in the present divided state of Christianity Christians must be loyal and active members of a particular denomination, while they yet remain ever mindful of the wider horizons and larger aims of Christ's kingdom. Living, as he once put it, "in one apartment of the great temple of God, as we must do if we are to live in the temple at all," we should, nevertheless, be hospitable and friendly toward the occupants of all the other apartments and work together with them in Christ's larger cause. [1]

Schaff himself participated energetically and actively, as in all of his undertakings, in the life of those two churches that were his denominational home in the United States: first the German Reformed church and then he Presbyterian church in the U. S. A. He changed his denominational affiliation in 1870, when he joined the faculty of Union Theological Seminary and was subsequently received into the New York Presbytery. Schaff joined the Presbyterian Church at a most propitious moment, for a year earlier the Old School and the New School, divided since 1837, were reunited. Nearly twenty years of harmony followed, until in 1889 the General Assembly unexpectedly voted in favor of revising the hallowed

---

[1] Schaff, *Christ and Christianity* (New York, 1885) 151.

Westminster Confession of Faith. This Confession, as Schaff was quick to note, unlike the sixteenth-century Reformed confessions, showed in its doctrinal formulations the impact both of Calvinism's opposition to Arminianism and of the scholasticism of seventeenth-century Reformed theology. A lively controversy ensued throughout the church, in which Schaff eagerly participated as an advocate of revision, forcefully propagating its aims by writing articles, making speeches and publishing a lengthy brochure, *Creed Revision in the Presbyterian Churches.* "I take my stand," he declared unequivocally, "on the side of a revision of the Westminster Creed, in accordance with the advanced stage of theology and Christianity; as some years ago I took an active part in the revision of the English Version of the Bible." He was convinced that the two movements "are parallel, and look to the same end."[2] Through their participation in the World Alliance of Reformed Churches American Presbyterians had kept in touch with sister churches in Scotland, England and on the Continent. Hence they knew that the Presbyterian churches in Scotland and England had taken the lead in the revision of the inherited creedal standard. Schaff was able to inform his readers, for instance, that the English Presbyterian church had adopted "the more radical course of preparing a new Confession, together with a Declaratory Statement, which is to be used alongside of the old for practical purposes," and he included both documents as an appendix in his brochure.[3] In the United States the Congregational churches had replaced the Westminster Confession with a new creed in 1883.[4]

As the author of the monumental *Creeds of Christendom* (3 vols., 1877) Schaff could be expected to be an expert in creedal matters. He had found creeds to be both necessary for a variety of reasons and relative in at least three respects. Like a mirror they reflect the Bible, as the Bible in turn mirrors Christ; therefore, creeds are relative because we must never "look *at* the mirror, but *through* the mirror to the glorious object which it reveals."[5] Furthermore, as

---

[2] Schaff, *Creed Revision in the Presbyterian Churches,* v.

[3] Ibid., 52-63.

[4] See Schaff, *The Creeds of Christendom,* 6th ed. revised and enlarged by David S. Schaff (New York and London, 1931) 3:914-15.

[5] Schaff, *Christ and Christianity,* 135.

the human response to the eternal Word of God creeds are also bound to mirror the intellectual culture and historical circumstances of their origin. Consequently, as the church advances in its understanding of divine truth, and as civilization itself progresses, the creeds of the past may need to be revised, or the Spirit of God may even prompt the formulation of a new creed. Finally, human comprehension, finite as it is, will be able to grasp only selected aspects of the infinite divine truth. Therefore, creeds are also only partial manifestations of the Christian truth, even though for this very reason they are complementary and not contradictory in nature, so that only together will they fully manifest the divine truth. According to Schaff, the Apostles' Creed alone is permanently embedded in the very foundation of the universal church and ought to be accepted by all Christians, as it has always been.

Underlying Schaff's deliberations about the nature of creeds was his characteristic conviction that still more basic than doctrinal and creedal unity is "the unity of spiritual life, the unity of faith, the unity of love which binds us to Christ, and to all who love him, of whatever denomination or creed."[6] This emphasis on the spiritual life of faith and love, the source and object of which is Christ, is the meaning that Schaff must have had in mind when he vaguely spoke of the comprehensive and harmonious "Creed of Christ" which "by and by we shall reach, through the Creeds of Christendom."[7] He rejected those creedal or doctrinal unions that are "absorptive," "negative" or "eclectic," which he identified, in the same sequence, with the Roman Catholic claim of possessing the absolute truth, the biblicism of the Bible Societies and a proposal like Samuel S. Schmucker's *Fraternal Appeal to the American Churches With a Plan for Catholic Union on Apostolic Principles* (1838) that had taken snippets from the various confessions and combined them into a new consensus creed. Schaff advocated instead a "conservative" union, which accepted all the historic creeds as complementary landmarks of the Christian faith.[8] But additionally he favored a brief new confession for each denomination expressive of the fundamental be-

[6]Ibid., 183.

[7]Schaff, *The Creeds of Christendom*, 6th ed., 1:viii (preface to the 4th ed., 1884).

[8]Schaff, *Christ and Christianity*, 146-48.

liefs that are shared by all Christians, of whatever denomination.
Each denomination should leave the formulation of more specific
doctrinal positions, including "metaphysics and polemics," to scientific theology.[9] After all, the "logic of the heart" is superior to
the "logic of the head."[10] It should be obvious that Schaff identified the "advanced stage of theology and Christianity," which
mandated creedal revision, with the progressive orthodoxy and the
ecumenical impulses and tenets of his own kind of evangelical Protestantism.

Schaff himself pursued actively two approaches to the task of
updating the creedal formulations of the Reformed Confessions of
Faith: consensus creed and creed revision. He had been one of the
leaders in the formation of the World Alliance of Reformed
Churches at London in 1875, when the Alliance had accepted "the
consensus of the Reformed Confessions" as its doctrinal basis without attempting to state that consensus. Two years later, at the first
General Conference of the Alliance held at Edinburgh, Schaff presented his great address "The Consensus of the Reformed Confessions As Related to the Present State of Evangelical Theology."[11]
In response to his paper, the Alliance constituted a committee,
which Schaff was asked to chair, charging it to prepare an historical
and comparative survey of Reformed creeds in preparation for the
possible future formulation of "the consensus of the Reformed
Confessions." Schaff himself believed that such a consensus might
well resemble the doctrinal basis, the Nine Articles, of the Evangelical Alliance. But at the Belfast meeting of the Alliance in 1884,
to Schaff's great disappointment, all attempts at formulating a
creedal consensus were terminated, though Schaff believed that the
Alliance had "practically defined [such a consensus] in a liberal sense
by admitting the semi-Arminian Cumberland Presbyterians."[12] As
this statement makes clear, a "liberal" interpretation of the creed
meant for Schaff no more than placing the scriptural or Arminian
emphasis on God's universal love and human responsibility along-

---

[9]Schaff, *Creed Revision in the Presbyterian Churches*, 51.

[10]Schaff, *Christ and Christianity*, 308.

[11]The address was reprinted in *Christ and Christianity*, 153-83.

[12]Ibid., 183n.

side of Calvinism's insistence on God's sovereignty, even though, as he readily admitted, such affirmations are logically irreconcilable. Broadly speaking, the difficulty was, as Schaff had realized from the beginning, that the Anglo-American churches "would require a maximum of orthodoxy," while the churches on the Continent "would be content with a minimum of orthodoxy."[13] However, there were also sterner, orthodox voices on the Continent such as the *Evangelische Kirchenzeitung,* which now presented Schaff to its readers as "a mediating theologian who is on principle inclined to every daring treatment of the traditional doctrinal teaching and has lost himself in an hazy unionism."[14]

Neither was the creedal revision movement in the Presbyterian church to succeed, at least not during Schaff's lifetime. Like many friends of creedal revision, among whom was now also Charles A. Briggs, Schaff favored both, a brief new confession and such alterations in the Westminster Confession as were called for by the theology and sensibilities of evangelical Protestantism in the late nineteenth century. In *Creed Revision in the Presbyterian Churches* he reviewed briefly previous revisions of various creeds, including the Westminster Confession, where, as he noted, the articles on church and state had been altered in 1788 in response to the revolutionary, constitutional principle of the separation of church and state of the newly born United States. He then discussed at length those "objectionable passages" in the Confession that are related to the Calvinistic doctrine of predestination, as stated in chapter 3, "Of God's Eternal Decree." He also found offensive the phrase "elect infants" in chapter 10 with the implication that there were "reprobate infants" who would be lost forever. Schaff took delight in calling attention to a "highly significant, although almost incredible" manifestation of the old orthodoxy in his colleague Shedd's *Dogmatic Theology,* with its three pages on Heaven and eighty-seven pages on Hell![15] He also addressed the issue of biblical criticism but held it to be without relevance to the question of creed revision—

---

[13]Ibid., 182.

[14]Quoted by Gustav Frank, *Die Theologie des neunzehnten Jahrhunderts,* ed. George Loesche, vol. 4 of *Geschichte der protestantischen Theologie,* 4 vols. (Leipzig, 1862–1905) 252.

[15]Schaff, *Creed Revision in the Presbyterian Churches,* 14n.1.

unlike Briggs, who insisted on changing the reference to creation in six days in chapter 9, "On Creation."[16] But as one might expect, Schaff proposed to excise the Confession's references to the papacy as "antichrist" and to Roman Catholics as "idolaters."

Selections from *Creed Revision in the Presbyterian Churches* are here included that are representative of Schaff's position. Schaff appended to his essay a brief paper, "Plea for the Revision of the Westminster Confession," which he presented at the meeting of the New York Presbytery in November 1889, after his colleague Shedd had spoken in opposition to the revision. In the second edition of *Creed Revision* Schaff allowed himself to be carried away by local pride and his usual enthusiasm, claiming that the ensuing debate in the New York Presbytery in January of the following year, which lasted 12 days and ended with a substantial majority voting for the revision, was "the greatest doctrinal discussion held in this country, and forms an epoch-making chapter in the history of American theology." And he added: "No such important and lengthy public debate has taken place since the Synod of Dort and the Westminster Assembly, except in the Vatican Council."[17]

The ultimate defeat of the revision movement in the General Assembly of 1893 was largely due to the uproar which Charles A. Briggs's inaugural lecture "The Authority of Holy Scripture" in January of 1891 had caused, when he assumed the newly created chair for Biblical Theology at Union Theological Seminary. An outspoken, at times abrasive advocate of the "higher criticism" of the Bible, although evangelical in all of his fundamental convictions, he initiated a controversy that culminated in his trial for heresy, and the proceedings of this trial then superseded all other concerns.[18] One might point out that as Schaff's own heresy trial had marked the beginning of his American career, so Briggs's heresy trial was to mark its end. In both instances controversy was caused by the new theological currents—different, though, as they

---

[16]See Max Gray Rogers, "Charles Augustus Briggs: Heresy at Union," in *American Religious Heretics. Formal and Informal Trials in American Protestantism,* ed. George H. Shriver (Nashville and New York, 1966) 95.

[17]Schaff, *Creed Revision in the Presbyterian Churches,* 2nd ed. (1890) 69.

[18]For a detailed discussion of the Briggs trial, see Rogers, "Charles Augustus Briggs: Heresy at Union," in *American Religious Heretics,* 89-147.

were in these two cases, separated by fifty years —that emanated from the studies and lecture halls of German universities. Only the affirmation of a probationary "middle state" proved to be controversial in both instances. Schaff never doubted that Briggs was an "evangelical," and he knew that in Germany "Dr. Briggs would be classed with the conservative and orthodox rather than with radicals and rationalists."[19] When in the spirited defense of his colleague and former student he approvingly repeated the statement, "As between liberty and orthodoxy, give me liberty," it was therefore far from Schaff's mind, as his biographer correctly adds, to endorse an unrestricted freedom of research and teaching, the German *Lehrfreiheit.*[20] What he did endorse was the freedom of evangelical scholarship to carry its investigation "beyond the narrow bounds of the creeds of the seventeenth century."[21] The trial, in which Briggs was acquitted by the New York Presbytery but subsequently condemned by the General Assembly in 1893, was to affect permantly "the fortunes of himself, the seminary he loyally served, and the Church he loved."[22] Briggs later joined the ministry of the Protestant Episcopal church; Union Theological Seminary, which steadfastly supported its beleaguered professor, declared its independence from the Presbyterian church in 1892; and the Presbyterian church itself, where the revision movement marked, indeed, an important milestone, continued to struggle with the unavoidable tension created by attempts at retaining the integrity of the orthodox faith and at coming to terms with the new intellectual currents alive in the modern sciences and a progressive theology. But since the basic outline of creedal revision had been established, the revision movement was revived, though still unexpectedly, in 1900 and succesfully concluded three years later.[23]

---

[19]Schaff, "Other Heresy Trials and the Briggs Case," *The Forum* 12 (January 1892): 626.

[20]David S. Schaff, *Life of Schaff,* 423-33.

[21]Schaff, *Theological Propaedeutic* (New York, 1893) 319n.

[22]Lefferts A. Loetscher, *The Broadening Church. A Study of Theological Issues in the Presbyterian Church Since 1869* (Philadelphia, 1954) 49.

[23]The revision resulted in a brief declaratory statement, changes in three chapters (including excision of the offensive references to the Pope and Roman Cath-

This revision then made possible the reunion of the Presbyterian church and the Cumberland Presbyterian church with its "semi-Arminian" Creed in 1906. The final success of the revision and the subsequent union of the two churches would have delighted Schaff, whose labors had done so much to help to prepare the ground for both events.

CREED REVISION IN THE PRESBYTERIAN CHURCHES*

A Progressive Age

Revision is in the air. Some years ago it was the revision of the Bible; now it is the revision of creeds. The former has been successfully accomplished without doing any harm either to the Bible or to Bible readers; the latter will be accomplished at no distant day, with the same result of sundry improvements in minor details without detriment to the substance. The Bible-revision movement extended over the whole Protestant world, and resulted in a material improvement of the Authorized English, German, Dutch, Swedish and Danish versions; the Creed revision movement, so far, is confined to the Presbyterian churches of America and Great Britain, but may soon spread to other evangelical denominations which have formulated confessions of faith. The result will be to bring them nearer together, on the basis of consensus in essentials, liberty in non-essentials, and charity in all things.[1]

We live in an age of research, discovery, and progress, and whosoever refuses to go ahead must be content to be left behind and to

---

olics), two new chapters on the Holy Spirit and Missions, and a brief new creed in sixteen articles. See Loetscher, *The Broadening Church,* 83-89, and Schaff, *The Creeds of Christendom,* 6th ed., 3:919-24.

Creed Revision in the Presbyterian Churches (New York, 1890) 1, 13-14, 30-31, 33-42.

[1](Ed.) Petrus Meiderlin (1582–1651), an irenic Lutheran pastor in Augusburg who wrote (under the pseudonym Rupert Meldenius) *Pareneses votiva pro pace ecclesiae* (1626), apparently first used the ecumenical peace formula: *In necessariis unitas, in non necessariis libertas, in utrisque caritas.*

be outgrown. Whatever lives, moves; and whatever ceases to move, ceases to live. It is impossible for individual Christians or churches to be stationary; they must either go forward, or go backward.

[After reviewing the state of the revision movement in the United States and Great Britain, Schaff continues.]

Grounds of Dissatisfaction

These facts prove that the desire for some change is deep, general, and irresistible; while throughout the Anglo-American branches of the Presbyterian family there is a considerable difference of opinion as to the manner and extent of revision. A growing number of ministers, elders, and students are calling for relief from bondage to certain doctrines which the theology of the age has outgrown, which are no more taught in the pulpit and would not be tolerated in the pews. Some theologians still defend them, but few students believe them. I know of no Presbyterian minister in these United States who preaches the decree of reprobation or preterition, the irresponsibility of the sinner for not accepting the gospel, the limitation of the atonement to the small circle of the elect, and the eternal condemnation of non-elect infants dying in infancy, and the damnation of the non-Christian world—heathen, Jews, and Mohammedans—who still constitute by far the greatest part of mankind. And yet these doctrines are supposed to be taught expressly or implicitly by the Westminster standards. If not, then let us disown them publicly and officially beyond the power of contradiction.

What cannot be preached in the pulpit ought not to be taught in a Confession of Faith, either expressly or by fair logical inference. On the other hand, what is taught in the Confession ought to be preached in the pulpit.

The great and most serious objection to the Westminster Confession is the overstatement of divine sovereignty, at the expense, if not to the exclusion, of human responsibility, and the overstatement of the doctrine of particular or partial election, to the exclusion of the general love of God to all his creatures. The last is nowhere mentioned. It is a confession for the exclusive benefit of the elect. To this small inside circle all is bright and hopeful; but outside of it all is dark as midnight. It is the product of the most polemical and most intolerant age of Christendom.

The Mystery of Predestination

The doctrine of predestination, as the Confession truly says (ch. III, 8), is a "high mystery," and should be "handled with special prudence and care." But the Confession fails just in presuming to know and to teach too much about this transcendent mystery, and in handling it as if it were a mathematical problem. It gives it a disproportionate importance and devotes much more space to it than to the Holy Trinity and other vital doctrines.

The very terms *pre*ordination and *fore*ordination involve a metaphysical impossibility; for in God there is neither before nor after; neither forethought nor afterthought; nor can we fix any point in eternity when he formed a resolution and passed a decree. The Calvinists assert that foreordination precedes foreknowledge; the Arminians reverse the order; both forget that all is simultaneous and eternal before God. We reason from our human standpoint, and ought, therefore, to be cautious and modest.

We have to stop somewhere in the flight of speculation, and must admit the boundaries of our knowledge. There is a moral as well as an intellectual logic—a logic of the heart as well as of the head. Our conscience forbids us to bring a God of infinite purity and holiness into any contact with sin, direct or indirect, except that he punishes and overrules it for good by his infinite wisdom and goodness. Speculation would drive us, with irresistible force, from absolute sovereignty to fatalism, from infralapsarianism to supralapsarianism, from supralapsarianism to pantheism or universalism; but theoretic speculation is checked by the Bible, by the Christian consciousness, and by practical experience. Christian humility claims no merit whatever, and gives all the glory of our salvation to God alone, but those who are lost are exclusively lost by their own guilt.

This is the ground on which every Calvinist practically stands as a preacher and worker, whatever be his theory as a theologian. He preaches and works as if all depended on man, and he prays as if all depended on God. He addresses his hearers as responsible beings to whom the Gospel salvation is sincerely offered, without exception, on the terms of repentance and faith. If this is an illogical inconsistency, then it is at least a necessary, happy, and useful inconsistency, and is supported by the authority of the great Apostle of faith, who exhorts us: "Work out your own salvation with fear and trembling; for it is God who worketh in you both to will and to work for his good pleasure" (Phil. 2:13).

The Anti-popery Clauses of the Confession

Finally, we venture to raise an objection which has not been touched at all in this discussion, as far as I have seen and is probably not contemplated by the General Assembly, but which I feel very strongly, both on moral as well as exegetical and historical grounds. I will mention it at the risk of provoking the opposition of many Presbyterian friends whom I highly esteem.[2] It is the declaration of the confession that the Pope of Rome is the Antichrist,[3] and that Papists, that is, all Roman Catholics, are idolaters.[4]

---

[2]In this I was happily mistaken. Quite a number of influential voices have since responded to my protest and advocated an elimination of the unfortunate attacks of the Confession upon a venerable and powerful Christian Church. Two theological professors also, who are decided anti-revisionists, have assured me privately that on this point they heartily agreed with me, and would support an excision.

[3][*The Westminster Confession*] ch. 25.6: "The Pope of Rome . . . is that Antichrist, that man of sin and son of perdition, that exalteth himself, in the Church, against Christ and all that is called God." This section was likewise anticipated by the Irish Articles, Art. 80. See Schaff, *Creeds*, 3 [1877] 540.

[4][*The Westminster Confession*] ch. 24.3, forbids marriage "with infidels and idolaters." There is not a Roman Catholic who would not indignantly reject the charge of idolatry as a calumny. The Roman divines distinguish between different degrees of worship (*latria, doulia,* and *hyper-doulia*) and claim the highest degree for God alone, as the giver of every good gift. We must respect their honest convictions and judge them by their doctrinal standards, however much we, from our Protestant standpoint, may oppose Mariolatry and hagiolatry, as a refined form of semi-idolatry. How differently did Paul deal with the Athenians, who were real idolaters. He gave them credit for being even "over-religious," or "very religious," in their anxiety to worship all gods—known and unknown. Acts 17,22.

I protest against this judgment as untrue, unjust, unwise, uncharitable, and unsuitable in any Confession of Faith. It is a colossal slander on the oldest and largest Church of Christendom. It is the passionate outburst of an intensely polemical age, but absolutely unjustifiable now. It can only do harm and no possible good. Instead of converting Romanists, it must repel them and intensify and perpetuate their prejudices against Protestantism. It will become more and more obnoxious and hurtful as the Roman Catholic Church grows in numbers and influence in our country.

The Pope of Rome is the legitimate head of the Roman Church, and as such he has the same rights and privileges as the Eastern Patriarchs or the Archbishops of Canterbury and York have over their respective dioceses. He is older than any one of them, and his line goes back in unbroken succession to Clement of Rome at the end of the first century. There were not a few wicked popes, and many bad bishops, as there were wicked high-priests in the history of Israel; the first connived at the worship of the golden calf, and the last demanded the death of the Messiah, who came to save his people. Dante, who was a good Catholic, puts five popes into hell, two into purgatory, and saw none in heaven, at least none who attracted his attention. We go further and admit that there is an anti-Christian element in the *papacy* as a system—namely, the claim of the pope to be the head of *all* Christendom and the vicar of Christ on earth. Even Pope Gregory I, or the Great, rebuked this assumption as "anti-Christian," and preferred to be called "the servant of the servants of God," rather than oecumenical or universal bishop.[5] But this does not make every or any pope "that Antichrist," or "that man of sin," and "that son of perdition that exalteth himself against Christ and all that is called God." The alleged prooftext in 2 Thess. 2:3,4 refers to "the mystery of lawlessness" (not "iniquity" as the Authorized Version has it), which was "at work already" (v. 7) in the time of Paul, before there was any popery. If he had had popery in mind, he

---

[5](Ed.) For Gregory I's protest against the title of "oecumenical patriarch" and for his preferred self-designation, see Jeffrey Richards, *Consul of God: The Life and Times of Gregory the Great* (London, 1980) 217-20, 248 (with source references).

would have warned against it in the Epistle to the Romans, and not in that to the Thessalonians. "Lawlessness," moreover, is not the characteristic mark of popery, which is just the reverse—namely, tyranny. As to the term "antichrist," it only occurs in the Epistle of John (1 John 2:18, 22; 4:3; 2 John 7), and is not used of a future individual, but of contemporaries of the Apostle, of heretical teachers in Asia Minor, who had been members of the Church, and left it, and who denied the incarnation and the real humanity of Christ. The pope has never done this, but, on the contrary, has ever held those doctrines with the utmost tenacity, and can never give them up.

The misinterpretation of these anti-popery pet texts, which has long since been exploded among scholars, furnished a pretext for the repeated attempts made in the General Assembly to unchurch the Church of Rome, and to unbaptize or to heathenize her two hundred millions of members. It seems incredible that a body of intelligent and well-educated Christian ministers, as the majority of Presbyterians undoubtedly are, should be able to entertain such a monstrous proposition. It outpopes the Pope who recognizes Protestant baptism, and it would unchurch all the churches of the Reformation which received their ordinances from the Mediaeval Catholic Church.

The last attempt of this kind was made in the General Assembly of the Presbyterian Church, at Cincinnati, in 1885, but was fortunately defeated by the good sense of the majority.[6] I thank God that, as a delegate, I helped to oppose and defeat this unreasonable anti-popery fanaticism. The action of the United Assembly of 1885 nullifies the contrary action of the Old School Assembly, likewise held in Cincinnati forty years earlier (1845), which declared Romish baptism invalid. But this decision was opposed, with irrefragable arguments, by Dr. Charles Hodge, of Princeton, and later, in 1853 and 1854, when the same question came up in the New School Gen-

---

[6]One of the arguments used by a clerical delegate and Doctor of Divinity in that Assembly against the validity of Romish baptism was, that the Pope sometimes baptized donkeys; to which my neighbor good-humoredly replied in a whisper: "And *we* ordain them."

eral Assembly, by Dr. Henry B. Smith, of New York.[7] These honored divines, now in their graves, did by this protest immense service to the cause of truth and righteousness, and prepared the way for the rejection of the anti-popery clauses of the Confession.

It is high time that we should abandon the policy of intolerance, prejudice, and bigotry against our Roman Catholic fellow-Christians, and adopt the policy of justice and charity which will lead to better results. I hope that the day may not be far distant when American Protestants will no longer envy and oppose, but hail with joy the progress of the Catholic, as well as any other Christian Church which preaches the gospel and promotes piety and virtue among the people.

Liberal Terms of Subscription

The views I have here expressed are not new. I have held and taught them for nearly fifty years. But how, then, could I ever subscribe to the Westminster Confession? I may as well answer this question. I honestly stated my objections to the Heidelberg Catechism (the eightieth question) before I signed it, after my call from the University of Berlin to a professorship in the German Reformed Church of the United States in 1844;[8] and I honestly stated my objections to the Westminster Confession when I was called (in view of all my previous publications) to a professorship in the Union Theo-

---

[7](Ed.) Henry Boynton Smith (1815–77) taught Church History (since 1850) and Systematic Theology (since 1853) at Union Theological Seminary in New York. The leading theological spokesman of New School Presbyterianism, he was, since his two years of study at Halle and Berlin (1838–40), like Schaff deeply influenced by the German mediating theology.

[8](Ed.) The eightieth question, "What difference is there between the Lord's Supper and the papal Mass?," which was missing in the first edition and included in its present form only in the third edition of the *Heidelberg Catechism* (1563), denounces the Roman Catholic mass as "a denial of the one sacrifice of Christ, and as an accursed idolatry." Of this question Schaff elsewhere wrote: "The wisdom of inserting controversial matter into a catechism for the instruction of the youth has been justly doubted. The eightiest question disturbs the peaceful harmony of the book, it rewards evil for evil, it countenances intolerance, which is un-Protestant, and un-evangelical" (*Creeds of Christendom*, 6th ed. [1931] 1:536).

logical Seminary of the Presbyterian Church in 1869; and on both occasions I was assured by men then highest in authority (as Drs. John W. Nevin, William Adams, Henry B. Smith, E. F. Hatfield, and others) that the terms of subscription were so liberal as to leave ample room for all my dissenting views on these and other points.[9]

It is well understood that ministers and elders generally are allowed, according to the "Form of Government" (chs. XIII, XIV, and XV), liberty of dissent in all those articles of the Confession which are not necessary or essential to what is termed (somewhat inaccurately) "the system of doctrine taught in the Holy Scriptures."[10]

But I confess I do not altogether like this mode of subscription. Would it not be wiser and safer so to alter and abridge the Confession

---

[9](Ed.) William Adams (1807–80) was the pastor of the Madison Square Presbyterian Church (1853–73), where Schaff liked to worship, and from 1873 until his death president of Union Theological Seminary. Edwin Francis Hatfield (1807–83) was the stated clerk of the New School Assembly of the Presbyterian church (1846–70) and, after the union of the Old School and the New School Presbyterians, of the united body (1870–83). In 1883 he was elected moderator of the Presbyterian church.

[10]I say "inaccurately," for the Bible is much more and much less than a logically constructed "system," and much higher, deeper, and broader than the Calvinistic or any other human system. It would be better to say, "the teaching of the Bible." The precise formula of subscription for ministers, elders, and deacons is this: "Do you sincerely receive and adopt the Confession of Faith of this Church, as containing the system of doctrine taught in the Holy Scriptures?" The proof text quoted is 2 Tim. 1:13: "Hold fast the form of sound words," etc. (Ed.) "The Form of Government of the Presbyterian Church in the United States of America," ch. 13, 4:2. The form of subscription required of Union Seminary faculty members until 1905 was as follows: "I believe the Scriptures of the Old and New Testament to be the word of God, the only infallible rule of faith and practice; and I do now, in the presence of God and the Directors of this Seminary, solemnly and sincerely receive the Westminster Confession of Faith as containing the system of doctrine contained in the Holy Scriptures. I also, in like manner, approve of the Presbyterian Form of Government; and I do solemnly promise that I will not teach or inculcate anything which shall appear to me to be subversive of said system of doctrines, or of the principles of said Form of Government, so long as I shall continue to be a Professor in the Seminary." (See Robert T. Handy, *A History of Union Theological Seminary in New York* [New York, 1987] 7.)

as to make it less objectionable and more generally acceptable? Unless some change takes place, it will become, I fear, more and more difficult after this revision question has been agitated, to secure the services of intelligent and conscientious elders and deacons. This has been made very apparent during the recent discussions in meetings of Presbyteries and in public papers.

Different Modes of Relief

Let us now briefly consider the different modes of relief.

1. The easiest mode is to widen the terms of subscription and reduce it to a general approval of the Confession, with a distinct reservation of dissent from some of its doctrines. This is demoralizing, and would virtually neutralize the subscription. Better do away with subscription altogether. The terms are already liberal enough.

2. The second mode is a supplement or declaratory statement such as the United Presbyterian Church of Scotland adopted in 1870. But this amounts to two Confessions which flatly contradict each other in several important articles. It does not remove the stumbling-blocks, and gives no permanent relief.

3. A third mode is a revision of the confession itself by omissions and modifications. This is in accordance with the tradition of the American Presbyterian Church, which has already revised four articles on Church and State, and one article on remarriage, and has appointed a committee for the revision of the proof-texts. This is the course adopted by the Assembly of the Free Church of Scotland, with which the American Church is most in sympathy. Revision can be made without difficulty by the simple omission of the hard doctrine of reprobation and preterition, the wholesale condemnation of the heathen world, and the anti-popery clauses. If we can remove these stumbling-blocks, why not do so? Is it not our duty to do so? If we can make our system clearer, more acceptable, and less liable to misunderstanding by friend or foe, we ought not to hesitate for a moment. It will be a great gain and an important step toward a new, shorter, and simpler Confession, which at no very distant time will express the living faith of the Church in the nineteenth or twentieth century, as the Westminster Confession expressed the faith of the Presbyterian Church in the seventeenth century.

4. The most radical cure would be, of course, a new Confession. The English Presbyterian Church has taken this course, and produced a document which retains all that is good in the Westminster Confession, and skilfully avoids all the objectionable points which we have mentioned, omitting also the anti-popery clauses. The Congregational Churches of England and the United States, which formerly accepted the Westminster system of doctrine, have likewise made new statements of faith which seem to give reasonable satisfaction. Such a work requires much learning, wisdom, and a secondary inspiration. Only the Holy Ghost can inspire creeds that will live. But he has done it repeatedly, and can do it again. He is as mighty and active now as he was in any former age.

A new creed of the Presbyterian Church should be undertaken by the Pan-Presbyterian Council, which is based upon "the consensus" of the Reformed Confessions, but has not defined it as yet. This was the very first subject of discussion at the Council in Edinburgh, 1877, and led to a laborious report of a committee on creeds and subscription to creeds. The report was accepted by the second Council in Philadelphia, 1880, and another international committee was appointed to consider the expediency of formulating "the consensus." The American branch of this international committee, at a meeting in the chapel of the Union Theological Seminary of New York, and including such wise and orthodox divines as Dr. Shedd, Dr. A. A. Hodge, and Principal Cavan, unanimously recommended the preparation of a Consensus creed, as expedient and desirable.[11] But Dr. Hodge, for reasons unknown, changed his mind, and voted against a Consensus creed when the several branches of the committee met at Edinburgh. The cautious conservatives feared a *minimum,* the advanced liberals feared a *maximum* of orthodoxy, and so the whole movement was crushed between the upper and lower millstone at the third Council, in Belfast, 1884. But the conservatives could not pre-

---

[11](Ed.) William Greenough Thayer Shedd (1820–94) was Schaff's colleague at Union Theological Seminary as professor of Biblical Literature (1863–74) and Systematic Theology (1874–90). Alexander Archibald Hodge (1823–86) succeeded his father at Princeton Theological Seminary where he taught from 1877 until his death.

vent the admission of the semi-Arminian Cumberland Presbyterians into the Council of the Pan-Presbyterian Alliance. I was told at the time by Dr. Oswald Dykes[12] (the chief framer of the new English Presbyterian creed) and several foreign missionaries, that since the Pan-Presbyterian Council refused to help them in this matter, they must help themselves, and prepare a simple and popular creed for the benefit of their churches, and for the foreign mission fields, which it is folly to disturb with the theological controversies and subtleties of the seventeenth century.

Whether the consensus-creed movement will ever be revived in the Council, nobody can tell. But there is a growing desire for some new statement of the old faith in the language of the present age, a statement less metaphysical and more practical, less denominational and more catholic than the Westminster Confession. It will come in God's own good time—perhaps in this or the next generation.

Conclusion

Let us be honest, and confess that old Calvinism is fast dying out. It has done a great work, and has done it well, but cannot satisfy the demands of the present age. We live in the nineteenth, and not in the seventeenth century. Every age must produce its own theology and has its own mission to fulfil. We may learn wisdom and experience from the past, but we ought not to be slaves of the past, and recognize no final and infallible authority but that of Christ. We must believe in the Holy Spirit, who is guiding the Church to ever higher life and light. He produced reformations in the past, he will produce greater reformations in the future.

I yield to no man in sincere admiration for St. Augustin of Hippo, and for John Calvin of Geneva, and have stated it more than once in public print. They were as pure and holy in character as they were strong and deep in intellect. They stand in the front rank of theologians of all ages, and their influence will be felt to the end of time. The truths which they brought forth from the mine of God's Word

---

[12](Ed.) James Oswald Dykes (1835–1932), a Scottish Presbyterian, who in 1869 became the minister of the Regent Square Presbyterian Church in London.

can never die or lose their power. St. Augustin impressed his mind upon every page of history, and his doctrines of sin and grace controlled the theology of the Reformers. These doctrines tend to humble man and to glorify God. They will always remind us that we cannot have too deep a hatred of man's sin and too high an estimate of God's mercy.

But Augustin ran his system to an untenable extreme. It leaves no room for freedom, except in the single case of Adam, who by one act of disobedience involved the whole human race in the slavery of sin. It suspends the history of the world upon that one act. It condemns the whole race to everlasting woe for a single transgression committed without our knowledge and consent six thousand years ago.[13] Out of this mass of corruption God by his sovereign pleasure elected a comparatively small portion of the human family to everlasting life, and leaves the overwhelming majority to everlasting ruin, without doing anything to save them. Calvinism intensified this system, and produced heroic races like the Huguenots of France, the Puritans of Old and New England, and the Covenanters of Scotland. But the Augustinian system was unknown to the ante-Nicene and Eastern Church. The Latin Church only half adopted it, and virtually condemned it by condemning Jansenism. The Lutheran Church accepted the doctrine of the slavery of the human will in the strongest form, and also the unconditional decree of election, therein following the extravagant views of Luther's book against Erasmus, but repudiated the decree of reprobation, and taught the universal offer of salvation. The Reformed Confessions of the sixteenth century wisely confined themselves to the positive part of predestination—the decree of election, but the Westminster Confession added to it the negative decree of reprobation and sharpened it into a two-edged sword against Arminianism and against itself.

---

[13](Ed.) Only at the very end of his life did Schaff briefly take notice of the "modern scientific theory of development in nature" as corresponding to the previously developed "theory of development in history" (*Theological Propaedeutic* [1893] 241). He now allowed that the Bible "does not determine the age of the earth or man" (see p. 333, below).

Arminianism arose and progressed in the heart of the Reformed Church in opposition to scholastic Calvinism, and through Wesleyan Methodism it has become one of the strongest and best organized agencies for the revival of practical religion and for the conversion of the world, so that in the United States this youngest of the great evangelical denominations outnumbers all others. This fact is a lesson and a warning more powerful than any argument.

And yet Arminianism and Methodism have not solved the theoretical problems on which they differ from Calvinism. We must look to the future, when God will raise another theological genius, like Augustin or Calvin, who will substitute something better, broader, and deeper than the narrow and intolerant system which bears their honored names.

We need a theology, we need a confession, that starts, not from eternal decrees, which transcend the utmost limits of our thoughts, nor from the doctrine of justification by faith, nor from the Bible principle, nor from any particular doctrine, but from the living person of Jesus Christ, the God-man and Saviour of the world. This is the burden of Peter's confession, the fruitful germ of all creeds; this is the central fact and truth on which all true Christians can agree. We need a theology and a confession that is inspired and controlled, not by the idea of Divine justice, which is a consuming fire, but by the idea of Divine love, which is life and peace. For "God is love" [1 John 4:8] and love is the key which unlocks his character and all his works. And this love extends to his creatures, and has made abundant provision in Christ for the salvation of ten thousand worlds. Love is the chief of Christian graces, the true sign of discipleship, and the bond of perfection. We need a theology and a confession that is more human than Calvinism, more Divine than Arminianism, and more Christian and catholic than either; a confession as broad and deep as God's love, and as strict and severe as God's justice. We need a theology and a confession that will not only bind the members of one denomination together, but be also a bond of sympathy between the various folds of the one flock of Christ, and prepare the way for the great work of the future—the reunion of Christendom in the Creed of Christ.

CHAPTER 9

The Quest for Christian Unity

EDITORIAL INTRODUCTION

Schaff heartily endorsed the World's Parliament of Religions, which was held in conjunction with the World's Columbian Exposition at Chicago in 1893 in commemoration of the four-hundredst anniversary of the discovery of the Americas.[1] Never doubting for a moment that Christianity is the true religion and the Christian God the only true God, Schaff yet believed, broadminded as always, that in that Heavenly Father's house there are many mansions, not only for each of the historic Christian denominations but also for each of the world's great religions. However imperfectly these religions might represent their share of the truth, they do, nonetheless, all share in that truth. Hence they should be willing to come to know each other and to learn from each other. But Schaff firmly believed that the final outcome of such interreligious dialogue will be the common worship of the one and only true God and his Son Jesus Christ who is "the Way and the Truth and the

---

[1]For a recent scholarly study see Clay Lancaster, *The Incredible World's Parliament of Religions at the Chicago Columbian Exposition of 1893: A Comparative and Critical Study* (Fontwell, Sussex, 1987).

Life."[2] In poor health after his stroke of the previous summer, and having been counseled that he would endanger his life if he were to attend the World's Parliament of Religions, he nonetheless insisted on travelling to Chicago. Too weak to read his paper "The Reunion of Christendom" during one of the sessions on 25 September, the Rev. Dr. Simon J. McPherson read it for him, while Schaff sat on the stage listening and then receiving an ovation from the large and attentive audience. During the second week of October the Evangelical Alliance also met (as did innumerable other religious congresses) in connection with the Columbian Exposition. This time Schaff heeded the doctor's advice and did not return to Chicago, as the Alliance had begged him to do. Again his paper "The Reunion of Christendom" was presented, the Rev. Joachim Elmendorf being the reader.

One should note that on these two occasions not the expanded and therefore final version of Schaff's paper but only parts of it, and apparently not even the same parts, were read. This may explain why shorter and in part different versions, reflecting perhaps what was actually read at Chicago in September and October, are found in *The World's Parliament of Religion*, ed. John Henry Barrows (Chicago, 1893) 2:1192-1201; in *The World Congress of Religions*, ed. J. W. Hanson (Chicago and Philadelphia, 1893) 615-27; and in *Neely's History of the Parliament of Religions and Religious Congresses at the World's Columbian Exposition*, ed. Walter R. Houghton (Chicago, 1893) 711-20. The latter two share the same text. The fact of three competing editions of the proceedings of the World's Parliament of Religions certainly testifies eloquently to the widespread popular interest in this event. The complete version of Schaff's paper was published twice, as *Evangelical Alliance Document* No. 33 and in the official record of the Chicago conference of the Evangelical Alliance, *Christianity Practically Applied. The Discussions of the International Christian Conference Held in Chicago, October, 8-14, 1893, In Connection With the World's Congress Auxiliary of the World's Colum-*

---

[2]The organizers of the World's Parliament of Religions were themselves convinced, just like Schaff, that Christianity was superior to all other religions, and they were eager to prove it. See concluding section "Grandeur and Final Influence of the Parliament," in *The World's Parliament of Religions*, ed. John Henry Barrows (Chicago, 1893) 2:1568-82.

bian Exposition And Under the Auspices and Direction of the Evangelical Alliance for the United States, 2 vols. (New York, 1894) 1:305-40. In the latter an editorial hand shows itself in the adaptation of capitalization and punctuation to a more modern usage and in the omission of all footnotes found in the text of the Evangelical Alliance document, which on this evidence can be taken to be the final text Schaff himself prepared. Hence it is this text that is here included.

Not included, however, is a lengthy appendix in the Evangelical Alliance document (also omitted in *Christianity Applied*) that contains a remarkable collection of written responses to Schaff's paper, some of which he still received and read during the last days of his life. Those responses—some negative, some positive, some similar, some diverging from Schaff's views—represent a wide spectrum of ecumenical positions and views. They thus reflect quite accurately the ferment of the ecclesiastical situation at the century's end, where Schaff, as was usual with him, saw only sunshine and some passing clouds beckoning the church to even more glorious days ahead. Adolf Harnack, for instance, wrote that he did not want to offer his personal opinion since he had thought too little about this matter, but then remarked: "So much I am sure of, that with their present organization the Protestant churches can negotiate with no one, for they are now passing through a crisis, and if they come out of it successfully they will assume new forms of life and doctrine. Then we may be able to negotiate."[3] By contrast, the Anglican Alfred Plummer quoted Döllinger's reply to the question, Is reunion possible?—"Es *muss* ja möglich sein, denn es ist *Pflicht*." He then added the remark: "Never did the Kantian principle, 'We ought, therefore we can,' come home to me so forcibly as in that striking application of it. We ought to be reunited; therefore it can be done. This is the right antidote for the pessimism which would tell us that a reunited Christendom is the dream of enthusiasts and that to spend time working for it is sheer waste."[4] Truly, it was the indomitable and enthusiastic spirit of such an application of the Kantian principle that motivated and permeated Schaff's whole career!

---

[3]*Evangelical Alliance Document* 33:54.

[4]Ibid., 50.

An earlier address, "The Discord and Concord of Christendom," which Schaff had delivered at the Eighth General Conference of the Evangelical Alliance held at Copenhagen in 1884,
anticipated his paper "The Reunion of Christendom." But it is this
paper which is here included, not only because it was Schaff's last
literary work but also, and most of all, because it was, as Schaff
himself declared, "the sum of my life and of my theological activity, and my testament to the church and to my contemporaries."[5]
Indeed, this paper marked the culmination of a life abounding in
ecumenical aspirations and accomplishments; it was the end result
of the long road Schaff had travelled—from Chur to Chicago.

The paper itself is remarkable for a variety of reasons. Truly
comprehensive was Schaff's discussion of the various ecumenical
strategies: ethical union of committed individuals, federation of
churches, organic union of churches. Equally comprehensive was
his survey of successful ecumenical endeavors along the lines of each
of those three approaches. His ecumenical outreach was also all-in-
clusive, as was demonstrated by his eager embrace of Eastern Orthodoxy, Roman Catholicism and the various churches of
Protestantism, including the Salvation Army. He insisted that the
closer we come to Christ the more likely we are to manifest our oneness in Christ, for he had appropriated from his teacher Neander as
his own motto Pascal's words: "In Jesus Christ all contradictions
are resolved."[6] All this, besides much else, is an eloquent testimony to the prophetic and pioneering character of Schaff's ecumenical efforts. It is further noteworthy that in keeping with the
evangelical cast of his ecumenical outlook Schaff downplayed the
significance of doctrinal differences (for which some of his critics
had taken him to task).[7] He even insisted that all Christians have

---

[5]David S. Schaff, *Life of Schaff*, 483.

[6]See p. 41n33, above.

[7]For instance, William Julius Mann, Schaff's life-long friend, who had firmly
embraced the Lutheran confessionalist position, later was as outspoken in opposing
the "unionistic" indifference of the Evangelical Alliance and of Schaff as he had
earlier, during the Mercersburg years, freely criticized the "romanizing tendencies" of his friend's high-church views (see Spaeth, *D. William Julius Mann*, 73-
78). And Friedrich Loofs, in reviewing Schaff's *Christ and Christianity*, referred

always been in basic agreement on the essential doctrines of their common faith. Still, he singled out three obstacles that remain stumbling blocks on the path leading toward Christian unity: the "historic episcopate" of the Anglicans for Protestants, the *filioque* of the western tradition for Eastern Orthodoxy, and the theory and institution of the papacy for all non-Roman Catholics. In each instance, though, Schaff proposed intriguing, if somewhat simplistic solutions to the ecumenical dilemma. At the Second Old Catholic Reunion Conference at Bonn in 1875, which brought together Old Catholic, Orthodox and Anglican theologians, Schaff, for instance, pleaded for the resolution of the controversy of the *filioque* clause by the simple expedient of adopting the language of certain statements in the Gospel of John and the letters of Paul. To this proposal the venerable and scholarly Ignaz von Döllinger curtly replied: "If his opinions are shared by the other members of the Conference, it follows that we all of us should have done far more wisely if we had remained at home."[8]

However, if we want to perceive the true significance of Schaff's last ecumenical utterance, then we need to recall once more and summarize the various strands in the rich and complex web of his ecumenical thought. No doubt, foremost was his sincere belief that he had found the key to the meaning of the history of Christianity in the principle of historical development as molded by the romantic-idealistic currents of early nineteenth-century German culture. For this principle had made it possible for him to explain and solve the puzzling, scandalous contradiction between the biblical concept of the unity of the church and the historical reality of the mul-

---

(admittedly with an air of teutonic superiority) to Schaff's "unionistic conviction of a typically American kind..., the practical motifs of which are clearer than its dogmatic development," lamented the fact that the author's own views "repeatedly rise above the opposites only by virtue of their indefiniteness," and concluded that with Schaff "the sharp distinctness of the confessional individuality" and "a unionistic conviction" are mutually exclusive (*Theologische Literaturzeitung* 11 [1886]: 150).

[8]*Alfred Plummer: Conversations with Dr. Döllinger, 1870–1890,* ed. Robrecht Boudens (Leuven, 1985) 134. Plummer added: "I have seldom seen a man so quietly, and at the same time so effectually, snuffed out as Dr. Schaff was by this remark from Dr. Döllinger." It appears, moreover, that Schaff, who was not a conference delegate, had somewhat tactlessly insisted on being heard.

tiplicity of Christian churches. Schelling's great ecumenical scheme in particular, centered as it was in the idealistic dialectics, was so attractive to him because it seemingly accomplished the nearly miraculous: It made it possible for him to trace the historical diversity of Christianity back to the very source of divine revelation, biblical Christianity itself; it showed him the necessity of the major historical types of Christianity as sequential stages, both logically and chronologically, in the dialectical unfolding of biblical truth; and it had finally opened for him the beautiful vision of the johannean church of the future, the church of "evangelical catholicism," the grand synthesis, in which the development of Christianity will at long last come to its fulfillment and rest. I should add that in 1854 Schaff had asked the dying Schelling whether he still was convinced of the truth of his grand ecumenical vision of the history of the Christian church. According to Schaff, Schelling "emphatically replied in the affirmative, but added that he had, on further reflection, made room for James as the representative of the Greek Church, in distinction from the Roman or Petrine Church." Schaff thought this modification contained "a grain of truth."[9] He offered later an adjustment of his own, when he claimed that "Jerusalem, Rome, and Petersburg are in different degrees on the side of Peter; Wittenberg, Geneva, and Oxford—at various distances and with temporary reactions—follow the standard of Paul."[10]

The romantic principle of individuality—the romantic belief that all living unity involves diversity, multiplicity and fulness—by contrast, had taught him that the Christian spirit manifests itself in history only in a variety of individual ecclesiastical forms, of which all are equally necessary for a complete representation of the life of Christ in his followers. Hence these romantic notions had made it possible for him to view the diverse forms of Christian piety and church life as simultaneous and not merely successive manifestations of the Christian spirit in history. In fact, the polarity and interplay of unity and diversity belong to the very nature of the historical life of Christianity; therefore, denominational diversity is also

---

[9]Schaff, *History of the Christian Church*, vol. 1, 3rd ed. (New York, 1890) 517n.1.

[10]Schaff, *The Epistle of Paul to the Galatians* (New York, 1881) 30 ("Excursus on Controversy of Peter and Paul").

essential to Christian unity. This was the other meaning implied, especially during the later years of Schaff's life, in his cherished ideal of "evangelical catholicism." And these romantic notions had soon prompted him to insist on the importance of drawing a careful distinction between "denominationalism" and "sectarianism." At the Seventh General Conference of the Evangelical Alliance held at Basle in Switzerland in 1879, he had implored his European friends to accept this distinction, for "the former is compatible with true catholicity of spirit; the latter is nothing but extended selfishness, which crops out of human nature everywhere and in all ages and conditions of the church." Then he had added the provocative remark: "The American denominations are really more united in spirit than the different theological schools and church parties of national churches under one governmental roof, and manifest this underlying unity by hearty cooperation in common enterprises."[11] At the end of his life, at Chicago, he affirmed the denominational diversity of Protestantism as a "blessing." Already early in his American career an exegetical discovery had taught him that Christ had prayed for the oneness of his "flock" (John 10:16)—and not "fold," as the Vulgate and the King James Version have it. Therefore, as he would subsequently time and again repeat, Christ's one flock might continue to be made up of many different "folds," which are the historic denominations, as long as they view each other as complementary in nature and mission and are drawing closer to each other in spirit and in doing God's work.

We should also remember that Schaff had at first expected America to be the "Phoenix grave" of all the Christian churches, from which in due time will issue the visible "reunion of Christendom." Later, when he tended to think of Christianity as a "garden" with a great variety of individual flowers, he came to understand the prevailing ecclesiastical situation as a "mosaic" (and not, to use a later metaphor, a "melting pot"), to which each of the historic denominations makes its own unique contribution, though complementary of all the others. Cooperative efforts of committed individual Christians for the furtherance of God's work

---

[11]Schaff, "Christianity in the United States" (A Report Prepared for the Seventh General Conference of the Evangelical Alliance, held at Basle, Switzerland, September 1879), *Evangelical Alliance Document* 14:26-27.

on earth, confederations of churches and organic unions must, of course, continue to take place and should be supported by all churches and Christians. But Schaff had soon come to view the abolition of all denominational distinctions in a final, visible "reunion of Christendom" as an eschatological event. It should also be noted that Schaff at no time offered a specific blueprint for the "faith and order" of the church toward which all ecumenical endeavors should be directed as their ultimate goal. Still, the ecumenical vision that guided him, I believe, was something akin to the Prussian Union church, only on a vaster, universal scale, including all the Christian churches: Orthodox, Roman Catholic and Protestant.[12] This ecumenical arrangement—Schaff liked to call it a "conservative, not absorptive" union—provided for a common church structure but allowed for the continuance of different historic creeds and traditions, just as was true of the Prussian Union church. If this was the broad and truly catholic nature of Schaff's ecumenical vision, it was still the ecumenical outlook of an evangelical Christian. Thus Schaff became a driving force in the Evangelical Alliance—the decline of the American branch of the Evangelical Alliance is usually dated from his death. He would later be singled out as one of the pioneers and prophets who, together with still others, had prepared the way for the Federal Council of the Churches of Christ.[13] Beyond the horizons of the present historical moment, however, Schaff always perceived the possibility of the transforming power of God's Spirit causing marvellous new surprises and reformations. This great expectation and hope is also, and perhaps even most of all, a part of Schaff's lasting ecumenical legacy.

Finally, one can say that Schaff's ecumenical position is perhaps best described as representing, in Schelling's words, "Christianity in the totality of its development."[14] Christianity, Schaff held, can

---

[12]See, for instance, Schaff's discussion of the Prussian church in *History of the Christian Church,* vol. 6 (1888) 599, as well as his earlier discussion of the larger significance of the Prussian union in *Amerika,* 2nd ed. (Berlin, 1858) 261-62.

[13]See John A. Hutchison, *We Are Not Divided: A Critical and Historical Study of The Federal Council of the Churches of Christ in America* (New York, 1941) 19.

[14]F. W. J. Schelling, *Sämmtliche Werke,* ed. F. K. A. Schelling (Stuttgart and Augsburg, 1856–61) sec. 2, 4:310.

only be identified with its first historical form, the apostolic church. No other historical form of the Christian church is to be absolute or normative. For the fulness of biblical Christianity is not contained in any one of these churches nor in any one century of church history, but unfolds its riches only in all churches and in all centuries. He was, therefore, opposed to all those churches which, in one way or another, identify their own church with the true church of Christ to the exclusion of all the other churches. It is true, though, that we can be Christians only by belonging to a certain historical church. Not this church, however, but only its source, Christ and the apostolic witness to him, are the fountain of our salvation. Gazing far into the future, he also held that the true unity and catholicity of the Christian church consist not only in the union of the various churches, but also in a simultaneous synthesis of church and world, of Christianity and culture, for ultimately Christ and his church will reign trimphantly over the whole human race and all human life.

On Friday, September 22, which was the twelfth day of the World's Parliament of Religions, the morning session, so the official record states, "began with silent devotion and the recital of the Lord's Prayer by the venerable Dr. Philip Schaff." After the prayer, Schaff spoke as follows:

This is short notice to speak to be given to one who has just risen from the dead. A little more than a year ago I was struck down by apoplexy; but I have recovered, through the mercy of God, and I am a miracle to myself. I was warned by physicians and friends not to come to Chicago. They said it would kill me. Well, let it kill me. I was determined to bear my last dying testimony to the cause of Christian Union, in which I have been interested all my life. But I think the Lord will give me strength to survive the Parliament of Religions. The idea of this Parliament will survive all criticism. The critics will die, the cause will remain. And as sure as God is the Truth and as sure as Christ is the Way and the Truth and the Life, his Word shall be fulfilled, and there shall be one flock and one Shepherd.[15]

---

[15]*The World's Parliament of Religions,* ed. Barrows, 1:138.

As the nineteenth century dawned, Friedrich Schleiermacher had written words that perfectly fit Schaff's life, which was now about to be completed: "The highest and most cultured always see a universal union, and, in seeing it, establish it."[16]

THE REUNION OF CHRISTENDOM*

Neither for these only do I pray, but for them also that believe on me through their word; that they may all be one; even as thou, Father, art in me, and I in thee, that they also may be in us: that the world may believe that thou didst send me.

—John 17:20-21

The Difficulty of the Problem

"With men this is impossible, but with God all things are possible" (Matt. 19:25-26).

This answer of our Saviour to the question of his disciples "Who can be saved?" may well be applied to the question, "How shall the many sections of the Christian world be united?"

When St. Paul entered the eternal city as an obscure prisoner, chained to a rude heathen soldier, no philosopher or historian could have foreseen the conversion of the Roman empire to the religion of Jesus of Nazareth; and yet in less than three hundred years the crowned successor of Nero appeared, as a worshipper of Christ, among the bishops of the Council of Nicaea, and the symbol of shame and defeat had become the symbol of glory and victory.

When Augustin, an humble monk, baptized the painted Anglo-Saxon savages of Kent, he did not dream that he was laying the foundation of Christian England with his missions encircling the globe.

Columbus died in the belief that he had discovered, not a continent, but merely a western passage to the East Indies, and Pope Alexander VI, in the exercise of his authority as the arbiter of Chris-

---

[16]F. Schleiermacher, *On Religion. Speeches to its Cultured Despisers,* trans. J. Oman (New York, 1958) 154.

*"The Reunion of Christendom," *Evangelical Alliance Document* 33 (1893): 1-45.

tendom, divided the New World between Catholic Spain and Portugal; but Providence intended to give the control of North America to the Anglo-Saxon race and to make it a home of religious freedom and progress.

Deus habet suas horas et moras.[1] A thousand years are with God as one day, and he may accomplish in one day the work of a thousand years. Sooner or later, in his own good time, and in a manner far better than we can devise or hope, he will, by the power of his Spirit, unite all his children into one flock under one Shepherd.

The Existing Unity

The reunion of Christendom presupposes an original union which has been marred and obstructed, but never entirely destroyed. The theocracy of the Jewish dispensation continued during the division of the kingdom and during the Babylonian exile. Even in the darkest time, when Elijah thought that Israel was wholly given to idolatry, there were seven thousand—known only to God—who had never bowed their knees to Baal. The Church of Christ has been one from the beginning, and he has pledged to her his unbroken presence "all the days to the end of the world" [Matt. 28:20]. The one invisible Church is the soul which animates the divided visible Churches. All true believers are members of the mystical body of Christ.

> The saints in heaven and on earth
> But one communion make:
> All join in Christ, their living Head,
> And of his grace partake.[2]

Let us briefly mention the prominent points of unity which underlies all divisions.

Christians differ in dogmas and theology, but agree in the fundamental articles of faith which are necessary to salvation: they believe in the same Father in heaven, the same Lord and Saviour, and

---

[1](Ed.) Freely translated: "God has his own time-table."

[2](Ed.) From Isaac Watts's hymn, "Not to the Terrors of the Lord," last verse (wording differs slightly).

the same Holy Spirit, and can join in every clause of the Apostles' Creed, of the *Gloria in Excelsis,* and the *Te Deum.*

They are divided in church government and discipline, but all acknowledge and obey Christ as the Head of the Church and chief Shepherd of our souls.

They differ widely in modes of worship, rites and ceremonies, but they worship the same God manifested in Christ, they surround the same throne of grace, they offer from day to day the same petitions which the Lord has taught them, and can sing the same classical hymns, whether written by Catholic or Protestant, Greek or Roman, Lutheran or Reformed, Calvinist or Methodist, Episcopalian or Presbyterian, Paedo-Baptist or Baptist. Some of the best hymn-writers—as Toplady and Charles Wesley—were antagonistic in theology; yet their hymns, "Rock of Ages," and "Jesus, Lover of my soul," are sung with equal fervor by Calvinists and Methodists. Newman's "Lead, kindly Light," will remain a favorite hymn among Protestants, although the author left the Church of England and became a cardinal of the Church of Rome. "In the Cross of Christ I glory," and "Nearer, my God, to Thee," were written by devout Unitarians, yet have an honored place in every trinitarian hymnal.[3]

There is a unity of Christian scholarship of all creeds, which aims at the truth, the whole truth, and nothing but the truth. This unity has been strikingly illustrated in the Anglo-American Revision of the Authorized Version of the Scriptures, in which about one hundred British and American scholars—Episcopalians, Independents, Presbyterians, Methodists, Baptists, Friends, and Unitarians, have harmoniously co-operated for fourteen years (from 1870 to 1884). It was my privilege to attend almost every meeting of the American Revisers in the Bible House at New York, and several meetings of the British Revisers in the Jerusalem Chamber of Westminster Abbey; and I can testify that, notwithstanding the positive convictions of the scholars of the different communions, no sectarian issue was ever raised; all being bent upon the sole purpose of giving the most faithful idiomatic rendering of the original Hebrew and Greek. The En-

---

[3](Ed.) John Bowring (1792–1872) and Sarah F. Adams (1805–48).

glish Version, in its new as well as its old form, will continue to be the strongest bond of union among the different sections of English-speaking Christendom—a fact of incalculable importance for private devotion and public worship.

Formerly, exegetical and historical studies were too much controlled by, and made subservient to, apologetic and polemic ends; but now they are more and more carried on without prejudice, and with the sole object of ascertaining the meaning of the text and the facts of history upon which creeds must be built.

Finally, we must not overlook the ethical unity of Christendom, which is much stronger than its dogmatic unity and has never been seriously shaken. The Greek, the Latin, and the Protestant Churches, alike, accept the Ten Commandments as explained by Christ, or the law of supreme love to God and love to our neighbor, as the sum and substance of the Law, and they look up to the teaching and example of our Saviour as the purest and most perfect model for universal imitation.

The Divisions of Christendom

The unity and harmony of the Christian Church were threatened and disturbed from the beginning, partly by legitimate controversy, which is inseparable from progress, partly by ecclesiastical domination and intolerance, partly by the spirit of pride, selfishness and narrowness which tends to create heresy and schism. Hence the frequent exhortations of the Apostles to avoid strife and contention, and to "keep the unity of the Spirit in the bond of peace" [Eph. 4:3].

The Church had hardly existed twenty years when it was brought to the brink of disruption by the question of circumcision as a condition of church-membership and salvation, and would have split into a Jewish Church and a Gentile Church, had not the wisdom and charity of the Apostles prevented such a calamity at the Council of Jerusalem. Not long afterward the same irritating question produced at Antioch a temporary alienation even between Paul and Peter.

The party spirit which characterized the philosophical schools of Greece, manifested itself in the congregation at Corinth, and created four divisions, calling themselves respectively after Paul, Apollos, Cephas, and Christ (in a sectarian sense). Against this evil the Apos-

tle raised his indignant protest: "Is Christ divided? was Paul crucified for you? or were ye baptized into the name of Paul?" (1 Cor.
1:13). If it is wrong to give a Church the name of an inspired Apostle, can it be right to call it after an uninspired teacher, though he
be as great as Luther or Wesley?

1. Many schisms arose in the early ages before and after the
Council of Nicaea. Almost every great controversy resulted in the ex-
communication of the defeated party, who organized a separate sect,
if they were not exterminated by the civil power. The Nestorians,
Armenians, Jacobites, and Copts, who seceded from the Orthodox
Greek Church, continue to this day as relics of dead controversies.
The schism of the Donatists, who were once as numerous and as well
organized in North Africa as the Catholics, was extinguished not so
much by the arguments of St. Augustin, the last great African, as by
the barbarian invasion which overwhelmed both parties in a common
ruin.

2. In the ninth century, the great Catholic Church itself was split
in two on the doctrinal question of the procession of the Holy Spirit,
and the ecclesiastical question of the primacy of the bishop of Rome.
The Greek schism lasts to this day and seems as far from being healed
as ever. It is even intensified by the two modern dogmas of the Roman Church—the immaculate conception of the Virgin Mary, and
the infallibility of the pope. It is strange that the Greek and Latin
Churches, which agree most in doctrine, worship, and government,
should be most antagonistic and irreconcilable in spirit and feeling,
so as to defy every attempt at reunion. The Pope of Rome and the
Czar at St. Petersburg are the greatest rivals in Christendom. The
Sultan still holds the key to the Holy Sepulchre, and Turkish soldiers
keep watch to prevent Greek and Latin monks from fighting on the
sacred spot in passion week!

In view of this greatest, and yet least justifiable, of all schisms,
neither the Greek nor the Latin Church should cast a stone upon the
divisions of Protestantism. They all share in the sin and guilt of
schism, and should also share in a common repentance.

3. In the sixteenth century, the Latin or Western Church was rent
into two hostile camps, the Roman and the Protestant, in consequence of the evangelical reformation and the papal reaction.

Protestantism, again, appeared first in three main divisions: Lutheran, Reformed (Calvinistic), and Anglican. The former two divided the field with the Roman Catholic Church on the Continent, and acquired an equal legal status in Germany after the terrible ordeal of the Thirty Years' War, by the Treaty of Westphalia (1648), in spite of the protest of the pope. In France, the Protestants were given legal toleration by the Edict of Nantes in 1598, which, however, was revoked in 1685. In Holland the Reformed Church triumphed in the great struggle for political and religious liberty against Spain. In England and Scotland, the whole nation became Protestant. Southern Europe and the greater part of Ireland remained Roman Catholic.

4. In England, a new era of division dates from the Toleration Act of 1688 [sic], which secured to the orthodox dissenters—Presbyterians, Independents, Baptists, and Quakers—a limited toleration, while the Episcopal Church remained the established or national religion in England, and the Reformed or Presbyterian Church remained the national religion in Scotland.

The principle of toleration gradually developed into that of religious freedom, and was extended to the Methodists, Unitarians, and Roman Catholics.

Under the reign of freedom, there is no limitation to the multiplication of denominations and sects, and there ought to be none. We cannot have the use of freedom, which is the greatest gift of God, without the risk of its abuse by sinful and erring men.

We find, therefore, the largest number of denominations in England and America where religious freedom is most fully enjoyed; while on the Continent of Europe, especially in Roman Catholic countries, freedom of public worship is denied or abridged, although of late it is making irresistible progress.

5. In the United States, all the creeds and sects of Europe meet on a basis of liberty and equality before the law, and are multiplied by native ingenuity and enterprise.

We are informed by Dr. Carroll, the official editor of the religious statistics of the census of 1890, that there are no less than 143 religious denominations in the United States, besides a number of independent congregations.[4]

This bare statement, it is true, would give a false impression, and must be corrected by the additional statement, on the same authority, that 119 of these denominations fall into 18 groups or families, leaving only 24 which are separate and distinct.

This would make 42 different denominations. Some of these are not Christian, or are very insignificant, and might as well be omitted. But even this reduced number is much too large, and a reproach to the Christian name. For these divisions promote jealousies, antagonisms, and interferences at home and on missionary fields abroad, at the expense of our common Christianity. The evil is beginning to be felt more and more.

The cure must begin where the disease has reached its crisis, and where the Church is most free to act. For the reunion of Christendom, like religion itself, cannot be forced, but must be free and voluntary.

Christian union and Christian freedom are one and inseparable.[5]

Division Not an Unmixed Evil

Before we discuss reunion, we should acknowledge the hand of Providence in the present divisions of Christendom.

There is a great difference between denominationalism and sectarianism: the first is consistent with Church unity as well as military corps are with the unity of an army, or the many monastic orders with the unity of the papacy; the second is nothing but extended selfish-

---

[4](Ed.) See also Henry King Carroll, *The Religious Forces of the United States*, vol. 1 of The American Church History Series (New York, 1893).

[5]The United States census statistics of 1890 count 17 branches of Methodists, 13 branches of Baptists, 12 Lutheran, and 12 Presbyterian organizations, which are separate and independent, yet essentially agree. There are 12 kinds of Mennonites, 4 kinds of Dunkards, 2 kinds of Christians, 4 kinds of Plymouth Brethren, 6 kinds of Adventists, etc. It is remarkable that England, which still has a national Church, should even have a larger number of sects than the United States, namely 254, according to Whitacker's *Almanack* for 1892, p. 249. But the report of the registrar-general in 1877 numbered only 122.

ness and bigotry. Denominationalism is a blessing; sectarianism is a curse.

We must remember that denominations are most numerous in the most advanced and active nations of the world. A stagnant Church is a sterile mother. Dead orthodoxy is as bad as heresy, or even worse. Sects are a sign of life and interest in religion. The most important periods of the Church—the Nicene age, and the age of the Reformation—were full of controversy. There are divisions in the Church which cannot be justified, and there are sects which have fulfilled their mission and ought to cease. But the historic denominations are permanent forces and represent various aspects of the Christian religion which supplement each other.

As the life of our Saviour could not be fully exhibited by one Gospel, nor his doctrine fully set forth by one Apostle, much less could any one Christian body comprehend and manifest the whole fullness of Christ and the entire extent of his mission to mankind.

Every one of the great divisions of the Church has had, and still has, its peculiar mission as to territory, race and nationality, and modes of operation.

The Greek Church is especially adapted to the East, to the Greek and Slavonic peoples; the Roman, to the Latin races of Southern Europe and America; the Protestant, to the Teutonic races of the North and West.

Among the Protestant Churches, again, some have a special gift for the cultivation of Christian science and literature; others for the practical development of the Christian life; some are most successful among the higher, others among the middle, and still others among the lower classes. None of them could be spared without great detriment to the cause of religion and morality, and without leaving its territory and constituency spiritually destitute. Even an imperfect Church is better than no Church.

No schism occurs without guilt on one or on both sides. "It must needs be that offenses come, but woe to that man by whom the offense cometh" [Matt. 18:7]. Yet God overrules the sins and follies of man for his own glory.

The separation of Paul and Barnabas, in consequence of their "sharp contention" [Acts 15:39] concerning Mark, resulted in the enlargement of missionary labor. If Luther had not burned the pope's bull, or had recanted at Worms, we would not have a Lutheran Church, but be still under the spiritual tyranny of the papacy. If Luther had accepted Zwingli's hand of fellowship at Marburg, the Protestant cause would have been stronger at the time, but the full development of the characteristic features of the two principal Churches of the Reformation would have been prevented, or obstructed. If John Wesley had not ordained Coke, we would not have a Methodist Episcopal Church, which is the strongest denomination in the United States. If Chalmers and his friends had not seceded from the General Assembly of the Kirk of Scotland in 1843, forsaking every comfort for the sake of the sole headship of Christ, we would miss one of the grandest chapters in modern Church history.

All divisions of Christendom will, in the providence of God, be made subservient to a greater harmony. Where the sin of schism has abounded, the grace of future reunion will much more abound.

Variety Essential to Unity

Taking this view of the divisions of the Church, we must reject the idea of a negative reunion, which would destroy all denominational distinctions and thus undo the work of the past.

History is not like "the baseless fabric of a vision" that leaves "not a rack behind." It is the unfolding of God's plan of infinite wisdom and mercy to mankind. He is the chief actor, and rules and overrules the thoughts and deeds of his servants. We are told that our heavenly father has numbered the very hairs of our head, and that not a sparrow falleth to the ground without his will. The labors of confessors and martyrs, of missionaries and preachers, of fathers, schoolmen and reformers, and of the countless host of holy men and women of all ranks and conditions who lived for the good of the world, cannot be lost. They constitute a treasure of inestimable value, for all future time. The Apostle encourages his brethren to be "steadfast, unmoveable, always abounding in the work of the Lord," because their "labor is not in vain in the Lord" (1 Cor. 15:58). Whatever is built upon the foundation of Jesus Christ shall stand.

Variety in unity and unity in variety is the law of God in nature, in history, and in his kingdom. Unity without variety is dead uniformity. There is beauty in variety. There is no harmony without many sounds, and a garden encloses all kinds of flowers. God has made no two nations, no two men or women, not even two trees or two flowers, alike. He has endowed every nation, every Church, yea, every individual Christian, with peculiar gifts and graces. His power, his wisdom, and his goodness are reflected in ten thousand forms.

"There are diversities of gifts," says St. Paul, "but the same Spirit. And there are diversities of ministrations, and the same Lord. And there are diversities of workings, but the same God, who worketh all things in all. But to each one is given the manifestation of the Spirit to profit withal" (1 Cor. 12:4-7).

We must, therefore, expect the greatest variety in the Church of the future. There are good Christians who believe in the ultimate triumph of their own creed, or form of government and worship, but they are all mistaken and indulge in a vain dream. The world will never become wholly Greek, nor wholly Roman, nor wholly Protestant, but it will become wholly Christian, and will include every type and every aspect, every virtue and every grace of Christianity— an endless variety in harmonious unity, Christ being all in all.

Inclusiveness, Not Exclusiveness

Every denomination which holds to Christ the Head will retain its distinctive peculiarity, and lay it on the altar of reunion, but it will cheerfully recognize the excellences and merits of the other branches of God's kingdom. No sect has the monopoly of truth. The part is not the whole; the body consists of many members, and all are necessary to each other.

Episcopalians will prefer their form of government as the best, but must concede the validity of the non-episcopal ministry.

Baptists, while holding fast to the primitive mode of immersion, must allow pouring or affusion to be legitimate baptism.

Protestants will cease to regard the pope as the Antichrist predicted by St. Paul and St. John, and will acknowledge him as the legitimate head of the Roman Church; while the pope ought to recognize the respective rights and privileges of the Greek patriarchs, and evangelical bishops and pastors.

Those who prefer to worship God in the forms of a stated liturgy, ought not to deny others the equal right of free prayer, as the Spirit moves them. Even the silent worship of the Quakers has Scripture authority; for there was "a silence in heaven for the space of half an hour" (Rev. 8:1).

Doctrinal differences will be the most difficult to adjust. When two dogmas flatly contradict each other, the one denying what the other asserts, one or the other, or both, must be wrong. Truth excludes error and admits of no compromise.

But truth is many-sided and all-sided, and is reflected in different colors. The creeds of Christendom, as already remarked, agree in the essential articles of faith, and their differences refer either to minor points, or represent only various aspects of truth, and supplement one another.

Calvinists and Arminians are both right, the former in maintaining the sovereignty of God, the latter in maintaining the freedom and moral responsibility of man: but they are both wrong, when they deny one or the other of these two truths, which are equally important, although we may not be able to reconcile them satisfactorily. The conflicting theories on the Lord's Supper which have caused the bitterest controversies among mediaeval Schoolmen and Protestant Reformers turn, after all, only on the *mode* of Christ's presence; while all admit the essential *fact* that he is spiritually and really present, and partaken of by believers, as the bread of life from heaven. Even the two chief differences between Romanists and Protestants concerning Scripture and tradition, as rules of faith, and concerning faith and good works, as conditions of justification, admit of an adjustment by a better understanding of the nature and relationship of Scripture and tradition, of faith and works. The difference is no greater than that between St. Paul and St. James in their teaching on justification; and yet the Epistles of both stand side by side in the same canon of Holy Scripture.

We must remember that the dogmas of the Church are earthly vessels for heavenly treasures, or imperfect human definitions of divine truths, and may be improved by better statements with the advance of knowledge. Our theological systems are but dim rays of the sun of truth which illuminates the universe. Truth first, doctrine next, dogma last.

> Our little systems have their day;
>> They have their day and cease to be;
>> They are but broken lights of thee,
> And thou, O Lord, art more than they.[6]

Every denomination should prepare a short popular and irenic creed of the essential articles which it holds in common with all others; and leave the larger confessions of faith to theologians, whose business it is to investigate the mysteries and solve the problems of faith.

Different Kinds of Christian Union

The Reformation of the sixteenth century ended in division; the Reformation of the twentieth century will end in reunion. The age of sectarianism is passing away, the age of catholicity is coming on. The progress has begun in earnest. Though many experiments may fail, the cause of union is steadily gaining.

There are three kinds of union: individual, federal, and organic.

1. Individual union is a voluntary association of Christians of different Churches and nationalities for a common purpose.

2. Federal or confederate union is a voluntary association of different Churches in their official capacity, each retaining its freedom and independence in the management of its internal affairs, but all recognizing one another as sisters with equal rights, and coöperating in general enterprises, such as the spread of the gospel at home and abroad, the defense of the faith against infidelity, the elevation of the poor and neglected classes of society, works of philanthropy and charity, and moral reform.

Such an ecclesiastical confederation would resemble the political confederations of Switzerland, the United States, and the modern German Empire. The beauty and strength of these confederate governments lie in the union of the general sovereignty with the intrin-

---

[6](Ed.) Alfred Tennyson, *In Memoriam A. H. H.* (1850) "Prologue," stanza 5. Also hymn, "Strong Son of God, Immortal Love," verse 4.

sic independence of the several cantons, or states, or kingdoms and duchies.

3. Organic or corporate union of all the Churches under one government. The Roman Catholic Church claims to be the one and the only Church of Christ, governed by his vicar in the Vatican; and undoubtedly she presents the most imposing organization the world has ever seen. The Roman Church goes back in unbroken line to the days of the Apostles; she extends over five continents, and is controlled by an aged, unmarried priest, whose encyclicals command the attention of every reader in Christendom. Proud of her past, she confidently hopes to absorb at no distant time the Greek schism and all the Protestant sects.

But this is an impossibility. The history of the Greek Church and of the Protestant Churches cannot be undone, as little as that of the Roman Church. The last three or four hundred years have done as much, or more, for Christianity and civilization than the Catholic middle ages. Christ needs no vicar: he is the ever-living Head of his Church, present everywhere and at all times. He promised us one *flock* under one shepherd, but not one *fold*. The famous passage, John 10:16, has been mistranslated by the Latin Vulgate, and the error has passed into King James's Version. Christ's flock is one, but there are many folds, and there will be "many mansions in heaven" [John 14:2].

Voluntary Associations of Individual Christians

Protestant Christians of different denominations have associated for common objects in voluntary societies, such as Bible Societies, Tract Societies, Sunday-school Unions, Young Men's and Young Women's Christian Associations, Evangelical Alliances, and Christian Endeavor Societies. These societies are all of comparatively recent growth, and are doing great service to the cause of Christian union. We mention the two largest and most influential.

1. *The Evangelical Alliance* was founded in London in 1846 by representative men of Europe and America, for the promotion of Christian union and the defense of Christian liberty. It has manifested, on a large scale, the great fact that Christians of different creeds, nationalities, and tongues are one in Christ.

The Alliance has national branches in different countries, but holds from time to time general conferences for the promotion of its objects. These conferences have proved a signal blessing to the countries in which they were held. The first General Conference met in London, 1851, the second in Paris, 1855, the third in Berlin, 1857, the sixth in New York, 1873 (the largest and most enthusiastic of all), the seventh in Basel, 1879, the eighth in Copenhagen, 1884, the ninth in Florence, 1891.[7]

It is probable that in 1896 all branches of the Alliance will meet in London to celebrate the first semi-centennial of the society, and make a new start on an enlarged scale as a Pan-Christian Alliance.

The Alliance has also done great service in the defense and promotion of religious liberty. It has first proclaimed the principle that Christian union and religious liberty are inseparably connected.

2. *The Christian Endeavor Societies* are scarcely more than a dozen years old, and have spread with wonderful rapidity from New England over Protestant Christendom. They carry the spirit of union and coöperation into local Churches, and unite young men and women for greater efficiency in prayer and active Christian work.

These societies have likewise assumed an interdenominational and international character. The last general meetings, held in New York, July, 1892, and in Montreal, July, 1893, have surprised the world by the extraordinary enthusiasm and vitality of our rising Christian youth, and are among the most hopeful signs of the times. Even the Roman Catholic Mayor of Montreal heartily welcomed the Convention as "an ally in the battle of belief against unbelief."

---

[7] I attended, as honorary secretary, the General Conferences at New York, Basel, and Copenhagen, and furnished papers on Christianity in the United States (1857 and 1879), on the Old Catholic Movement (1873), on the Discord and Concord of Christendom (1884), and on the Renaissance and the Reformation (for the conference in Florence, 1891), and edited, with Dr. Prime, the Proceedings of the Conference of 1873.

(Ed.) For details of these publications, see below the chapter "A Chronology: Schaff's Life and Published Writings." Schaff's "paper" on the Old Catholic Movement, however, was nothing more than a brief introduction to a letter from the Old Catholic Congress which he read at the New York Conference (see *Evangelical Alliance Conference, 1873,* 485-89).

The sense of the superiority of the common creed of Christendom over sectarian creeds is strengthened by the best preaching of the day, and by religious periodicals which are undenominational yet thoroughly evangelical, and surpass in circulation and influence many sectarian organs.

Confederate Union

We now pass beyond the union of individuals to the union of Churches. The first step in this direction is the confederation of the several branches of those denominations which profess the same creed (as the Augsburg Confession, or the Heidelberg Catechism, or the Westminster Confession), but differ as to interpretation, or in the rigidity of subscription, or in a number of minor differences of government and discipline, or in methods of church work.

Family feuds are often the most bitter and painful; hence it is more difficult to heal the divisions of different branches of the Lutheran, Presbyterian, Methodist, Baptist, and other Church families than to unite distinct and separate denominations. Nevertheless several such attempts have been actually made, with more or less success.

1. *The Alliance of the Reformed Churches*, usually called the "Pan-Presbyterian Alliance," was organized in the English Presbyterian College at London, July, 1875, by representative divines and laymen of Europe and America, most of whom had taken a leading part in the Evangelical Alliance. It embraces the Churches which hold to the consensus of the Reformed confessions of faith and the Presbyterian system of government. Its object is to bring them into closer communion and coöperation in mission fields, and for the support of the weaker branches, as the Waldensians and the Reformed Bohemians. The Alliance does not claim any legislative authority. The doctrinal consensus has not been defined, but it is generally understood to embrace only the fundamental articles of the evangelical faith, which the German Reformed and the semi-Arminian Cumberland Presbyterians hold in common with the high Calvinists.

The Alliance holds from time to time General Councils in different capitals. The first of these councils met at Edinburgh in 1877, the second at Philadelphia in 1880, the third at Belfast in 1884, the fourth at London in 1888, the fifth at Toronto, Canada, in 1892.[8] The sixth will meet at Glasgow in 1896. It is to be hoped that Geneva, the common mother of the Reformed Churches, will not be overlooked in selecting a place for future meetings. It may also be expected that the Churches represented in this Alliance will ultimately agree upon a brief popular and irenic consensus creed, which is suggested in the constitution and was discussed at Edinburgh, 1877, and in subsequent Councils.

2. *The Pan-Methodist Conference.* The various branches of the aggressive and progressive Methodist family have followed the example of the Presbyterians and held an enthusiastic international Conference at London, 1881, and a second one at Washington, the capital of the United States, in 1892, where delegates from the Pan-Presbyterian Council of Toronto were kindly received as Christian brethren notwithstanding the doctrinal differences.

3. *The Congregationalists* of England and America held an International Congress at London in 1891, and discussed all the religious questions of the day with great ability.

4. *The Anglican Council* consists of all the bishops of the Protestant Episcopal Churches of Great Britain, the British Colonies, and the United States. It has so far held three meetings at Lambeth Palace, London, under the presidency of the Archbishop of Canterbury, the first in 1867, the second in 1878, and the third in 1888.

The third council was by far the most important. It was attended by one hundred and forty-five bishops of Great Britain and America, and adopted, with slight modifications, a program for the reunion of Christendom which had been previously proposed by the House of Bishops in the General Convention of the Protestant Episcopal Church of the United States at Chicago in 1886.

---

[8]I took part, as a delegate, in the formation of the Alliance in 1875, attended all the Councils except the last, and prepared addresses on the Consensus of the Reformed Confessions (1877) and on the Toleration Act of 1688 [*sic*] (for the London Council in 1888).

The Four Anglican Articles of Reunion

This Anglican program consists of four articles as "a basis on which approach may be by God's blessing made toward home reunion." The articles are as follows:

I. The Holy Scriptures of the Old and New Testaments, as 'containing all things necessary to salvation,' and as being the rule and ultimate standard of faith.

II. The Apostles' Creed, as the Baptismal Symbol; and the Nicene Creed, as the sufficient statement of the Christian faith.

III. The two Sacraments ordained by Christ himself—Baptism and the Supper of the Lord— ministered with the unfailing use of Christ's words of institution, and of the elements ordained by him.

IV. The Historic Episcopate, locally adapted in the methods of its administration to the varying needs of the nations and peoples called of God into the unity of his Church.

This conference earnestly requests the constituted authorities of the various branches of our communion, acting, as far as may be, in concert with one another, to make it known that they hold themselves in readiness to enter into brotherly conference (such as that which has already been proposed by the Church in the United States of America) with the representatives of other Christian communions in the English-speaking races in order to consider what steps can be taken, either toward corporate reunion, or toward such relations as may prepare the way for fuller organic unity hereafter.[9]

This overture looks toward a confederation of all English-speaking Evangelical Churches, and possibly even to an organic union. As it comes from the largest, most conservative, and most churchly of all the Protestant communions, it is entitled to the highest respect and to serious consideration. It commends itself by a remarkable degree of liberality. It says nothing of the Thirty-nine Articles, nor of the Book of Common Prayer, and leaves the confederate Churches free to keep their own confessions of faith and modes of worship. What a difference between this liberality and the narrow policy of the six-

---

[9]See *The Lambeth conferences* of 1867, 1878, and 1888; edited by Randall T. Davidson, London, 1889, pp. 280, 281.

teenth and seventeenth centuries, which by legislative acts of conformity would force one creed, one discipline, and one liturgy upon England, Scotland, and Ireland! Instead of the Thirty-nine Articles, the Lambeth Articles, and the Irish Articles, which embody a whole system of divinity, we have but four. The first and third articles are already agreed upon by all Protestants. The same may be said of the Apostles' Creed, and the Nicene Creed, except that the latter would exclude Unitarian Christians, and that the Western addition of *Filioque* would never be accepted by the Oriental Church.

The only serious difficulty is the "historic episcopate." This is the stumbling-block to all non-episcopalians, and will never be conceded by them as a condition of Church unity, if it is understood to mean the necessity of three orders of the ministry and of episcopal ordination in unbroken historic succession. Christ says nothing about bishops any more than about patriarchs and popes, and does not prescribe any particular form of church government. All scholars, including the most learned of the ancient Fathers—as St. Jerome or St. Chrysostom—and of the modern Episcopalians—as Bishop Lightfoot—admit the original identity of bishops and presbyters, as is evident from the New Testament and the post-apostolic writings before the Ignatian Epistles.[10]

And as to an unbroken episcopal succession, it is of little avail without the more important succession of the spirit and life of Christ, our ever-present Lord and Saviour, who is as near to his people in the nineteenth century as he was in the first. Even where two or three are

---

[10]The Preface to the Ordinal of the Episcopal Church is not sustained by the facts of history when it affirms that, "it is evident unto all men diligently reading the Holy Scriptures and Ancient Authors, that *from the Apostles' time* there have been these orders of ministers in Christ's Church: Bishops, Priests, and Deacons." The Preface is ascribed to Cranmer (1549), but it was altered in 1662. The earliest testimony to the three orders is that of Ignatius of Antioch (after A. D. 107); but he represents the bishop, surrounded by a college of elders and deacons, as the head of a single congregation, not of a diocese. This is congregational episcopacy. Diocesan episcopacy appears toward the end of the second century in the writings of Irenaeus and Tertullian.

gathered together in his name, he is in the midst of them. *Ubi Christus, ibi Ecclesia.*[11]

The Church of England recognized in various ways, directly or indirectly, the validity of Presbyterian ordination, and held communion with Lutheran and Calvinistic Churches on the Continent from the Reformation down to the Restoration in 1662, when the Ordinal was introduced in its present form.

Archbishop Cranmer, the greatest Anglican liturgist, called Martin Bucer, a mediator between the Lutheran and Swiss Reformers, from Strassburg to the chair of systematic theology in Cambridge, and Peter Martyr, a strict Calvinist, in the same capacity, to the University of Oxford, and consulted them freely in the preparation of the Articles of Religion and the Book of Common Prayer. The Elizabethan bishops, who during their exile under Queen Mary had sought refuge in Zürich, Basel, and Geneva, wrote letters overflowing with gratitude for the hospitality and kindness received from the Swiss Reformers and preachers, and addressed them as spiritual fathers and brethren. Bullinger's *Decades* and Calvin's *Institutes* were the highest authorities in the universities of England, and the influence of Beza's editions of the Greek Testament, his text and notes, is manifest in the Authorized Version of King James. The "judicious" Hooker, the standard writer on church polity, expressed profound veneration for Calvin as "the wisest man that ever the French Church did enjoy" and he expressly admitted "an extraordinary kind of vocation . . . where the Church must needs have some ordained and neither hath nor can have possibly a bishop to ordain; in case of such necessity, the ordinary institution of God hath given oftentimes, and may give, place. And therefore we are not simply without exception to urge a lineal descent of power from the Apostles by continued succession of bishops in every effectual ordination."[12]

Even James I, who hated the Presbyterians, sent five delegates, including three bishops (George Carleton, John Davenant, and Jo-

---

[11](Ed.) "Where Christ is, there is the Church."

[12](Ed.) Richard Hooker, *Of the Laws of Ecclesiastical Polity,* preface, ch. 2.1, and book 7, ch. 14.11, vols. 1 and 3 of The Folger Library Edition of the Works of Richard Hooker, 4 vols. (Cambridge MA, 1977–82).

seph Hall), to the Calvinistic Synod of Dort, who raised no question about the necessity of the episcopate for the being or the well-being of the Church.

Let us learn something from history. All respect for the historic episcopate! It goes back in unbroken line almost to the beginning of the second century, and no one can dispute its historical necessity or measure its usefulness. But God has also signally blessed the Lutheran, the Presbyterian, and the Congregational ministry for many generations, with every prospect of growing usefulness for the future; and what God has blessed no man should lightly esteem. The non-episcopal Churches will never unchurch themselves and cast reproach on their ministry. They will only negotiate with the Episcopal Church on the basis of equality and a recognition of the validity of the ministry. Each denomination must offer its idol on the altar of reunion.

But it is to be hoped that the Episcopal Church will give the historic episcopate, as "locally adapted," such a liberal construction as to include "the historic presbyterate," which dates from the apostolic age and was never interrupted, or will drop it altogether, as a term of reunion. At the Reunion Conference at Grindelwald in 1892, which is to be repeated at Lucerne in 1893, Episcopal dignitaries conferred with Dissenting ministers as Christian brethren.

In any case, we hail the Episcopal proposal as an important step in the right direction, and as a hopeful sign of the future. It is in the line of a noble project of Archbishop Cranmer, who was deeply grieved at the distractions of the Church, and invited Melanchthon, Bullinger, and Calvin to a conference in Lambeth Palace for the purpose of drawing up a consensus creed of the Reformed Churches. Calvin replied that for such a holy purpose he would cross not only the English Channel, but ten seas.

Organic Union

1. An organic union between the *Lutheran* and *German Reformed Churches,* into which German Protestantism has been divided since the sixteenth century, was effected in 1817 in connection with the third centennial of the Reformation, under the lead of Frederick William III, King of Prussia and father of the first emperor of unified

Germany. He was German Reformed, like his ancestors from the time of John Sigismund of Brandenburg (1614), but a majority of his subjects were Lutherans. Hence the traditional tendency of the House of Hohenzollern towards union. The name of *The United Evangelical Church* was substituted for the two separate denominational names, but freedom was allowed to retain the Lutheran or Reformed creed, and to use the Augsburg Confession or the Heidelberg Catechism, according to custom or preference. The Prussian Union, therefore, is not an absorptive, but a conservative, union of two confessions under the same government and administration.

Several other German States, as Baden and Würtemberg, have followed the example of Prussia to their advantage; while those States which were exclusively Lutheran, as Saxony and the Saxon Duchies, adhere to their Lutheran name and tradition.

The Evangelical Union has been accompanied and strengthened, since the days of Schleiermacher and Neander, by a corresponding type of theology, which combines Lutheran and Calvinistic elements. This theology, divided into different schools, prevails in all the Prussian universities, as also in Heidelberg and Tübingen, and is the most progressive theology of the age.

2. In our country, the recent history of the *Presbyterian* Church furnishes an example of organic union. The *Old School* and the *New School,* which were divided in 1837 on doctrinal questions, were reunited by a free and simultaneous impulse in the year 1869 on the basis of orthodoxy and liberty, and have prospered all the more since their reunion, although the differences between conservative and progressive tendencies still remain, and have, within the last few years, come into collision on the questions of a Revision of the Westminster Standards, and the historical criticism of the Bible.

3. The four divisions of *Presbyterians* in *Canada* have forgotten their old family quarrels, and have been united in one organization since 1875.

4. The *Methodists* in *Canada,* who, till 1874, were divided into five independent bodies, have recently united in one organization.

Union with the Catholic Church

If all the Protestant Churches were united by federal or organic union, the greater, the most difficult, and the most important part of the work would still remain to be accomplished; for Christian union must include the Greek and the Roman Churches. They are the oldest, the largest, and claim to be the most orthodox; the former numbering about 84,000,000 members, the latter 215,000,000, while all the Protestant denominations together number only 130,000,000.

If any one Church is to be the center of unification, that honor must be conceded to the Greek or the Roman communion. The Protestant denominations are all descended, directly or indirectly, from the Latin Church of the Middle Ages; while the Greek and Latin Churches trace their origin back to the apostolic age, the Greek to the congregation of Jerusalem, the Latin to the congregation of Rome.

The Greek and Roman Churches

First of all, the two great divisions of Catholicism should come to an agreement among themselves on the disputed questions about the eternal Procession of the Holy Spirit, and the authority of the Bishop of Rome.

On both points, the Greek Church is supported by the testimony of antiquity, and could not yield without stultifying her whole history. The original Nicene Creed does not teach a double Procession, which is a later addition, made in Spain and Gaul, and first disapproved by Pope Leo III, but accepted by his successors; and the Ecumenical Councils, all of which were held in the East and called by the Greek emperors, concede to the Bishop of Old Rome only a primacy of honor among five patriarchs of equal rights and independent jurisdiction.

The first difficulty could easily be solved by omitting the *Filioque* from the Nicene Creed, or by substituting *"sent by* the Father and the Son," for *"proceeds from* the Father and the Son." For the Greek Church never denied the double *Mission* of the Spirit which began with the day of Pentecost, while the *Procession* is an eternal intertrinitarian process, like the eternal generation of the Son from the Father.

The second difficulty is far greater.

Will Rome ever make concessions to the truth of history? We hope that she will.

PHILIP SCHAFF

The Old Catholic Union Conferences

Under the auspices of the Old Catholic Church, and under the lead of Dr. Döllinger of Munich, who, before he was excommunicated on account of his protest against the Vatican dogma of papal infallibility, was esteemed in the Roman Church as her most learned historian and divine, two conferences were held at Bonn, in 1874 and 1875, with a view to prepare for a confederation and intercommunion of the Old Catholic, the Orthodox Greek and Russian, and the Anglican Churches, on the basis of the ecumenical consensus of the ancient Church before the division, and of the Episcopal succession.

These conferences were attended by some of the ablest and most learned dignitaries of these three communions, and agreed upon a doctrinal basis of fourteen articles, and the settlement of the *Filioque* controversy by a compromise which substitutes the Procession of the Holy Spirit from the Father *through* the Son for the Latin doctrine of the Procession of the Holy Spirit from the Father *and* the Son. [13]

These important conclusions of the Bonn Conferences have not been officially ratified by any of the Eastern or Anglican Churches, but may be revived and acted upon at some future time.

---

[13]See the German and Latin text of the Bonn Consensus, with a historical Introduction, in Schaff's *Creeds of Christendom*, vol. 2, 545-554. Dr. Döllinger regarded the Vatican dogma of infallibility and the order of the Jesuits as the chief obstacles to the reunion of Churches, but hoped that the agreement at Bonn might be a means for orientation and a basis for future transactions at a more favorable political conjunction. See his lectures on the *Wiedervereinigung der christlichen Kirchen* (Nördlingen, 1888). These lectures were delivered at Munich, 1872, translated into English by [Henry Nutcome] Oxenham from manuscript and newspaper reports ([*Lectures on the Reunion of the Churches,*] London, 1872) and from English into French by Mrs. Hyacinthe-Loyson (*La réunion des églises,* Paris, 1880) and finally published by the author himself (1888). I was present, as an invited guest, at the Second Conference in Bonn, and listened with admiration to Döllinger's speeches, which were brimful of information and delivered in excellent English with youthful vigor, although he was then seventy-six years old. He seemed to know more about the subject than all the other delegates. Repeated efforts were made, even by Pope Leo XIII, to win him back, but he died excommunicated in 1890, in his ninety-second year. See *Briefe und Erklärungen von J. von Döllinger über die Vatican-ischen Decrete, 1869–1887* (edited by Prof. Reusch), München, 1890.

There is a party among the Anglo-Catholics which is more anxious for union with the Old Catholic and the Graeco-Russian Church than with any Protestant denomination nearer home, although the Greek and Russian delegates at Bonn expressed doubts as to the validity of Anglican orders.

The conferences with the Old Catholics were resumed in Switzerland in 1892.

Papal Infallibility

The difficulty of union with the Roman Church is apparently increased by the modern dogma of papal absolutism and papal infallibility, declared by the Vatican Council in 1870. This dogma is the logical completion of the papal monarchy, the apex of the pyramid of the hierarchy. But it can refer only to the Roman Church. The official decisions of the pope, as the legitimate head of the Roman Church, are final and binding upon all Roman Catholics, but they have no force whatever for any other Christians.

The antichristian feature of the papacy to which the Reformers objected, begins where the pope claims jurisdiction over all Christendom. It is no less than a pope, and one of the very best of them, Gregory I, who protested in official (and therefore infallible) letters against the assumption by the Greek patriarchs of the title of "ecumenical" or "universal bishop," which, he says, belongs to Christ alone. He branded such an assumption as "antichristian," and preferred to call himself "the servant of the servants of God."[14]

What if the pope, in the spirit of the first Gregory and under the inspiration of a higher authority, should infallibly declare his own fallibility in all matters lying outside of his own communion, and invite Greeks and Protestants to a fraternal pan-Christian council in Jerusalem, where the mother-church of Christendom held the first council of reconciliation and peace?

---

[14](Ed.) See p. 284, above.

But whether in Jerusalem or Rome, or (as Cardinal Wiseman thought)[15] in Berlin, or (as some Americans like to think) on the banks of the Mississippi, the war between Rome and Constantinople, and between Rome, Wittenberg, Geneva and Oxford, will be fought out to a peaceful end when all the Churches shall be thoroughly christianized and all the creeds of Christendom united in the creed of Christ.

Restatement of Confessional Differences in the Interest of Truth and Peace

The reunion of the entire Catholic Church, Greek and Roman, with the Protestant Churches, will require such a restatement of all the controverted points by both parties as shall remove misrepresentations, neutralize the anathemas pronounced upon imaginary heresies, and show the way to harmony in a broader, higher, and deeper consciousness of God's truth and God's love.

In the heat of controversy, and in the struggle for supremacy, the contending parties mutually misrepresented each other's views, put them in the most unfavorable light, and perverted partial truths into unmixed errors. Like hostile armies engaged in battle, they aimed at the destruction of the enemy. Protestants in their confessions of faith and polemical works denounced the pope as "the Antichrist," the papists as "idolaters," the Roman mass as an "accursed idolatry," and the Roman Church as "the synagogue of Satan" and "the Babylonian harlot,"—all in perfect honesty, on the ground of certain misunderstood passages of St. Paul and St. John, and especially of the mysterious Book of the Revelation, whose references to the persecutions of pagan Rome were directly or indirectly applied to papal Rome.[16] Rome answered by bloody persecutions; the Council of Trent closed with a double anathema on all Protestant heretics, and the pope annually repeats the curse in the holy week, when all Christians should humbly and penitently meet around the cross on which the Saviour died for the sins of the whole world.

---

[15](Ed.) When Pope Pius IX restored the Roman Catholic hierarchy in England in 1850, Nicholas Patrick Stephen Wiseman (1802–65) was appointed archbishop (later cardinal) of Westminster.

[16](Ed.) See pp. 284-85, above.

When these hostile armies, after a long struggle for supremacy without success, shall come together for the settlement of terms of peace, they will be animated by a spirit of conciliation and single devotion to the honor of the great Head of the Church, who is the divine concord of all human discords.

Peter and Paul

There is truth and comfort in the idea that the apostolic age anticipated the war and peace of subsequent ages.

The Apostles who thus far have most influenced the course of Church history are Peter and Paul. The Apostle whose spirit will preside over the final consummation is John, the bosom friend of Jesus, the Apostle of love.

Peter, the Apostle of Authority, represents Jewish and Roman Christianity; while Paul, the Apostle of freedom, who was called last, and called irregularly, yet none the less divinely, is a type of Gentile and Protestant Christianity. Peter was called "Rock" [Matt. 18:19], but also "Satan" [Matt. 16:23], by his Master. He first confessed Christ; he even hastily drew the sword in his defense; and then denied him three times. But Christ prayed for him that his faith "fail not," and prophesied that he would "turn again and strengthen his brethren" (Luke 22:32). All popes have confessed Christ, and many have drawn the sword, or caused temporal princes to draw it, against heretics; some have denied Christ by their wicked lives: will not some future pope "turn again and strengthen his brethren"?

The same Peter boldly defended the liberty of the Gentile converts at the Council of Jerusalem and protested against the intolerable yoke of bondage; yet afterward, in consistent inconsistency, he practically disowned that liberty at Antioch, and withdrew from fellowship with the Gentile brethren (Gal. 2:11 sqq.). Has not the pope again and again unchurched all Protestant Churches, and denied that liberty wherewith Christ has made us free?

Peter accepted the severe rebuke of the younger Apostle of the Gentiles, and both died martyrs in Rome, to live forever united in the grateful memory of the Church. If the pope should acknowledge the sins of the papacy and extend the hand of brotherhood to his fellow-Christians of other Churches, he would only follow the example of him whom he regards as his first predecessor in office.

Orthodoxy and Progress

The whole system of traditional orthodoxy, Greek, Latin, and Protestant, must progress, or it will be left behind the age and lose its hold on thinking men. The Church must keep pace with civilization, adjust herself to the modern conditions of religious and political freedom, and accept the established results of biblical and historical criticism, and natural science. God speaks in history and science as well as in the Bible and the Church, and he cannot contradict himself. Truth is sovereign, and must and will prevail over all ignorance, error, and prejudice.

Exegetical Progress

The history of the Bible is to a large extent a history of abuse as well as use, of imposition as well as exposition. No book has been more perverted.

The mechanical inspiration theory of the seventeenth century, which confounded inspiration with dictation and reduced the biblical authors to mere clerks, has been superseded by a spiritual and dynamic theory, which alone can account for the obvious peculiarities of thought and style, and which consists with the dignity of God and the freedom of man.

Textual criticism has, after two or three centuries of patient comparison of manuscripts, versions, and patristic quotations as they gradually came to light, purified the traditional text of the Greek Testament, correcting many passages and omitting later interpolations. The criticism of the Hebrew Bible text and the Septuagint has begun the same fundamental process.

Historical criticism is putting the literature of both Testaments in a new light, and makes it more real and intelligible by explaining its environments and organic growth until the completion of the canon.

The wild allegorical exegesis, which turns the Bible into a nose of wax and makes it to teach anything that is pious or orthodox, has been gradually superseded by an honest grammatical and historical exegesis, which takes out the real meaning of the writer instead of putting in the fancies of the reader.

Many proof texts of Protestants against popery, and of Romanists against Protestants, and of both for orthodoxy or against heresy, can no longer be used for partisan purposes.

Historical Progress

Church history has undergone of late a great change, partly in consequence of lost documents and deeper research, partly on account of the standpoint of the historian and the new spirit in which history is written.

1. Many documents on which theories and usages were built, have been abandoned as untenable even by Roman Catholic scholars. We mention the legend of the literal composition of the Apostles' Creed by the Apostles, and of the origin of the creed which was attributed to Athanasius, though it did not appear till four centuries after his death; the fiction of Constantine's Donation; the apocryphal letters of pseudo-Ignatius, of pseudo-Clement, of pseudo-Isidorus, and other post-apostolic and mediaeval falsifications of history, which were universally believed till the time of the Reformation, and even down to the eighteenth century.

2. Genuine history is being rewritten from the standpoint of impartial truth and justice. If facts are found to contravene a cherished theory, all the worse for the theory; for facts are truths, and truth is of God, while theories are of men.

Formerly Church history was made a mere appendix to systematic theology, or abused and perverted for polemic puposes.

The older historians, both Roman Catholic and Protestant, searched ancient and mediaeval history for weapons to defeat their opponents and to establish their own exclusive claims. Flacius, the first learned Protestant historian, saw nothing but antichristian darkness in the Middle Ages, with the exception of a few scattered *Testes Veritatis,* and described the Roman Church from the fifth to the sixteenth century as the great apostasy of prophecy.[17] But modern

---

[17](Ed.) The German Lutheran Matthias Flacius Illyricus was the author of *Catalogus testium veritatis* (1556) ("Catalogue of the Witnesses of the Truth").

Protestant historians, following the example of Neander, who is called "The Father of Church History," regard the Middle Ages as the period of the conversion and the civilization of the barbarians, as a necessary link between ancient and modern Christianity, and as the cradle of the Reformation.

On the other hand, the opposite type of historiography, represented by Cardinal Baronius, traced the papacy to the beginning of the Christian era, maintained its identity through all ages, and denounced the Reformers as arch-heretics and the Reformation as the foul source of revolution, war, and infidelity, and of all the evils of modern society.[18] But the impartial scholars of the Roman Catholic Church now admit the necessity of the Reformation, the pure and unselfish motives of the Reformers, and the beneficial effects of their labors upon their own Church. We may refer to the remarkable judgments of Döllinger on Luther and of Kampschulte on Calvin, based upon a through knowledge of their writings.[19]

A great change of spirit has also taken place among the historians of the different Protestant denominations. The early Lutheran abhorrence of Zwinglianism and Calvinism has disappeared from the best Lutheran manuals of Church history. The bitterness between Prelatists and Puritans, Calvinists and Arminians, Baptists and Paedobaptists, has given way to a calm and just appreciation.

The impartial historian can find no ideal Church in any age. It was a high-priest in Aaron's line that crucified the Savior; a Judas

---

[18](Ed.) Caesar Baronius (1538–1607), Roman Catholic historian and cardinal, author of *Annales Ecclesiastici* (12 vols.), which was a reply to the Lutheran *Magdeburg Centuries*.

[19]See these judgments quoted in Schaff's *Church History*, vol. VI, pp. 741sq., and vol. VII, pp. 285, 412. It is true, Döllinger and [Franz Wilhelm] Kampschulte died excommunicated on account of their opposition to the Vatican dogma of papal infallibility, but they were good Catholics in every other respect. [Johannes] Janssen's *History of the German People* [trans. from the German, 16 vols., London, 1896–1910] and [Ludwig] Pastor's *History of the Popes of the Renaissance* [vols. 1-3 of his monumental *History of the Popes*, trans. from the German, 1899ff.] were written from the modern ultramontane standpoint, but even they after all differ considerably in tone from the older Roman Catholic historians.

was among the Apostles; all sorts of sins among church-members are rebuked in the Epistles of the New Testament; there were "many antichrists" [1 John 2:18] in the age of St. John, and there have been many since, even in the temple of God. Nearly all Churches have acted as persecutors when they had the chance, if not by fire and sword, at least by misrepresentation, vituperation, and abuse. For these and all other sins, they should repent in dust and ashes. One only is pure and spotless— the great Head of the Church, who redeemed it with his precious blood.

But the historian finds, on the other hand, in every age and in every Church, the footprints of Christ, the abundant manifestations of his Spirit, and a slow but sure progress toward that ideal Church which St. Paul describes as "the fullness of him who filleth all in all" [Eph. 1:23].

The study of Church history, like travel in foreign lands, destroys prejudice, enlarges the horizon, liberalizes the mind, and deepens charity. Palestine by its eloquent ruins serves as a commentary on the life of Christ, and has not inaptly been called "the fifth Gospel." So also the history of the Church furnishes the key to unlock the meaning of the Church in all its ages and branches.

The study of history—"with malice toward none, but with charity for all"—will bring the denominations closer together in an humble recognition of their defects and a grateful praise for the good which the same Spirit has wrought in them and through them.

Changes of Opinions

Important changes have also taken place in traditional opinions and practices once deemed pious and orthodox.

The Church in the Middle Ages first condemned the philosophy of Aristotle, but at last turned it into a powerful ally in the defense of her doctrines, and so gave to the world the *Summa* of Thomas Aquinas and the *Divina Commedia* of Dante, who regarded the great Stagirite as a forerunner of Christ, as a philosophical John the Baptist. Luther, likewise, in his wrath against scholastic theology, condemned "the accursed heathen Aristotle," but Melanchthon judged differently, and Protestant scholarship has long since settled upon a just estimate.[20]

Gregory VII, Innocent III, and other popes of the Middle Ages claimed and exercised the power, as vicars of Christ, to depose kings, to absolve subjects from their oath of allegiance, and to lay whole nations under the interdict for the disobedience of an individual. But no pope would presume to do such a thing now, nor would any Catholic king or nation tolerate it for a moment.

The strange mythical notion of the ancient Fathers, that the Christian redemption was the payment of a debt due to the devil, who had a claim upon men since the fall of Adam, but had forfeited it by the crucifixion, was abandoned after Anselm had published the more rational theory of a vicarious atonement in discharge of a debt due to God.

The unchristian and horrible doctrine that all unbaptized infants who never committed any actual transgression, are damned forever and ever, prevailed for centuries under the authority of the great and holy Augustin, but has lost its hold even upon those divines who defend the necessity of water-baptism for salvation. Even high Anglicans and strict Calvinists admit that all children dying in infancy are saved.

The equally unchristian and fearful theory and practice of religious compulsion and persecution by fire and sword, first mildly suggested by the same Augustin, and then formulated by the master theologian of the Middle Ages (Thomas Aquinas), who deemed a heretic, or murderer of the soul, more worthy of death than a murderer of the body, has given way at last to the theory and practice of toleration and liberty.

The delusion of witchcraft, which extended even to Puritan New England and has cost almost as many victims as the tribunals of the Inquisition, has disappeared from all Christian nations forever.

---

[20](Ed.) The Index volume of the Weimar Edition of Luther's *Works*, 58:163, contains a long list of "characteristic expressions" for Aristotle.

The Church and Science

A few words about the relation of the Church to natural and physical science.

Protestants and Catholics alike unanimously rejected the Copernican astronomy as a heresy fatal to the geocentric account of creation, in Genesis; but after a century of opposition which culminated in the condemnation of Galileo by the Roman Inquisition under Urban VIII, they have adopted it without a dissenting voice, and "the earth still moves."

Similar concessions will be made to modern geology and biology, when they have passed the stage of conjecture and reached an agreement as to facts. The Bible does not determine the age of the earth or man, and leaves a large margin for difference of opinion even on purely exegetical grounds. The theory of the evolution of animal life, far from contradicting the fact of creation, presupposes it; for every evolution must have a beginning, and this can only be accounted for by an infinite intelligence and creative will. God's power and wisdom are even more wonderful in the continual process than in a single act.

The theory of historical development, which corresponds to the theory of physical evolution, and preceded it, was first denounced by orthodox divines (within my own recollection) as a dangerous error leading to infidelity, but is now adopted by every historian. It is indorsed by Christ himself in the twin parables of the mustard-seed and the leaven. "First the blade, then the ear, and after that the full corn in the ear," this is the order of the unfolding of the Christian life, both in the individual and the Church.[21] But there is another law of development no less important, which may be called the law of creative headships. Every important intellectual and religious movement begins with a towering personality which cannot be explained from antecedents, but marks a new epoch. Take as illustrations: Moses and the history of Israel, Socrates and the Greek philosophers, Caesar and the Roman emperors, Constantine the Great and the Byzantine

---

[21](Ed.) From the second verse of Henry Alford's hymn, "Come you thankful people, come."

emperors, Charlemagne and the German emperors, Washington and the American presidents, Napoleon and his generals, Dante and the Italian poets, Shakespeare and the English poets, Raphael and his school of painters, Luther and the Lutheran divines, Calvin and the Reformed divines, Spener and the Pietists, Zinzendorf and the Moravians, Wesley and the Methodists, and, above all, Jesus Christ, who is the great central miracle of history, the beginning, the middle, and the end of Christianity.

The Bible, we must all acknowledge, is not, and never claimed to be, a guide of chronology, astronomy, geology, or any other science, but solely a book of religion, a rule of faith and practice, a guide to holy living and dying. There is, therefore, no room for a conflict between the Bible and science, faith and reason, authority and freedom, the Church and civilization. They run in parallel lines, independent, and yet friendly and mutually helpful, tending to the same end—the salvation and perfection of man in the kingdom of God.

Means of Promoting Christian Union

Before the reunion of Christendom can be accomplished, we must expect providential events, new Pentecosts, new reformations—as great as any that have gone before. The twentieth century has marvelous surprises in store for the Church and the world, which may surpass even those of the nineteenth. History now moves with telegraphic speed, and may accomplish the work of years in a single day. The modern inventions of the steamboat, the telegraph, the power of electricity, the progress of science and of international law (which regulates commerce by land and by sea, and will in due time make an end of war), link all the civilized nations into one vast brotherhood.

Let us consider some of the moral means by which a similar affiliation and consolidation of the different Churches may be hastened.

1. The cultivation of an irenic and evangelical-catholic spirit in the personal intercourse with our fellow-Christians of other denominations. We must meet them on common rather than on disputed ground, and assume that they are as honest and earnest as we in the pursuit of truth. We must make allowance for differences in educa-

tion and surroundings, which to a large extent account for differences of opinion. Courtesy and kindness conciliate, while suspicion excites irritation and attack. Controversy will never cease, but the golden rule of the most polemic among the Apostles—to "speak the truth in love" [Eph. 4:15]— cannot be too often repeated. Nor should we forget the seraphic description of love, which the same Apostle commends above all other gifts and the tongues of men and angels— yea, even above faith and hope.

2. Cooperation in Christian and philanthropic work draws men together and promotes their mutual confidence and regard. Faith without works is dead. Sentiment and talk about union are idle without actual manifestation in works of charity and philanthropy.

3. Missionary societies should at once come to a definite agreement, prohibiting all mutual interference in their efforts to spread the gospel at home and abroad. Every missionary of the cross should wish and pray for the prosperity of all other missionaries, and lend a helping hand in trouble. "What then? only that in every way, whether in pretense or in truth, Christ is proclaimed; and therein I rejoice, yea, and will rejoice" [Phil. 1:18].

It is preposterous, yea, wicked, to trouble the minds of the heathen or of Roman Catholics with our domestic quarrels, and to plant half a dozen rival Churches in small towns, where one or two would suffice, thus saving men and means. Unfortunately, the sectarian spirit and mistaken zeal for peculiar views and customs very materially interfere with the success of our vast expenditures and efforts for the conversion of the world.

4. The study of Church history has already been mentioned as an important means of correcting sectarian prejudices and increasing mutual appreciation. The study of symbolic or comparative theology is one of the most important branches of history in this respect, especially in our country, where professors of all the creeds of Christendom meet in daily contact, and should become thoroughly acquainted with one another.

5. One word suffices as regards the duty and privilege of prayer for Christian union, in the spirit of our Lord's sacerdotal prayer, that his disciples may all be one in him, as he is one with the Father.

Conclusion

We welcome to the reunion of Christendom all denominations which have followed the divine Master and have done his work. Let us forgive and forget their many sins and errors, and remember only their virtues and merits.

The Greek Church is a glorious Church: for in her language have come down to us the oracles of God, the Septuagint, the Gospels, and Epistles; hers are the early confessors and martyrs, the Christian fathers, bishops, patriarchs, and emperors; hers the immortal writings of Origen, Eusebius, Athanasius, and Chrysostom; hers the Ecumenical Councils and the Nicene Creed, which can never die.

The Latin Church is a glorious Church: for she carried the treasures of Christian and classical literature over the gulf of the migration of nations, and preserved order in the chaos of civil wars; she was the *Alma Mater* of the barbarians of Europe; she turned painted savages into civilized beings, and worshipers of idols into worshipers of Christ; she built up the colossal structures of the papal theocracy, the canon law, the monastic orders, the cathedrals, and the universities; she produced the profound systems of scholastic and mystic theology; she stimulated and patronized the Renaissance, the printing-press, and the discovery of a new world; she still stands, like an immovable rock, bearing witness to the fundamental truths and facts of our holy religion, and to the catholicity, unity, unbroken continuity, and independence of the Church; and she is as zealous as ever in missionary enterprise and self-denying works of Christian charity.

We hail the Reformation which redeemed us from the yoke of spiritual despotism, and secured us religious liberty— the most precious of all liberties, and made the Bible in every language a book for all classes and conditions of men.

The Evangelical Lutheran Church, the first-born daughter of the Reformation, is a glorious Church: for she set the word of God above the traditions of men, and bore witness to the comforting truth of justification by faith; she struck the keynote to thousands of sweet hymns in praise of the Redeemer; she is boldly and reverently investigating the problems of faith and philosophy, and is constantly making valuable additions to theological lore.

The Evangelical Reformed Church is a glorious Church: for she carried the Reformation from the Alps and lakes of Switzerland "to the end of the West" (to use the words of the Roman Clement about St. Paul);[22] she furnished more martyrs of conscience in France and the Netherlands alone, than any other Church, even during the first three centuries; she educated heroic races, like the Huguenots, the Dutch, the Puritans, the Covenanters, the Pilgrim Fathers, who by the fear of God were raised above the fear of tyrants, and lived and died for the advancement of civil and religious liberty; she is rich in learning and good works of faith; she keeps pace with all true progress; she grapples with the problems and evils of modern society; and she sends the gospel to the ends of the earth.

The Episcopal Church of England, the most churchly of the Reformed family, is a glorious Church: for she gave to the English-speaking world the best version of the Holy Scriptures and the best Prayer-Book; she preserved the order and dignity of the ministry and public worship; she nursed the knowledge and love of antiquity, and enriched the treasury of Christian literature; and by the Anglo-Catholic revival under the moral, intellectual, and poetic leadership of three shining lights of Oxford, Pusey, Newman, and Keble—she infused new life into her institutions and customs, and prepared the way for a better understanding between Anglicanism and Romanism.

The Presbyterian Church of Scotland, the most flourishing daughter of Geneva—as John Knox, "who never feared the face of man," was the most faithful disciple of Calvin[23]—is a glorious Church: for she turned a barren country into a garden, and raised a poor and semi-barbarous people to a level with the richest and most intelligent nations; she diffused the knowledge of the Bible and a love of the Kirk in the huts of the peasant as well as the palaces of the noblemen; she has always stood up for church order and discipline,

---

[22](Ed.) *Clement's First Letter* (to the Church in Corinth) 5.7.

[23](Ed.) According to Schaff, 'Here lies he who never feared the face of man' was spoken over Knox's grave and "has since been accepted as the best motto of his life" (*Creeds,* 6th ed. [1931] 1:677).

for the rights of the laity, and first and last for the crown-rights of King Jesus, which are above all earthly crowns, even that of the proudest monarch in whose dominion the sun never sets.

The Congregational Church is a glorious Church: for she has taught the principle, and proved the capacity, of congregational independence and self-government based upon a living faith in Christ, without diminishing the effect of voluntary cooperation in the Master's service; and has laid the foundation of New England, with its literary and theological institutions and high social culture.

The Baptist Church is a glorious Church; for she bore, and still bears, testimony to the primitive mode of baptism, to the purity of the congregation, to the separation of Church and State, and the liberty of conscience; and has given to the world the *Pilgrim's Progress* of Bunyan, such preachers as Robert Hall and Charles H. Spurgeon, and such missionaries as Carey and Judson.

The Methodist Church, the Church of John Wesley, Charles Wesley, and George Whitfield— three of the best and most apostolic Englishmen, abounding in useful labors, the first as a ruler and organizer, the second as a hymnist, the third as an evangelist—is a glorious Church: for she produced the greatest religious revival since the day of Pentecost; she preaches a free and full salvation to all; she is never afraid to fight the devil, and she is hopefully and cheerfully marching on, in both hemispheres, as an army of conquest.

The Society of Friends, though one of the smallest tribes in Israel, is a glorious Society: for it has borne witness to the inner light which "lighteth every man that cometh into the world" [John 1:9]; it has proved the superiority of the Spirit over all forms; it has done noble service in promoting tolerance and liberty, in prison reform, the emancipation of slaves, and other works of Christian philanthropy.

The Brotherhood of the Moravians, founded by Count Zinzendorf—a true nobleman of nature and of grace—is a glorious Brotherhood: for it is the pioneer of heathen missions, and of Christian union among Protestant Churches; it was like an oasis in the desert of German rationalism at home, while its missionaries went forth to the lowest savages in distant lands to bring them to Christ. I beheld with wonder and admiration a venerable Moravian couple devoting their lives to the care of hopeless lepers in the vicinity of Jerusalem.

Nor should we forget the services of many who are accounted heretics.

The Waldenses were witnesses of a pure and simple faith in times of superstition, and having outlived many bloody persecutions, are now missionaries among the descendents of their persecutors.

The Anabaptists and Socinians, who were so cruelly treated in the sixteenth century by Protestants and Romanists alike, were the first to raise their voice for religious liberty and the voluntary principle in religion.

Unitarianism is a serious departure from the trinitarian faith of orthodox Christendom, but it did good service as a protest against tritheism, and against a stiff, narrow, and uncharitable orthodoxy. It brought into prominence the human perfection of Christ's character, and illustrated the effect of his example in the noble lives and devotional writings of such men as Channing and Martineau. It has also given us some of our purest and sweetest poets, as Emerson, Bryant, Longfellow, and Lowell, whom all good men must honor and love for their lofty moral tone.

Universalism may be condemned as a doctrine; but it has a right to protest against a gross materialistic theory of hell with all its Dantesque horrors, and against the once widely spread popular belief that the overwhelming majority of the human race, including countless millions of innocent infants, will forever perish. Nor should we forget that some of the greatest divines, from Origen and Gregory of Nyssa down to Bengel and Schleiermacher, believed in, or hoped for, the ultimate return of all rational creatures to the God of love, who created them in his own image and for his own glory.

And, coming down to the latest organization of Christian work, which does not claim to be a Church, but which is a help to all Churches,—the Salvation Army: we hail it, in spite of its strange and abnormal methods, as the most effective revival agency since the days of Wesley and Whitefield; for it descends to the lowest depths of degredation and misery, and brings the light and comfort of the gospel to the slums of our large cities. Let us thank God for the noble men and women who, under the inspiration of the love of Christ, and unmindful of hardship, ridicule, and persecution, sacrifice their lives to the rescue of the hopeless outcasts of society. Truly, these good Samaritans are an honor to the name of Christ and a benediction to a lost world.

There is room for all these and many other Churches and societies in the kingdom of God, whose height and depth and length and breadth, variety and beauty, surpass human comprehension.

O the depth of the riches both of the wisdom and the knowledge of God! how unsearchable are his judgments, and his ways past tracing out! For who hath known the mind of the Lord? or who hath been his counselor? or who hath first given to him, and it shall be recompensed unto him again? For of him, and through him, and unto him, are all things. To him be the glory forever. Amen. [Rom. 11:33-36]

EPILOGUE
BERLIN 1842–NEW YORK 1892

EDITORIAL INTRODUCTION

In 1892, at the age of seventy-three and less than a year before his death, Philip Schaff had the privilege of being able to look back at half a century of teaching and scholarship. On that occasion he received a number of official congratulatory letters, which, together with his replies, were privately published (the German letters also in an English translation) in a slim volume entitled *Berlin 1842–New York 1892. The Semi-Centennial of Philip Schaff*. One of these letters came from the Theological Faculty of the University of Berlin. Fifty years earlier it had granted Schaff the *venia legendi* (the right to lecture in his chosen specialty); in 1854 it had bestowed upon him an honorary doctor of divinity degree. Though this letter was signed by the New Testament scholar Bernhard Weiss, who was then the Dean, its author was the church historian Adolf Harnack.[1] Three years earlier Harnack had delivered an address commemorating the centennial of the birth of his great predecessor (and Schaff's teacher) August Neander, who stands at the begining of that impressive mountain range of nineteenth-century Protestant church historiography just as Harnack, far removed in theological outlook and scholarly aims, stands at its end. At that time Harnack had made Schaff the recipient of one of his famous

---

[1] Postcard of Harnack to Schaff, dated 17 February 1893 (Union Theological Seminary Collection, New York): "I am glad that our letter to you pleased you. It was written by me."

postcards, thanking him for his recent election as an honorary member of the American Society of Church History and expressing his hope that the Society would always prosper and flourish. Then he mentioned that he had mailed a copy of his Neander address to Schaff, asking him to "judge [it] leniently: it was not an easy task for me."[2] In the congratulatory letter of 1892, however, Harnack obviously found it an easy task to pay tribute to the life of Neander's greatest follower, for with graceful ease and sincere appreciation he honored Schaff by highlighting with brief comments his most important publications and activities. Schaff could not have asked for a finer tribute to his long career as the historian and ambassador of the universal church. In a spirit of genuine humility and piety, he himself offered a summary of his life in far simpler terms in his reply to the congratulatory letter sent him by the students of Union Theological Seminary: "The greatest art is the art of living, and this consists in making temporal life on earth a forecourt of life eternal in heaven."[3] This was the voice of the Württemberg pietism of his youth, this was spirit of Neander's spirit. Over a long and fruitful life Philip Schaff had, in fact, learned to perfect the art of the living of the life of a Christian and a scholar, or better still, of a Christian scholar, for to be a Christian scholar had been his lifelong aspiration. Fittingly, Harnack's letter and Schaff's reply conclude our selection of Schaff's writings.

---

[2]Postcard, dated 21 June 1889 (Union Theological Seminary Collection, New York). For Harnack's address "August Neander," see *Reden und Aufsätze,* vol. 1, 2nd ed. (Gieszen, 1906) 193-218.

[3]*Berlin 1842–New York 1892. The Semi-Centennial of Philip Schaff,* 42.

CONGRATULATORY ADDRESS
FROM THE THEOLOGICAL FACULTY
OF THE UNIVERSITY OF BERLIN*

Berlin, November 16, 1892

Most Worthy Sir, Most Honored Colleague:

On this, the anniversary of the day when fifty years ago you won in our High School the *venia legendi,* the Theological Faculty of the Frederick-William-University would present to you, most honored colleague, their heartiest good wishes and prayers.

You entered upon your work as Academical Instructor in our High School at the time when the study of Church History, under the lead of Neander and Baur, had taken on a marked impetus. Erbkam, Piper, Kahnis, and Jacobi were among your immediate predecessors; Reuter followed two months later; these, with yourself, all grateful pupils of Neander and filled with the noble spirit that animated him, were one in your determination to seek the welfare of the Church by mastering with loving zeal the distinctive features of Christian life and thought in order faithfully to impart the results to others.[1]

Of this circle of six teachers of Church History who taught together for one year in our Faculty and then passed into other High

---

Berlin 1842–New York 1892. The Semi-Centennial of Philip Schaff (privately printed, 1893) 9-13.

[1](Ed.) Neander succeeded only during the last decade of his life in gathering a group of gifted followers around him. Those under his influence who took their second academic degree (*Habilitation*) and began their teaching career as *Privatdozent* at Berlin were Wilhelm Heinrich Erbkam (1810–84) in 1838, Karl Wilhelm Ferdinand Piper (1811–89) in 1840, Justus Ludwig Jacobi (1815–88) in 1841, Karl Friedrich August Kahnis (1814–88) in 1842, the same year as Schaff, and Hermann Ferdinand Reuter (1817–89) in 1843. All distinguished themselves later as university teachers, scholars and churchmen.

Schools, you alone are left remaining, now that our dear colleague Piper also has been called away from his fruitful field of labor.

You remained with us but a few semesters. In 1844 you left Berlin to find a new home in North America, where at first in the German Theological Seminary at Mercersburg, then afterward in Union Theological Seminary, New York, you found scope for your activity.

What you have accomplished in these forty-eight years for the Evangelical Churches of that great country, and the position you have achieved for yourself, is an imperishable part of your life story.

Like Martin Bucer, who three hundred years before you had crossed over to England to carry thither the light of German theological science, you went over to the New World to sow there the seeds of the same culture, and thus became, through your tireless and richly blessed work the Theological Mediator between the East and the West. If to-day the famous theological seminaries in the United States have become nurseries of theological science, so that the old world no longer gives to them alone, but receives from them instruction in turn, this is owing chiefly to your activity.

You have introduced into your new Fatherland in English translations an array of valuable and weighty works of German theology, thus naturalizing there that science and causing it to be appreciated.

This, however, forms but a small part of your great and fruitful work. You have advanced the science of Theology by works both in German and English, particularly by your great works, the "History of the Apostolic Church," the "History of the Christian Church," and the *Bibliotheca Symbolica Ecclesiae Universalis* ["The Creeds of Christendom"], together with numerous treatises on subjects pertaining to Church History, which are the fruits of your own independent studies. Your "Church History" in particular has taken a most honorable rank among the Church Histories of the day, by virtue of the thoroughness of its execution and the clearness of its style. It is the most notable monument of universal historical learning produced by the School of Neander.

In addition to this, and thereby resembling the great Mediator between the Greek and the Latin Church in the past, you have shown the most lively interest in both the original text of the New Testament and its translation into English. Your "Companion to the Greek

Testament and the English Version" has become a very useful hand-book. And as President of the American Bible Revision Committee in co-operation with the English Committee, you have played a most prominent part in bringing that great work to a happy conclusion.

But, unlike Jerome, your aim was not to introduce into one country the theological conflicts of another, nor to draw party lines of doctrine as strictly as possible, but, on the contrary, you have ever made it your task to promote reconciliation, to draw together the various parties in the Church, and everywhere to bring about "the speaking of the truth in love" [Eph. 4:15].

If the signs of the times do not deceive us, your work in this re-gard also has been crowned with special blessing. The various Evan-gelical denominations of your new home are indeed drawing nearer to one another, and their ecclesiastical and scholarly emulation no longer minister to strife, but to mutual recognition and co-opera-tion.

Lastly, we may not forget what your efforts on behalf of the Ger-man Evangelical congregations in America have accomplished in the production of a Hymn Book, and of a Liturgy, not to mention a number of other works having an immediate bearing on Church life.

The fruitfulness of your academical activity is borne eloquent witness to by many pupils, some of whom are already themselves professors. In this connection we can ourselves, and with ever-in-creasing emphasis, bring testimony; for every year adds to the num-ber of pupils who come from you across the ocean to continue with us their studies. We desire here to give expression to the special plea-sure with which we welcome American students to our University life; for they are distinguished above all others by the depths of their interest and the ardor of their diligence.

The Lord Almighty has vouchsafed to you, most honored col-league, to pass the threshold of your seventieth year with activity and strength undiminished. Within the past few years you have begun two great undertakings, the founding of an American Society of Church History, whose President you have become and in the fore-front of whose work you stand, and the editing an English transla-tion of a Nicene and Post-Nicene Library of the Fathers.

That your health and strength may long abide unimpaired in order that you may bring to a successful issue all you have undertaken, is our most heartfelt wish.

In communicating to you to-day these, our good wishes, we would at the same time express our gratitude that you have not only never forgotten the old ties that bind you to our Faculty, but that you have ever cherished them most lovingly.

Be assured that we, on our part, bear you in most affectionate rememberance, and ever rejoice most thankfully in all that God the Lord has bestowed upon you.

With feelings of the highest regard and honor for your worthiness,

The Faculty of the Royal Frederick-William-University,

B. Weiss, Dean

To the Most Worthy,
    The Professor of Church History,
    Dr. Philip Schaff,
    New York.

Dr. Schaff's Reply[*]

New York, December 24, 1892

Most worthy Sirs; Highly-esteemed Colleagues:

Your semi-centennial *Epistola congratulatoria* of November 16th reached me on the 12th of December,—the very day when, fifty years ago, I began my regular course of academic lectures in Berlin.

I could not wish a nobler and more honorable testimonial to my humble labors. The Theological Faculty of Berlin, from the days of Schleiermacher and Neander, has directed the progressive movements of Protestant Theology, and will continue to exercise a controlling influence from the metropolis of Germany upon the rising generation of divines in the old and the new world.

Your letter carries me back to the happy spring-time of my life, when with a number of like-minded friends and future historians I sat at the feet of Neander, Twesten, Marheineke, Hengstenberg, Ritter, and Ranke, who were then at the height of their influence.[2] I received the first theological impulse at Tübingen from my revered teachers, Schmid, Baur, and Dorner. Dr. Baur made a profound impression upon me by his philosophical and critical grasp of the intellectual processes of Apostolic and post-Apostolic Christianity, and first gave me a clear conception of a progressive development in history; but the negative results of his researches of the Gospels and the

---

[*]*Berlin 1842–New York. The Semi-Centennial of Philip Schaff,* 16-17.

[2](Ed.) Schaff had little contact with Marheineke, though it was Marheineke who gave a farewell party for Schaff shortly before his departure for America. August Detlev Christian Twesten (1789–1876), Schleiermacher's successor in 1835, held to a conciliatory, mediating position between Marheineke's Hegelianism and Hengstenberg's strict Lutheran orthodoxy, which attracted Schaff; he presided at both of Schaff's doctoral examinations. Karl Ritter (1779–1859) was the distinguished professor of geography at Berlin since 1820. Schaff visited Leopold von Ranke one more time shortly before his death and included a sketch of him in *August Neander, Erinnerungen* (1886).

Pauline Epistles repelled me. Dr. Neander—that Christian Israelite without guile, who was led by Moses and Plato to Jesus the Messiah—attracted me still more by his original personality, his childlike simplicity, his evangelical catholicity, and his deep spiritual insight into the religious and moral forces of history. He wrote in my album the Pauline motto: *Theologia crucis, non gloriae.*[3]

My removal to the United States gave me a new home without alienating my affections from Europe. But the new situation and surroundings modified my views and directed my course. German learning and thought cannot be effectively transplanted to American soil unless they are freely reproduced in the English language and practically adapted to the wants of a free Church in a free State. If I have in any measure succeeded in the mission of an international and interdenominational mediator, which in common with American friends you kindly assign to me, it is due not to personal merit, but to the peculiar circumstances and relations into which Providence has placed me.

The high testimony which you bear to the Alumni of the Union Seminary and other American students in Berlin, confirms what I have heard more than once from your lips, and is especially gratifying to me and my colleagues. Ever since the establishment of two "Prize Fellowships," in 1877 (which I suggested after the example of the *Repetentenstiftung* in Tübingen), the Union Seminary has sent annually one or two of our best graduates, for two years, to German Universities, and particularly to Berlin, to finish their studies. It will be gratifying to you to learn that soon after their return they were called to positions of influence in various literary and theological institutions of the country, and I take the liberty of adding a list of them.[4] Their success is the best evidence of the appreciation of German learning in America.

---

[3](Ed.) "Theology of the cross, not of glory." Cf. especially Gal. 6:14 and 1 Cor. 1:17-18.

[4](Ed.) The *Repetententstiftung* provided for tutorial fellowships at the Protestant divinity school of the University of Tübingen. The most famous *Repetent*, no doubt, was David Friedrich Strauss (1833–35). Included in Schaff's list of 16 names were

We shall continue to send you our most promising Alumni, that in this way a living contract [*sic*] between Europe and America may be kept up for their mutual benefit, in the common pursuit of Christian truth and Christian life.

Wishing you all many happy New-Years of health and usefulness,

I remain,

Thankfully, your friend and brother in Christ,

[Philip Schaff]

To the Very Reverend Theological Faculty
of the University of Berlin

---

those of Francis Brown, then his colleague at Union Theological Seminary as professor of Hebrew and the Cognate Languages; Arthur C. McGiffert, who succeeded Schaff in 1893; and William Adams Brown, who joined the Union faculty in 1892 as instructor in church history (with Schaff paying his salary of $1,500 out of his own pocket) and was appointed Roosevelt professor of Systematic Theology in 1898.

A CHRONOLOGY
OF SCHAFF'S LIFE AND PUBLISHED WRITINGS

Note: References to foreign language translations (other than German and English) are taken from the extensive bibliography in David S. Schaff, *The Life of Philip Schaff: in Part Autobiographical* (New York, 1897) 511-18.

1 Jan 1819   Born in Chur, Switzerland

1834/1835   Boys' Academy at Kornthal, Württemberg

1835–1837   Gymnasium, Stuttgart

1837–1839   University of Tübingen

1838   Preached his first sermon, on John 3:16—his life-long, favorite text—at Gomaringen near Stuttgart

1839/1840   University of Halle (winter semester only)

1840–1841   University of Berlin

Spring 1841   Licentiate in theology, University of Berlin

Die Sünde wider den heiligen Geist, und die daraus gezogenen dogmatischen und ethischen Folgerungen. Eine exegetisch-dogmatische Abhandlung, nebst einem historischen Anhang über das Lebensende des Francesco Spiera. Halle. 210 pp.

1841–1842   Italian journey (14 months)

1842   *Habilitationsschrift: venia legendi* granted by the University of Berlin

Das Verhältnis des Jakobus, Bruder des Herrn, zu Jakobus Alphäi, auf's neue exegetisch und historisch untersucht. Berlin. 99 pp.

<u>1842–1844</u> Lecturer (*Privatdozent*), University of Berlin (three se-
mesters)

<u>April 1844</u> Ordination at Elberfeld, Westphalia

<u>May/June</u> Visit to England

<u>July 28</u> Aboard ship, first sight of the United States

<u>October 25</u> Inaugural lecture at Reading, Pa.: "The Principle of
Protestantism"

<u>1844–1863</u> Professor of Church History and Biblical Literature,
Mercersburg Seminary of the German Reformed church,
Mercersburg, Pa.

<u>1845</u> Heresy trial and acquittal

Marriage to Mary Elizabeth Schley (of eight children, five
died in their youth)

D. D., Marshall College

Das Princip des Protestantismus. Chambersburg, Pa.,
xiv + 180 pp. Translated, with an introduction, by John
W. Nevin, *The Principle of Protestantism, as related to the
present state of the Church.* Chambersburg PA, 1845. 215
pp.

<u>1846</u> Death of first child, Anna, aged six days

Threatened with a second heresy trial

*What Is Church History? A vindication of the Idea of His-
torical Development.* Translated by John W. Nevin. Philadelphia. 128 pp.

*Der Anglogermanismus. Eine Rede gehalten den 10ten März,
1846, vor der Schillergesellschaft des Marshall-Collegiums zu
Mercersburg, Pa.* Chambersburg PA. 22 pp. Translated
by J. S. Ermentrout, *Anglogermanism, or the significance of
the German nationality in the United States.* Chambersburg
PA, 1846. 24 pp.

*Dante's Divina Commedia. An Address delivered before the
Goethean Literary Society of Marshall College, August 28,
1846.* Translated by Jeremiah H. Good. Chambersburg
PA. 47 pp.

<u>1848–1853</u> Editor, *Der Deutsche Kirchenfreund. Organ für die gemein-
samen Interessen der amerikanisch-deutschen Kirchen.* Vols.
1-6. Mercersburg PA. Schaff contributed the majority

of articles, some of which were also published, in translation, in *The Mercersburg Review*. Schaff's friend, William (Wilhelm) Julius Mann, continued as editor for another six years, 1854–1860.

1851 *Geschichte der christlichen Kirche, von ihrer Gründung bis auf die Gegenwart.* Vol. 1 (*Die allgemeine Einleitung und die erste Periode, vom Pfingstfest bis zum Tode des heil. Johannes {a. 30–100}, oder die apostolische Kirche*). Mercersburg PA. xvi + 576 pp. Second edition, revised and enlarged, *Geschichte der apostolischen Kirche, nebst einer allgemeinen Einleitung in die Kirchengeschichte*. Leipzig, 1854. xvi + 680 pp. Second German edition translated by Edward D. Yeomans, *History of the Apostolic Church, with a General Introduction to Church History*. New York, 1853. 684 pp. Translated also into Dutch.

1852 *Systematic Benevolence*. Mercersburg PA. 32 pp. Enlarged version of the first sermon Schaff preached in English.

1852–1857 Chairman of the Liturgical Committee of the German Reformed church

1853 Death by accident of son Philip William, aged 2 years

Late 1853–1854 First European Journey: Scotland, England, France, Germany, Austria, Switzerland (lectures on America in Germany)

1854 D.D., University of Berlin

Amerika. Die politischen, socialen und kirchlich-religiösen Zustände der Vereinigten Staaten von Nord-Amerika mit besonderer Rücksicht auf die Deutschen, aus eigener Anschauung dargestellt. Berlin. xxi + 278 pp. Second and enlarged edition, Berlin 1858. xxiv + 366 pp. Translated by Edward D. Yeomans, *America. A sketch of the political, social, and religious character of the United States of America, in Two Lectures, Delivered at Berlin, with a Report read before the German Church Diet at Frankfort-on-the-Main, Sept., 1854.* New York 1855. xxiv + 291 pp. Translated also into Dutch.

Der heilige Augustinus. Sein Leben und Wirken für Freunde des Reiches Gottes dargestellt. Berlin. vi + 129 pp. Translated by Thomas C. Porter, *The Life and Labour of St. Augustine, A Historical Sketch*. London and New York, 1854. viii + 98 pp.

<u>1856</u> *American Nationality. An Address before the Irving Society of the College of St. James, Maryland.* Chambersburg PA. 24 pp.

<u>1857</u> Evangelical Alliance Conference in Berlin—the first Evangelical Alliance Conference to which Schaff contributed a paper

Germany: Its Universities, Theology, and Religion. With sketches of Neander, Tholuck, Olshausen, Hengstenberg, Twesten, Müller, Ullmann, Rothe, Dorner, Lange, Ebrard, Wichern, and other distinguished German divines of the age. Philadelphia. 418 pp.

Editor, *A Liturgy: or Order of Christian Worship. Prepared and published by the direction and for the use of The German Reformed Church in the United States of America.* Philadelphia. 408 pp.

<u>1857–1861</u> Coeditor, *The Mercersburg Review.* Vols. 9-13. Chambersburg PA.

<u>1858</u> *History of the Christian Church.* Vol. 1 (*From the Birth of Christ to the Reign of Constantine, A.D. 1-311*), translated by Edward D. Yeomans. New York. xiii + 535 pp.

<u>1859</u> Editor, *Deutsches Gesangbuch. Eine Auswahl geistlicher Lieder aus allen Zeiten der christlichen Kirche. Nach den besten hymnologischen Quellen bearbeitet und mit erläuternden Bemerkungen über Verfasser, Inhalt und Geschichte der Lieder versehen.* Philadelphia. xiv + 663 pp. Enlarged edition, 1874.

<u>1861</u> *The Moral Character of Christ, or The Perfection of Christ's Humanity, A Proof of His Divinity. A Theological Tract for the People.* Chambersburg PA. 53 pp.

Entwurf eines Katechismus mit Bibelsprüchen für Sonntags-Schulen. Chambersburg PA. 80 pp. Revised and enlarged as *Christlicher Katechismus mit Bibelsprüchen für Schule und Haus,* Philadelphia 1863. 192 pp. Another enlarged edition by Georg Pfleiderer, *Philip Schaff's christliche Glaubens-und Sittenlehre.* Stuttgart 1874. 279 pp. Also English, *A Christian Catechism for Sunday-Schools and Families.* Philadelphia 1862. 167 pp. Various authorized and unauthorized editions, both German and English. Translated into Nestorian, Arabic, Chinese, Bulgarian, and other languages.

Slavery and the Bible. A Tract for the Times. Chambersburg PA. 32 pp.

1862/1863 Teaching at Andover Seminary (because of war unrest at Mercersburg)

Fall 1863 Requested two years leave of absence from Mercersburg Seminary

Moved to New York City where, since 1878, he resided at 15 East 43rd Street; his study was at Bible House of the American Bible Society at the corner of Ninth Street and Fourth Avenue

Der Heidelberger Katechismus. Nach der ersten Ausgabe von 1563 revidirt, und mit kritischen Anmerkungen, sowie einer Geschichte und Characteristik des Katechismus versehen. Philadelphia and Bremen. 168 pp. Second revised edition, 1866.

Editor, *Gedenkbuch der dreihundertjährigen Jubelfeier des Heidelberger Katechismus in der Deutsch-Reformirten Kirche der Vereinigten Staaten.* Chambersburg and Philadelphia. 449 pp.

The Anglo-American Sabbath. An Essay read before the National Sabbath Convention, Saratoga, August 11, 1863. New York. 68 pp. New York Sabbath Committee, Doc. 26. Translated by J. G. Zahner, *Der Anglo-Amerikanische Sonntag. . . .* New York 1863. 32 pp. New York Sabbath Committee, Doc. 27.

1863–1866 Editor, *Evangelische Zeugnisse aus den deutschen Kirchen in Amerika. Eine homiletische Monatsschrift.* Vols. 1-3. Philadelphia.

1863–1867 Editor, *Documents of the New York Sabbath Committee.* Nos. 26-34. New York.

1864 Death from illness of son Philip, aged seven years

Editor, *Gesangbuch für Deutsche Sonntagsschulen. Sammt einem Anhang ausgewählter Englischer Lieder.* Philadelphia and New York. 272 pp.

1864–1870 Corresponding Secretary of the New York Sabbath Committee

1864–1880 Editor, *A Commentary on the Holy Scriptures. Critical, Doctrinal, and Homiletical. With Special Reference to Ministers and Students. By John P. Lange D.D., in connection with a number of emiment European divines. Translated from the German, and Edited, with Additions, by Philip Schaff, D.D., in connection with American Scholars of Various Evangelical Denominations.* 25 vols. New York and Edinburgh. Schaff wrote all prefaces, translated and edited *Matthew, Luke* (first three chapters), wrote the annotations in *John* and *Romans* (chapters 1-9), and "A General Introduction to the Poetical Books" in the volume on *Job.*

1865 Second European Journey: England, Germany, Switzerland (Sabbath observance and Sunday School movement; lectures on Civil War in Germany and Switzerland)

Upon return from Europe, official resignation from Mercersburg Seminary

Die Person Jesu Christi: das Wunder der Geschichte. Sammt einer Widerlegung der falschen Theorien und einer Sammlung von Zeugnissen der Ungläubigen. Gotha. 234 pp. Also English, *The Person of Christ: The Perfection of His Humanity Viewed as a Proof of His Divinity. With a collection of impartial testimonies.* Boston 1865. 375 pp. Various later editions, German and English, also revised and enlarged, sometimes with changes in the title. Translated into Dutch, French, Italian, Greek, Russian, Bulgarian, Japanese, and other languages.

Der Bürgerkrieg und das christliche Leben in Nord America. Vorträge gehalten in Berlin und mehreren Städten Deutschlands und der Schweiz. Berlin. 72 pp. Translated by C. C. Starbuck, "Dr. Schaff's Lectures on America Delivered in Europe, 1865," *The Christian Intelligencer* 37/9-20 (1866) (March 1–May 17).

1867 Organisation of the American Branch of the Evangelical Alliance

Geschichte der alten Kirche von der Geburt Christi bis zum Ende des 6ten Jahrhunderts. Leipzig. xvi + 1250 pp. Second edition in three vols., 1869. Translated by Edward D. Yeomans, *History of the Christian Church*, vols. 2 and 3 (*From Constantine the Great to Gregory the Great, A.D. 311–600*). New York 1867–1868. 1083 pp.

<u>1867–1893</u> Associated with the American Branch of the Evangelical Alliance, as:

> 1867–1871—Member of the Executive Committee
> 1870–1873—Corresponding Secretary (with S. Irenaeus Prime and others)
> 1874–1875—One of many Vice-Presidents
> 1876–1884—Corresponding Secretary (with S. Irenaeus Prime)
> 1885–1893—After incorporation of the Evangelical Alliance in 1885, member of the Board of Managers and Honorary Corresponding Secretary

<u>1868–1871</u> Visiting lecturer in church history at Hartford Seminary

<u>1868</u> Editor, *Christ in Song. Hymns of Immanuel.* New York. xx + 701 pp.

<u>1869</u> Third European Journey: England, Scotland, France, Holland, Germany, Switzerland (preparation of New York Conference of the Evangelical Alliance)

<u>1869–1884</u> Editor, *Documents of the Evangelical Alliance,* nos. 3-15. New York.

<u>1870–1893</u> Professor at Union Theological Seminary, New York City—held chairs of Theological Encyclopedia and Christian Symbolics, 1870; Hebrew, 1873; Biblical Literature, 1874; Church History, 1887

<u>1870</u> Joined New York Presbytery of the Presbyterian church in the U.S.A.

Death by accident of son John, aged nine years

The Report of the Rev. Dr. Philip Schaff, of his Mission to Europe in Behalf of the Alliance. Evangelical Alliance Doc. 3:20-33.

<u>1871</u> Fourth European Journey: Germany, Switzerland, France, England (for the American Branch of the Evangelical Alliance presentation of memorial to the Csar of Russia on behalf of the Protestants in the Baltic Provinces; Bible Revision)

<u>October 18</u> Inaugural Lecture at Union Theological Seminary: "The Theology for Our Age and Country"

December First meeting of the American Committee on Bible Revision

*Report of the Deputation of the American Branch of the Evan-
gelical Alliance, Appointed to Memorialize the Emperor of
Russia in Behalf of Religious Liberty submitted by Samuel F.
B. Morse President and Philip Schaff Secretary.* Evangelical
Alliance Doc. 6. 32 pp.

Die Christusfrage. Berlin. 39 pp. English translation,
"Christ His Own Best Witness," in *Christ and Christianity* (1885) 23-44.

1871–1874 Coeditor, with Henry B. Smith, *Theological and Philosophical Library: A Series of Text-Books, Original and
Translated, for Colleges and Theological Seminaries.* New
York. Only works published: Überweg's *History of Philosophy* and van Oosterzee's *Christian Dogmatics and Practical Theology.*

1872 Fifth European Journey: Scotland, Ireland, England,
France, Holland (preparation of New York Conference
of the Evangelical Alliance; Bible Revision)

October Official Organisation of the American Committee on
Bible Revision

*The Theology for Our Age and Country. Address delivered Oc-
tober 18, 1871, in the Fourth Avenue Presbyterian Church,
at the inauguration of Philip Schaff., D.D., Professor . . .
in the Union Theological Seminary, New York.* New York.
27 pp.

1872–1884 President of the American Committee on Bible Revision—the New Testament Company, of which Schaff was
a member, completed its work in 1880, the Old Testament Company in 1884

1873 Sixth European Journey: England, France, Germany,
Austria, Switzerland, France (preparation of New York
Conference of the Evangelical Alliance; Bible Revision)

2-12 October New York Conference of the Evangelical Alliance—the
first Evangelical Alliance Conference which Schaff attended

"Introduction" to J. B. Lightfoot, R. C. Trench, and
C. J. Ellicott, *The Revision of the English Version of the New
Testament.* New York. Separately published, *The Revi-
sion of the English Version of Holy Scriptures, by Cooperative*

Committees of British and American Scholars of different denominations. New York 1875. xlix pp.

1874 Coeditor, with S. Irenaeus Prime, *Evangelical Alliance Conference, 1873. History, Essays, Orations, and other Documents of the Sixth General Conference of the Evangelical Alliance, Held in New York, 2-12 October 1873.* New York. 773 pp.

Coeditor, with Roswell D. Hitchcock and Zachary Eddy, *Hymns and Songs of Praise for Public and Social Worship.* New York. 597 pp.

1875 Seventh European Journey: Scotland, England, Germany (Bible Revision; Alliance of Reformed Churches; Second Old Catholic Conference at Bonn)

History of the Vatican Council, Together with the Latin and English Text of the Papal Syllabus and the Vatican Decrees, in W. E. Gladstone, *The Vatican Decrees in Their Bearing on Civil Allegiance.* New York. 168 pp.

1876 Death from illness of daughter Meta, aged twenty years

L.L.D., Amherst College

In Memoriam. Our Children in Heaven. Privately printed.

1876–1877 Eighth European Journey: England, France, Switzerland, Italy, Egypt and Palestine, Constantinople, Greece, Switzerland, Germany, Scotland (Visit to the Holy Land; Bible Revision; Evangelical Alliance; First Council of the Alliance of Reformed Churches at Edinburgh)

1877 *Bibliotheca symbolica ecclesiae universalis. The Creeds of Christendom.* New York and London. vol. 1 (*The History of Creeds*) xvii + 941 pp.; vol. 2 (*The Greek and Latin Creeds. With Translations*) vii + 607 pp.; vol. 3 (*The Evangelical Protestant Creeds. With Translations*) vii + 914 pp.

The Harmony of the Reformed Confessions, as related to the Present State of Evangelical Theology. An essay delivered before the General Presbyterian Council at Edinburgh, July 4, 1877—Together with the action of the Council on confessions and formulas of subscription. New York and Edinburgh. 70 pp.; also in *Christ and Christianity* (1885) 153-83.

Summer 1878 Journey to the Midwest and Pacific Coast (on behalf of Bible Revision)

Through Bible Lands. Notes of Travel in Egypt, the Desert, and Palestine. New York and London. 434 pp.

1879 Ninth European Journey: England, Scotland, Germany, Bohemia, Switzerland (Bible Revision; Committee on Consensus of Reformed Confessions; Evangelical Alliance Conference at Basel)

Editor, *Anglo-American Bible Revision. By Members of the American Revision Committee.* Philadelphia and London. iv + 192 pp.

Christianity in the United States of America. A Report, Prepared for the Seventh General Conference of the Evangelical Alliance, held in Basle, Switzerland, September 1879. Evangelical Alliance Doc. 14. 67 pp.

1879–1882 Editor, *The International Illustrated Commentary on the New Testament.* 4 vols. New York and Edinburgh. Based on the Text of the Authorized Version. Schaff prepared, together with M. B. Riddle, the introduction, the commentaries on Matthew, Mark, Luke, and Romans, and alone Galatians. Also published separately, *The Epistle of Paul to the Galatians.* New York 1881. 66 pp. The whole series also was published under the title *A Popular Commentary on the New Testament. By English and American scholars of various evangelical denominations.* Revised edition, 1882–1884 (see below).

1880 A founding member of the Society of Biblical Literature and Exegesis which held its preliminary meeting in Schaff's study at 42 Bible House

A Dictionary of the Bible. Including Biography, Natural History, Geography, Topography, Archaeology, and Literature. Philadelphia. 960 pp. Fifth edition revised, 1890. Translated into Italian, Arabic, Marathi, and other languages.

Coeditor, with Arthur Gilman, *A Library of Religious Poetry.* New York. xxxi + 1004 pp.

1881 "Introduction" (89 pp.), to B. F. Westcott and F. J. A. Hort, *The New Testament in the Original Greek.* New York. Fifth edition revised, 1893.

"The Anglo-American Revision," in Alexander Roberts, *A Companion to the Revised Version of the English New Testament, with Supplement by a Member of the American Committee of Revision.* London and New York. Pp. 154-206.

1882–1892 *History of the Christian Church.* The final edition.

1882 *History of the Christian Church,* vol. 1 (*Apostolic Christianity*). New York. xvii + 871 pp. Revised edition, 1890. A thoroughly revised edition, in two volumes, of *History of the Christian Church,* vol. 1 (1858).

1882–1884 Coeditor, with Samuel M. Jackson and David S. Schaff. *A Religious Encyclopedia: or, Dictionary of Biblical, Historical, Doctrinal, and Practical Theology, Based on the Real-Encyklopädie of Herzog, Plitt, and Hauck.* 3 vols. New York. Revised 1887. Third edition, revised and enlarged, in 4 vols., 1891. This edition, in vol. 4, includes *Encyclopedia of Living Divines and Christian Workers of all Denominations in Europe and America,* edited by Schaff, with Samuel M. Jackson, New York, 1887.

The New Schaff-Herzog Encyclopedia of Religious Knowledge. 12 vols., appeared 1908–1914, with Samuel M. Jackson as editor-in-chief. This final edition is based on the third edition of the *Real-Encyklopädie.*

Editor, The International Revision Commentary on the New Testament, Based on the Revised Version of 1881. By English and American Scholars and Members of the Revision Committee. 6 vols. (only through Acts). New York. This was a revised edition of *The International Illustrated Commentary on the New Testament* (1879–1882). Schaff prepared vol. 1, *A Commentary on the Gospel according to Matthew.* 416 pp.

1883 *History of the Christian Church,* vol. 2 (*Ante-Nicene Christianity, A.D. 100-325*). New York. xiv + 877 pp. Revised editions, 1885 and 1889. Second volume of thoroughly revised edition of *History of the Christian Church,* vol. 1 (1858).

A Companion to the Greek Testament and the English Version. With facsimile illustrations of MSS. and of standard editions of the New Testament. New York. xvii + 616 pp. Revised editions, 1885, 1888, 1892.

<u>1884</u> Tenth European Journey: England, Scotland, Ireland,
Norway, Sweden, Russia, Germany (Bible Revision;
Third Council of Alliance of Reformed Churches at Bel-
fast; Evangelical Alliance Conference at Copenhagen)

Union Theological Seminary moved to new quarters at
700 Park Avenue and 69th Street (from 9 University
Place between Waverly Place and Eighth Street)

History of the Christian Church, vol. 3 (*Nicene and Post-Nicene Christianity: From Constantine the Great to Gregory the
Great, A.D. 311–600*). New York. xv + 1049 pp. Revised edition, 1889. A reprint, with the addition of recent literature, of *History of the Christian Church*, vols. 2
and 3 (1867–1868).

*The Discord and Concord of Christendom, Or, Denomina-
tional Variety and Christian Unity*, in *The Discord and
Concord of Christendom. Report on the Copenhagen Conference
of the Evangelical Alliance and the Scandinavian Meeting in
New York, with Addresses.* Evangelical Alliance Doc.
18:21-39. Also in *Christ and Christianity* (1885) 293-
310. Translated also into German and Danish.

<u>1885</u> Eleventh European Journey: England, Scotland, France,
Germany (visiting the theological faculties of German
and Swiss universities)

*Christ and Christianity. Studies in Christology, Creeds and
Confessions, Protestantism and Romanism, Reformation Prin-
ciples, Slavery and the Bible, Sunday Observance, Religious
Freedom, and Christian Union.* New York. 310 pp.

*The Teaching of the Twelve Apostles, or The Oldest Church
Manual. The Didache and kindred Documents in the Original, with translations and discussions of postapostolic teaching, baptism, worship, and discipline, and illustrations and
facsimiles of the Jerusalem MS.* New York and Edinburgh.
301 pp. Third edition, revised and enlarged, 1889.

Editor, *Documentary History of the American Committee on
Revision, prepared by order of the Committee for the Use of the
Members.* New York. 186 pp. Private and confidential
(only 100 copies printed). An abridged version, by Timothy Dwight, *Historical Account of the American Committee
of Revision of the Authorized English Version of the Bible, pre-*

pared from the documents and correspondence of the Committee. New York, 1885. 74 pp.

1885–1887 "Sketches of German universities and their theological faculties," in *New York Independent,* 1885 (pp. 1094, 1159, 1222), 1886 (pp. 1040, 1100, 1136, 1198, 1261), and 1887 (p. 488).

1886 Twelfth European Journey: England, Scotland, Spain, France, Germany (preparatory work for edition of Nicene and Post-Nicene Fathers; delegate to Fifth Centennial of the University of Heidelberg; visiting German universities)

History of the Christian Church, vol. 4 (*Medieval Christianity: From Gregory I to Gregory VII, A.D. 590–1073*). New York. xiii + 799 pp.

Saint Augustin, Melanchthon, Neander. New York. 168 pp. The section on Neander also in German, with additions, *August Neander. Erinnerungen.* Gotha, 1886. viii + 76 pp.

1886–1892 Editor, *A Select Library of the Nicene and Post-Nicene Fathers of the Christian Church.* First Series, 14 vols., New York 1886–1890. Second Series, with Henry Wace, 14 vols., New York and Oxford 1890–1900. Of the Second Series, Schaff supervised vols. 1 and 2 and wrote the preface for vol. 3.

1887 D.D., St. Andrews University

The English Language: heterogeneous in formation, homogeneous in character, universal in destination for the spread of Christian civilization. A Lecture delivered before Vanderbilt university, January 3, 1887. Enlarged and published by request of the faculty. Nashville. 61 pp.

1888 Organization of the American Society of Church History in the study of Schaff's house, 15 East 43rd Street, New York City (March 23)

Thirteenth European Journey: Germany, Italy, England, Scotland (delegate to Eighth Centennial of the University of Bologna; Fourth Council of the Alliance of Reformed Churches in London)

History of the Christian Church, vol. 4 (*Modern Christianity: The German Reformation, A.D. 1517–1530*). New York. xv + 755 pp. Revised edition, 1892.

The Toleration Act of 1689. A Contribution to the History of Religious Liberty. London. 59 pp.

Church and State in the United States, or the American Idea of Religious Liberty and Its Practical Effects, with Official Documents. New York. 170 pp. Also in *Papers of the American Historical Association* 2 (1888): 383-543.

1888–1893 President of the American Society of Church History

1889 *The Progress of Religious Freedom as Shown in the History of Toleration Acts.* New York. 126 pp. Also in *Papers of the American Society of Church History* 1 (1889): 1-126.

The Eighth Centenary of the University of Bologna. Report delivered before the University of the City of New York at the celebration of Founder's Day, April 18, 1889. New York. 29 pp.

1890 Fourteenth European Journey: Italy, Switzerland, Germany (Vatican Library and Papal Archives; visiting German universities)

Creed Revision in the Presbyterian Churches. New York. 67 pp. Second edition enlarged, 1890.

Literature and Poetry. Studies in the English Language, the Poetry of the Bible, Dies Irae, Stabat Mater, Hymns of St. Bernard, the University—ancient and modern, Dante Alighieri and the Divina Commedia. New York. xi + 436 pp.

History of the Edict of Nantes. An Address delivered before the Huguenot Society of America, March 21, 1889. New York. 29 pp.

Dante's Theology. New York. 21 pp. Also in *Papers of the American Society of Church History* 2 (1890): 53-73.

1891 General Conference of the Evangelical Alliance at Florence—Schaff sent a paper on Renaissance and Reformation

St. Chrysostom and St. Augustin. Studies in Christian Biography. New York. 158 pp.

The Renaissance and the Reformation, in *The Evangelical Alliance in Florence . . . Proceedings and Papers.* Evangelical Alliance Doc. 30:17-31. Translated into Italian.

The Renaissance. The Revival of Learning and Art in the 14th and 15th Centuries. New York. 132 pp. Also in *Papers of the American Society of Church History* 3 (1891): 3-132.

Coeditor, *Wilmore's New Analytical Reference Bible.* New York. 2189 pp. Schaff wrote the preface and revised and edited the section "Comprehensive Bible Helps."

1892 Suffered stroke (July)

D.D., University of the City of New York

History of the Christian Church, vol. 7 (*Modern Christianity: The Swiss Reformation*). New York. xvii + 890 pp. David S. Schaff, who utilized materials left by his father in the first four chapters, wrote and published two volumes on the Middle Ages, vol. 5, part 1 and part 2 (sometimes also numbered vols. 5 and 6), 1907 and 1910.

The Friendship of Calvin and Melanchthon. New York. 21 pp. Also in *Papers of the American Society of Church History* 4 (1892): 143-63.

Spring 1893 Resigned from the faculty of Union Theological Seminary

September Attended Parliament of Religions in Chicago at the risk of his life

20 October Died at his home in New York City. Buried at Woodlawn Cemetery

Theological Propaedeutic. A General Introduction to the Study of Theology, Exegetical, Historical, Systematic, and Practical, including Encyclopaedia, Methodology, and Bibliography. A Manual for Students. New York. xii + 596 pp.

Berlin 1842—New York 1892. The Semi-Centennial of Philip Schaff. Privately printed.

The Reunion of Christendom. A Paper prepared for the Parliament of Religions and the National Conference of the Evangelical Alliance held in Chicago, September and October 1893. Evangelical Alliance Doc. 33. 70 pp.

Coeditor, The American Church History Series, 13 vols., 1893–1897. Schaff initiated this series.

SELECT BIBLIOGRAPHY

Note: David S. Schaff, *The Life of Philip Schaff, in Part Autobiographical* (New York, 1897), not only remains the best source for biographical data but also offers a nearly complete bibliography of Schaff's published writings, including references to foreign-language translations. A similar bibliography is included in *Berlin 1842— New York 1892. The Semi-Centennial of Philip Schaff* (New York, 1893). Schaff also published innumerable articles in newspapers, magazines, and journals. It can be safely stated, however, that they usually add little that is new to his books since Schaff had the ability of repeating himself endlessly in print. Manuscript materials (for example, diaries, notebooks, letters) can be found in the Burke Library of Union Theological Seminary in New York and in the Philip Schaff Library and the archives of the Evangelical and Reformed Historical Society at Lancaster Theological Seminary, Lancaster, Pennsylvania.

1. Schaff: Recent Editions and Reprints

History of the Christian Church. Eight volumes. Grand Rapids MI, 1959–1960.

Editor. *A Commentary on the Holy Scriptures: Critical, Doctrinal, and Homiletical, with Special Reference to Ministers and Students. By John Peter Lange.* Translated from the German and edited, with additions, by Philip Schaff. Twelve double volumes. Grand Rapids MI, 1960.

America. A Sketch of the Political, Social, and Religious Character of the United States of North America. Edited by Perry Miller. Cambridge MA, 1961.

The Principle of Protestantism. Edited by Bard Thompson and George H. Bricker. Volume 1 of the Lancaster Series on the Mercersburg Theology. Philadelphia, 1964.

The Mercersburg Theology. Edited by James Hastings Nichols. New York, 1966.

Church and State in the United States, or the American Idea of Religious Liberty and Its Practical Effects, with Official Documents. Religion in America, Series 2. New York, 1972.

Through Bible Lands. Notes of Travel in Egypt, the Desert, and Palestine. America and the Holy Land—Reprint Series. Seventy-two volumes. Edited by Moshe Davis. New York, 1977.

Reformed and Catholic: Selected Historical and Theological Writings of Philip Schaff. Edited by Charles Yrigoyen, Jr., and George M. Bricker. Pittsburgh, 1979.

The Principle of Protestantism and *What is Church History?* American Religious Thought in the 18th and 19th Centuries 21. Thirty-two volumes. Edited by Bruce Kuklick. New York and London, 1987.

More Important Secondary Works

A. German

Bárczay, Gyula. *Ecclesia semper reformanda. Eine Untersuchung zum Kirchenbegriff des 19. Jahrhunderts*. Zurich, 1961.

Elert, Werner. *Der Kampf um das Christentum. Geschichte der Beziehungen zwischen dem evangelischen Christentum in Deutschland und dem allgemeinen Denken seit Schleiermacher und Hegel*. Munich, 1921.

Fagerberg, Holsten. *Bekenntnis, Kirche und Amt in der deutschen konfessionellen Theologie des 19. Jahrhunderts*. Uppsala, 1952.

Hausrath, Adolf. *David Friedrich Strauss und die Theologie seiner Zeit*. Two volumes. Heidelberg, 1876–1878.

————. *Richard Rothe und seine Freunde*. Two volumes. Berlin, 1902–1906.

Hermelink, Heinrich. *Geschichte der evangelischen Kirche in Württemberg von der Reformation bis zur Gegenwart*. Stuttgart, 1949.

Hirsch, Emmanuel. *Geschichte der neuern evangelischen Theologie*. Five volumes. Second edition. Gütersloh, 1960.

Holte, Ragnar. *Die Vermittlungstheologie. Ihre theologischen Grundbegriffe kritisch untersucht*. Uppsala, 1965.

Müller, Karl. *Die religiöse Erweckung in Württemberg am Anfang des 19. Jahrhunderts*. Tübingen, 1925.

Schnabel, Franz. *Deutsche Geschichte im 19. Jahrhundert*. Four volumes. Third edition. Freiburg, 1954-1955. Volume 4: *Die religiösen Kräfte*.

Schoeps, Hans Joachim. *Das andere Preussen. Konservative Gestalten und Probleme im Zeitalter Friedrich Wilhelms IV*. Second edition. Honnef, 1957.

Spaeth, Adolf. *D. Wilhelm Julius Mann*. Reading PA, 1895.

Staehelin, Ernst. *Schweizer Theologen im Dienst der reformirten Kirche in den Vereinigten Staaten*. Zurich, 1919.

Stephan, Horst. *Geschichte der deutschen evangelischen Theologie seit dem deutschen Idealismus*. Second edition revised by Martin Schmidt. Berlin, 1960.

B. English

Appel, Theodore. *The Life and Work of John Williamson Nevin*. Philadelphia, 1889.

Baird, Robert. *Religion in America, or An Account of the Origin, Relation to the State, and Present Condition of the Evangelical Churches in the United States. With Notices of the Unevangelical Denominations*. New York, 1856. Reprint: edited by Henry Warner Bowden. New York, 1970.

Bebbington, D. W. *Evangelicalism in Modern Britain: A History from the 1730s to the 1980s*. London, 1989.

Billington, Ray Allen. *The Protestant Crusade, 1800–1860*. New York, 1938.

Binkley, Luther J. *The Mercersburg Theology*. Lancaster PA, 1953.

Bowden, Henry Warner. *Church History in the Age of Science*. Chapel Hill NC, 1971.

_____, ed. *A Century of Church History: The Legacy of Philip Schaff*. Carbondale and Edwardsville IL, 1988.

Brillioth, Yngve. *The Anglican Revival*. London, 1933.

_____. *Three Lectures on Evangelicalism and the Oxford Movement*. London, 1934.

Brown, Colin. *Jesus in European Protestant Thought, 1778–1860*. Studies in Historical Theology 1. Durham NC, 1985.

Brown, Jerry Wayne. *The Rise of Biblical Criticism in America, 1800–1870: The New England Scholars*. Middletown CT, 1969.

Bruce, F. F. *The English Bible. A History of Translations*. New York, 1961.

Chadwick, Owen. *From Bossuet to Newman: The Idea of Doctrinal Development*. Cambridge, 1957.

_____. *The Victorian Church*. Two volumes. London, 1966–1970.

Conser, Walter H., Jr. *Church and Confession. Conservative Theologians in Germany, England, and America, 1815–1866.* Macon GA, 1984.

Dubbs, Joseph Henry. *A History of the Reformed Church, Germany, in the United States.* American Church History Series 8. New York, 1894.

Goliber, Thomas J. "Philip Schaff (1819–1893): A Study in Conservative Biblical Criticism." Ph.D. dissertation, Kent State University, 1976.

Good, James I. *History of the Reformed Church in the United States in the Nineteenth Century.* New York, 1911.

Graham, Stephen R. " 'Cosmos in Chaos': A Study of Philip Schaff's Interpretation of Nineteenth-Century American Religion." Ph.D. dissertation, The University of Chicago, 1989.

Handy, Robert T. *A Christian America: Protestant Hopes and Historical Realities.* Second edition, revised and enlarged. New York, 1984.

—————. *A History of Union Theological Seminary in New York.* New York, 1987.

Herbst, Jurgen. *The German Historical School in American Scholarship. A Study in the Transfer of Culture.* Ithaca NY, 1965.

Hodgson, Peter C., ed. and trans. *Ferdinand Christian Baur: On the Writing of Church History.* New York, 1968.

Jordan, Philip D. *The Evangelical Alliance for the United States of America, 1847–1900: Ecumenism, Identity, and the Religion of the Republic.* New York, 1982.

Klein, H. M. J. *The History of the Eastern Synod of the German Reformed Church in the United States.* Lancaster PA, 1943.

Loetscher, Lefferts A. *The Broadening Church.* Philadelphia, 1957.

Marsden, George M. *The Evangelical Mind and the New School Presbyterian Experience.* New Haven, 1970.

Maxwell, Jack Martin. *Worship and Reformed Theology: The Liturgical Lessons of Mercersburg.* Pittsburgh, 1976.

McLoughlin, William G., ed. *The American Evangelicals, 1800–1900. An Anthology.* New York, 1968.

McNeill, John T., and James Hastings Nichols. *Ecumenical Testimony: The Concern for Christian Unity Within the Reformed and Presbyterian Churches.* Philadelphia, 1974.

Nichols, James Hastings. *Romanticism in American Theology: Nevin and Schaff at Mercersburg.* Chicago, 1961.

Penzel, Klaus. "A Chapter in the History of the Ecumenical Quest: Schelling and Schleiermacher." *Church History* 33 (September 1964): 322-37.

_____. "A Nineteenth-Century Ecumenical Vision: F. W. J. Schelling." *Lutheran Quarterly* 18 (November 1966): 362-78.

_____. "Church History in Context: The Case of Philip Schaff." In *Our Common History as Christians,* ed. John Deschner et al. 217-60. New York, 1975.

_____. "The Reformation Goes West: The Notion of Historical Development in the Thought of Philip Schaff." *Journal of Religion* 62 (July 1982): 219-41.

_____. "Philip Schaff—A Centennial Appraisal." *Church History* 59 (June 1990): 207-21.

Pfleiderer, Otto. *The Development of Theology in Germany Since Kant, and Its Progress in Great Britain Since 1825.* Translated by J. Frederick Smith. London, 1890.

Pranger, Gary Keith. "Philip Schaff (1819–1893): Portrait of an Immigrant Theologian." Ph.D. dissertation, University of Illinois at Chicago, 1987.

Prentiss, George Lewis. *The Union Theological Seminary in the City of New York: Historical and Biographical Sketches of its First Fifty Years.* New York, 1889.

_____. *The Union Theological Seminary in the City of New York: Its Design and Another Decade of Its History.* Asbury Park NJ, 1899.

Richards, George Warren. *History of the Theological Seminary of the Reformed Church in the United States, 1825–1934, Evangelical and Reformed Church, 1934–1952.* Lancaster PA, 1952.

Rouse, Ruth, and Stephen Charles Neill, eds. *A History of the Ecumenical Movement, 1517–1948.* Philadelphia, 1954. Especially chapters 5–7 (The Nineteenth Century).

"Schaff Memorial Number." *Bulletin: Theological Seminary of the Evangelical and Reformed Church* 15 (October 1944).

Schaff, David S. *The Life of Philip Schaff: in Part Autobiographical.* New York, 1897.

Schweitzer, Albert. *The Quest of the Historical Jesus. A Critical Study of Its Progress from Reimarus to Wrede.* Translated by W. Montgomery. London, 1910; New York, 1959.

Shriver, George H., ed. *American Religious Heretics. Formal and Informal Trials in American Protestantism.* Nashville and New York, 1966.

_____. *Philip Schaff. Christian Scholar and Ecumenical Prophet. Centennial Biography for the American Society of Church History.* Macon GA, 1987.

Stevenson, Louise L. *Scholarly Means to Evangelical Ends: The New Haven Scholars and the Transformation of Higher Learning in America, 1830–1890.* Baltimore, 1986.

Strauss, David Friedrich. *The Life of Jesus, Critically Examined.* Translated by George Eliot [Mary Ann Evans] (1846). New edition: edited with an introduction by Peter C. Hodgson. Lives of Jesus Series. Philadelphia, 1972; London, 1975.

Thompson, Robert E. *A History of the Presbyterian Church in the United States.* American Church History Series 6. New York, 1895.

Welch, Claude. *Protestant Thought in the Nineteenth Century.* Two volumes. New Haven, 1972, 1985.

INDEX

Abelard, 197n
Achilli, G. G., 107
Acton, Lord, lii, 14
Adams, John Quincy, 167n
Adams, Sarah F., 304n
Adams, William, 18, 287
Adler, Carl M., 13-14
Africa, 176, 182
Albigenses, 102
Alexander the Great, 137
Alexander II, Csar, 19
Alexander VI, Pope, 302
Alexander, Joseph Addison, 128
Alford, Henry, 262, 333n
Ambrose, 46, 99
America, xvi; Bible, church, and sabbath secure Christian character of, lxii, 15; and Europe, xxxvi n, 155, 214-15, 238, 245, 258, 348-49; fate of Reformation to be decided in, 180; general significance of, 151-58, for kingdom of God, 151, 153, 176-83; main theater of church history, 140; Phoenix grave of all churches and sects, 166-67, 175-76; rationalism spreading in, 207; religious composition of, 159-76, 307-8; significance of Reformation for, 142; unitive reformation will occur in, xliii, 93, 140, 154

American Bible Society (Bible societies), lx, 163, 172, 181, 247, 264, 267, 314
American Christianity. See Christianity, American
Americanization. See Schaff, Philip: Life
American religion, 151; churches and sects, 153, 166-76; essentially Protestant, 159-60, 179-80; liberal and conservative, 154-55; millenianism, messianism, and racism of, liv, lvi; voluntaryism of, 153, 155, 164-66, 179. See also Religious liberty; Sectarianism; Separation of church and state
American Society of Church History. See Schaff, Philip: Major Projects
American Tract Society (Tract societies), 163, 172, 181, 314
Anabaptism, 46, 339
Andover Seminary, 1, 226
Anglicanism, 102, 297, 307, 324, 332, 337; Articles of Reunion, 317-21; high-church party in, 235, 325; a Reformed variant, 118, 157; romanizing tendencies in, 86. See also Church of England; Episcopal church; Historic episcopate; Puseyism
Anglo-Catholicism. See Puseyism
Angus, Joseph 252-53, 263
Anselm of Canterbury, 46, 197, 332